GLOBAL MOUNTAIN REGIONS

FRAMING THE GLOBAL BOOK STUDIES

The Framing the Global project,
an initiative of Indiana University Press and
the Indiana University Center
for the Study of Global Change,
is funded by the Andrew W. Mellon Foundation.

Hilary E. Kahn and Deborah Piston-Hatlen,
Series Editors

ADVISORY COMMITTEE

Alfred C. Aman Jr.
Eduardo Brondizio
Maria Bucur
Bruce L. Jaffee
Patrick O'Meara
Radhika Parameswaran
Richard R. Wilk

GLOBAL MOUNTAIN REGIONS

Conversations toward the Future

Edited by Ann Kingsolver and
Sasikumar Balasundaram

INDIANA UNIVERSITY PRESS

This book is a publication of

Indiana University Press
Office of Scholarly Publishing
Herman B Wells Library 350
1320 East 10th Street
Bloomington, Indiana 47405 USA

iupress.indiana.edu

Manufactured in the
United States of America

Cataloging information is available from
the Library of Congress.

ISBN 978-0-253-03685-8 (hdbk.)
ISBN 978-0-253-03686-5 (pbk.)
ISBN 978-0-253-03689-6 (web PDF)

1 2 3 4 5 23 22 21 20 19 18

We dedicate this volume to the world's mountain communities.
All royalties will be donated to the United Nations
Voluntary Fund for Indigenous Peoples.

Contents

Acknowledgments

WE WOULD LIKE to express our gratitude to all of the contributors to this volume and their communities; all mountain residents around the world; those in the University of Kentucky Appalachian Center who supported the Global Mountain Regions conference, especially Pam Webb and Shane Barton; the University of Kentucky College of Arts & Sciences; the staff of Indiana University Press; and everyone engaged in collaborative global work for equity and well-being. All royalties from this volume are being donated to the United Nations Voluntary Fund for Indigenous Populations.

GLOBAL MOUNTAIN REGIONS

Hard Times

Si Kahn

It's hard times in Washington
Hard times in Tennessee
Hard times for everyone
Hard times for you and me
It's hard times in the public places
Hard times in the factories
Hard times on the corporate farms
Hard times on the company seas
Hard times
It's hard times

It's hard to watch it all go down
Drowning like the setting sun
Hard to watch our freedoms taken
Hard to lose what we had won
It's hard to watch the towers tumble
Hard to watch the struggling town
Hard to watch the bastards smile
While they tear the Constitution down
Hard times
It's hard times

But it's hardly time to take a seat
Hardly time to lose your voice
Hardly fair to just complain

As if we never had a choice
For we are born to work and choose
We are born to rip and mend
We are born to win and lose
We are born to lose . . . and win
Hard times
It's hard times
Hard times
It's our time

CHAPTER 1

Introduction

LISTENING TO VOICES ACROSS
GLOBAL MOUNTAIN REGIONS

Ann Kingsolver and
Sasikumar Balasundaram

IN THE APPALACHIAN Mountains, there is a centuries-old recipe for apple stack cake, which is made for weddings and other collective events. It is a practice attributed to indigenous communities in the region and embodies the opposite of capitalist individuation and performative consumption. Each household contributes one very affordable flat, round sweetened pancake made in a frying pan, and then as people assemble, the flat cakes are stacked together with apple butter between the layers to make a large communal cake to share during the public event. This seems to us to be a good model for social theorizing, in the epistemological path of First Nations, womanist, and participatory knowledge practices—each person contributing an equally valued vantage point to a collective analysis.

Most of the contributions to this volume emerged from a Global Mountain Regions conversation we organized at the University of Kentucky in 2012 between artists, social scientists, and activists from mountain regions on five continents, with everyone's participation and translation fully funded by the University of Kentucky and its College of Arts & Sciences. Given the shared experiences of social, economic, and political marginalization of mountain communities within each of our sixteen nation-states (while acknowledging other forms of inequality, e.g., Global North, academic, and English-speaking privilege), we aspired to create a context in which one's voice or presence did not have to be justified or represent a "token" perspective, and all participants—using verbal, nonverbal, visual, and musical forms of communication—could compare notes on equal ground. Mountain regions across the world were at the center of the conversation rather than its edges.

The goal of this comparative conversation, which others in this collection have since joined, has been to compare histories, analyses, and strategies. Communities in mountain regions have been stigmatized, silenced, and displaced while having fueled global economic development through the extraction of vital natural resources and labor for centuries. Far from being isolated, upland regions have played a key role in nation-building, whether by providing lumber for ships' masts and railroads, minerals for currency and trade, or cash crops like tea, tobacco, coffee and coca. Mountainous regions are labeled, in many languages, as wild, remote, "backwater" zones. The paradox is that this label can be both used disparagingly as an indication of social inferiority and with reverence to refer to sacred zones at the heart of cultures and religions. Mountain ranges are often the sites of violent contestations of national borders, political philosophies, and resource ownership. Control of watersheds, for example, is an essential issue in the twenty-first century, with mountains as a focus. Mountain regions, as the source of forest and biosphere reserves, the headwaters of watersheds, and inexpensive land for those displaced by economic inequality and climate change, will be critical sites in the coming decades.

People from mountain regions have been engaged in diasporic networks nationally and transnationally for generations. Today, many young people are returning to mountain communities with ideas about developing more interconnected and sustainable livelihoods, and that is one of the themes in this book, as they discuss the possibilities of sustainable forestry, agriculture, and beekeeping; arts and media production; diverse economies; green energy jobs; and intergenerational education. Another theme of the book is examples of environmental and social justice, as indigenous activists from the Amazon, Andean, Appalachian, and Odishan regions share the strategies, ideas, and actions that have been most effective in their work toward sustainable futures. Instead of protecting only their own regions, many occupants of mountain zones are also fighting for the well-being of those downstream in the watersheds that begin in their regions but affect the major urban centers of the world. The authors in this collection represent multiple generations, languages, nations, religions, disciplines, professions, and identities. From conversations across mountain regions, we have learned that diversity is not only the strongest aspect of bioregions (mountain regions contribute to the planet's oxygen and the development of new medicines through their forests, for example), but it is also the strongest contribution of upland human communities.

Mountain communities provide expertise in looking beyond the binary, a much-needed skill in dominant discourses in which those models have run their course. Living in edge environments in which the human and nonhuman, the secular and the sacred, the very old and the very young, and insider and outsider meet daily and which have endured the shifting boundaries of political claims and recognize their arbitrariness, has taught residents to parse plurality with fluency. Rather than waiting for ideas and plans to find their way to mountain areas, we suggest, those mountain regions may be seen globally as a powerful source of ideas and practices, just as they are the source of the rivers that feed the world. The scale and scope of watersheds, and the way they link regions together, are more easily seen from above than below; in mountain regions, interdependence has long been recognizable. This volume does not simply document histories of marginalization, but also assertions of communal rights, for example, that have become models for other movements. Bolivians in Cochabamba (Olivera and Lewis 2004) demonstrated how to contest privatization of water resources and redemocratize water rights, and examples of standing up to land grabbing (an effort requiring constant vigilance) and working for the restitution and rearticulation of land rights may be found in a number of marginalized contexts (Fay and James 2009). In a world in which there is a continuum of complex private and public arrangement—beyond a simple binary—in supplying water, for example (Bakker 2010), or labor, mountain resident are experienced navigators.

As the contributors to this volume have made connections between languages, regions, and disciplines, we have found that one of the most powerful means of sharing experiences across mountain regions is through art. The paintings of Pam Oldfield Meade, an Appalachian resident who paints stories of place, with her words written in streams of flowing water, tree trunks, and the hair of generations of women—evoking simultaneously the everyday and the timeless—moved everyone at the Global Mountain Regions conference and made it possible to talk about loss and survival. When we gathered in 2012 to begin this conversation, her community had just survived an unusual and devastating mountain tornado. The poetry of Crystal Good and Jeremy Paden brought the rhythm of bulldozers and dancers into the room, and showed how similar the open wounds of extraction were in Appalachia and Haiti. The songs of social justice balladeer Si Kahn, in English and Spanish, drew everyone into the music together, remembering histories of those who have been ground down and those who have stood up, time after time, place after place. The lyrics of Si Kahn run like a river throughout this volume, uniting voices from across mountain regions. The format of this volume is interdisciplinary, a multimodal stack cake, and we believe each layer makes the consideration of global mountain regions stronger through its difference.

Global Mountain Regions

Mountains, like notions of the global, are culturally constructed. As Rebecca Adkins Fletcher (2016, 284) has noted, "place becomes an active ideology rather than a static space." Mapping is always a political act, and that includes the mapping and conceptualization of mountain regions. In talking about natural preserves (many of which are in mountain zones), Agustín Coca Pérez (2014) mentions that sometimes it is forgotten that these environments are concepts because of human agency. Residents have been defined in national or world heritage park discourses, for example, as a nuisance in the very regions they have co-constructed and stewarded.

What is the difference between a hill, a mountain, and a plateau? Such terms are defined through scientific and political discourses (often politically charged boundary discourses), as well as cultural (including religious) ones, and these often conflict. The Himalayas, for example, have different names in India and China and are actors in different development dramas, each with its own plans for tourism, hydropower, and political control. Mountains are often the sites of such contestation, partly because of their combination of inhabited and uninhabitable zones—making political boundaries both likely and hard to police—and their larger-than-human scale and terrain. Larry Price (1981, xix) has articulated the role of mountains on the earth in this way: "Mountains serve to delineate, accentuate, and modify the global patterns of climate, vegetation, soil, and wildlife. Mountains establish the fundamental scenery of the earth and set the stage upon which the terrestrial play takes place. The ebb and flow of wind and water, of life and living processes, are expressed against this backdrop."

Along with oceans, the vastness of mountain ranges facilitates biodiversity and the planet's water cycle, and, for the same reasons, they are increasingly being monitored for signs of climate change. The international scientific agenda began to be established in 1971 through the Man and the Biosphere agenda of UNESCO, the United Nations Educational, Scientific, and Cultural Organization (Messerli 2012, S55). The United Nations declared 2002 the International Year of the Mountains, and, since then, transnational and interorganizational collaborations focusing on the well-being of mountain environments and (secondarily) populations have grown. The Food and Agriculture Organization (FAO) convened a series of scientific research projects and conferences clustered under the "Mountain Agenda," which came out of the 1992 United Nations Conference on the Environment and Development (or Earth Summit) in Brazil. Agenda 21, chapter 13, of the plan of action emerging from the conference was called "managing fragile ecosystems: sustainable mountain development," and a number of entities have been formed for this purpose, for example, the Mountain Forum, the Mountain Research Initiative, the World Glacier Monitoring Service, the Global Mountain Biodiversity Assessment, and the journal Mountain Research and Development. In 2000, the first World Mountain Forum was held, leading to the organization of the World Mountain People Association (which cannot have individual members, but has governmental members). The United Nations established December 11 each year as International Mountain Day. There are now associations for most of the major mountain regions of the world, including the African Mountain Association, the Andean Mountain Association, and many others. As summarized by Debarbieux and Price (2012), the scholarship focused on mountain regions has led to findings that the greatest cultural and religious diversity, as well as biodiversity, can be found in mountainous areas, as well as high rates of political and food insecurity (with estimates of up to 50 percent). Arguments for mountain regions to be held as commons (for example, through World Heritage designations) have been both strongly advocated and strongly contested, related to the status of social movements (and their repression) based in mountain zones.

This global mountain regions conversation, then, joins a number of collaborations across mountain regions. The interdisciplinary and international Kassam Research Group, for example, is drawing on knowledge of centuries-old ecological calendars through which residents in the Pamir Mountains of Central Asia have been adapting to changes in their glacial environment to educate climate scientists about ways to attend to more earth-centered and embodied knowledge practices in global research conversations.[1] Sometimes such partnerships are spread across mountain regions, and sometimes their transnational and interdisciplinary focus is concentrated on the significance of a single mountain, like the Kailash Project of the India China Institute at the New School for Social Research, focusing on the plural understandings of Mount Kailash—a pilgrimage site in the Himalayas shared by India, Nepal, and China.

Mountains cover approximately a quarter of the earth's surface and are home to about one-eighth of the world's population (Debarbieux and Price 2012). Ironically, mountains figure in the widely accessible World Social Forum in relation to the voices of marginalized, often indigenous, mountain residents and also provide the site, in Davos, Switzerland, for the elitist World Economic Forum. Those inhabiting mountain regions may be "global citizens" with wealth and strong market participation, as in those who own personal ski resorts, or may be so economically and politically displaced as to not have citizenship or market participation in any national context. It must be noted that we do not claim to gloss mountain residents as homogeneous in identity or experience. But we do argue that there are, among mountain residents, those who share across national contexts experiences of (albeit in different forms) social, economic and political marginalization and also active efforts to analyze and counter such marginalization. The latter are those threads of conversation emphasized in this volume.

What does it mean to speak of global mountain regions? Hilary Kahn (2014, 4) has referred to "a plurality of globals that that emerge and come to rest in different guises, locales, and performances." One of the uniting discourses in this volume is a lived analysis of the extraction of material, labor, and political autonomy in regions considered "wild" by those in political and economic centers elsewhere, providing from the periphery the resources for building global trade networks for centuries that, as Andre Gunder Frank (1966) described, actively underdeveloped and stigmatized those responsible for the "development" of their oppressors. Such contorting power to name was brought home to us in the Global Mountain Regions Conference in the catalyzing moment Monica Chují described the Ecuadorian government labeling the snakes carried on the shoulders of her fellow indigenous Amazonian protestors in an organization she led as "'weapons of mass destruction,' and the activists as terrorists." The "threat" they represented to the state was blocking the extraction of oil from their communally held land for the global market, and speaking for means and foci of valorization other than capitalist logic; in the inversion Taussig (1987) speaks of as constitutive of the culture of terror, those who had been accused by their government of terrorism were actually being terrorized by logging, drilling, silencing by the state, and disappearances.

The editors, Ann Kingsolver and Sasikumar Balasundaram, met in a classroom at the University of Peradeniya in Sri Lanka in 2004, while Kingsolver was teaching a course on globalization. She had been listening to how differently situated individuals made sense of capitalist globalization and had acted on those understandings for several decades, especially in rural places (cf. Kingsolver 2001, 2011) like her home community on the edges of Appalachia, in Kentucky, where the economy had been based on tobacco cultivation. She was in the Upcountry (or central mountain region) of Sri Lanka to compare interpretations of globalization by those in the tea sector with those she had listened to in the tobacco sector in Kentucky. Balasundaram was an undergraduate who had come to Peradeniya as the first university student from the tea estate on which he grew up, where his mother and grandmother had plucked tea—his grandmother as an indentured worker from India in colonial times caught in the statelessness that promised no admission to Sri Lankan citizenship and no return to India. With other students in the multilingual, multiethnic classroom, and from their vantage points as social scientists from rural Appalachia and the Upcountry, they built an understanding of globalization from the ground up. Topics on the students' minds were the generation-long ethnic war, with the United States, China, and India intervening in more and less obvious ways for strategic interests (mostly in Sri Lanka's deepwater ports), and the high rates of youth unemployment and suicide. Sasikumar Balasundaram came to the University of South Carolina, where Ann Kingsolver was a faculty member, to earn a Ph.D. in anthropology (writing his dissertation on long-term refugee camps and structural violence—see Balasundaram 2014), and their commitment to facilitate conversations between, and not about, those most marginalized by global capitalism continued. This led in 2012 to their organization of the Global Mountain Regions Conference (and subsequent exchanges between participants), after Kingsolver had moved to the University of Kentucky to direct the Appalachian Center and Appalachian Studies Program with a global comparative focus.

Balasundaram, flying into the United States for the first time and trying to figure out where to go in the Atlanta airport, tells of going to the janitor for instruction because he was the person he saw who was most like him. How is it possible to navigate the global and valorize shared perspectives rather than the view of those who claim the power to name? Even the language of marginalization we are using in this introduction is problematic, since it incorporates the assumption that those whose voices are at the center of this volume and their communities are peripheral. Through weaving narratives across mountain regions into a different pattern, our hope is to bring into question dominating perspectives and the systems of valorization that inform them.

As noted earlier, mountain communities are not just now being touched by, or incorporated into, cultural and economic globalization. They have, in many cases, had the longest engagement with global capitalism in their nation-states, through the timbering and mining, for example, that made it possible to build the world's tall ships, early railroads, and factories. What does it mean to be a resident of a "sacrifice zone" for capitalism (see Moody 2007)? Beyond mercantile capitalism, the extraction has continued—of labor, and now of water, as dams provide hydropower and irrigation for lowland development. As Anthony Oliver-Smith (2009, 3–4) documents, "More people were involuntarily displaced in the twentieth century than in any other in recorded history," and "there can be no return to land submerged under a dam-created lake. . . . Many people displaced by development projects are never resettled and either succumb to the impacts of dislocation or find themselves consigned to the margins of society and the economy." Of the development-displaced, many are in mountain regions and somehow often fall outside accountability by nation-states or corporations— a process of alienation aided by widespread stereotypes of mountain people as simultaneously self-reliant and agentive, without the need of a safety net, and ignorant, uncivilized, and responsible for their own impoverishment. This is a dominant narrative about mountain people in many cultural contexts, even as, glaringly, their means of production is literally scooped out from under them. In this book, the authors try different means for communicating this experience of silencing and displacement. Saakshi Joshi, for example, who has been listening to people displaced by the Tehri Dam in the Himalayan region of Uttarakhand, India, writes from the vantage point of a piece of wood from a house in the submerged community that has been taken as a memory to "New Tehri," which residents say is a worse place to live than where they were before.

We do not claim this book to be representative of all mountain regions, or all voices in mountain regions. Some of the chapters represent new collaborations and others, decades-long partnerships (as in the Welsh–Appalachian conversations described by Tom Hansell and Patricia Beaver, also possible to learn about through the newly released film After Coal: Welsh and Appalachian Mining Communities). Another transnational group that was included in the Global Mountain Regions Conference as a model of collaboration was comprised of participants in an exchange between media collectives Appalshop in the United

States and Kommunitas Dokumenter Indonesia, Kiri Depan, and Kampung Halaman in Indonesia. Tommy Anderson, Elizabeth Barret, Machlyn Blair, Zamzam Fauzanafi, Maureen Mullinax, Dwi Sujanti Nugraheni, Patmawaty Taibe, Natasha Watts, and Somi Roy shared their experiences of learning through mountain-to-mountain youth exchanges for critical visual analysis. Their presentations were not submitted as a chapter for this volume, but Maureen Mullinax provided this summary of their collaboration:

> [which has been] a three-year cross-cultural exchange between media makers, artists, youth media educators, and curators from the eastern Kentucky-based media arts center, Appalshop, Inc., and thirteen arts organizations from Indonesia. These organizations share in common a commitment to using media as tools to tell cultural stories and to address social injustices. The Global Mountain Regions Conference facilitated this reflection by providing several exchange participants the opportunity to reunite and hold a thoughtful conversation about the project and its lasting impacts. At the center of this discussion were questions about what each organization and their members brought to and learned from the exchange. The participants explored the dialogues that the exchange open up. We were interested in discussing how the sharing of culture through artistic production can encourage new ways of thinking about and sustaining democratic practices, especially as related to the involvement of youth in their mountain communities.

Since the conversation across mountain regions shaping this volume is on sustainable futures, young people's voices, practical strategies, and uses of new means of global communication through multimodal media are emphasized. The keynote for the Global Mountain Regions Conference, for example, was Tammy Horn and Kunal Sharma's presentation on beekeeping in the Appalachian and Nilgiri Biosphere Reserves of the United States and India. Strip mining and clear-cutting have constituted a kind of everyday disaster in that the devastation is unrelenting and does not make headlines like a tsunami or earthquake. Beekeeping is one of the postmining strategies for making a living on land left to communities, and it contributes-like community forestry and other diverse livelihood strategies detailed in several chapters- to healing the headwaters, which is something that should, but does not seem to, concern everyone downstream from mountain regions.

In a salvage economy, as Anna Tsing (2015, 131–132) and her collaborators describe making a living from the "life in ruins" of sites of capitalist extraction, "patches of livelihood come into being as assemblages. Participants come with varied agendas, which do their small part in guiding world-making projects." The contributors to this volume have found that since nation-states have not had an interest in assisting residents of marginalized zones to create such postindustrial or postcapitalist livelihoods—since low-wage labor in precarious regions is a national resource still to be sold on the transnational market (for call centers, for example, and Amazon distribution warehouses)—we think it is a vital strategy to compare notes globally about how to envision a future in regions with common histories of abandonment. As Vaccaro, Harper, and Murray (2016, 12) put it, "How do individuals and communities respond to the massive ruptures, dispossession, and human suffering that happen when capital moves on to more profitable places? Imagining futures without the security of industrial workplaces—which may be a romanticized security that looks best in hindsight—can be a scary business." Isolation has been a capitalist strategy for mountain regions, where states have still not invested in transportation or information infrastructure, in addition to cultural stereotyping of mountain residents (who have engaged in national and transnational circuits of migration for generations) as "isolated" and "backward." Collaboration across mountain regions defies that label of isolation and provides models for new (or old) strategies to try, like beekeeping. There is no one industry that will replace coal, copper, tobacco, old growth timber, coca, coffee, or tea. There is no panacea, so "patching" strategies (mentioned by Tsing) are useful to compare and learn from.

There are myriad ways to understand the global (as Hilary Kahn noted, above), and many iterations of capitalism (Gibson-Graham 1996). It is not simple, the work of tracing the effects of these entanglements and crafting responses, and a reactive romanticization of the local can also be oppressive. Like Arif Dirlik (1996, 38, 42), the contributors to this volume ascribe to a "critical localism," a perspective that acknowledges that "the contemporary local is itself a site of invention; the present is ultimately the site for the global." Attention to the many processes of place-making and of inclusions and exclusions in community-making (based on gendered, classed, caste, ethnic, racialized, sexualized, age, insider/outsider, land-based or landless, long-term resident, new immigrant, citizen/non-citizen, and other ways to discern and discriminate), and to which voices are empowered to name places, histories, and future paths, is an important part of active critical localism. The contributors to this volume, when speaking across mountain regions, may not have the same places in mind or be dis/empowered in the same ways, or have experienced capitalism and its effects in the same ways, but they share a process of attending to environment, history, difference, and possibilities.

There are many paradoxes in rural mountain regions. One example is the emphasis in government and NGO-led development work on opening bars and distilling local forms of alcohol for tourists in an experience economy; another is the informal drug economy being the main livelihood option in many marginalized areas at the same time as there are local anti-alcohol, anti-drug, and swelling anti-corruption movements. One concern expressed among the participants in the Global Mountain Regions Conference across regions was that economic development discussions need to take into account the actual landscape of livelihoods, including the informal economy. Sex work and informal drug and alcohol sales tend to accompany extractive industries, and while the capital from mining and logging, for example, are not retained in the mountains, environmental toxins, addictions, and sexually transmitted diseases are. This is not to say there is a uniform conservativeness on this topic in mountain regions—women who pluck tea have often also made their own alcohol to address pain and monotony, and bars have created alternative safe spaces for LGBTQ rural residents, for example (see Gray 2009). High mountain zones have often been associated with areas "beyond the law" (in colonial Peru, literally, because the colonizers could not breathe at high altitudes—see Silverblatt 1987). Instead of stereotyping mountain residents as outlaws and addicts, however, what if we followed Otto Santa Ana's (2002) recommendation to use insurgent metaphors to contest stereotypes? Mountain people could be spoken of as protectors of water sources, and instead of drug addicts in the mountains, we could refer to lowland money addicts, and speak of inequality as toxic. Language can be a powerful force for political change, as poets like Victor Jara have exemplified. Despite mountain regions having been persistently stereotyped as sites of intolerance in many nations, they have often been at the forefront of social change. The Highlander Center in Appalachian Tennessee, for example, was an early organizing site for the Civil Rights movement in the United States. The song "We Shall Overcome" was written there.

At this moment, young people, especially, are using spoken words and music to assert a force countering the negative representations or silencing of marginalized voices. In North America, there are the Black Lives Matter and Native Lives Matter movements, and the rebel music movement Seventh Generation Rising, with lyrics fighting against rape, alcoholism, and suicide, and standing up for land rights. Young people (often using social media) are speaking up, speaking out, and speaking together across contexts. This is the threat to the capitalist strategy of keeping groups on the edge, isolated and politically and economically dependent, or silenced. What has happened to marginalized regions hurts all of us on the planet—much as Fanon (1967) pointed out that the colonizers were also damaged by colonialism, not only the colonized.

Land grabbing—the appropriation of large tracts of land, sometimes with the assistance of state military force, by external national or corporate actors—has been increasing exponentially in the last decade, often displacing people from (or to) mountain environments. In the name of securing the food supply in anticipation of climate change, for example, the People's Republic of China has been accumulating land in many nations. The food security for some guarantees food insecurity for others in this global dance. Land grabbing, along with the expansion of extractive industries in some mountain regions, is responsible for internal as well as transnational migration. Residents of some mountain regions, as in the state of Sikkim, in India, have organized recently to discourage land grabbing and work toward securing small-scale, sustainable organic livelihoods and discouraging corporate agricultural practices and holdings.

The mountains are everywhere, in that marginalized mountain zones have long exported people in far-reaching (largely invisible, to mainstream media) labor diasporas, and those mountain travelers have contributed cultural aesthetics and skills to many flatland contexts. People from mountains who have voluntarily or involuntarily migrated tend to find one another, in restaurants, picnics in parks, musical groups, fishing in rivers, and sometimes in religious sites. In a collaborative theater project we organized through the University of Kentucky Appalachian Center called Las Voces de los Apalaches, residents of Appalachia from Mexico and Central America spoke of forming a mountain soccer league, and of moving to eastern Kentucky from lowland cities in the United States because the mountains were beautiful. Transnational mountain migrants—like those recruited to Appalachia for work in coal mines from Eastern Europe in the early twentieth century—have long carried and traded ideologies, including strategies for labor organizing. In the middle of the company-owned coalfields of Kentucky and during the "coal wars" of Harlan and Pike Counties, for example, a group of Hungarians set up a collective, worker-owned coal camp. Laborers are more than working bodies, and there is power in not feeling alone.

There are silences in this book that we want to note—the voices and perspectives that are absent (urban and wealthy mountain regions, for example), the silence of the mountains themselves, and the absence of those mountains that have been removed entirely through mining, with homes, farms, streams, forests and cemeteries blasted away. It is too simple to draw moral lines around what could and should be in mountain regions—residents are very accustomed to living paradoxes every day, for example, relying for a living on sectors that ultimately represent the death of the mountain landscape. What we have found as common ground in discussions of the future of mountain regions is a commitment to the well-being of children as the future generation, and for that reason we emphasize listening to young people. We find inspiration in children's direct communication, as in the Children's Radio Foundation in Africa and the children's parliaments in refugee camps in India.

As we look to the future, mountains are increasingly conflict zones. Political, ethnic, and resource conflicts are intensifying, and as climate change displaces more coastal residents into uplands, private/public debates about land and water rights will only increase. Consider the massive project in China to reverse the flow of rivers—what will the long-term social repercussions be? There are new social hierarchies in mountain regions and new kinds of displacement as those with wealth look to "return to the land" and attempt to purchase or appropriate the social capital rural residents have constructed through years of daily interaction, and experience economies favor the construction of never-having-existed nostalgic landscapes over the visibility of the detritus of earlier waves of capitalist extraction. Crossing borders, in many senses, to listen to each other and compare notes is more essential now than ever.

Introduction of Contributions to This Collection

While readers cannot hear this book singing, lyrics by Si Kahn from his career of singing with mountain workers around the world connect all the contributions, and serve not as ornamentation but as the connective tissue of the volume and its collective arguments for co-constructed knowledge (a practice exemplified by music for social change). In general, the conversation among the chapters begins with histories of extraction of resources and labor, moving to mountain residents' organizing—sometimes with mountains as agentive partners—to speak up and back to those long, oppressive histories of marginalization, and ending with finding ways of building and imagining futures in global mountain regions.

In a collaboration initiated in the 1970s through Helen Lewis and John Gaventa of the Highlander Research Center in Appalachia and in Wales members of the National Union of Mine workers and the miners' choir Cor Meibion Onllwyn, Tom Hansell and Patricia Beaver in chapter 2 share what can be learned through long-term, equal exchanges of knowledge between workers in the same global industry in different mountain regions. They document the ways in which the coal mining industry deeply shaped every aspect of culture in the communities brought into conversation in this dialogue about the past, present, and future of coalmining regions, situating local experiences in a global political economic context. Given that the Welsh coal-mining industry collapsed earlier than the Appalachian industry (only now acknowledging that coal production has shifted to the western United States), the comparison affords Appalachian communities the opportunity to learn from how Welsh communities have handled the postcoal transition. The contributors urge readers to reframe the conventional debate about the coal industry from jobs versus environment to collective considerations of the long-term sustainable future of rural communities and provide examples of an alternative and equitable development model that has brought both employment and empowerment to postcoal communities in Wales.

Chapter 3, by Paul Ciccantell, also provides a comparative discussion of historical and transnational contexts of coal production, comparing the experiences of Canadian and U.S. mining communities in British Columbia and West Virginia. He focuses on the regulatory environment in Canada and the United States, and documents that the same mining technologies have been used with very different health outcomes because of the emphasis in Canadian regulations on the well-being of workers in the industry and of residents of communities in the vicinity of mining activities. By contrast the emphasis in the United States has been on deregulation of corporations with minimal oversight of occupational and environmental health and safety due to corporate pressures on legislators. With the Canadian example, Ciccantell demonstrates for Appalachian communities what health outcomes would be possible with stricter environmental and occupational regulatory measures.

Crystal Good is a member of the Affrilachian Poets, a group of poets who assert the voices of African Americans in Appalachia, an identity that is seemingly perpetually erased in dominant media stereotypes of a "white" Appalachia. Crystal Good speaks as a poet, a woman, an Appalachian, a person interested in particle physics, a mentor, and an advocate for cessation of mountain top removal mining. Her poem "Black Diamonds," included here as chapter 4, is a commentary on the effects of the coal industry on West Virginia communities. In another poem, "Boom Boom," not included in this volume, she draws parallels between gendered and environmental violence. She has read her poetry in many venues—bars, rallies, classrooms—and it always has a powerful effect on those who hear her read it.

Tony Milanzi, in chapter 5, describes the shaping of mountain environments of southern Malawi—including both the ecology and livelihoods—through historical colonial administrative practices. The introduction in the region of monocropping of tea, coffee, and tobacco by British planters led to eventual impoverishment of the residents. Mountain residents tend to be blamed for their own poverty in development sectors and national discourses. By contrast this chapter advocates linking the colonial history of marginalization to considerations of current livelihood options. Tony Milanzi, a cultural anthropologist, has long been involved in efforts to document and address economic disparities for rural residents in his home nation of Malawi.

Monica Chují's lecture from the Global Mountain Regions Conference is included in this volume, in translation, as chapter 6: "Voices for Community Rights in Amazonia." As an indigenous Ecuadorian, she grew up attending communal meetings with her parents and learning to think of nature as a living force with its own rights, as she has put it. She attended the Global Mountain Regions Conference as Chair of CONAIE, the Confederation of Indigenous Nationalities of Ecuador. She has been a leader of indigenous resistance movements since 1990. She has organized forums for indigenous people to share experiences in indigenous languages, including a film festival. She has worked with the United Nations on transnational organizing for indigenous rights. She helped write a new constitution for Ecuador that limited water privatization and recognized the inherent rights of nature, but argues that the government of Ecuador, in turn, has ignored and repressed those rights. In her chapter, she shares organizing strategies that have been successful in standing up to both government and corporate exploitation in the Amazonian region in which there is strong pressure to allow petroleum extraction on communal lands.

Chapter 7 is coauthored by Carmen Martínez Novo, an anthropologist who has done collaborative research with indigenous communities in Ecuador and Mexico on identity, human rights, and state policies; Shannon Bell, a sociologist whose participatory research has focused on community activism, especially by women, in the coal-mining region of West Virginia; Subhadra Channa, an anthropologist who has done collaborative research in many indigenous communities in India, including on discussions of cosmology in the Himalayan region; Annapurna Pandey, an anthropologist whose work has been in her home state of Odisha, India, with indigenous women activists defending communal lands from mining activities; and Luis Alberto Tuaza Castro, a social scientist from the indigenous community of Chimborazo, Ecuador, in the Andes who has worked with other indigenous communities on voicing their rights, drawing on the intersections of ethnicity, politics, and religion. In their comparative discussion across global mountain regions, they describe challenges faced by indigenous communities in relation to nation-states and private corporations and the resistance strategies they have used. For centuries, indigenous communities have been exploited in the name of nation-building and economic development, seeing the benefits of neither state projects nor economic development, as Chují also points out. Although there are many differences between those on whom this chapter focuses, there are shared experiences of colonization, discrimination, oppression, and exploitation. The authors argue that although struggles and resistance strategies are different, by comparing stories across contexts it is possible to learn from one another and establish a global solidarity that can be drawn on in conflicts with specific states and corporations. One lesson we have learned from this comparison of efforts to organize against extractive industries in mountain regions is that the most successful (as in Odisha) include the mountains as sacred actors and partners rather than as contested property.

Chapter 8 discusses both natural and human-made disasters in mountain regions, with attention to how communities rebuild in their aftermath. Contributors to the chapter include anthropologist Jude Fernando, who has done activist, collaborative work with communities after the tsunami in his home country of Sri Lanka and after the earthquake in Haiti; Jeremy Paden, who grew up in Italy, Central America, and the Caribbean, is a Spanish and Latin American literature scholar and author whose poem reflecting on the survivors of the earthquake in Haiti is included in the chapter; Lina Calandra, a geographer who works on environmental conflicts in Africa and Europe and who, as director of the Cartolab at the University of L'Aquila, in Italy, collaborated with residents of L'Aquila after an earthquake hit their community; Shaunna Scott and Stephanie McSpirit, participatory researchers and social scientists who have worked with Appalachian Kentucky residents to document the effects of environmental disasters—including a massive coal sludge spill—that regulatory bodies, along with the coal companies responsible, turned their backs on; and Pam Oldfield Meade, the Appalachian artist mentioned earlier in the chapter. The combination of poetry, social science, and art in this chapter convey the sense of shock, loss and abandonment experienced by survivors of human-made and natural disasters, and the transnational connections forged as individuals and communities and landscapes work to recover.

Daniel Joseph, a cultural anthropologist from Haiti, discusses in chapter 9 his current work with Dominicans of Haitian descent and undocumented Haitian migrants who were displaced from the Dominican Republic by legislative fiat in 2015 to the other, much less hospitable, side of the mountain region on the Haitian–Dominican border. Their daily challenges in forging a living in underresourced refugee camps in an arid zone demonstrate the human toll that political border-making and enforcing can take. The mountain landscape itself defies such arbitrary political lines and identities, as do people's livelihood strategies in such border regions.

Chapter 10 is another collaborative chapter between scholars working in Appalachia and another mountain region: the Chiapas mountains of Mexico. Mary Anglin is an anthropologist whose research in the United States is at the intersection of medical anthropology and public health, attending also to environmental and social justice and gendered, classed, and racialized oppressions and acts of resistance—from women working in mica factories in North Carolina to organizing for low-income breast cancer care in California. Gregory Button has studied environmental disasters as a journalist, public health researcher, and anthropologist. At the time of the Global Mountain Regions Conference, he was co-director of the Disasters, Displacement and Human Rights Program at the University of Tennessee, tracking the effects of a recent Tennessee Valley Authority coal ash spill. Dolores Molina Rosales, an anthropologist at El Colegio de la Frontera Sur in Mexico, has worked with indigenous mothers and midwives in Chiapas on dealing with emergencies and challenging transportation infrastructure as well as other human and environment interactions that exacerbate social inequalities. In this chapter, they discuss environmental justice and health disparities across mountain communities.

Rural newspapers do not have the budgets that urban news sources do and can also have different priorities. Journalism scholars Al Cross, a political reporter and director of the University of Kentucky Institute for Rural Journalism and Community Issues, and You You, a social science and communications scholar at Shanghai University, share the results of their comparative analysis of rural journalism in the United States and China in chapter 11. They focus on the circulation of news in rural areas, and discuss the new challenges posed by cable news and state-sponsored national media not representing the identities and issues of rural communities and undermining the importance of circulating local news.

Partnerships between education scholars working in mountain regions in the United States, Italy, and Pakistan are represented in chapter 12. Jane Jensen of the University of Kentucky, and Marco Pitzalis, of the University of Cagliari, compare educational challenges, educational institutions, resource allocations, and pedagogical methods in two mountain regions. Alan DeYoung and Mir Afzal Tajik, from the United States and Pakistan, respectively, do the same for Appalachia and the mountains of Pakistan. The four scholars argue that it can be empowering to compare different successful educational models as each region resists universalizing "solutions" and constructs culturally appropriate and equitable ways forward.

Sajjad Ahmad Jan, a political scientist in Pakistan, writes in chapter 13 about jirga, a tribal practice of informal negotiation, decision-making and dispute resolution in mountain villages of Pakistan along the border with Afghanistan. He argues that far from being a "backward" practice, this traditional form of daily peace-building has much to offer to nation-states, which seem to be increasingly challenged in having the listening skills necessary for avoiding and addressing conflict. The author points out the irony of modernist frameworks that classify informal dispute resolution practices like jirga as less developed than formally organized institutional practices, given the relative success of each in peace-building experience. He also discusses gendered critiques of jirga.

The authors of chapter 14, Stan Brunn (University of Kentucky) and Maria Paradiso (University of Sannio, Italy, and founder of the Italian network Geography of the Information Society), are both geographers. Their focus is on cartographic silences about, and lack of internet access in, mountain regions. Like Sajjad Ahmad Jan, their chapter points to another irony experienced by residents of mountain regions: they provide key resources for the global economy (raw materials, sources of energy, and water) while being denied another key resource of globalization, internet access. The authors advocate expansion of broadband internet, linking it especially to the potential of young people in "remote" regions to become equal partners on the global stage.

As noted earlier in the introduction, Saakshi Joshi, an anthropologist who has researched development-related displacement in the Himalayan region, experiments in chapter 15 with a writing strategy that gives voice to the material in "Artifacts of Home: The Landscape Speaks."

Jasper Waugh-Quasebarth, also a cultural anthropologist, is—like Joshi—attending to the voices of the nonhuman, in this case the trees that are made to "sing" by musical instrument makers in his Appalachian home state of West Virginia and in the Carpathian Mountains of Romania, where he follows the "tonewood" industry between mountain regions. In chapter 16, Waugh-Quasebarth draws on what he has learned about human and material interactions through apprenticing with instrument makers in Appalachia, following the process from tree selection to finished musical instruments.

Discussing another, more brief, Appalachian-Carpathian exchange in chapter 17, Jessica Murray and Iryna Galuschchak share their initial impressions of each other's home regions (the Appalachian United States and the Carpathian Ukraine), especially with regard to land use and sustainable food production. They each participated in a now-annual Appalachian–Carpathian conference, as Jasper Waugh-Quasebarth has. There have been several ongoing Appalachian exchanges with other mountain regions—the connection with Wales out of the Highlander

Research Center, continued by Appalachian State University; the Appalachian-Sardinian connection between the University of Kentucky and the University of Cagliari; and the multi-institutional Appalachian–Carpathian conference.

Long before the Global Mountain Regions Conference, Patrick Angel of the Appalachian Regional Reforestation Initiative (ARRI) initiated a mountain-to-mountain exchange between children in Colombia, South America, and the Appalachian United States to help them understand global environmental connections through the migration of the cerulean warbler, which migrates between their regions and relies on a forested habitat. In chapter 18, Regina Donour—an activist in Kentuckians for the Commonwealth, an environmental and social justice advocacy organization, and an elementary school teacher—describes what it was like for her students to participate in that pen-pal project.

Lisa Markowitz, a political economic anthropologist focused on food justice and collective movements, is engaged in long-term research on how highland Andean herders have fared in their relationship with the global economy, supplying alpaca fiber, for example, to the European fashion industry. In chapter 19, she describes Andean mountain producers' engagement with global economic circuits and sets this in the context of the effects of climate change on mountain communities.

Shifting focus from the Andes to another high-altitude zone, Dipak Pant discusses in chapter 20 what he has learned from working with nomadic herders in Mongolia that can be applied more broadly to sustainable development strategies in what he calls "extreme lands." Originally from Nepal, Pant heads the Interdisciplinary Unit for Sustainable Economy at Università Carlo Cattaneo (LIUC) in Italy and founded the Extreme Lands Program. His chapter describes the sustainable development planning partnership in which he is engaged with Mongolian herders, which could serve as an example for other mountain region collaborations focused on sustainable futures.

In chapter 21, Domenica Farinella, an Italian sociologist working with shepherds and farmers working on sustainable territorial development efforts in Sardinia, Italy; Ann Kingsolver, writing about Appalachia, in the United States; and Ismael Vaccaro and Oriol Beltran, who are both anthropologists and political ecologists working collaboratively in the Pyrenees, in Spain, trace histories of media stereotyping and development policies that have negatively affected mountain communities even as they purport to support them, and discuss the difference that national policies and interregional cooperation make to building sustainable experience economies in postmining and postindustrial regions, focusing especially on the efforts of young people to create diverse economies in rural places.

The keynote lecture for the Global Mountain Regions conference by Appalachian beekeeper and scholar Tammy Horn Potter and forest ecologist in the Nilgiri Biosphere Reserve Kunal Sharma comprises chapter 22. Tammy Horn

Potter is the author of *Beeconomy: What Women and Bees Teach Us about Local Trade and Global Markets*, and Kunal Sharma documents and educates others about indigenous ecological knowledge in India; he is one of the authors of *Honey Trails in the Blue Mountains*. Potter and Sharma have visited one another's environments and observed beekeeping practices. In this innovative essay they describe the role of bees in larger ecologies of wildlife corridors, and the centrality of mountain communities in maintaining those key pathways for the planet's health.

Aklilu Reda, in chapter 23, discusses a process common to many mountain regions: the appropriation of indigenous plants and knowledge by external actors, who may even commodify those resources as their own intellectual and material property and sell them back to mountain residents. In this case, Reda discusses the global spread of native coffee from Ethiopia, his home nation, where coffee has strong cultural significance as well as economic value. He briefly follows the story of arabica coffee from mountain forests to faraway Starbucks and considers strategies for mountain communities to retain or recover ecological and knowledge sovereignty.

In chapter 24, Nathan Hall, an Appalachian Kentucky agroforester, draws on both the local and transnational experience of mountain regions to discuss practical strategies for developing sustainable livelihoods in mountain regions. He has organized countless tree plantings on postmined lands in Appalachia with two of the authors of the next chapter, Barton and Angel, through Green Forests Work and the Appalachian Regional Reforestation Initiative (ARRI).

Christopher Barton, Kenton Sena, and Patrick Angel, in chapter 25, continue with the theme of reclamation of postmined lands through reforestation with diverse tree species that can contribute to sustainable economies in mountain regions. They describe their forestry reclamation approach (FRA), developed through ARRI and implemented now in a number of the world's regions that have been altered by mining activities. A major challenge they point out is the soil compaction due to the use of heavy equipment used to "restore" the soil to acceptable contours and the sterility of that soil, which does not resemble the topsoil built up over centuries in the forests preceding the strip or mountain top removal mining processes. Their team has developed a low-tech, low-cost way of reforesting such areas, and ARRI—with wide participation from civic organizations considered to be on all points of the political spectrum in relation to the issue of coal mining—is working successfully to reforest areas by addressing soil compaction. ARRI is partnering with the American Chestnut Foundation to replant hybrid chestnuts in areas that were once old growth chestnut stands and with beekeepers like Tammy Horn Potter, in this volume, to reclaim postmined lands in ways encouraging of sustainable futures.

Asma Jaber, a Palestinian American justice scholar and activist, and Michel Awad, a Palestinian experience economy professional, discuss their collaboration in chapter 26, and the possibilities of responsible tourism for residents of mountain regions—especially those characterized in broad strokes as conflict zones in the international media—to provide crosscultural education through everyday interactions while contributing to livelihoods through the experience economy.

In the concluding discussion, chapter 27, "Conversations toward the Future in Global Mountain Regions," Felix "Skip" Bivens, an international participatory development professional from Appalachian Tennessee with extensive experience supporting academic/community partnerships who facilitated the Global Mountain Regions Conference, and the editors of this volume share their perspectives on future directions for conversation and collaborative action.

Our goal, as organizers of the Global Mountain Regions conference, in subsequent conversations, and as editors of this volume, continues to be to find possibilities for equitable listening opportunities across mountain regions that generate further collaboration, especially among young people, activists, artists, and others whose voices have often not been heard in state-led decision-making processes in and about mountain regions. The mountains themselves, in their experiences of migration over geological time and their defiance of easily establishing, fencing, and policing borders, have much to teach all of us about plural and equitable relationships.

ANN KINGSOLVER is Professor of Anthropology and past director of the Appalachian Center and Appalachian Studies Program at the University of Kentucky. Her research in the United States, Mexico, and Sri Lanka has focused on how people make sense of all that gets called "globalization" and act on those understandings. Her books include *NAFTA Stories: Fears and Hopes in Mexico and the United States, Tobacco Town Futures: Global Encounters in Rural Kentucky,* and several edited volumes.

SASIKUMAR BALASUNDARAM is Assistant Professor of Anthropology at Southern Illinois University, Edwardsville. His research interests include refugees, humanitarian aid, global health, engaged anthropology with children and youth, and contemporary issues of the Up-country Tamils of Sri Lanka.

Note

1. See the website of Karim-Aly Kassam, International Professor of Environmental and Indigenous Studies in the College of Agriculture and Life Sciences at Cornell University, for more information about this transnational collaboration on indigenous cosmologies informing climate change research.

References

Bakker, Karen. 2010. *Privatizing Water: Governance Failure and the World's Urban Water Crisis.* Ithaca, NY: Cornell University Press.

Balasundaram, Sasikumar. 2014. "Children Matter: Including Camp Children's Perspectives in Refugee Research." *Practicing Anthropology* 36 (3): 38–42.

Coca Pérez, Agustín. 2014. "Los procesos de patrimonialización natural en cuestión: Legitimidad y usos de los recursos en el PN Los Alcornocales (Andalucía)." *Arxius de Sociología* 30: 31–44.

Debarbieux, Bernard, and Martin F. Price. 2012. "Mountain Regions: A Global Common Good?" *Mountain Research and Development* 32 (S1): S7–S11.

Dirlik, Arif. 1996. "The Global in the Local." In *Global/Local: Cultural Production and the Transnational Imaginary,* edited by Rob Wilson and Wimal Dissanayake, 21–45. Durham, NC: Duke University Press.

Fanon, Frantz. 1967. *Black Skin, White Masks,* translated by Charles Lam Markmann. New York: Grove.

Fay, Derrick, and Deborah James. 2009. *The Rights and Wrongs of Land Restitution: "Restoring What Was Ours."* New York: Routledge-Cavendish.

Fletcher, Rebecca Adkins. 2016. "(Re)introduction: The Global Neighborhoods of Appalachian Studies." In *Appalachia Revisited: New Perspectives on Place, Tradition, and Progress,* edited by William Schumann and Rebecca Adkins Fletcher, 275–290. Lexington: University Press of Kentucky.

Frank, Andre Gunder. 1966. "The Development of Underdevelopment." *Monthly Review* 18 (4): 17–31.

Gibson-Graham, J. K. 1996. *The End of Capitalism (As We Knew It): A Feminist Critique of Political Economy.* Cambridge, MA: Blackwell.

Gray, Mary L. 2009. *Out in the Country: Youth, Media, and Queer Visibility in Rural America.* New York: New York University Press.

Kahn, Hilary E. 2014. "Introduction: Framing the Global." In *Framing the Global: Entry Points for Research,* edited by Hilary E. Kahn, 1–17. Bloomington: Indiana University Press.

Kingsolver, Ann E. 2001. *NAFTA Stories: Fears and Hopes in Mexico and the United States.* Boulder, CO: Lynne Rienner.

———. 2011. *Tobacco Town Futures: Global Encounters in Rural Kentucky.* Long Grove, IL: Waveland.

Messerli, Bruno. 2012. "Global Change and the World's Mountains: Where Are We Coming From, and Where Are We Going To?" *Mountain Research and Development* 32 (S1): S55–S63.

Moody, Roger. 2007. *Rocks and Hard Places: The Globalization of Mining.* London: Zed.

Olivera, Oscar, with Tom Lewis. 2004. *¡Cochabamba! Water War in Bolivia.* Cambridge, MA: South End.

Oliver-Smith, Anthony. 2009. "Development-Forced Displacement and Resettlement: A Global Human Rights Crisis." Introduction. In *Development and Dispossession: The Crisis of Forced Displacement and Resettlement,* edited by Anthony Oliver-Smith, 3–23. Santa Fe, NM: School for Advanced Research.

Price, Larry W. 1981. *Mountains and Man: A Study of Process and Environment.* Berkeley: University of California Press.

Santa Ana, Otto. 2002. *Brown Tide Rising: Metaphors of Latinos in Contemporary American Public Discourse*. Austin: University of Texas Press.

Silverblatt, Irene. 1987. *Moon, Sun, and Witches: Gender Ideologies and Class in Inca and Colonial Peru*. Princeton, NJ: Princeton University Press.

Taussig, Michael. 1987. *Shamanism, Colonialism, and the Wild Man: A Study in Terror and Healing*. Chicago: University of Chicago Press.

Tsing, Anna Lowenhaupt. 2015. *The Mushroom at the End of the World: On the Possibility of Life in Capitalist Ruins*. Princeton, NJ: Princeton University Press.

Vaccaro, Ismael, Krista Harper, and Seth Murray. 2016. "The Anthropology of Postindustrialism: Ethnographies of Disconnection." In *The Anthropology of Postindustrialism: Ethnographies of Disconnection*, edited by Ismael Vaccaro, Krista Harper, and Seth Murray, 1–21. New York: Routledge.

Mother Jones' Farewell (I Was There)

Si Kahn

I have been a radical
For fifty years and more
Stood against the rich and greedy
For the workers and the poor
From Canada to Mexico
I traveled everywhere
Wherever trouble called me
I was there

Like stitches in a crazy quilt
That women piece and sew
Wherever there was suffering
I was bound to go
With angry words for cowardice
Comfort for despair
Whenever help was needed
I was there

I was there in the depressions
When times were at their worst
But we had them where we wanted
Like a dam about to burst

With fire in our bellies
Revolution in the air
For a moment we saw clearly
I was there

There were times I saw the issues
In quite a different light
And old friends turned against me
But I never left the fight
When stones were in my passway
And the road was far from clear
Whether I chose right or wrongly
I was there

On a day when hope goes hungry
And your dreams seem bound to fall
You may see me at the mill
Or just outside the union hall
When the clouds are empty promises
The sky a dark despair
Like an eagle from the mountain
I'll be there

And you, my brave young comrades
When the future sounds the call
Will you be there for the battle
Will you answer, one and all
When the roll is called up yonder
When the roll's called anywhere
Will you stand and answer proudly
We're still here
Can you stand and answer proudly
I was there

CHAPTER 2

After Coal, through Film

WELSH AND APPALACHIAN MINING COMMUNITIES

Tom Hansell and Patricia Beaver

AFTER COAL: WELSH *and Appalachian Mining Communities* is a long-term mul-
timedia community engagement project that works with communities in Wales
and Appalachia that are confronting their dependence on fossil fuels. The cen-
terpiece of this project is a feature-length documentary film, released in 2016,
that supports more than 40 years of exchange between these global mountain
regions. Whereas the Appalachian coalfields are struggling with chronic unemployment and environmental degradation, the Welsh coalfields were essentially
closed by the late 1980s and for over a quarter century Wales has experimented
with cultural, economic, and environmental strategies to rebuild communities.
After Coal considers the legacy of coal mining in Wales and Appalachia, from
common experiences of the past to opportunities for the future. Our central
questions are, How do industrial and economic forces shape culture and community? What happens when fossil fuels run out? What is the role of culture in
sustaining community? And how can lessons from these areas speak to other
resource-dependent regions throughout the globe?

    After Coal compares and contrasts the development of the Welsh and Appa-
lachian coalfields and examines the impact of each coalfield on the development
of the United Kingdom and the United States. This history provides valuable context as we explore the distinct Welsh and Appalachian responses to globalization.
Finally, we reflect on what the Welsh experience after coal means for Appalachian
communities that are facing their last generation of mining. We also consider

what comparing these two regions may mean for other mining communities, both in the United States and in developing nations.

Background

Coal reaches deep into our histories as both the United States and the United Kingdom move through the process of deindustrialization. The highly structured, centralized process of coal extraction has shaped communities, families, opportunities for women, the organization of labor, and the arts—especially music. Helen Lewis, Appalachian scholar-activist who has also conducted research in Wales observed, "The industrialized coal mining areas of South Wales and Central Appalachia share several common features: similar highland environments, a history of rural subsistence agro-pastoral economies, colonial experiences as a result of capitalist expansion, and industrialization based on extraction of minerals. Both regions have maintained viable subcultures and developed regional consciousness despite (or because of) their industrialization and integration into an international economy" (H. Lewis 1984, 50).

The roots of the *After Coal* project reach to 1974, when political sociologist John Gaventa videotaped striking coal miners in Wales and in Appalachia and came to Helen Lewis's classes in the Appalachian coalfields in Wise, Virginia. Lewis subsequently was awarded a fellowship from the National Science Foundation and went to Wales in 1975 to research coal-mining culture. Working with Gaventa and filmmaker Richard Greatrex, the team made over 150 videotapes of daily life in South Wales. Historian Hywel Francis helped provide support for the team. Then in 1979 Lewis developed exchanges of Welsh and Appalachian miners and the Center for Appalachian Studies at Appalachian State University has helped continue this exchange over the past three decades though Patricia Beaver's efforts as director of the center. The videotapes made by Lewis, Gaventa, and Greatrex are archived in the W. L. Eury Appalachian Collection archives of Appalachian State University's Belk Library. Over the last decade, Appalachian Collection librarian Fred Hay has overseen the archiving and digitization of all of the tapes that Lewis, Gaventa, and Greatrex made in Wales during the 1970s.

The social, economic, and environmental challenges to Wales and Appalachia in recent decades are at times tragically similar. The coal industry throughout the United Kingdom (including Wales) was privatized and mostly shut down in the 1980s, eliminating more than 85,000 jobs (H. Francis 2009). Meanwhile, according to the US Energy Information Administration, the Appalachian coalfields lost over 70,000 mining jobs between 1980 and 2000. During that same period, the US Environmental Protection Agency reports that more than 1,200 miles of Appalachian streams were buried by mountaintop removal coal mining operations. Throughout Appalachia, slurry dams, holding byproducts of coal production, still threaten communities, not unlike the famous coal tip that claimed the lives of 116 school children and their teachers in the 1966 disaster in Aberfan, Wales (McLean 2000).

Wales and Coal

South Wales is made up of 20 narrow valleys running north–south. Coal's history reaches deep into the seventeenth and eighteenth centuries in Wales through the copper and iron smelting industries, firing the rising industrial order. The advent of the steam engine and the use of coal in shipping and railways in 1840 pushed the expansion of coal mining into the 1,000 square miles that form the South Wales coalfield. The rural forests and farms along the hills and valleys of south Wales were transformed, and by the mid-nineteenth century the coal industry had become the major driver of the Welsh economy.

Comparing Wales and Appalachia, historian and project advisor Ronald Lewis observed: "Within this one-thousand-square mile coal region were anthracite reserves rivaled only by those found in Pennsylvania; the smokeless quality of the bituminous steam coal was unmatched anywhere in the world until the southern West Virginia coalfields were developed at the turn of the twentieth century" (2008, 22). The coalfields of Wales and Appalachia are separated by a vast ocean and regional cultures, yet bound by the common experiences of the hazardous work in coal as the Industrial Revolution enveloped both countries. Work in coal is dangerous and difficult, and mine owners were ruthless in crushing the rising unionism. In South Wales, mid-nineteenth century laws were enacted to ban the abusive work conditions under which women and young children labored in the mines. Welsh trade unions began to organize by 1831 and were firmly established by the 1870s. The South Wales Miners Federation, commonly known as "the Fed," emerged by 1898 and evolved into the South Wales Area of the National Miners Union in 1945 (Francis and Smith 1980, xvi). By the turn of the twentieth century the population of the South Wales mining areas had exploded and more than one quarter of the South Wales workforce worked in coal. In 1914, more than 230,000 men were employed by the coal industry in 485 pits (Davies 1993, 67). Faced with reduced wages, miners went on strike in the early 1920s. In the General Strike of 1926, miners were brutalized by the combined forces of police, troops, and courts.

Hywel Francis explained the impact that industrial unions had on Welsh culture and society: "For over a hundred years—from the 1880's to the 1980's—unions have held a major role in Welsh society. They created the 8 hour work day, formed social benefit clubs, built miners libraries, and offered continuing education as well as a guarantee of health and safety of the miners" (2009, 17). Francis further explained that the National Union of Miners (NUM) philosophy was to set up a system that would use natural resources to benefit the entire nation: "Decisions about how to run the mines were made with their impacts on

Fig. 2.1 The Kentucky Mine Supply building in downtown Harlan, Kentucky.
Photo credit: Tom Hansell

communities in mind—productivity was important, but it was not the only goal of the nationalized mines" (2009, 17).

Retired Welsh miner Terry Thomas, who spoke at the Global Mountain Regions Conference in 2012, reviewed the World War II effort in Britain around coal production, saying that not only was Britain and the rest of the developed world dependent on coal for its industrialization, it was also dependent on coal for fighting its wars. Between 1943 and 1948, 48,000 young men were drafted to work in the mines throughout Great Britain. They became known as the Bevin Boys because the minister responsible for the coal mining industry at that time was Ernest Bevin. His name was attached to the people who were conscripted into the mining industry. Thomas believes that the miners' efforts during World War II have often been overlooked, commenting: "Now, we should remember the people who went to the armed forces and sacrificed their lives in order to gain our freedom. But we should also remember the miners that were killed in the mines during that time and that made it possible for that freedom to be won and that victory to happen" (Thomas 2012).

After decades of labor disputes, the Welsh mines were nationalized in 1947 in a radical departure from the private ownership path of American mines. As Terry Thomas explained, coal tends to be in the mountainous areas and very often in remote areas. As the coal industry developed, it became inevitable that coal miners would form close-knit communities. They worked together, they lived together, they played together, and they fought together. In addition to the usual concerns over wages and safety conditions, the Welsh miners' unions developed social and cultural facilities that improved miner's lives including miners' libraries, male voice choirs, brass bands, and continuing education programs.

As Thomas recalled from that period, the union meant everything. The union became "what we termed 'the poor man's lawyer.' If anybody wanted advice, they couldn't afford to go to high-paid lawyers, and the only place they had to turn to for any protection, any advice, any guidance, was to the union. And that's what made the union so strong in areas like South Wales" (Thomas 2012).

Appalachia and Coal

Industrialization of the Appalachian coalfields began late in the nineteenth century and is part of a folk memory that is, as oral historian Alessandro Portelli describes, "short and intense." Portelli observes, "In Harlan County you feel the nearness of the beginnings. The stories go back to a pristine wilderness, the first migrations and settlements, the Revolution, yet this is a living memory, entrusted to generations of storytellers" (Portelli 2011, 14).

Following the American Civil War, the southern and central Appalachians were promoted as a "magnificent field for capitalists" for their wealth in coal, timber, iron, and water, all the ingredients for a growing industrial order (Eller 1982, 128). About 50 million acres of the Appalachian coalfields were made accessible by the expansion of the rail system into central Appalachia. Driven by late nineteenth-century economic expansion, the Appalachian coalfields, like the Welsh coalfields, experienced monumental growth. "By 1900, coal production in the region had tripled, and in the next three decades it multiplied again more than fivefold, coming to account for almost 80 percent of national production" (Eller 1982, 128).

The coal boom brought dramatic population increases and the recruitment of a diverse labor force. Appalachian natives were joined by African Americans from the Deep South and an international labor force from Italy, Hungary, Greece, Poland, and other European nations, including Welsh, English, and Irish immigrants who came to the southern mountains by way of Pennsylvania (R. Lewis 2008).

The eastern industrialists who financed Appalachia's mines were joined by foreign investors in a frenzy of land speculation, resulting in the concentration of land ownership and mineral rights by the coal industry (Gaventa 1980, 43). The level of control blocked economic diversification, and coal owners were strident in their opposition to unionization. Workers were often paid in company scrip, redeemable only at the company store. They lived in company-owned coal camps and coal towns, where companies also owned the schools, churches, houses, police, health care, recreation facilities, and every dimension of the miners' lives (H. Lewis 1984, 112).

Miners' attempts to organize for better wages and working conditions were met with violent resistance, as the Appalachian coalfields saw "bloody mine wars every decade from 1893 to 1933" (Eller 1982, 123). In Harlan County, Kentucky, the period 1931–1941 was especially brutal, "a war against starvation." Portelli observed, "Everyone involved describes the 1931–1941 period as a ten-year war. The *New York Times* reported: 'Harlan resembles a scene of war'" (2011, 187). The power and the tragedy are captured in Florence Reece's song, penned during the dramatic strike of 1931–1932, "Which Side Are You On?" As in Wales, deep mining in the Appalachian coalfields has been marked by danger and death. "In seventy-five years after the beginning of the industry, at least thirteen hundred men were killed in Harlan County mines" (Portelli 2011, 147).

After the labor reforms of the New Deal guaranteed workers' right to organize, the United Mineworkers of America (UMWA) by 1948 had become the largest union in the country. Unlike Wales, a change in labor laws and rapid mechanization of the industry during the 1950s weakened the union. United Mineworkers of America membership dropped from 600,000 in 1948 to 200,000 in 1990. By 1990, not a single union mine was operating in Harlan County or in all of eastern Kentucky.

In Appalachia, the 1950s saw massive unemployment, accompanying increases in poverty, major out-migrations from the region, and disillusionment with the union. At the same time, many big coal companies, largely untaxed and unregulated, made large profits. Living in Wise, Virginia, and teaching students from the coal communities, Helen Lewis saw firsthand the impoverishment of the coalfields and the wealth of the industry, and she recognized the connections between the local economy and the industrialization of this rural area by an extractive industry whose ownership and interests lay primarily outside the region: "People said the coal industry was dead, but the coal was still being mined and the industry was healthy. I became concerned about how the area of the state which produced the greatest wealth, could be the poorest part of the state, concerned about lack of roads, health care, education" (H. Lewis 2011b, 47).

Retired miner Carl Shoupe from Harlan County, Kentucky remembered: "Coal came in the twentieth century like blazing guns—and that was a good thing back then. But now it is the twenty-first century and coal, in my opinion, is a thing of the past. It was part of my past and it's part of my present, but I don't see it being part of my future or my grandchildren's future" (Shoupe 2012).

Coal Culture and Music

In both Wales and Appalachia, culture has become a buzzword in discussions of economic renewal strategies. However, as Welsh historian Dai Smith (2002, 22) reminds us: "Culture is one of the two or three most complicated words in the English language."

Since the Welsh mines closed, retired miner Allan Flash Pierce reminisces for tourists and school groups in his role as tour guide in the South Wales Mining Museum in the Afan Valley. Community development (in Appalachia) and regeneration (in Wales) are manifest in multiple forms of cultural expression: theater, public art, poetry and literature, museums, cultural and music festivals. Yet Smith warns us, as do other critics, of the perils of turning mining museums like the South Wales Mining Museum in Wales or the Portal 31 exhibition coal mine in Harlan County, Kentucky, into commercialized cultural fast foods. Smith's vision is "to breath[e] in again and fill the lungs with the fresher thought of how culture, as more than a mere commercial spin off, might yet become the unique deliverer of Wales' specific 21st century needs" (Smith 2002, 23).

In Appalachia and Wales, music has played a major role in shaping coalfield culture and identity, unifying resistance, giving voice to movements and to grieving. Scholars and community organizers alike have examined music, art, and popular culture "as key determinants of citizen identity; as contested terrains of political action; as forms of communication ideally suited for developing alternative visions of being and society; as prefigurative spaces in which new political ideas and practices emerge; and as essential and constitutive ingredients of a vital democracy" (Love and Mattern 2010, 463).

From 1974 to 1976 Helen Lewis, John Gaventa, and Richard Greatrex documented Welsh choirs, silver bands, and pub singing. At the same time in Appalachia, folklorists and indigenous groups such as the Appalshop Media Arts Center documented music created out of the coalfield experience by Nimrod Workman, Sarah Ogan Gunning, Florence Reece, the African Methodist Episcopal (AME Zion) Church Choir of Harlan County, Kentucky, and numerous others (see, for example, Wright 2007). Reflecting on these efforts, Helen Lewis says "I think what we did was to document the last generation of a real coal mining culture" (2011a). Although the mining jobs have left both Wales and Appalachia, the music remains a force that helps communities stay together.

Transitions through the 1970s: Documenting Wales and Appalachia

The 1970s was a pivotal time in both South Wales and Appalachia, foreshadowing unprecedented changes that would soon come to both regions. Project advisor John Gaventa reflects on this period: "In 1974 I was living in Clairfield, Tennessee, trying to understand how a British-owned multinational had developed its corporate power in rural east Tennessee and east Kentucky, as well as working with a bold group of citizens to challenge that power. This work informed my later book *Power and Powerlessness: Quiescence and Rebellion in an Appalachian Valley*. While students in Oxford, England, Richard Greatrex and I had done some very rough videotapes in Wales of the 1974 Miners' Strike. Helen [Lewis] invited me over to one of her classes at Clinch Valley College to show the tapes" (Gaventa 2011, 82).

For her part, Helen Lewis recalled her interest and motivation for traveling to Wales from the Appalachian coalfields.

> I had been teaching in the Appalachian coalfields for about 20 years, and I had developed a big interest in understanding what coal mining—in particular extractive industries or industrialization in general—did to mountain communities. . . . I got a postdoctoral fellowship from the National Science Foundation. . . . and went to Wales. . . . John Gaventa was over there. His friend Richard Greatrex, a Welsh filmmaker, had been in the States for a year working with Vanderbilt Center for Health Services and was going back home. He agreed to do videotapes in the mining communities if I would provide him with room and board. So I piggybacked this whole Welsh videotape production on my fellowship. Most weekends John would come to Wales, and he and Richard and I would videotape Welsh community scenes. We also used the grant for an exchange; we brought Hazel Dickens, Mike Seeger and that group of musicians—Rich Kirby, John McCutcheon, some of the Brookside mine women. . . . It was an invasion of the Americans in this mining community where they hadn't seen Americans since World War II (2011b, 85).

Their videotapes of Wales are far ranging, including miners' discussions of labor politics, memories of strikes, visits to mine sites, women's work and women's lives, marriage and family, village businesses—including the bakery, hotel, bicycle shop, and dairy—pub singing, brass band music, bingo nights, miners on the job, village scenes and landscapes, as well as preachers, teachers, and youth talking about Welsh culture and language. This documentation captures the last decade of full-scale mining and coalfield community life in South Wales and provides an anchor for the *After Coal* project.

Returning to the United States, Helen Lewis organized an exchange of coal miners in 1979, which brought a seven-man delegation from South Wales to Appalachia. Hywel Francis and Ron Reece were among them. Francis observed that the differences between Appalachia and Wales were "enormous," most notably in the United States the private ownership of the coal industry, the existence of women miners, poor safety standards, and the treatment and prevention of industrial diseases such as black lung. They also felt that "the American miners were living and struggling through a period which our parents and grandparents had already experienced but also we were seeing the all too obvious effects of the energy crisis and an economic slump which would ultimately affect our own coalfields." Yet in his report on the exchange, Hywel Francis concluded, "Miners throughout the world have much in common. As far as those of South Wales and Appalachia are concerned, more things unite us than divide us" (1979, 16).

In Appalachia, the 1970s signaled improvement in mine health and safety, as the Federal Mine Safety and Health Administration began to enforce the 1969 Coal Mine Health and Safety Act. Rank and file members of the UMWA were working to reform the union and oust corrupt leadership. The Black Lung

Movement was pushing for a compensation plan for coal miner's pneumoconiosis, a disease that had been recognized and compensated in Wales since the 1940s. Later in the decade, the Coal Employment Project pushed for the increased hiring of woman coal miners. These regional efforts in Appalachia were connected to national efforts in the United States such as the Equal Rights Amendment, the Clean Water Act, and the Clean Air Act.

Globalization and the 1980s

Hywel Francis recalled, "I had visited the Appalachian coalfields with six rank-and-file miners from Brynlliw and Maerdy in May 1979, just at the very moment that Margaret Thatcher won her momentous General Election victory. Our report, South Wales Miners in America, mirrored our own past and what was to be our own future—hostile employers, non-unionism, anti-union laws and expanding opencast mining" (2009, xi).

In the 1980s, the newly elected Conservative government began a policy of scrutinizing the profitability of the nationalized mines, and the Welsh coal industry faced the threat of expanded energy imports. Between 1980 and 1984, tens of thousands of jobs were eliminated as Welsh coal was replaced by coal from subsidized mines in Poland and apartheid labor conditions in South Africa. An additional move to cut jobs and close mines led the National Union of Miners to begin a nationwide strike in 1984.

The 1984–1985 coal strike was unprecedented in the involvement of both local community groups and elaborate support networks reaching across Wales, the United Kingdom, and internationally, especially women's support groups. Hywel Francis notes, "what made the local struggle so different was the role of women. They did not simply support; they led" (2009, xix). Welsh activist Mair Francis describes the importance of the work of women of the Welsh valleys during the strike: "the women in our support group became active on the political stage during the miner's strike. They spoke alongside union leaders, politicians (usually male), marched on demonstrations, and picketed" (M. Francis 2008).

The strikes of 1984–1985 bear witness to the depth and structure of the South Wales valley communities and the particular ways that community culture formed around coal. The culmination of what Hywel Francis calls that "terrible and glorious year" was the final disappearance of coal mining from much of the area, and feelings that were "apocalyptic. . . . In such remote communities, the closures of schools and libraries, the end of bus services, the demolition of houses, the loss of a doctor from a practice, even the disappearance of a telephone kiosk, were all cumulative symptoms of a long-term decline. But this last rundown of colliery closures severed the surviving link with an industry that had given birth to these communities barely a century before. And yet resilience, a community spirit, and a political consciousness, stiffened by the recent struggle remained" (2009, 78). Francis reflects "Everyone somewhere or other in Wales feels as if they have their roots in coal. Communities always change. Industries come and go, and it was foolish of us to think at the end of the '85 strike that it was the end of the world. It was the opportunity for a new beginning and we should have never really have been so committed to sustaining communities on the back of an industry like coal" (2012).

Meanwhile, in Appalachia, pressure from an increasingly global coal market caused many mining companies to reorganize, forming subsidiaries to escape the high labor cost of union contracts.

Different Paths: The 1990s

By the end of the 1980s, the British government had finally begun to propose strategies for economic regeneration. In Wales the Valleys Initiative was launched in 1988 to initiate "new and diverse jobs," as well as environmental and community improvements. Reclamation of abandoned mine sites became a cornerstone of the Welsh strategy for regeneration. Together with tourism initiatives centered around national parks and other sites such as the South Wales Mining Museum, many government efforts seemed designed to attract wealthy visitors to the region.

Community education and lifelong learning were another important element for economic regeneration. The Valley Initiative for Adult Education and the Dulais Valley Education Initiative (DOVE) provide examples of this approach. Project advisor Mair Francis helped start the DOVE workshops, and described her intent during a 2010 symposium at Appalachian State University: "Women in the area were given secondary roles, they were invisible. The organizations within the valley were controlled by men, men were the voices.... And so we knew that when we set up DOVE, it had to be run and organized by women for women."

By combining traditional and nontraditional teaching styles with public transportation and a day nursery, the DOVE has expanded into a national model for the role of education and economic development. Mair Francis recounted that "by 2009, a broad, formal curriculum met the needs of adults returning for personal development, health, and well-being, employment prospects and further, and higher-learning. Now we find that this type of work is being recognized nationally" (M. Francis 2010).

In Appalachia, the response to an increasingly globalized energy market was led by the coal industry; the nation's largest mining companies, together with railroads and electrical utilities, aggressively lobbied state and federal government for deregulation. As a consequence, during the past two decades, the Appalachian coalfields have suffered increased environmental problems from mountaintop removal coal mining, as well as a decline in enforcement of health, safety, and environmental regulations. The plight of the town of Benham, Kentucky, where the city council has sued the state to protect the town's water supply from being polluted by coal mining, provides an example of how Appalachian coalfield communities are responding to the pressures of a global economy.

Helen Lewis sees present day Appalachia in global context:

> In this new phase of capitalist expansion, we find that Appalachia and rural America become like third world economies and share their problems, high unemployment, lower wages, environmental degradation, community destruction, increasing poverty. . . . There has been a decline in democracy, growing distrust in and alienation from government and less participation in civic affairs. In the '30s when the social contract of the New Deal was being formed, people looked to the government to provide some protection and security from the failures of the economic system. This is now questioned. Public schools and social security are in danger of being privatized. For some the government is an enemy to be destroyed. (H. Lewis 2010, 8)

Imagining the Future, Honoring the Past

Increasing evidence points to the final days of coal in the Appalachian coalfields. The US Energy Information Administration reported that eastern coal production is in decline, from 188 million tons in 2011 to 112 million tons by 2015 (Rivard 2011). Alpha Natural Resources, one of the region's largest coal companies, claimed a "sharp drop in Appalachian coal production," confirmed by a March 2013 report from Kentucky's Cabinet for Energy and Environmental Protection, which placed coal production "at its lowest level since 1965." Meanwhile, the US Geological Survey has revised its estimate of the minable coal in Central Appalachia from 100 years to around 30 years. Coal is harder and more expensive to mine, not even considering the social and environmental costs of mountaintop removal mining. Deep mining accidents, like Massey's Upper Big Branch in April 2010, and the death of 29 miners, continue to jar America's consciousness.

As communities in Appalachia face the end of an industry that has defined much of the region, Helen Lewis explains how we must seek to bring people together to imagine the future:

There are many community grassroots groups trying to rebuild their communities, deal with environmental problems, develop coalitions. But people seem less confident of what to do about the many problems. . . . We need something today to bring people together to deal with the destruction of our communities, degradation of the environment, growing poverty, economic distress and alienation and not just in our country but worldwide. We cannot hide from the fact that we are part of a global economy, but we can work to be cooperative, helpful and not exploitive. We live on a fragile planet–we are all spinning around together and need to come together to save us all (H. Lewis 2010, 7).

In Wales, Appalachia, and other coalfields communities, cultural owner-ship through community is necessary for regeneration, and local groups within Wales and Appalachia must "own themselves in different ways" through culture and education (Smith 2002, 24). Welsh historian Dai Smith has written about the importance of "building anew so that the texture of the vanished histori-cal environment is captured again, in its detail, but in other forms of retention. Transforming a landscape into a mindscape. And, if possible, a fresh building of purpose" (2002, 23).

After Coal has brought together coalfield residents and scholars to consider how to face the challenges of their future. Love and Mattern (2010, 464) have asked questions that inform our quest: "In what concrete ways are contemporary art and popular culture forms used to increase the capacities of individuals and groups to act effectively in the world?"

Conclusion

We are interested in changing the conversation from the narrowly defined debate over jobs versus environment to the broader question, "What is good for local communities?" The exchange between Appalachia and Wales that Helen Lewis and John Gaventa pioneered in the 1970s provides an opening that may move the conversation forward. In May of 2012, we went to Wales to document the Welsh approach to economic transition, or what the Welsh call "community regenera-tion," Here's what we found:

1. There is no magic bullet—former mining communities in the Welsh Valleys are doing better than in the 1980s, but population has dropped and employ-ment remains low.
2. The first step they took was the "greening the valleys" government programs to clean up mine waste piles (called "tips"), acid mine drainage, and other sources of pollution.
3. Government needs to be part of the solution. For it to be part of the solution, people need to be actively involved in the process of government.
4. Grassroots groups also need to be part of the solution. The longest lasting initiatives are where people started their own program to meet their own needs (for example, the DOVE workshop in Banwen, Wales).
5. Perhaps most important, energy is still an intensely debated issue. In some areas coal is making a small resurgence—the latest figures have about 1,000 miners working in Wales. But a critical difference in Wales is the existence of strict reclamation laws so that communities know that within a certain number of years, with strip mines or open-cast mines, the contours of the land and vegetation will be restored.
6. Meanwhile, energy corporations and the Welsh government have made a serious commitment to wind power—spinning turbines are commonplace

above the former mining valleys. The government has partnered with private power companies to develop these wind farms and is now exploring large-scale tidal power.

On the surface this all sounds productive. However, these former mining communities have well-founded concerns about outside corporations developing these energy sources and not leaving anything behind in the community. When we look at the proposal for a wind farm with 87 new wind turbines to overlook the Afan Valley, we must ask ourselves "Who benefits?" It is the local communities or the stockholders of some offshore corporation?

Response to *After Coal*

The *After Coal* documentary was released in 2016, opening at the Hay Festival in Wales and at the Princeton Environmental Film Festival in the United States. Over the past year, the documentary has been shown at more than 70 locations, including public television broadcasts in Kentucky and West Virginia. Citizens groups have used the films to start conversations about a "just transition" from fossil fuels. The idea of a just transition includes providing new opportunities for laid-off miners and community members impacted by dramatic changes in global energy markets. *After Coal* may not offer all of the answers for economic prosperity, but our hope is that the people featured in the film will inspire other coal-impacted communities to articulate their hopes for the future. A companion book for the documentary will be published in 2018.

Postscript: Remembering Terry Thomas

Terry Thomas died in 2016 at the age of 78. He was an important voice in the *After Coal* film and in the education of the filmmakers. Terry began work in coal in 1960 in the Garngoch No. 3 Colliery in Gorseinon, and then moved to Brynlliw Colliery (H. Francis 2017). He soon became active in the NUM and was elected local branch secretary. Terry went on to serve as vice president of the South Wales NUM between 1983 and 1989, coordinating difficult negotiations throughout the 1984–1985 national strike year. He later served as a chairman of the Wales Executive Committee of the Labour Party (see Gaventa 2017).

We met Terry while researching the film. He led us on a tour of many south Wales mining sites. In 2012 Terry Thomas came to Appalachia where he joined us for the presentation discussing *After Coal* at the Global Mountain Regions Conference sponsored by the Appalachian Center at the University of Kentucky, which provides the basis for this book. At the conference, Terry spoke passionately about the strength of communities, the history of the Bevin Boys, and the hard organizing work of Welsh labor during the past century. Then he traveled to Harlan County, Kentucky, where he met retired miner Carl Shoupe for a spirited exchange and tour of mining sites in Benham, Kentucky, which is featured in *After Coal*. Terry was wise, passionate, adventurous, and full of stories, and we will miss him.

Tom Hansell is Assistant Professor of Appalachian Studies and codirector of University Documentary Film Services at Appalachian State University. He is a documentary filmmaker and installation artist who has worked on creative placemaking projects in Appalachia for more than twenty years. His films and artwork have been broadcast, screened, and exhibited nationally and internationally. He directed *After Coal: Wales and Appalachian Mining Communities* and authored a companion book.

Patricia Beaver is Professor Emerita of Anthropology at Appalachian State University, where she was the founding director of the Center for Appalachian Studies. She has authored and edited numerous articles and books and is co-producer of the documentary film *After Coal: Wales and Appalachian Mining Communities*.

References

Davies, John. 1993. *A History of Wales*. London: Penguin.

Eller, Ronald. 1982. *Miners, Millhands and Mountaineers: Industrialization of the Appalachian South, 1880–1930*. Knoxville: University of Tennessee Press.

Francis, Hywel, ed. 1979. *South Wales Miners in America: Report of the First Rank and File British Miners' Delegation to Visit the United States Coalfields*. Brynlliw and Mardy Lodges of the NUM, May.

———. 2009. *History on Our Side: Wales and the 1984–1985 Miners' Strike*. Fernbank, Ferryside, Wales: Iconau.

———. 2012. Interview for *After Coal* film project, Crynant, UK, June.

———. 2017 "Tribute to Terry Thomas (1938–2016)." Gorseinon Workingmen's Club, South Wales. January 20.

Francis, Hywel, and David Smith. 1980. *The Fed: History of the South Wales Miners in the Twentieth Century*. London: Lawrence and Wishart.

Francis, Mair. 2008. *Up the DOVE! The History of the DOVE Workshop in Banwen*. Banwen, Neath, UK: Dove Workshop.

———. 2010. "Wales after Coal: The DOVE." Symposium on Coal and after Coal, Appalachian State University, Boone, NC. October 14–16.

———. 2012. Interview for *After Coal* film project, Crynant, UK, June.

Gaventa, John. 1980. *Power and Powerlessness: Quiescence and Rebellion in an Appalachian Valley*. Urbana: University of Illinois Press.

———. 2011. "Local to Global, 1977–1985." In *Helen Matthews Lewis: Living Social Justice in Appalachia*, edited by Patricia Beaver and Judith Jennings, 82–84. Lexington: University Press of Kentucky.

———. 2017. "Remembering Terry Thomas." Gorseinon Workingmen's Club, South Wales, January 20.

Lewis, Helen M. 1984. "Industrialization, Class and Regional Consciousness in Two Highland Societies: Wales and Appalachia." In *Cultural Adaptation to Mountain Environments,* edited by Patricia D. Beaver and Burton L. Purrington, 50–70. Athens: University of Georgia Press.

———. 2010. "A Clean Glass of Water for Every Appalachian Child," Appalachian Transition Initiative, University of Colorado, Denver, January.

———. 2011a. Interview for *After Coal* Project. Eastern Kentucky University, March 22.

———. 2011b. *Helen Matthews Lewis: Living Social Justice in Appalachia,* edited by Patricia Beaver and Judith Jennings. Lexington: University Press of Kentucky.

Lewis, Ronald. 2008. *Welsh Americans: A History of Assimilation in the Coalfields.* Chapel Hill: University of North Carolina Press.

Love, Nancy S., and Mark Mattern. 2010. "Introduction." *New Political Science: A Journal of Politics and Culture* 312 (4): 463–469.

McLean, Iain. 2000. "Corporatism and Regulatory Failure: Government Response to the Aberfan Disaster." Project Director's Report. Economic & Social Research Council.

Portelli, Alessandro. 2011. *They Say in Harlan County: An Oral History.* New York: Oxford University Press.

Rivard, Ry. 2011. "CEO Forsees Decline of WVA Coal." *Charleston Daily Mail*, May 30.

Shoupe, Carl. 2012. Interview for *After Coal* Project, Harlan, Kentucky, June 6.

Smith, Dai. 2002. "Wales, Culture & Regeneration." *Bevan Foundation Review* 1: 23–24.

Thomas, Terry. 2012. "After Coal: Welsh and Appalachian Mining Communities." Global Mountain Regions Conference, University of Kentucky, Lexington, KY, October 24.

Wright, Jack. 2007. *Music of Coal: Mining Songs from the Appalachian Coalfields.* Big Stone Gap, VA: Lonesome Records & Publishing BMI.

Wigan Pier

Si Kahn

The mines are closed in the northwest country
Time like the colliery wheel stands still
Children at play where the work once called us
The work is gone but we're still living here
Living on the road to Wigan Pier

Memory settles like early evening
Light like the Davey Lamps all gone down
Colliery theme parks and miners' statues
Are all the proof that we were here
Living on the road to Wigan Pier

Who will stand and who remember
Who still hears that whistle blow
Who will wait beside the window
For the black-faced miner
Coming down the road

Time marches on just like Coxey's Army
Were those the bad or the good old days?
We live in fear of the dream that failed us
The dream is done but we're still here
Living on the road to Wigan Pier

CHAPTER 3

Mountains, Coal, and Life in British Columbia and West Virginia

Paul S. Ciccantell

MOUNTAINTOP REMOVAL COAL mining in Appalachia has been increasingly criticized for its negative impacts on the environment, human health, and local communities. However, the same mining technology has been employed to mine coal in southeastern British Columbia for more than four decades with far fewer negative environmental and social impacts and generally much greater economic benefits for local communities. This chapter presents a comparison of these two cases to analyze the differences between the two regions. The major causes of the differences identified in this analysis are the natural characteristics of the rock in the Canadian Rockies versus the Appalachian Mountains, the more stringent environmental regulation and enforcement in Canada than in the United States, and, probably most important, the very different historical uses and legacies of these uses, with far less extensive and less negative historical legacies in Canada in comparison with Appalachia.

Same Raw Material, Different Worlds

Coal has been a central economic pillar of the economies of West Virginia and Kentucky in the Appalachian Mountains and southeastern British Columbia in the Canadian Rockies for decades. Millions of tons of high-quality coal have been extracted via mountaintop removal techniques from both areas and shipped to distant markets by firms typically headquartered far from these extractive peripheries. In both regions, the scale of production has increased dramatically, output per worker has soared, and total employment in coal mining has fallen as mountaintop removal has become the key technology for extracting coal.

However, despite the many material similarities, the differences between these regions are even more striking. In southeastern British Columbia, the Elk River is one of the world's best trout fisheries, while eating fish caught in Appalachia is often not advisable. Average household income is more than twice as high, and average house prices are more than three times higher in the Regional District of East Kootenay (RDEK) in southeastern British Columbia than in two comparable counties in southern West Virginia, Raleigh and Fayette, the area where both of my grandfathers worked as coal miners. Perhaps most telling, the negative economic, social, and environmental impacts of the coal industry in Appalachia have been the subject of a great deal of analysis at least since the early 1960s (Caudill 1962), a stream of research that has expanded dramatically as mountaintop removal has become the key technology of extraction (see, e.g., Burns 2007; Reece 2006; Ahern et al. 2011a, 2011b; Zegre et al. 2013; Griffith et al. 2012; Hendryx and Zullig 2009; Hendryx et al. 2008; Collins et al. 2012; Wishart 2012; Perdue and Pavela 2012; Austin and Clark 2012; Bell and York 2012; Burns, Evans, and House 2009; Johannsen et al. 2005). However, no comparable literature exists in regard to southeastern British Columbia, despite its even greater reliance on mountaintop removal. This raises a fundamental question: why are these two coal-mining regions so different? Given my experiences in my family's home area of southern West Virginia, my first visit to southeastern British Columbia was rather disconcerting; answering this question about the reasons for these differences became a long-term research interest.

This chapter is a first cut at identifying the causes of these dramatic differences. The analysis in this chapter is based on a wide variety of data, including government census and environmental reports, industry documents, interviews and observations from several field visits to southeastern British Columbia, a variety of academic literatures, and media reports.

In this chapter, I briefly outline the similar natural and social histories of coal mining in the two regions from the late 1800s through 1960. Next I describe the shift to mountaintop removal mining (MTR) in the Elk Valley as the coal industry underwent a long boom and then a subsequent bust of coal mining that was driven by demand for coal in Japan from the mid-1960s through the 1990s. I will also briefly compare this to the rise of MTR and changing markets for southern West Virginia coal during this period. I then examine the China-driven global coal boom and the efforts to diversify southeastern British Columbia's economy and move away from sole dependence on coal by increasing investment in tourism, in comparison to the expansion of MTR in southern West Virginia and the much less effective efforts to diversify the economic base of southern

Table 3.1 Comparative data, population, housing, and coal production

	Raleigh Co., WV	Fayette Co., WV	RDEK, BC
Population 2016	76,601	44,323	60,439
Median household income[a]	41,032	36,293	79,764
Median housing price	101,700	77,100	300,715
Surface-mined coal 2015	2.7	0.42	0
MTR coal production 2013[b]	1.76	0.37	25

[a]Median household income and median housing price: WV average 2011–2015; Regional District of East Kootenay (RDEK), BC data for 2011.
[b]MTR, mountain top removal mining; in millions of tons.
Sources: Statistics Canada, US Census Bureau.

West Virginia. The concluding section offers an outline of the key factors that led to the dramatic differences between these two regions.

Similar Natural and Social Histories from the Late 1800s through 1960

The Canadian Rockies in British Columbia and the Appalachian Mountains in southern West Virginia share a number of key natural similarities. Both regions contain large amounts of high-quality metallurgical coal (used for producing coke to process iron ore into steel and to process other ores, including copper) and steam coal (used for generating electricity). The geologic processes that created mountains in both regions produced this high-quality coal but covered it with overburden and created coal seams that are often discontinuous and angled. Further, the mountainous topography makes transporting the extracted coal difficult and expensive. In short, the coal in both regions has long been attractive to mining and coal-using firms because of these natural characteristics, but extracting and transporting the coal is challenging and costly.

However, several natural differences are worthy of note. Coal seams in British Columbia are generally larger and lie in higher (up to 11,000 feet) and extremely steep mountains in comparison to West Virginia (most mines are between 2,000 and 3,600 feet in elevation), but the surrounding rock is much less likely to release acid when disturbed via mining than is the case in Appalachia. Coal is more accessible in West Virginia, but potentially much more disruptive of surrounding ecosystems because of these natural differences. Further, the climate in British Columbia is much colder and more severe than in West Virginia, and, in combination with differences in topography, British Columbia had limited arable land and less timber coverage than was the case in West Virginia (Ramsey 1997; Cohen 1984), all of which meant that opportunities for alternative economic uses of the area for farming and logging were much less in British Columbia than in West Virginia.

These natural characteristics, in combination with the long distances to potential coal markets, meant that coal extraction on a significant scale in British Columbia had to await the arrival of railroads. In the Elk Valley, the arrival of the Canadian Pacific Railway via the Crowsnest Pass line in 1898 opened the area for coal exploration and development. Although small deposits were already known (Ramsey 1997), employees of the Canadian Pacific located extensive deposits on the Alberta side of the border in the Crowsnest Pass region and in the Elk Valley on the British Columbia side of the border. The area's proximity to the metal mining and smelting industry of Montana and to the mainline of the Great Northern Railway (GNR) in the United States owned by J. J. Hill also led to exploration and coal development by affiliates of the GNR (some of the deposits Hill's affiliates developed in the Elk Valley and the Crowsnest Pass region were actually purchased from the Canadian Pacific Railway [CPR], which for a time had little interest in coal mining) and the construction of a branch line across the border to transport coal and coke to Montana and other US markets (Den Otter 1984; Ramsey 1997).

In West Virginia, the coalfields of Fayette and Raleigh counties, including the very large New River coalfield, became viable after the construction of rail lines into the area by the Chesapeake and Ohio Railroad in the 1870s, which could transport coal both east to the Virginia coast for shipment to the US Northeast and for export and west and north to industrial centers across the Midwest. The Norfolk and Western Railroad reached southern West Virginia in 1881 and shipped coal east to the Virginia coast as well. The third railway serving the region, the Virginian, arrived much later (in the early 1900s) and shipped coal east to its own port facilities on the Virginia coast (Dixon 2009). Thus, the Elk Valley and Fayette and Raleigh counties became major coal producers for distant domestic and international markets between 1880 and 1910 after the arrival of rails, and both regions expanded coal mining rapidly in the early years of the twentieth century.

Once the entry of the railroads solved the transport problem presented by the mountainous terrain and remote locations of the coal deposits in West Virginia and British Columbia, the coal-mining industry in both areas developed along similar lines. The railroads themselves provided a market for these areas' coal and some of the capital needed to develop these coal deposits. Once the initially discovered small outcrops of coal had been mined, firms in both regions moved on to small and then progressively larger underground mines in the first half of the twentieth century as underground mining technology slowly increased in scale. Ownership of coal mines in both regions was almost all in the hands of external owners who used the regions' naturally produced coal for their own interests: the Canadian Pacific Railway based in Toronto and the Great Northern Railway with its owners based in Seattle, Spokane, and Minneapolis in the

British Columbia case (Ramsey 1997; Den Otter 1984; Davies 1998), and a variety of mining and steel firms based in New York, Pittsburgh, and other industrial cities in the case of West Virginia.

Because of the small non–Native American populations in both regions, coal companies typically built company-owned towns to house workers and engaged in extensive efforts to bring in miners from eastern cities and from southern and eastern Europe; many Italians, for example, arrived in both regions in the first third of the twentieth century (Basile and Byers 2011; Giuliano 2002). Working and living conditions in these coal camps were very difficult in both regions, and companies often used ownership of houses and stores as means of labor control (Caudill 1962; Ramsey 1997, 1990; Norton and Miller 1998; Norton and Langford 2002; Buckley 2004). Despite often strong opposition from mining companies and governmental units, the United Mine Workers and other unions successfully organized coal miners in both West Virginia and British Columbia. Repeated prolonged conflicts between management and labor became endemic in both regions during the twentieth century (Ramsey 1990, 1997; Cohen 1984; Savage 1990; Blizzard 2004; Corbin 1990; Lunt 1992). During my first visit to British Columbia in the 1990s, my reaction to the stories told by longtime residents about life in the coal camps was always "that sounds exactly like life in the West Virginia coal camps where my grandparents and parents lived."

In terms of the local impacts of the coal mines in the first half of the twentieth century, the stories in both regions were also similar: few local linkages to other forms of economic activity were created. Some local processing of coal into coke in coke ovens did occur in both regions, but this largely disappeared by the mid-twentieth century in both regions (Ramsey 1997; Cohen 1984). Other than this highly polluting form of initial processing, no other coal was used locally in this period for potential forward linkages such as coal-fired power plants, and no inputs (backward linkages) into coal-mining equipment or even into agriculture to supply food became important sources of employment or economic development in either region. Coal-fired electricity generation became a significant coal consumer in mid-twentieth century West Virginia, but no coal-fired generation facility has ever been built in the Elk Valley, despite several efforts to do so over the decades.

Both southeastern British Columbia and southern West Virginia endured a series of booms and busts in the coal industry in the first half of the twentieth century, including a boom during World War I and much of the 1920s, a bust during the Great Depression, and a revival during mobilization for World War II. Moreover, both regions entered similar stages of stagnation and decline during the 1950s for similar reasons. The railroads in both the United States and Canada shifted rapidly from coal to diesel power (Dixon 2009), and oil became a dominant fuel source, not just for transport but also for electricity generation.

In both regions, coal output declined, many workers lost their jobs or were able to work only a limited number of days each month, and coal-dependent regional economies and communities faced severe economic difficulties and pressure for unemployed workers, their families, and young people to leave in search of other economic opportunities (Caudill 1962).

In terms of alternatives to coal mining as an economic activity, the natural characteristics of southeastern British Columbia and southern West Virginia presented very different possibilities during the late 1800s and first half of the 1900s. In British Columbia, the steep mountainous terrain, high altitude, harsh winters, and extreme climate that limited the growing season combined to severely limit potential agricultural use, other than in small areas of land along rivers and streams. Forestry is possible in some areas of southeastern British Columbia, but the harsh climate limits the diversity of the forests; much of the forest cover is evergreens. Logging has been a secondary economic activity in the Elk Valley for more than century, but it is dwarfed by the coal industry. In contrast, the lower altitudes and more temperate climate of much of Appalachia resulted in much more diverse forests, with many large hardwood trees that were decades or even centuries old by the time the railroads opened the region for logging. The rapid expansion of logging and the resulting deforestation of much of West Virginia by the mid-1950s (Lewis 1998; Williams 2002) was an important economic alternative for the region's population, but one that left a legacy of lost topsoil, ecosystem degradation, and rapid rainwater runoff and erosion that continue to plague people and ecosystems today. However, the scale of the logging industry has decreased dramatically since the mid-twentieth century. The older, more weathered mountains of Appalachia also created larger river valleys with greater agricultural potential than was the case in southeastern British Columbia, making agriculture a more important economic activity in West Virginia.

Mountaintop Removal, the Japan-Driven Coal Boom, and Boom and Bust Cycles, 1960s–1990s

From the mid-1960s through the early 1980s, both areas experienced a period of renewed coal-fueled growth, although for somewhat different reasons. In British Columbia, rapid economic growth in resource-poor Japan led by the development of the world's largest steel industry created tremendous demand for and a huge wave of investment in the Elk Valley's metallurgical coal deposits to fuel Japanese economic development (Bunker and Ciccantell 2005, 2007). In West Virginia, rising oil prices after the first oil crisis in 1972 and 1973 led to a shift back to coal as a source of fuel for electricity generation. Despite the ongoing decline of the US steel industry during the 1970s and 1980s, rising demand for metallurgical coal in Japan led to the expansion of the export of US coal from West Virginia to Japan.

The boom and bust cycles of both of these coal-dependent regions moved back to bust from the mid-1980s until the late 1990s, although for very different reasons. In West Virginia, increasing regulation of air pollution produced by burning higher sulfur-content Appalachian coals led to a long-term shift to the use of less polluting but lower quality coal from the Powder River Basin in Wyoming and Montana. In British Columbia, strategic small investments and signing of long-term contracts with a large number of new coal mines in the Elk Valley, northeastern British Columbia, and Australia by Japanese steel mills led to excess global coal mining capacity, a situation that the Japanese steel firms used to drive down prices. The result was the bankruptcy of some mining companies, long-term strikes by labor unions in the face of efforts by firms to cut labor costs, and a severe depression in the Elk Valley (Bunker and Ciccantell 2005, 2007).

The technological evolution of the coal industry in both regions has been remarkably similar as well. The small, labor-intensive, relatively high-cost underground mines of the first half of the twentieth century have increasingly been supplanted by large-scale surface mines in both West Virginia and British Columbia. The process that Caudill (1962) begins to describe in Appalachia in the late 1950s and early 1960s has expanded and transformed into something barely recognizable to coal miners from the 1950s. Large underground mines can extract a million tons or more of coal a year due to larger, faster cutting and hauling machines in Appalachia (technologies that have never been introduced in British Columbia). However, the move in both West Virginia and British Columbia from the use of small-scale bulldozers, loaders, and dump trucks in the early 1960s in conventional surface mines that could only access coal deposits relatively close to the surface to monstrous drag lines, shovels, loaders and dump trucks that can move 420 tons of coal or rock in one load in mountaintop removal mines has been far more transformative of the coal industry, topography, and ecosystems in both southern West Virginia and the Elk Valley of British Columbia.

It is important to emphasize that both regions now employ the same technology of mountaintop removal mining, although both the absolute size and the scale of these operations are quite different. In the Elk Valley today, five MTR mines produce 25 million tons of coal per year, while in Raleigh County MTR mines produce only 2.74 million tons per year and in Fayette County only 0.28 million tons per year. One coal executive in Canada put it to me succinctly when I asked him about the environmental impacts of coal mining in western Canada, "we're tearing down mountains." The same large-scale equipment and blasting that has attracted so much negative attention in Appalachia in recent years (see, e.g., Burns 2007; Reece 2006; Austin and Clark 2012; Bell and York 2012; Burns, Evans, and House 2009; Johannsen et al. 2005) is used in the Elk Valley, but on a far larger scale and with far fewer negative impacts than in West Virginia. This seeming paradox is central to my research, because the reasons for it, along with the role of the ski tourism and second home industry, lie at the heart of the dramatic differences to be seen in southern West Virginia and the Elk Valley today.

The regulation of coal mining, particularly the respect for and enforcement of these regulations, differs markedly in West Virginia and British Columbia. While both federal as well as state and provincial government agencies are involved in regulating mining, much of the responsibility for monitoring environmental impacts and enforcing regulations rests with the West Virginia state and British Columbia provincial government agencies. Further, both West Virginia and British Columbia rely heavily on the mining firms themselves for monitoring and reporting environmental impacts. However, the attitudes and behaviors of firms in the two regions appear to differ markedly. Many observers in West Virginia are highly critical of MTR mining firms' behavior with respect to the environment, while the firm that owns the five coal mines in the Elk Valley, Teck Corporation, is seen by both industry and government as a leader in environmental protection in Canada and globally. The attention paid to control of drainage from mining areas, protection of wildlife, restoration of soil and plant life after mining is completed, and many other areas of environmental impact by miners and the mining company in the Elk Valley has been striking in my conversations with miners, government officials, and area residents. Moreover, the lack of downstream consequences from these huge mines (some of the world's best trout fishing is located directly downstream from these mines, for example) is further evidence of the success of the attention paid by the mining firm and regulatory agencies. The only downstream impact of concern that has emerged in the region is elevated concentrations of selenium. It has been recognized in recent years that selenium, an essential ingredient for life in small quantities, presents severe environmental problems in higher concentrations for birds, animals, humans, and many forms of aquatic life (Lemly 2004; Hamilton 2004; Lenz and Lens 2009). As awareness of the potential problems from selenium release from coal mining has grown in the last few years, in British Columbia Teck and provincial and federal environmental agencies have worked together to evaluate the extent of threat. This cooperative effort has resulted in ongoing investments of more than C$600 million dollars by the mining firm in water treatment that seeks to address this potential but apparently still relatively minor concern (Teck Resources 2014). The situation in British Columbia stands in stark contrast to the highly polluted water, noise and dust pollution, and other negative health and environmental impacts, that characterize MTR coal mining in West Virginia and other areas of Appalachia (Burns 2007; Reece 2006; Ahern et al. 2011a, 2011b; Zegre et al. 2013; Griffith et al. 2012; Hendryx and Zullig 2009; Hendryx et al. 2008; Collins et al. 2012; Wishart 2012; Perdue and Pavela 2012; Austin and Clark 2012; Bell and York 2012; Burns, Evans, and House 2009; Johannsen et al. 2005).

One of the most important differences in living conditions between southeastern British Columbia and southern West Virginia has resulted from very different government policies towards the social impacts of coal mining in the two regions during the 1960s and 1970s. Pictures of coal mining camps in British Columbia and West Virginia circa 1960 are basically indistinguishable. For example, cheap wooden housing construction, the separation of lower quality housing for miners from higher quality housing for managers, and high levels of pollution evident in coal dust covering buildings and streets are virtually identical. However, in West Virginia, despite the pleas of regional leaders such as Harry Caudill and the antipoverty programs such as the Appalachian Regional Commission that were part of the Great Society efforts that began during the Johnson administration, the poor living conditions of the early 1960s have only worsened over the ensuing half century. The housing stock is even older and in poorer repair, many families continue to live in decades-old homes built by the coal companies and later sold at inflated prices to miners, and many communities have even fewer stores and professional services available in the early twenty-first century than they had in the early 1960s. In my grandparents' home town of Mt. Hope in Fayette County, for example, the large downtown department store closed years ago and has been replaced by an antiques dealer, the large family-owned hardware store that had been in operation for decades recently closed, and there are only a few small locally owned restaurants and stores and one bank still in operation. Compared to Mt. Hope's peak as a population and commercial center in the 1920s, or even to the early 1960s, the economic activity of the town is now a pale shadow of what it once was.

In sharp contrast, the old coal camps of Michel and Natal that lined the main highway entering southeastern British Columbia from neighboring Alberta are long gone, replaced by a planned community in Sparwood built in cooperation between the provincial government and the mining consortium that developed one of the world's largest coal mines on a mountain overlooking the old and new communities in the late 1960s. While some of the provincial government's motivation for removing the old coal camps was the desire to make the gateway to the province more attractive to visitors, a larger part was the desire to capture the benefits of resource extraction for the residents of the province. The provincial government used its negotiating leverage with Canadian, US, and Japanese firms that sought to gain access to the area's coal to resolve the problem of poor living conditions that had long characterized the area's coal mining camps. The community of Sparwood possesses an endowment funded by the original coal-mining firm that has grown, through careful management of day-to-day operations and ongoing tax payments from the coal mine located on the edge of the city, into a total reserve of C$78 million in 2013 in a city of 4,200. City services are well maintained and up to date, and the growing housing stock is in good condition. The other four mines in the region are located closer to Elkford, a community of 2,500 that was built by the coal-mining subsidiary of the Canadian Pacific Railway in the 1970s. This remote community, literally at the end of the paved road and located at the highest elevation of any community in the province of British Columbia, has quality housing stock and a variety of amenities. The oldest mining community, the city of Fernie, has a population of 4,800. While some coal miners still live in Fernie, this city has been the center of the dramatic economic diversification in the area based on developing ski tourism and building second homes for ski enthusiasts from Calgary and elsewhere. To put it bluntly, the choice of whether to live in Fernie, Sparwood, or Elkford versus Mt. Hope, Beckley, Oak Hill, or other communities in Raleigh and Fayette Counties in the abstract is easy to make; by any measure, quality of life is far higher in southeastern British Columbia than it is in southern West Virginia.

The China-Driven Global Coal Boom and Economic Diversification Efforts since 2000

By 2000, a new coal-induced boom swept into both regions: the rapid economic development of China created rapidly growing demand and fast-rising prices for coal (and many other raw materials) around the world. Demand increased for metallurgical coal to supply China's steel industry, which became the world's largest in the early 2000s, as well as to supply the resurgent US and European steel industries that rode the China-driven boom; demand for thermal coal for electricity generation in China drove demand for Appalachian thermal coal as well (Bunker and Ciccantell 2005, 2007; Ciccantell 2009). Metallurgical coal prices exceeded $150 per ton in the early 2010s, and mining companies earned high profits and could afford to pay high wages to attract and keep employees. By 2014, this China-driven raw materials boom was waning, and prices for both types of coal were falling, raising important questions about the future contribution of coal mining to the economies of both West Virginia and British Columbia. Changing US environmental regulation of coal burning and the declining use of coal for electricity generation in the United States present huge challenges for the future of coal production in southern West Virginia.

Since the early 2000s, a very different economic sector has emerged as a key economic driver in the Elk Valley: tourism and second home ownership, largely focused on the ski industry. The state government in West Virginia has made efforts to promote tourism throughout the state, including the southern coal counties on which I focus here, and ski tourism has become an important factor in the eastern part of West Virginia, but these efforts and their impacts pale in comparison to what has taken place in the Elk Valley. Centered first in the community of Fernie, the location of the area's largest ski hill, which had been purchased by a major Canadian investor in skiing-based tourism in other areas of

British Columbia and neighboring Alberta in the late 1990s, this new economic sector has spread in recent years to other areas of the Elk Valley. This ski tourism (more than 300,000 skiers visit Fernie from around the world each year) and building second homes for ski enthusiasts from the city of Calgary (financial and managerial capital of the oil sands boom in neighboring Alberta) and from around the world have driven an almost unbelievable economic and social transformation in the Elk Valley. During my first visit to the region in 1998 housing values averaged C$105,000, and it was almost impossible to give away homes vacated by miners who lost their jobs in the bust. Average home prices in the Elk Valley now exceed $300,000, and dozens of homes in Fernie are worth more than $1 million. This economic diversification effort, which did receive some support from local and provincial governments in an effort to avoid the horrible impact of the last coal bust period, has been transformative. The city has dozens of restaurants and stores, and the number and diversity of types of businesses continue to grow.

This skiing-based boom is not unqualifiedly positive for the Elk Valley, despite the economic benefits of seasonal residents and visitors and of the construction of these second homes. The dramatic increase in housing prices has created a lack of affordable housing for workers in the service and construction sectors, and even for well-paid coal miners, with some relocating from the skiing center of Fernie to Sparwood and Elkford further up the valley. Despite this important concern, coal mining and tourism coexist in the Elk Valley rather successfully.

The state of West Virginia has made extensive efforts in recent decades to promote tourism throughout the state and in Raleigh and Fayette Counties. The oldest and most significant form of tourist development has been the creation of a whitewater rafting and adventure sports tourism destination in the New River Gorge area of Fayette County, an area that was once the center of the area's coal production. Eleven rafting and adventure sports businesses and other businesses such as hotels and restaurants also benefit from this activity. The state of West Virginia built and owns a folk art sales center at Tamarack on Interstate 77 near Beckley, an effort to promote this form of economic activity via sales to people passing through the region. The most recent tourist-related form of development has been the construction of a Boy Scout ranch in the Mt. Hope area that has taken over a large number of properties in the region. While some local residents hope that this will create new business opportunities, it is difficult to imagine how the movement of large numbers of Boy Scouts into and out of the area for camping, hiking, and other outdoor experiences will make much of a contribution to the local economy. In short, tourism has been a huge new economic activity in the Elk Valley, but a much smaller and less significant activity in Fayette and Raleigh Counties.

Conclusion: Why Are These Regions So Different?

To return to the central question motivating my research, how can these major differences between two seemingly similar regions be explained? In terms of the impacts of natural characteristics, the Elk Valley was favored by having some larger coal deposits than those in southern West Virginia, less extensive and less diverse timber coverage that inhibited the development of a large logging industry and its attendant negative impacts, and mountains that do not produce acid mine drainage as is the case in southern West Virginia and that are amenable to use as a global skiing destination. National as well as state and provincial policies have played an important role, particularly in the form of capturing a greater share of earnings from coal for local communities in the Elk Valley, including building a planned community that replaced coal company camps and greater attention to environmental regulation by government agencies and especially coal-mining firms in British Columbia. More generally, MTR in the Elk Valley takes place in a natural and social setting that had suffered many fewer negative impacts from earlier periods of logging and mining, which makes MTR less environmentally and socially destructive there than in Raleigh and Fayette counties.

PAUL S. CICCANTELL is Professor of Sociology in the Department of Sociology at Western Michigan University. His current research is on the global coal industry and its impacts on British Columbia, Appalachia, and a variety of other locations around the world.

References

Ahern, Melissa et al. 2011a. "The Association between Mountaintop Mining and Birth Defects among Live Births in Central Appalachia, 1996–2003." *Environmental Research*, no. 111, 838–846.

Ahern, Melissa et al. 2011b. "Residence in Coal-Mining Areas and Low-Birth-Weight Outcomes." *Maternal and Child Health Journal*, no. 15, 974–979.

Austin, Kelly, and Brett Clark. 2012. "Tearing Down Mountains: Using Spatial and Metabolic Analysis to Investigate the Socio-Ecological Contradictions of Coal Extraction in Appalachia." *Critical Sociology* 38 (3): 437–457.

Basile, Victor, and Judy Byers. 2011. *Italians in West Virginia*. Charleston, SC: Arcadia.

Bell, Shannon Elizabeth, and Richard York. 2012. "Coal, Injustice, and Environmental Destruction: Introduction to the Special Issue on Coal and the Environment." *Organization and Environment* 25 (4): 359–367.

Blizzard, William. 2004. *When Miners March*. Gay, WV: Appalachian Community Services.

Buckley, Geoffrey. 2004. *Extracting Appalachia: Images of the Consolidation Coal Company 1910–1945*. Athens: Ohio University Press.

Bunker, Stephen, and Paul S. Ciccantell. 2005. *Globalization and the Race for Resources*. Baltimore: Johns Hopkins University Press.

———. 2007. *An East Asian World Economy: Japan's Ascent, with Implications for China*. Baltimore: Johns Hopkins University Press.

Burns, Shirley Stewart. 2007. *Bringing Down the Mountains: The Impact of Mountaintop Removal on Southern West Virginia Communities*. Morgantown: West Virginia University Press.

Burns, Shirley Stewart, Mari-Lynn Evans, and Silas House, eds. 2009. *Coal Country: Rising Up Against Mountaintop Removal Mining*. San Francisco: Sierra Club.

Caudill, Harry. 1962. *Night Comes to the Cumberlands: A Biography of a Depressed Area*. Boston: Little, Brown.

Ciccantell, Paul. 2009. "China's Economic Ascent via Stealing Japan's Raw Materials Peripheries." In *China and the Transformation of Global Capitalism*, edited by Ho-fung Hung, chap. 6. Baltimore: Johns Hopkins University Press.

Cohen, Stan. 1984. *King Coal*. Charleston, WV: Quarrier.

Collins, Alan, Evan Hansen, and Michael Hendryx. 2012. "Wind versus Coal: Comparing the Local Economic Impacts of Energy Resource Development in Appalachia." *Energy Policy*, no. 50: 551–561.

Corbin, David, ed. 1990. *The West Virginia Mine Wars: An Anthology*. Charleston, WV: Appalachian Editions.

Davies, David. 1998. "The Crows Nest Southern Railway." In *The Forgotten Side of the Border: British Columbia's Elk Valley and Crowsnest Pass*, edited by Wayne Norton and Naomi Miller, 58–65. Kamloops, BC: Plateau.

Den Otter, A. A. 1984. "Bondage of Steam: The CPR and Western Canadian Coal." In *The CPR West: The Iron Road and the Making of a Nation*, edited by Hugh Dempsey, 191–207. Vancouver: Douglas & McIntyre.

Dixon, Thomas. 2009. *West Virginia Railroads*. Forest, VA: TLC.

Giuliano, Mary. 2002. "'Noi andiamo a Farnie bee chi': Italian Experience in the Elk Valley." In *A World Apart: The Crowsnest Communities of Alberta and British Columbia*, edited by Wayne Norton and Tom Langford, 72–77. Kamloops, BC: Plateau.

Griffith, Michael, et al. 2012. "The Effects of Mountaintop Mines and Valley Fills on the Physicochemical Quality of Stream Ecosystems in the Central Appalachians: A Review." *Science of the Total Environment* 417–418 (February): 1–12.

Hamilton, Steven. 2004. "Review of Selenium Toxicity in the Aquatic Food Chain." *Science of the Total Environment*, no. 326: 1–31.

Hendryx, Michael, Kathryn O'Donnell, and Kimberly Horn. 2008. "Lung Cancer Mortality Is Elevated in Coal-Mining Areas of Appalachia." *Lung Cancer*, no. 621–617.

Hendryx, Michael, and Keith Zullig. 2009. "Higher Coronary Heart Disease and Heart Attack Morbidity in Appalachian Coal Mining Regions." *Preventive Medicine*, no. 49, 355–359.

Johannsen, Kristin, Bobbie Ann Mason, and Mary Ann Taylor-Hall, eds. 2005. *Missing Mountains: We Went to the Mountaintop but It Wasn't There*. Nicholasville, KY: Wind.

Lemly, A. Dennis. 2004. "Aquatic Selenium Pollution Is a Global Environmental Safety Issue." *Ecotoxicology and Environmental Safety*, no. 59, 44–56.

Lenz, Markus, and Piet Lens. 2009. "The Essential Toxin: The Changing Perception of Selenium in Environmental Sciences." *Science of the Total Environment*, no. 407, 3620–3633.

Lewis, Ronald. 1998. *Transforming the Appalachian Countryside*. Chapel Hill: University of North Carolina Press.

Lunt, Richard. 1992. *Law and Order vs. the Miners: WV 1906–1933*. 2nd ed. Charleston, WV: Appalachian Editions.

Norton, Wayne, and Tom Langford, eds. 2002. *A World Apart: The Crowsnest Communities of Alberta and British Columbia*. Kamloops, BC: Plateau.

Norton, Wayne, and Naomi Miller, eds. 1998. *The Forgotten Side of the Border: British Columbia's Elk Valley and Crowsnest Pass*. Kamloops, BC: Plateau.

Perdue, Robert Todd, and Gregory Pavela. 2012. "Addictive Economies and Coal Dependency: Methods of Extraction and Socioeconomic Outcomes in West Virginia, 1997–2009." *Organization and Environment* 25 (4): 368–384.

Ramsey, Bruce. 1990. *The Noble Cause: The Story of the United Mine Workers of America in Western Canada*. Calgary: District 18, United Mine Workers of America.

———. 1997. *The Elk River Valley: 100 Years of Coal Mining*. Altona, Manitoba: Friesens Corporation.

Reece, Erik. 2006. *Lost Mountain: A Year in the Vanishing Wilderness*. New York: Riverhead.

Savage, Lon. 1990. *Thunder in the Mountains: The West Virginia Mine War 1920–21*. Pittsburgh: University of Pittsburgh Press.

Teck Resources. 2014. *Elk Valley Water Quality Plan*. Vancouver, BC: Teck Resources, http://www.teckelkvalley.com/res/vpl/documents/_ces_portal_meta/_portal _pages/documents/elk_valley_water_quality_plan_teck_resources.pdf.

Williams, John. 2002. *Appalachia: A History*. Chapel Hill: University of North Carolina Press.

Wishart, Ryan. 2012. "Coal River's Last Mountain: King Coal's Après moi le Déluge Reign." *Organization and Environment* 25 (4): 470–495.

Zegre, Nicolas, et al. 2013. "Characterizing Streamflow Response of a Mountaintop-Mined Watershed to Changing Land Use." *Applied Geography*, no. 29, 5–15.

CHAPTER 4

Black Diamonds

Crystal Good

for Mrs. Sweet Genny Lynch

Whatchu know about black diamonds, black diamonds, black diamonds?
Whatchu know about soooul?
Whatcha know about coooal?

Whatchu know about the pressure
of the earth
turning soil to coal
turning coal to diamonds?

They say
they say . . . one day
millions and millions of years of pressure
       of pressure
       of pressure
formed diamonds
in colors: black, pink, yellow, green.

Today, this pressure forms black diamonds
       from blood
       from sweat
       from love
from slaves buried in unmarked graves.

Black diamonds form on days like April 5th 2010.
That day started just like all the other days

just like all the other days
the other days
the hundreds of days,
like for hundreds of years
      that the earth fell
      in on
      miners
trapping them underground with nothing
but their prayers

This time on April 5th 2010
29 men died
in what they call a "mine disaster"
others, "industrial homicide"
      homicide
      homicide.
DEAD, 29 MINERS, two black men

Whatchu know about black diamonds . . .

You See, When Mrs. Lynch
when sweet Mrs. Genny Lynch
heard the news
that her husband would not be coming home
she knew that there would be no more
      "I love you's"
no more three kisses at 4am
no more coffee on the stove by your pail
honey.
Her high school sweetheart
her husband of 34 years
her Rosie,
      would not
      be coming
      home.

When sweet Genny sheds a tear
when every coal wife
sheds a tear
there comes the pressure

      compacted
      compacted
      compacted
and every time Mrs. Lynch, Mrs. sweet Genny cries
and her tears hit the earth
        There
        There
in the mountains of West Virginia, forms a priceless
black diamond
no coal company can ever sell.

These jewels of Appalachia
women who love their men deep into the earth
this special breed
this diamond
forming diamonds
compacted
compacted
        of tears
        of love
        of human slavery
        of the company store
        of "we're sorry for your loss"
        of black black lung

this/ our history, is scattered
you have to find it in poems
called Black Diamonds
in pages where black ink fades
until somebody digs
and some brave heart will always hear the call
from deep inside the earth and dig
so that millions and millions of years from now . . .
they will hold up and marvel at our diamonds,
and wonder at their timeless love
formed by pressure
        and pressure
        and pressure
and the salt
        of her tears.

CRYSTAL GOOD is a writer, poet, and advocate in West Virginia. She is a member of the Affrilachian Poets, an Irene McKinney Scholar, and performs with Heroes Are Gang Leaders, a New York–based free/avant-garde jazz experimental improvisation ensemble. Her debut collection of poetry, *Valley Girl,* explored themes in quantum physics, Appalachian culture, and the destructive coal mining practice known as mountaintop removal.

CHAPTER 5

Historicizing Poverty and Marginalization in the Southern Mountain Regions of Malawi

Tony Milanzi

THIS CHAPTER TAKES a historical approach to account for the political, social, and economic dynamics that are the root of poverty and marginalization for people of the mountain regions of southern Malawi, and to account for ways in which these dynamics have in turn affected the environment and the social development of the region and the country at large. The southern mountain region refers to the districts surrounding the Mulanje and Thyolo Mountains, and these are Mulanje, Thyolo, and Phalombe districts. They are all part of the Shire Highlands, which include other districts such as Chiradzulu, Blantyre, and Zomba. This region is critical in the history of Malawi as it is where early colonial settlers, drawn by a favorable climate, first established tea and coffee plantations, making the region the birthplace of modern agriculture in Malawi—and a sector linked inextricably to the processes of state building. The mountain regions played a critical role in shaping the social and political landscape of pre- and postcolonial Malawi through the movement of labor, which brought knowledge of this type of agriculture to other regions of Malawi. The political processes that culminated in the alienation of land from locals, which in turn triggered the massive exodus of labor, have ensured continued poverty and underdevelopment of a region marked by acute land shortages, low agricultural productivity, low incomes, and stagnating social and human development.

As a Malawian researcher, my work centers on rural livelihoods and agricultural and rural development. My interest in and understanding of the mountain regions of southern Malawi came through my research on the historical development of modern export-oriented agriculture in Malawi, particularly tobacco. Although tobacco is produced primarily in the central and northern regions of Malawi, historical and contemporary sources point to the contributions of the southern mountain region to the growth of agriculture in the central region as well as to the political and socioeconomic development of the country at large. Furthermore, my work as an economic justice activist has taken me to the region on numerous occasions. On these trips I got a close and intimate experience of the grinding poverty and the deteriorating environmental situation that affects the region. Recognition of the historical marginalization of the region is a necessary foundation for transformative initiatives, which would need to include land reform and sustained investments in the agricultural value chain, as well as in integrated rural development projects, to address imbalances and improve the welfare of people from the region.

The Setting

The defining feature of the mountain region in southeastern Malawi is the majestic Mulanje Mountain that rises dramatically over the Phalombe plain. The massif covers 650 square kilometers, and one of its peaks, the Sapitwa peak (at an elevation of 3,200 meters) is southeastern Africa's highest point. The mountain serves important ecological functions, including acting as a water catchment for surrounding areas. In addition, it is home to valuable plant and bird species including the Mulanje cedar (*Widdringtonia whytei*), a valuable timber tree that grows up to 40 meters high and is only found on Mulanje Mountain. To the north and northwest of Mulanje Mountain lie the Shire Highlands proper, the southern portion of which is dominated by Thyolo Mountain (Spriggs n.d.). Known to many for its scenic tea plantations, the region is also home to other plantation crops including tung (a tree with seeds pressed for oil), coffee, and macadamia nut trees. It is also the most densely populated region in Malawi. According to the 2008 Malawi Population Census, Thyolo had a population density of 342 persons/km², Mulanje 254 persons/km², and Phalombe 225 persons/km². These densities are higher than those of districts with the largest urban centers in Malawi, except for Zomba. In 2008, Malawi as a whole had a population density of 139 persons/km² (NSO 2008). At the time Britain declared Nyasaland a protectorate in the 1890s, the importance of plantation crops to the colonial state put the region at the center of state-making processes primarily through the promotion of export agriculture, which also entailed control of native labor and alienation of native land. The effects of these processes shaped not just the region but also the country as a whole.

The Colonial State and Agriculture

Export-oriented agriculture has been widely implicated in the entrenchment of the colonial system. In a bid to make colonies self-sustaining, Britain and other colonial powers looked to develop plantation crops like coffee, sugar, tobacco, and tea (Vail 1982; Rotberg 1982; Shillington 2012). In the same vein, realizing the need to generate taxes for the administration of the protectorate, and considering that Nyasaland had no mineral deposits worth exploiting, the colonial government in Nyasaland (present-day Malawi) considered agriculture the engine of economic growth. Further believing in the supremacy of European plantation agriculture, the government of Sir Harry Johnston, the first governor of Nyasaland, was keen to attract a white settler community to stay in Nyasaland and practice export-oriented agriculture, which was expected to drive the economy (Malekano 1999). At the time Nyasaland was declared a British protectorate in 1891, coffee was the major export crop grown by a small settler community. Most of these individual settlers and companies such as the Blantyre & East Africa Company, British Central Africa Company, and the Africa Lakes Company started growing tobacco at their estates in Mulanje, Blantyre, Zomba, Chiradzulu, Mulanje, and Thyolo districts (Wilshaw 1994; Rangeley 1957). Here they grew coffee as a main cash crop, alongside tea. Later, when coffee farming proved unprofitable due to falling world prices, the settlers began to allocate more land to other crops such as cotton and tobacco.

In the early years of the Protectorate, most of the settler farmers were too undercapitalized to successfully undertake agriculture on the scale desired by government. But through the powerful Chamber of Commerce and Agriculture, they pressured the colonial government to facilitate profitable production of plantation agriculture and allow them to have a monopoly over local trade (Chipeta 1986). The colonial government was only too happy to oblige, and thus began a series of agricultural policies and interventions to promote settler agriculture—most of which came at the expense of smallholders in these districts. The most notable interventions of the colonial government on behalf of settler farmers were the alienation of land and extraction of native labor. These key interventions shaped the social, economic, and political development of the region and the country at large.

Alienation of Land

The earliest intervention of the colonial government was through alienation of land from local African populations, accomplished through the conquest and pacification of Yao, Chewa, and Ngoni chiefs. Harry Johnston appropriated over 3 million hectares of native land between 1891 and 1894, which was given to companies, individual settlers, and companies. Most of the alienated land was in the Shire Highlands, especially Thyolo and Mulanje, where settlers opened up tea and coffee estates, later venturing into tobacco (Chipeta 1986; Wilshaw 1994).

The development of estates in the Shire Highlands resulted in severe land shortages for the local population that were further compounded by the arrival of Lhomwe immigrants from Portuguese East Africa (Mozambique). This land shortage became a source of unrest among the local African population and together with other grievances culminated in an uprising in 1915. Settler farmers and companies resisted efforts of the colonial government to address the land shortage for locals. Baker (1993) relates that at one point the colonial government sought to buy back idle land from the British Central African Company to resettle the displaced local population, a move that was resisted by the company. The coming of independence in 1964 did little to change land ownership patterns, as foreign companies still continue to hold large segments of land. Currently, Eastern Produce Ltd., a subsidiary of the British company Camellia PLC (the biggest producer of tea in Malawi) owns 21 estates in Mulanje and Thyolo districts (Kateta 2013). Just two estate landowners, Barron Estates Ltd. and Conforzi Estates Ltd., hold one-third of the land in Thyolo district (Kandodo 2001). This foreign ownership of land explains why people from these districts have some of the smallest land sizes in the country. A baseline survey for a livelihoods project conducted in 2005 showed that residents of Thyolo and Mulanje had average landholdings of less than one acre (MVAC 2005).

In addition to giving land to white settler farmers, the colonial government enacted a number of laws and regulations to create a labor reserve for settler farmers. From 1892, the government imposed a hut tax on men and a poll tax on women to ensure that instead of working on their own farm plots for subsistence, local residents would find paid employment on settler estates, earn a wage, and pay their taxes (Vail 1982). To further ensure availability of labor for the white farmers and to solve the problem of landless immigrants from Mozambique, a system called "thangata" was promoted. The system required native male heads of households living on settler estates to work on the estates in lieu of rent. Thangata was associated with labor abuses by the settlers. For example, household heads were required to work one month in a year for rent and another month for hut tax. Often estate owners would arbitrarily extend the period to up to six months (Kandawire 1977).

The move to tax natives of the region triggered two key processes that affected local agriculture and the social landscape of the country at large. First, apart from pushing locals into wage labor, the imposition of taxes also pushed them into commodity agriculture; they began to grow crops for sale. Mostly, the locals grew food crops for sale to meet increased demand from a growing population in the Shire Highlands (McCracken 2012). Those who were able took to commercial production of dark and sun-fired tobacco (Rangeley 1957; Wilshaw 1994). Thus, through trying to promote plantation agriculture at the expense of the subsistence of local populations, the colonial government inadvertently triggered the growth of peasant commodity agriculture. Second, following the imposition of taxes some local residents began to migrate to Southern Rhodesia (Zimbabwe) and South Africa to take advantage of higher wages in mines and plantations there. Nyasaland settler farmers were locked in a competition for labor with labor recruiters from those two countries. The poor working conditions on settler estates in the Shire Highlands made it difficult for them to attract enough locals willing to work for them (Chipeta 1986).

Southern Labor and Tobacco in the Central Region

Having been introduced to migration for economic opportunity, people from the agriculturally advanced mountain regions went on to play a key role in establishing the tobacco industry in the central region.

Prior to 1920, agricultural development in Nyasaland was concentrated in the Shire Highlands. This changed in 1920 when two settler farmers, Andrew F. Barron and Roy J. Wallace (who already had established tobacco estates in Zomba) ventured to the central province. Lured by good soil and abundant labor, they obtained land at Mbabzi and Lingadzi, west of Lilongwe, the present-day capital of Malawi. Here Barron set up an estate to grow flue-cured tobacco to sell to the Imperial Tobacco Company. In 1922, he invited Africans to grow fire-cured (also known as dark-fired) tobacco as tenants on his estate, and, shortly after, this expanded into an outgrower scheme. This scheme attracted native African growers from the southern region who already had experience growing tobacco and found the conditions on these outgrower schemes better than the thangata system prevailing in the south (Prowse 2010). In 1927 another settler, Inaco Conforzi, leased 5,000 acres in Lilongwe, around Namitete, and initiated a visiting tenancy, which drew an estimated 4,000 visiting tenants, mostly from the south. His scheme was such that tenants grew sun-cured tobacco, which he transported for processing at his factory in Thyolo, from where it was exported to Belfast (Wilshaw 1994).

Historical Marginalization and Its Impacts on Current Livelihoods and the Environment

Despite the fact that labor migration was triggered by unfair and punitive state policies such as land alienation and punitive taxation, people from the mountain regions of the south made an immense contribution to the growth of the tobacco industry and to the socioeconomic development of Malawi. From its humble beginnings as a tobacco-growing region in the 1920s, the central region surpassed the southern region to become the hub of tobacco production in Malawi. Today, tobacco is the biggest foreign exchange earner, generating 60 percent of exports and contributing 13 percent of GDP. Tobacco also generates up to 23 percent of the tax base and employs between 600,000 and 2 million out of a workforce of 5 million people (Jaffee 2003). Unfortunately, the historical marginalization that came with being the first region to welcome settler farmers persists, and their contributions to the development of agriculture in Malawi has not done much to reduce poverty in the region. Land constraints in the region have resulted in low agricultural productivity and low incomes for the people. For many, the only option is to take on low-paying seasonal jobs with tea companies. Tea companies employ up to 50,000 tea pickers at harvest time, which runs from October to April for a fortnightly wage of 11 euros. After the harvest season, workers are laid off (Kateta 2013). Land constraints have further led to environmental damage and loss of bio-diversity as people encroach into the mountains, causing a loss of forest and valuable plant and bird species. Mulanje cedar, valued for its fine timber, its fragrance, and its pest-resistant sap, has been dwindling due to illegal logging and forest fires. A study published in 2007 showed that there were 845.3 hectares of the cedar on Mulanje Mountain, 32 percent of which were dead, representing a loss of 616.7 hectares over 15 years (Bayliss et al. 2007). In addition, some of Mulanje Mountain's evergreen forest bird species have been accorded the International Union for Conservation of Nature's endangered status (Thyolo Alethe, spotted ground-thrush, *Zootheraguttata,* and yellow-throated Apalis, *Apalis flavigularis*), and one species has been accorded the status of vulnerable species (white-winged Apalis, *Apalis chriessa*) (Spottiswode et al. 2008). Thyolo Mountain has also suffered its share of deforestation. Between 1999 and 2003, much of the Thyolo forest reserve was destroyed for subsistence agriculture, going from 10 square km to 0.27 square km with most of the remaining forest being on private land (Spottiswode et al. 2008).

The bleak economic prospects mean that people from the south have continued to trek to the central and northern regions to work as tenants on tobacco estates. A recent study showed that 77 percent of tenants on tobacco estates originate from the most densely populated and land-scarce districts in the southern region such as Machinga, Mangochi, Phalombe, Thyolo, Mulanje, and Zomba. They cite poverty, food insecurity, lack of land, lack of resources to buy agricultural inputs, and lack of alternative employment opportunities as the primary factors that push them into becoming tenant labor (Kanyongolo and Mussa 2015). The tobacco tenancy system is synonymous with labor exploitation. Tenants bear heavy workloads for very low wages (Phiri 2004), and they are exposed to deplorable working conditions including poor housing, inadequate food, unsafe drinking water, and lack of access to health services (CFSC 2015).

Poverty, lack of land at home, and poor working conditions on the labor migration circuit have long been causes of disquiet in the region, but now the dissatisfaction is becoming more overt as some people in the region, especially in Thyolo, have started to agitate for the government to give them land. There have been attempts at land redistribution before. In the late 2000s, a project funded by the World Bank attempted to resettle people from Thyolo and Mulanje to the districts of Machinga and Mangochi (Chinsinga 2008). Although the project was hailed as a success for providing land and increasing productivity of the 15,000 (Simtowe, Mendola, and Mangisoni 2011), it was not enough, as demand for land is still very high. Recently, a movement of Thyolo residents led by Vincent Wandale took matters into their own hands and encroached on land owned by Conforzi Tea Estate, ostensibly to reclaim their ancestral land. He and some of his followers were arrested and charged with trespassing. Since his conviction, which resulted in a suspended sentence, his movement seems to have become invigorated.

Conclusion

The problems of the mountain regions need to be placed in a political and historical context, and solutions need to be well integrated to address the multiple dimensions of the problem. Development analysts as well as conservation experts recognize that landlessness, poverty, and environmental degradation are interlinked, and this trio is at the center of underdevelopment in the region. But efforts to address these problems have been fragmented. Initiatives aimed at improving the economic and social well-being of people in the region must take a holistic approach by enhancing local livelihoods while tackling environmental degradation and biodiversity loss. Since most people depend on agriculture, there is need for a land reform program to get idle land from tea estates which must be redistributed to the locals. Furthermore, there is need to increase productivity and incomes through integrated rural development services, including agricultural extension, produce markets, health facilities, and education. There is also need to invest in good road infrastructure to facilitate production of food crops for the nearby urban places in Blantyre and Zomba. Development planning must aim to unlock the potential of the region to develop a specialized high-value economy. The region's potential for tourism is well known, but investment and purposeful initiatives are needed to ensure that tourism benefits locals. In addition, the region has a climate and soils favorable to fruit production and legumes. If adequately supported to increase productivity and value-added activities, these could support the livelihoods of people in the region.

TONY MILANZI is a postdoctoral fellow in anthropology at the University of Kentucky. His research and teaching interests include agrarian change, food studies in local and global contexts, and the anthropology of development. He has done extensive research with tobacco farmers in Malawi and has managed projects in the areas of economic governance and social justice in Malawi, particularly economic literacy.

References

Baker, Colin. 1983. *Seeds of Trouble: Government Policy and Land Rights in Nyasaland, 1946–1964*. London: British Academic.

Bayliss, J., S. Makungwa, J. Hecht, D. Nangoma, and C. Bruessow. 2007. "Saving the Island in the Sky: The Plight of the Mount Mulanje Cedar *Widdringtonia whytei* in Malawi." *Oryx* 41: 64–69.

CFSC (Center for Social Concern). 2015. *Tobacco Production and Tenancy Labor in Malawi: Treating Individuals and Families as Mere Instruments of Production*. Lilongwe, Malawi: CFSC.

Chinsinga, Blessings. 2008. "Exploring the Politics of Land Reforms in Malawi: A Case Study of the Community Based Rural Land Development Program (CBRLDP)." Research Program Consortium for Improving Pro-Poor Growth Institutions, discussion paper series no. 20. University of Manchester.

Chipeta, Mapopa. 1986. *Labor in Colonial Malawi: A Study in the Development of the Malawian Working Class C, 1891–1964*. PhD diss. Dalhousie University.

Jaffee, Steve. 2003. "Malawi's Tobacco Sector: Standing on One Strong Leg Is Better Than on None." Africa Region working paper series no. 55. World Bank.

Kandawire, J. A. K. 1977. "Thangata in Pre-Colonial and Colonial Systems of Land Tenure in Southern Malawi with Special Reference to Chingale." *Africa* 47 (1): 185–191.

Kandodo, Fredrick. 2001. *Land Reform in Regional Context: Malawi Experiences*. Lilongwe, Malawi: Catholic Commission for Peace and Justice.

Kanyongolo, Ruth, and Richard Mussa. 2015. *A Rapid Assessment of the Tobacco Sector in Malawi: Consolidated Report*. Lilongwe: ILO.

Kateta, Madalitso. 2013. *A Bitter Brew: Malawi's Plantations*. Equal Times Online Report. Accessed March 31, 2017. https://www.equaltimes.org/a-bitter-brew -malawi-s-tea?lang=en#.WN7Y5G_yvIV.

Malekano, Lawrence. 1999. *Peasants, Politics and Survival in Colonial Malawi, 1891–1964*. PhD diss., Dalhousie University.

McCracken, John. 2012. *A History of Malawi: 1859–1966*. Suffolk, UK: James Currey.

MVAC (Malawi Vulnerability Assessment Committee). 2005. *Malawi Baseline Livelihood Profiles*. Ministry of Economic Planning and Development, Government of Malawi.

NSO (National Statistics Office of Malawi). 2008. *Population and Housing Census*. Zomba, Malawi: NSO.

Phiri, M. Alexander R. 2004. Assessment of the Potential Impact of the Abolition of the Tenancy Labor System in Malawi. Report prepared for the International Labor Organization, Malawi Commercial Agriculture Program. Lilongwe: ILO.

Prowse, Martin. 2010. A Century of Growth? A History of Tobacco Production and Marketing in Malawi, 1890–2005. Working Paper / 2011.10. Antwerp: Institute of Development Policy and Management, University of Antwerp, Belgium.

Rangeley, W. H. J. 1957. "A Brief History of the Tobacco Industry in Nyasaland, Part 1." *Nyasaland Journal* 10 (1): 62–83.

Rotberg, Robert, ed. 1982. *Imperialism, Colonialism, and Hunger: East and Central Africa*, Introduction. Lexington, MA: Lexington.

Shillington, Kevin. 2012. *History of Africa*. New York: Palgrave Macmillan.

Simtowe, Franklin, Mariapia Mendola, and Julius Mangisoni. 2011. "Independent Project Impact Evaluation of the Community Based Rural Land Development Project (CBRLDP) in Malawi." Report prepared for Italtrend.

Spottiswode, Claire, I. Hassam Patel, Eric Herrmann, Jonathan Timberlake, and Julian Bayliss. 2008. "Threatened Bird Species on Two Little-Known Mountains (Chiperone and Mabu) in Northern Mozambique." *Ostrich* 79 (1): 1–7.

Spriggs, Amy. n.d. "Southern Africa: Southern Malawi into Mozambique." Accessed May 9, 2017. http://www.worldwildlife.org/ecoregions/at1014.

Vail, Leroy. 1982. "The State and Creation of Malawi's Agricultural Political Economy." In *Imperialism, Colonialism, and Hunger: East and Central Africa*, edited by Robert Rotberg. Lexington, MA: Lexington.

Wilshaw, Colin. 1994. *A Century of Growth: Malawi's Tobacco Industry 1893–1993*. Blantyre, Malawi: Central Africana.

Momma Was a Union Woman

Si Kahn

Wake up, Sally, don't you sleep so late
Don't you sleep so long
Daddy just went off to work
Momma soon be home
Don't you see that old sun shining
Climbing up the hill
Can't you hear that whistle whining
Home from the mill

Momma was a union woman
Tried to raise us right
Momma was a union woman
Hoot owl shift each night
Momma was a union woman
Two hard working hands
She raised up a union woman
And a union man

Do you remember hard times, Sally
Just before the war
Seemed the world was out on strike
In 1934

Momma on the back of a pickup truck
Shouting to the crowd
Where'd that woman get the strength
Wish I had it now

Sally, what would Momma do
If she was here today
By God I know she's never stand
To see us done this way
The way she taught us how to fight
I never will forget
She's with us on this picket line
Walking with us yet

CHAPTER 6

Voices for Community Rights in Amazonia

Monica Chují

[This is the transcript of a keynote lecture given in 2012 at the Global Mountain Regions conference at the University of Kentucky; it was presented in Spanish and in English translation.]

GOOD EVENING, EVERYBODY. First, I would like to thank the Appalachian Center and the University of Kentucky for giving us the opportunity to be here with you tonight. My name is Monica Chují, and I am an indigenous person from the Amazon in Ecuador. I am vice president of the Confederation of Indigenous Nationalities of the Ecuadorian Amazon region. It is a pleasure to be here with you and share the reality of our situation in Ecuador, and share with you information about what we are doing. When I saw what the conference was going to be about, including the resistance of peoples in mountainous regions, I was very interested in the theme. It was very surprising to me that here in the United States people are talking about this, and that this kind of situation exists in the United States as well.

I would like to explain how others want to take control of our natural resources and what is going on in response to that. In Ecuador, we have 14 million people and four regions. One of the biggest regions is the Amazon. In the Ecuadorian Amazon, we have ten nationalities or communities that are indigenous, each with its own language and its own land. To this I would also add an eleventh nationality, the mestizos.

Most of the natural resources of the country come from the Amazon region. Before talking about the situation, I would like to tell you about how we think about our region, where I come from in the Amazon. As you know, indigenous communities have a relationship with our land that is very important. We consider that we live in nature, and that in nature, everything is alive. We have to live with respect for everything that is around us.

I would like to explain why the territory is so important to us, and why we defend it so. If we have a right to our life, then we consider that right to live is linked to our territory. If we violate the rights to our territory and of our land, we could also say we are in violation of our right to live. Our territory is our space where we have our life, where we create science, culture, technology, and if we have that taken away from us, they are also taking our life away. A Quichua friend of mine used to say that.

There is a Quichua [or Kichwa] term, *Sumak Kawsay*, that is hard to translate, even into Spanish; it helps explain why we fight for our land. It means a harmonious life, or a fullness of life. This concept and vision of Sumak Kawsay conveys a lot; it is starting to have broader relevance and is being taken up in academic discussions. This vision includes a vision of how we want to be, how we want to live our life, and how we relate to our environment. It comes into direct conflict with the modern view. In our country it is very common for people to refer to us, the indigenous people from the Amazon, as the people of nature. We are called "natural" because of the importance of nature and the environment to our life, but from a "modern" view and a modern standpoint, that is equated with being ancient or premodern. So of course that would mean that if we are moving away from nature, then we are moving into modern times, but that vision is being questioned now. That is a good thing; even minimal questioning of that perspective is a good thing. It is being debated and being retheorized in these times.

With this great territory and the vision that I have talked about, we see that there is great cultural richness in the Amazon valley that touches nine different countries. There are about 400 indigenous communities and a great deal of biodiversity across the entire region. Then we ask ourselves why—when we have more and more laws, and constitutions get renewed all the time and new rights are given to people—at the same time the territories are being threatened more and more. These threats to our territory exist because this is where our natural resources are. There are those who mean to exploit all those natural resources. Some of these agents are the multinational companies that are looking to exploit them—oil, mining companies, and pharmaceutical companies, and I would even add the tourism companies that take advantage of the Amazon region. Then, of course, we have the government. The state, with its power, is also trying to gain the rights to the natural resources that are in the Amazonian territories. Of course we need to consider our own actions: all of the nations, the communities that have lived in these territories for millennia. We are concerned about the land not just because of the natural resources that are there, but also because it is the place where we live. Rights to water as a natural resource are especially being disputed. Water is such a basic resource for communities. Herein lies a great contradiction: the government, the entity that should protect the rights of indigenous communities, is instead treating us as enemies. State entities have said this openly and repeatedly—that we are their enemy.

At the center of this dispute are the natural resources, those that can be renewed and the nonrenewable ones. Oil has been of great interest to those wanting to exploit our resources, but now water is also featured in this group of contested natural resources. Because of the interests of all of these groups that want to exploit the same resources, there is an ongoing confrontation between us and multinational companies and against the government; all the time we are fighting this exploitation we are in a disadvantaged position. Although we are marginalized, we are still generating consciousness about the problem. There is currently a strong surge in this exploitation of natural resources versus our view, the indigenous view, of conservation and living well, expressed in the concept we talked about, the Sumak Kawsay. On the one hand, we have Sumak Kawsay; on the other hand, we have the development framework. They are in conflict: our view and the view of exploiting the natural resources as the primary goal. Our organizing resistance causes the government to try to show interest in our communities, but we think that this is just an excuse for exploiting our territory. The government is saying that the natural resources are for the good of everyone. They say they will use them to fight poverty, but we think this is an excuse to go against the rights of our people. While they are saying they will fight poverty, what they actually do is violate and diminish our rights, the rights of the people, in the interest of the government's rights. The government forgets all the people's rights.

I would like to clarify what we want to accomplish through our resistance, what our goals are. We are cultures and communities like any other. What we are asking is that the government return to us the capacity to govern ourselves and make our own choices and our own decisions with respect to our own future. We are not saying that we are a perfect community, but we want to be listened to and not stepped on. There are institutions within the indigenous communities that we want the state to recognize as part of our own government. We want to contribute to building a society that will live alongside other societies and other cultures, not as unequals, but as different peoples who have the same rights.

There are 10 indigenous communities in the Ecuadorian Amazon. I would like to talk now about the resistance of our communities, how are we organized, the problems we are facing, and what we are doing and not doing. Just the fact that we have been able to organize ourselves and have organizations at the local level and at the national level has been a great thing in empowering us to participate in society.

Starting in 1998, there were some rights that were recognized for the indigenous communities. Before that, we had always just had a resistance strategy. However, starting in 1998, these rights that were guaranteed for the people gave us another set of tools—the use of the law. We were more able, then, to mount a legal defense from a traditional standpoint. One of the protests that was organized by one of the biggest indigenous organizations was called Water, Life, and Dignity. We camped out to make our resistance known. In the Amazon we have been organizing a lot of resistance movements, and some of them are very strong movements. One of the benefits of all this is that we have been able to organize. It has given us strength in that the smaller communities are organized into larger regional communities. This political organization gives us more strength. One of the biggest movements from the past was in 1992, the protest that lasted almost a month and went from the Amazon to Quito. We asked the government for the property title to our Quichua territories. At that time, we still had not been granted those rights.

There have been two legal cases that have been very important and historic in that they have gone to international organizations for judgment. The first one was against Texaco. That company extracted oil from the Amazon region for many years. Indigenous communities sued the company. Our case has finally been won at a judicial level, but it is still a fight because the payments have not been received from that. That case, and its finding, is based on the harm that Texaco is causing the environment. The second, most recent case is one brought by a community in the south of the Amazon. It went to trial and even went up to the Inter-American Court of Human Rights. The community was successful in convicting the government of having violated the right to prior consultation of indigenous communities, which had been granted through the 1989 Indigenous and Tribal Peoples Convention Agreement 169 [brokered by the International Labor Organization] recognizing self-determination of indigenous communities in the region and rights over natural resources in our territories.

We have had several strategies for resistance. We have organized a political, judicial, and now a social movement. This is a central theme. The movement has helped us exercise the right (through Agreement 169) to prior consultation, which is the right we have to be consulted before the government does something. Before, they used to come and just start taking natural resources violently from the land without asking us. This right is also being interpreted incorrectly, because the government of Ecuador is saying that we are going to socialize resources, so we do not need to be asked. All the resources are going to belong to the state. So the fight is centered around this: they are asking us, but at the same time they are telling us they are socializing us and our resources. If they are going to do what they want, why even ask us? That is what the resistance movement is focused on.

The government has given concessions for 13 oil wells in the Amazon. The government has made up rules to consult with us, but we did not know anything about this. According to the Constitution, we should be consulted prior to their coming in and working, and we should continue to be informed. This never actually happens. They really do not ask us. So what is happening in the Amazon? What are we facing? We are facing a governmental policy that supports an economy that is about exploiting the natural resources. To connect with what Carmen Martínez Novo says about the leftist governments and their speeches [see chapter 7], their speeches are justifying this policy of extraction of natural resources in the name of broader resource distribution and the ending of poverty. These fights have generated a lot of confrontations between the government and indigenous communities, and there has been persecution of indigenous leaders.

One of the rationales that the government uses for that persecution of us is to say that we are terrorists and are sabotaging the government. There was a protest two years ago, and our people from the Amazon had taken a boa constrictor with them. At the rally they were holding up the boa in front of them as they were facing off with the police, who were mounted on horseback. The indigenous protestors did not know that the horses were scared of snakes. When the Amazonians showed the boa, the horses got spooked and started running away. The Amazonians were able to turn in the letter that they had carried there to the president, but then the government used that they had the snake to accuse the indigenous people of having weapons of mass destruction and being terrorists. I could not believe that I was seeing that, but those were the words that were written in the legal accusation against them after they were arrested: that the snake and their spears were weapons of mass destruction being used against the government of Ecuador. This was because when the horses started running, the police lost their handcuffs.

In these processes of resistance, besides persecution by the state, there are also media campaigns being conducted against indigenous leaders, trying to show that we are dangerous criminals. It could be that people think we are attacking them because the Amazonians were shown in pictures with the snake after the protest, but before that we had also presented the government with many alternatives, and those have not been covered by the media in the same way. I want to concentrate on two proposals we have made to the government in our resistance movement. The main proposal, which I have already mentioned, centers on the Sumak Kawsay: we want to live in harmony with our environment and to protect life for the generations to come. We also have proposed the transformation of the national government into one that recognizes that in Ecuador we have 14 different indigenous nationalities and 20 different communities. These proposals are in the Constitution, and now what we want is for our own indigenous government to be recognized. We are organizing another movement soon because we disagree with the government's plans to sell a big part of the Amazonian region to China. So as we prepare this social movement, we know we are going to face strong government opposition to it. But we have learned through time and through our own mistakes, and we know where our strengths are. Obviously, the main thing we have is the capacity to organize and to maintain our unity.

MONICA CHUJÍ has served as chair of the Constituent Assembly Committee on Natural Resources and Biodiversity in Quito, Ecuador. She was an active participant and young leader in the 1990 indigenous uprising that thrust issues of indigenous rights and demands onto Ecuador's national stage, and she has been working for indigenous rights throughout her career.

Blue Ridge Mountain Refugee

Si Kahn

I'm working in a factory
And thinking how it feels
To be bringing home good money
Like my Daddy never seen
But a feeling follows after me
Like a hound dog at my heels
'Cause I know that I'll never see
My mountain home again

Oh they say that
You can't go home again
Never sit and talk
Among your childhood friends
Never live among
Your neighbors and your kin
No, you'll never see
Your mountain home again

Down by the railway station
In the early afternoon
You can see them carrying bundles
That are all done up in twine

And they hear the whistle from the South
They're saying their goodbyes
And they say they'll be back
But they're leaving for all time

Don't they know that
They can't go home again
Never sit and talk
Among their childhood friends
Never live among
Their neighbors and their kin
No, they'll never see
Their mountain homes again

In Cincinnati, Baltimore,
Chicago and Detroit
You can find us by the thousands
With our husbands and our wives
If you wonder what we're doing here
So far from our mountain homes
We're Blue Ridge Mountain Refugees
Fighting for our lives

And we know that
We can't go home again
Never sit and talk
Among our childhood friends
Never live among
Our neighbors and our kin
No, we'll never see
Our mountain homes again

CHAPTER 7

Indigenous Social Movements in Mountain Regions

Carmen Martínez Novo, Shannon
Elizabeth Bell, Subhadra Mitra Channa,
Annapurna Devi Pandey, and Luis
Alberto Tuaza Castro

THIS CHAPTER FOCUSES on social movements struggling to preserve the natural environment and traditional livelihoods in mountain regions on three continents: the Himalayas; the Eastern Ghats in Odisha, India; Appalachia; and the Andes. These regions are all rich in natural resources and are exploited by nation-states, private corporations, or a combination of both, as well as by the local population. In the four regions discussed, local populations are constructed as marginal to the nation-state and are often stigmatized as isolated, primitive, and opposed to development and modernization. Development processes in these regions tend to benefit national elites, middle classes, and corporations much more than those living in the area. In addition, the exploitation of natural resources is producing severe environmental problems, which are placing the livelihoods and health of each of these local groups at risk. In this context, the authors are witnesses to the consolidation of local identities and social movements. Challenging the stereotype that local populations are static and primitive, the authors show how mountain and indigenous people organize to question global capitalist transformations and to propose alternative futures. As Kingsolver (2011) has noted, global processes can call localities into existence, because the locale can be a site of resistance to capital—and, we would like to add, to the state.

Although social movements in these regions have much in common in regards to their origin and their strategies for resistance, there are also important differences in how global processes of extraction and development are internalized and resisted within local and national contexts. There are also differences in how social movements are organized on the basis of particular traditions and cultures. Social movements may have different histories and trajectories in these regions: whereas local peoples confront neoliberal policies and activities and are consolidating their organizations in the Himalayas, Appalachia, and Odisha, Andean populations have already been able to challenge neoliberalism through a full-blown social movement, and are facing new challenges posed by governments that call themselves postneoliberal but that continue traditional forms of development based on the extraction of nonrenewable resources.

This chapter reflects a collaboration among social scientists working in different areas: Subhadra Mitra Channa in the Himalayas of India, Annapurna Devi Pandey in the state of Odisha in southeastern India, Shannon Elizabeth Bell in West Virginia in US Appalachia, and Carmen Martínez Novo and Luis Alberto Tuaza Castro in the Andes. We envision this collaboration as an opportunity to learn from other groups' problems, strategies, successes, and mistakes. As Kingsolver (2011, 2) has argued: "if people involved in global production were able to cross language, national, and cultural divides and compare experiences, it may make a difference." This chapter is an attempt to carry out precisely this kind of intercultural effort. We have crossed national as well as language barriers, translating our collective work into English thanks to the opportunity we had to meet at the Global Mountain Regions Conference organized by Ann Kingsolver and Sasikumar Balasundaram at the University of Kentucky. We hope that this collaboration fulfills the ambitious goals set by Kingsolver in her volume *Tobacco Town Futures* (2011, 9). She argues: "I believe that if more people in communities around the world could speak directly with each other about their situations, comparing notes, it would be useful in making sense of these larger events."

We propose thinking about the challenges confronted by the four regions and their respective social movements through two theoretical concepts that, although having roots in international Marxist and decolonial theory, were developed more systematically in Latin America in the 1960s and 1970s and have reemerged more recently (González Casanova 2006): the concept of internal colonialism (Gonzalez Casanova 1969, 2006; Stavenhagen 1970) and the concept of regions of refuge (Aguirre Beltrán 1991 [1967]). Internal colonialism refers to a colony that has become an independent nation but that, despite independence, retains within the nation colonial relations—political, economic, and cultural domination—that benefit a dominant ethnic group or groups and hurt an ethnically and culturally distinct population. Peoples colonized by the nation-state suffer conditions similar to those of international colonialism: they do not have decision-making power over their own territory and resources and are unequal, disempowered, and discriminated against in relation to the dominant ethnic group or groups. According to González Casanova (2006), the concept of internal colonialism may be expanded to regional differences in which surplus is extracted from some regions for the benefit of other dominant regions. González Casanova (2006) adds that, today, internal colonialism has become articulated with international and transnational domination. Peoples within the nation-state confront simultaneously internal and transnational forms of exploitation. The social movements of these oppressed peoples can also be, according to González Casanova, international avant-gardes, or models for other peoples on how to resist different forms of neocolonial relations.

These forms of domination and oppression of one culturally distinct people over another resulting from conquest and colonialism but reproduced after independence, tend to take a territorial form, as dominated ethnic groups tend to inhabit regions of inhospitable geography where they either have lived traditionally or were pushed by conquest: particularly mountain regions, jungles, and rainforests. According to Aguirre Beltrán (1991 [1967]) in these "regions of refuge" on the one hand colonial relations perpetuating discrimination are preserved to a greater degree than in urban or central areas of the nation. On the other hand, Aguirre Beltrán (1991) points out that many of the nation's nonrenewable natural resources can be found in regions of refuge. The conflicts that we describe below reflect this articulation between internal colonialism and the struggle by national and transnational elites over the resources of mountain regions and natural reserves where stigmatized groups live. Since both the concept of internal colonialism and the concept of regions of refuge are based on relations of domination between ethnically distinct populations, there is the question as to what degree these ideas can be applied to Appalachia, although there is a long history of oppression of, and resistance by, indigenous communities in the region. We discuss this issue in the conclusion. The concepts can definitely be applied to the Andes, the Himalayas, and India, since they are postcolonial areas where indigenous groups still suffer colonial forms of discrimination and exploitation.

Indigenous Social Movements in the Himalayas

I (Subhadra Mitra Channa) have spent decades as an ethnographer learning from and with marginalized communities in India, especially in its northern reaches. The Himalayas are one of the newest mountain chains in the world, forming the borders between the countries of India, China, Nepal, Bhutan, and Chinese-occupied Tibet. This region rich in natural resources has been the peripheral zone for the mainland of India, and, as documented by Guha (1989), the dense forests, flora and fauna of this region have been systematically exploited over the years, the most intensive draining outof resources having commenced from the early period of British colonization of this area. Even in the postcolonial period the power holders of the center, located in the plains of New Delhi, have continued treating Himalayan resources as if they were meant for the benefit of the mainland populations rather than the local people, who, deprived of their livelihoods as a result of depletion of their resource base, have become more and more marginalized on their own lands. Like in the American South (S. Scott 2012, 39), the major landowners of this region, especially the royalty, have been largely absentee landowners dependent on revenue rather than on the produce of the land. Yet, as shown by Guha (1989), there has always been a culture of protest and resistance from the peasants who have made their voice heard through novel forms of resistance like Chipko, a movement with several strands organized to stop industrial-scale deforestation in the Himalayan region of northern India.

My own work is based on the study of local peasant farmers and shepherds of the upper Himalayan regions who, in India, are included in the group of Scheduled Tribes (ST), which corresponds roughly to what in the United States are called Native Americans. These people are generally seen to be outside the fold of mainstream Hindu populations and are also often characterized as not possessing a "civilized" way of life (Unnithan-Kumar 1997, Guha 1999). The stereotypical image of "primitiveness" focuses on eating habits (meat-eating and alcohol-drinking), sexual life (promiscuity, especially on the part of women), non-*sanskritic* lifestyles (meaning not conforming to Brahmanical rituals), and—in the context of present-day urbanity—not "modern." In this way, they correspond to what Stewart (2011, 3) has called the "misconceptions and stereotyping" of the US mountain South. As in southern Appalachia, the people of this region have been seen as dispensable and not important enough to be given much weight when planning and policy making for the so-called development of the mainland population. As a consequence, the Himalayan region is witnessing the building of a large number of dams, ostensibly to provide energy to power-starved cities like New Delhi.

One example is the large dam being built on the Bapsa River in Kinnaur in the Indian state of Himachal Pradesh, where the Kinnauries, who depend on shepherding and subsistence agriculture and horticultural activities, live. Although they claim to be high-caste Hindus (Rajputs), the local people are not served by Brahmins (an essential aspect of being high caste) and have an economy of almost total self-sufficiency. This region remains snowbound for most of the year, and the people herd large numbers of sheep, whose wool is used for making clothes and shawls as well as being sold commercially in the markets. Earlier, when trade across the Indo-Tibet border was prominent, they depended a great deal on barter. Nowadays, the woolen products such as colorful shawls woven by the women are part of a national and international market network. There is subsistence farming on the slopes of the mountains, and the local forest provides fuel wood, fodder, and grazing pastures for the animals; medicinal herbs and spices; almost anything else that the Kinnauries require as supplemental food such as mushrooms, a variety of fruits, walnuts, and a local nut called *chilgoza*; and building material in the form of evergreen conifers such as *deodar*. The numerous mountain streams not only provide fresh water for drinking but also serve as a small-scale energy source for running water mills for grinding locally produced wheat and millet. These water bodies were also used for small hydroelectric dams providing electricity to their homes.

There are, however, several outside forces at work that threaten this self-sufficiency and the peaceful life of these people. The most prominent of these is the building of large dams. There is also the aggressive policy of the state (both regional and national governments) to introduce cash crops and thus wean people away from a self-reliant subsistence economy and integrate them into the cash economy, the propagation of which has been a prime motivation of the Indian government ever since it opted for economic liberalization and neoliberal policies in 1992. Thus, the local farmers have been persuaded to give up subsistence farming in favor of apple farming, and apples have emerged as a major cash crop in this region. The third factor is tourism—an aftereffect of the dam-building activities that have not only improved road connections to this area, but also ensured that the roads are kept open through the use of earth movers and snow removers by the dam-building companies, which have also brought in large numbers of skilled and unskilled workers. The tourist traffic and the presence of large numbers of outsiders have opened up the local markets to the flow of consumer goods, which has further increased the desire of the local people to have more cash income; the local investment in cash-cropping and tourism, then, is increasing.

The combined effects of these changes are the rapid degradation of the local environment and the disappearance of local means of livelihood like sheepherding and subsistence farming. The Himalayas comprise an unstable mountain chain, and the heavy boring done by the dam builders is shaking up the mountainsides, bringing about massive landslides that are destroying fields on the slopes used for cultivation by the local people. During my research, I was shown agricultural fields that had once been fertile but now were covered with huge boulders that had come crashing down the mountainside. The apple farmers are encouraged by the state agencies to use pesticides and chemical fertilizers that are polluting their once pristine mountain streams and environment. The deforestation caused by the heavy construction used to build dams and hotels has caused many glaciers to melt and has also given rise to intense mountain floods that devastate the local ecology. In a visit in 2008 to this area, I found that flash floods and melting glaciers were the prime concerns of the villagers of this region, and in their wisdom they attributed most of these problems to the dam builders and the external interference with their environment.

They are also aware that they have little power of their own. In the democratic system, they lack the one major power base: namely, numbers. Historically, these are sparsely populated areas, and the number of the local people is still insufficient to evoke much political interest. In addition to the stigma of being labeled "primitive," they have merited little governmental attention. Lacking any powerful human lobbies, the locals have turned to their supernatural beings for both solace and protection. Their two major forms of protest are building up rhetoric to oppose the dams as being "outside" their social and economic world and invoking the power of their deities for protection and intervention.

None of the locals seek employment in these dams, which they consider as being made to "provide electricity to outsiders as far away as America." The local people insist that the abode of the gods, who live in various spots in the landscape such as rivers, caves, underground, and various types of aboveground locations, has been disturbed by all these activities. They vehemently opposed the building of ski slopes on the upper regions of Himachal by saying that the local gods are totally opposed to it. As I have described elsewhere (Channa 2010a, 2010b), the local gods are not icons in temples (as in mainstream Hinduism) but living beings who are active members of the social world of the villagers, who all consider themselves to be the *praja*, or followers of the king or the village deity (see also Galey 1994; Mazumdar 1998; and Sax 2002).

In recent times these gods are in consultation about how to save their people from the onslaught of the environmental disasters that are befalling them. I saw the local gods going from village to village in processions to consult each other, and entire villages including local officials congregating to listen to them. The involvement of the deities ensures that the matters are not only common knowledge, but also part of community discourses, and issues like dam building and environmental degradation are increasingly becoming part of the collective consciousness. More important, these issues are also assuming a moral dimension such that saving the environment is no longer a secular issue but part of a sacred debate. It is this lack of boundaries between the material and the nonmaterial world that exists in so many societies that lends credence to the power of beliefs in motivating action. As Geertz (1973) put it, we can see that the sacred is a powerful stimulator of setting "moods and motivations" and in initiating actions. Where nature is not a utilitarian resource but a sacred dimension of the cosmological world, saving the environment can become a powerful motivation and can initiate protests of significant proportions.

The Tribal Resistance Movement against Mining in the Kondhmal Region of Odisha, India

This section is devoted to a resistance movement in Odisha led by the Dongria Kondh Tribe of the Niyamagiri Hills. Tribal communities—including men, women, and children—mobilized against a bauxite mining operation run by the

Vedanta Corporation of the United Kingdom. I (Annapurna Devi Pandey) argue that the state of Odisha has developed a partnership with multinational corporations to exploit the natural resources of the state—most of it in the areas inhabited by its tribal people. The people's resistance movement I have documented is primarily in opposition to such projects, which have harmed their social and natural environment. I worked among the Dongria Kondhs during January and February 1987, followed by brief return visits in 2004 and 2012. I found the contrast between the earlier visit and the later ones quite disturbing because of the changing conditions for the mountain residents.

Several missionaries and anthropologists have studied the Dongria Kondh since the late nineteenth century. The most impressive anthropological study is by Felix Padel and Samarendra Das, and it has been reported in several books, articles, and videos (Padel, 2011; Padel and Das, 2010). Odisha is known for its distinct tribal population—every fourth person out of 42 million belongs to one or the other of its 62 Scheduled Tribes (STs).[1] In the statistical profile of the state, tribal residents constitute 22.1 percent of the total population of 42 million; it is the second largest tribal population in the country (as per the 2011 census). The state of Odisha holds about 9 percent of the tribal population of the country and has the highest number (13) of Particularly Vulnerable Tribal Groups (PVTGs)[2] out of a total 62 tribal communities. In the name of the special protection of the scheduled tribes, "tribal areas (called 'Scheduled Areas') further benefited from being treated as separate administrative categories in order to protect the rights of Scheduled Tribes over their land, forests, and water. The Constitution's Fifth Schedule and Sixth Schedule carried over the principles of the Scheduled Districts Act of 1874 which excluded these 'Scheduled Areas' from the operation of ordinary laws in British India" (Shah 2007, 1813). Ironically, nearly half of the state's area is under Schedule V of the Indian constitution,[3] some of the most impoverished areas in the country (Elwin 1936). Despite being extremely rich in resources, 72 percent of the tribal households in Odisha live beneath the poverty line. Since much of the country's mineral resources are located in these protected scheduled areas, they are constantly amended by the state to extract all the rich resources and help the state rapidly improve its growth rate (as measured in GDP).

Kondhs are the largest tribal group in the state of Odisha with a population of over a million (Padel 2011). They are largely concentrated in the Kondhmal, Koraput, Rayagarha, Nabarangpur, Kalahandi, and Gajapati Districts. When I visited Kondhmal in 1986–1987, I was struck by the natural beauty of the area and the simple lifestyle of the Kuttia Kondhs and nearby Dongria Kondhs living in the area. I was studying, at that time, the exploitation going on in this area with the influx of people from the plains: namely, government officials, businessmen, contractors, moneylenders, and other entrepreneurs grabbing land and living well at the expense of the Kondhs.

In the 1960s and early 1970s, the Kondhmal area attracted many people from all over India in search of a better life. In the name of progress, mega-construction projects took place in Kalahandi and G.udayagiri (transliterated spelling) and the capital city of Phulbani (predominantly a Kondh district), which have witnessed a massive influx of the mainstream population into the tribal areas. Many of the officials and businessmen were temporarily assigned to work in the forests of Odisha in fulfillment of government or forestry contracts, to build roads, and to work in the steel mining projects.

It became a common practice among these migrants to marry Kondh women with a meager bride price and the exchange of a few gifts. However, most of the men were already married and had families in their native states. They knew full well that this new marriage was not in compliance with the Hindu Marriage Act (1956), but local custom supporting the independence of Kondh women sanctioned their living with a Kondh woman as their wife. This arrangement was indeed extremely beneficial for the man: in his Kondh wife, he got a sex provider, caretaker, housekeeper, and cook, all for a meager sum. In a few years they would have children. Being the wife of a Hindu, the Kondh woman would start wearing vermilion, bangles, and anklets and cover her head as a symbol of marriage. But this fairy-tale marriage did not last long. The men, as I said, had a parallel family back home; eventually, at the end of the business contract or state transfer, they left the area, promising they would come back soon to collect their beloved wife and children, but very few ever returned. This practice introduced a growing number of abandoned wives and children in G.udayagiri, which became popularly known as Premnagar ("Pleasure Town"). It attracted lots of tourists in search of sexual pleasure for free. The abandoned women felt too dejected and disgraced to return to their own communities.

This major social problem gave rise to an indigenous women's organization known as Ghumusar Mahila Sangathan (GMS) led by Maka Naik, a Kondh woman, in 1979. With support of other activist groups and student organizations, GMS attracted a lot of media attention. Ghumusar Mahila Sangathan challenged the men in court and succeeded in getting traditional marriages recognized as legal. As a result of the GMS' own work, in 40 cases, women were declared legal wives entitled to financial support. The state ultimately acknowledged the helpless situation these women were in and provided adequate compensation for them and their children. The men were also charged with human rights violations. As a result, this practice of men working in the region marrying a Kondh woman when they are already married elsewhere has decreased greatly.

Now with bauxite mining in the area, new problems have emerged: massive displacement of the tribal people from their own land; the depletion of the forests due to large-scale mining; and urban migration for livelihoods that, for women, often end up being sex trafficking due to poverty and unemployment.

When I visited that area in 2004, the community house (Dhangari Ghara) where boys and girls used to socialize was almost deserted. When I asked about that, I was told that Kondhs had faced continuous rampage by the outside community. In fear for the safety and security of their women, they had stopped the practice of young men and women meeting on a casual basis and getting to know each other. Women were wearing vermilion and covering their faces so as not to be teased and mistreated by the mainstream Hindu society. Even though there had been a consistent effort to improve the education of boys and girls in the area, the constant threat of rape and abduction of the Kondh girls, even by their nontribal teachers, made the schools an unsafe place to be in.

Since the tribal women have traditionally been equal partners with men in producing and collecting food from the jungle, their relationships have been disrupted by the multiple levels of oppression they experience due to the multinational corporate mining venture and the urbanization and industrialization of this region. They see a correlation between the rise in alcohol consumption by men and their violence toward women; between women's lack of access to the forest resources and their poverty; between changing gender roles and sexual exploitation; and between cultural loss and a broader identity crisis. Ghumusar Mahila Sangathan today focuses on many aspects of tribal women's challenges related to poverty, violence against women, decreasing biodiversity, negative media attention, and the need for an increased focus on health and nutrition, economic development, education, training and empowerment, and greater participation in decision making (Mishra 2001). In the development model borrowed from the West, I see a clear discrepancy between the state's ideology and the existing cultural, social, and economic realities of tribal women in Odisha and elsewhere in India. As Kim Berry observes (2003, 78), "Ideas about women and their needs are created out of and are nested within unequal power relations"; the increasing role of state and capitalist ideologies and practices in the region is particularly oppressive to Kondh women.

Odisha has the following percentages of India's mineral reserves: 27 percent of its coal reserves, 33 percent of its iron ore, 55 percent of India's bauxite (used in aluminum production), 92 percent of its nickel, and 95 percent of its chromate.[4] As Padhy and Panigrahy (2011, 25) report, since independence, Odisha has set up 190 mining development projects, which have deforested 24,124 hectares of land, the basic source of livelihood of the tribal people.

The exploitation of the Kondhs is nothing new. It has gone on for a very long time, as F. G. Bailey and other scholars have reported. During the British colonial period, their land was classified and became available for profitmaking, leading to their land alienation. The role of missionaries, moneylenders, and *zamindars* (large landowners), and the British punitive rules and regulations, were major sources of their exploitation (Bailey 1957, 1960, 1969). What is new is robbing them of their land and their livelihood through state-supported and state-sponsored multinational mining projects.

The state of Odisha, especially the southern belt comprised of the Koraput, Balangir and Kalahandi Districts (KBK), is endowed with 1,733 million tons (70 percent) of the total bauxite resources of the country. In the postliberalization period, this mineral resource has attracted many multinational corporations both from within and outside the country, dragging this state into the globalization arena. The state whole-heartedly supports these initiatives, attracting huge revenues from the mining. During the period 1992–1997, bauxite resources in Odisha have pulled in US$20.5 billion. Vedanta Aluminium Ltd. has set up and is operating a 1 million-ton aluminum refinery at Lanjigarh, in the district of Kalahandi, based on a memorandum of understanding signed with the Government of Odisha that up to 150 million tons of bauxite for the plant will be supplied from the nearby Niyamagiri Hills (VedantaResources, PLC 2012). However, with the protest of the local Dongria Kondhs, the Union Ministry of Environment and Forest has disallowed bauxite excavation at Niyamgiri.

These mining projects have had an adverse impact on the local tribal people, leading to their physical displacement, loss of land, and loss of access to the forest and its resources, affecting their indigenous livelihoods. The state is getting plenty of revenue and has fervently promoted mining as a sure way to curb unemployment among the youth in Odisha. Ambitious middle-class youth and entrepreneurs from different parts of the state have flocked to these areas and have found a quick way of making money. But the mining project areas are inhabited by tribal people—they live and breathe around these mines.

The Niyamagiri Hills provide the the Dongria Kondhs their source not only of food and water, but also of their identity and spirituality. In their origin myth, Donger *raja* is their god, ancestor, and the source of their being. They realize that with bauxite mining in the area, their kin and clan are displaced and have suffered severe blows.

The depletion of forest resources has become the biggest threat in the wake of mining projects in the surrounding districts. This has been accompanied by the "piling up of solid effluents such as red mud and tons of sodium hydroxide, leaving a high PH level in the soil and loss of vegetation and natural habitats" (Padhi and Panigrahi 2011, 43), a major health hazard.

Ironically, the state advertises the establishment of bauxite mining by the National Aluminium Company (NALCO) at Damanjodi only 110 kilometers from Kashipur as a symbol of state pride. In reality, bauxite mining has adversely affected the tribal people and their livelihood. With the depletion of the forest resources, people are being displaced from their own land and are forced to perform wage labor. Around every bauxite mine, local people testified that their water sources that had been perennial have dried up; this is just one of the dangers faced by farmers in the area. I observed similar situations while visiting the Aditya Birla mining project in the neighboring city of Barbil in Keonjhar District. There are 80 iron ore mines operating in this region around Barbil, as it is known as the fifth largest deposit of iron ore and manganese ore in the world. I was shocked to see the thick red dust covering the trees, roads, and houses. While visiting the mining sites, I could see opencast mining mile after mile; the hills have been cut down and piles of iron ore mounted and transported by trucks to the nearby railway station. The people who have moved away from the hills and are living in small makeshift houses were standing in line to work in the mines. All the managerial jobs are held by the nontribal *babus,* while the low-paying manual jobs are given to the tribal people. Clearly, one can see that there was no fair sharing of the profit made by the mines. Even though the multinational mining corporations are making excessive profit and illegal mining is common and has created scores of millionaires coming from the plains, the tribal people remain poor and mostly illiterate.[5]

It is because of the dedication and the courage shown by the Dongria Kondhs that the Niyamgiri Hills are still untouched (apart from the refinery below). For the people, the Niyamgiri Hills are too precious to be touched. Everyone knows that once the machines move in, it is a slippery slope and those hills could be destroyed. The Dongria Kondhs in the Niyamgiri Hills have raised their voices against such megadevelopment projects. They have questioned these development projects by asking, "Development for whom, and at whose cost?" noting that it robs tribal people of their livelihood resources. This is one of the reasons there have been protests by the tribal people in Odisha against the state-sponsored bauxite mining operations in 1985, 1996, 1997, 2000, and 2005 (Padhy and Panigrahy 2011). This shows the conflict between state-sponsored development, which favors industrialization and mining, and the people, who prefer a sustainable livelihood provided by their environment. In all these movements, women have taken an active part through picketing, processions, and public hearings. The emergence of indigenous leadership has made all these movements more widespread.

Since 1991, when the state liberalized its policies and got rid of the permit quota system, different business interest groups have been competing in the global arena to maximize their own profits. This has decreased the protections the state had provided in the name of the uplift of the tribal people. Many people have made a lot of money—legally or illegally—from mining operations, and some of that money has gone into financing state enterprises. Unless and until the state rises up to meet its obligation to protect all citizens—marginalized as well as privileged—these tribal peoples are going to be exploited and their lives and livelihoods will be threatened.

India, by all accounts, is becoming a very different country. It is no longer a predominantly agrarian society. Due to world-class information technology and the revolution in telecommunications, it has been pushed to become the third largest economy in Asia, with a rising middle class that is now about as large as the total population of the United States. Both domestic and foreign industries and corporations have contributed to this massive growth since the advent of liberalization and globalization in early 1990s.

Odisha—known as a "backward" state—also wants to have its share of the benefits of globalization. The state has much of the country's mineral reserves (a million tons), mostly concentrated in its tribal areas. To increase its per capita income, it has collaborated with many multinational corporations and big industries in India in mining, which is affecting the life of the people in many adverse ways. The state has adopted neoliberal policies to promote growth without taking into account the impact it is bound to have on the health and well-being of the tribal people living in the area.

Despite all the protest movements described in this section, in July 2013 came the news that the refinery in Lanjigrh reopened after seven months of being closed due to the lack of availability of bauxite. With the protest of the local tribals, called the Niyamgiri Suraksha Samiti (NSS), the Supreme Court of India ordered the state of Odisha to halt any mining operation until ascertaining the views of the local people through the Palli Sabhas (Village Panchayats). The tribal people expressed fear that money power, coupled with the muscle power, would coopt some of their leaders, who would then favor the state's agenda in promoting the interest of the Vedanta mining corporation against their own people. Unless and until a wider movement resisting the oppression of local residents by the state and corporations is organized, it will be challenging to preserve the land and livelihoods of the tribal people in that region. Toward that end, the indigenous women's leadership, particularly, has demonstrated successful resistance strategies in collaboration with the sacred mountain itself.

Appalachian Women and the Fight for Environmental Justice in Mountain Communities

The central Appalachian region of the United States, which includes West Virginia, eastern Kentucky, southwest Virginia, and eastern Tennessee, is one of the largest and oldest coal-producing regions in the nation. For a number of years, I (Shannon Elizabeth Bell) have been doing collaborative research with the activists, primarily women, who are standing up to mountaintop removal mining in West Virginia. While employment in the coal industry has long been on the decline due to technological advances that have increased productivity within the industry, the historical connections between coal and regional identity are still deeply felt (Bell and York 2010; R. Scott 2010). "Friends of Coal" bumper stickers and license plates are a common sight along the roadways in Central Appalachia, and this loyalty to coal extends into the county and state levels of government as well. Some residents contend that the coal industry's political power in the region has given the industry a free pass to employ methods of coal mining and processing that are causing great environmental harm and threatening the health and safety of local residents.

Throughout the past two decades, mountaintop removal mining has become pervasive throughout Central Appalachia. In this type of mining, powerful explosives are used to blow apart mountains to provide access to thin coal seams, which are then scraped from the flattened surface with giant draglines. The earth that once made up the mountain above the coal is pushed into adjacent valleys, creating "valley fills," which cover streams and harm delicate ecosystems. Mountaintop removal mining has destroyed more than 1 million acres of land and over 500 mountains in Central Appalachia (Geredien 2009).

Coal mining and coal processing have many significant consequences for residents living proximal to industry operations, including acute flood events, coal waste impoundment breaches, coal dust air pollution, structural damage to homes from blasts, projectile rocks and boulders, water contamination, and higher rates of birth defects, cancer, and chronic illnesses (Flood Advisory Technical Taskforce 2002; Orem 2006; EPA 2005; Erikson 1976; Scott et al. 2005; Bell 2010; Bell and York 2010; Bell and Braun 2010; Palmer et al. 2010; Hendryx, Ahern, and Nurkiewicz 2007; Hendryx 2008; Hendryx and Ahern 2008; Ahern and Hendryx 2008).

Despite the coal industry's power, the injustices it has caused in Central Appalachia have not gone without resistance. Over the past 15 years, a grassroots struggle for environmental justice has emerged in the region, and working-class women have been at the forefront of this fight. The fact that local women initiated this struggle and populate the front lines of the movement is not atypical among environmental justice groups across the United States. A large body of research has found that despite their lower rates of participation than men in the mainstream environmental movement,[6] women "are heavily represented in both the leadership and the membership" of environmental justice organizations, representing upwards of 70 percent of the activists in local and state organizations that are fighting such hazards as chemical plants, toxic waste dumps, and nuclear facilities (Brown and Ferguson 1995, 148–150; Kaplan 1997; 1992; Cable 1992).

A substantial number of studies have found that working-class women often attribute their involvement in social movements to their roles as mothers. Motherhood is called on both as a justification and as a resource for environmental justice activism (Krauss 1993; Culley and Angelique 2003; Brown and Ferguson 1995; Peeples and DeLuca 2006; Epstein 1995; Bell and Braun 2010). Parallel findings can be seen among women environmental justice activists in Central Appalachia that I interviewed from 2006 to 2009. One of the most prevalent themes throughout the interviews I conducted is that these women consider activism against the injustices of the coal industry is an extension of their identities—and obligations—as mothers and grandmothers.

One example of this pattern is Maria Gunnoe, whose family experienced a terrifying flood in June 2003 that nearly washed away their house. The experience of the flood was so traumatizing that it left psychological scars on Maria's children, especially her young daughter, who, Maria told me, suffered from post-traumatic stress disorder from the flood. Anytime there was a thunderstorm or a weather alert, her daughter would not sleep. As Maria relates,

> That is what *pissed me off*. How *dare* they steal that from my child! The security of being able to sleep in her own bed. The coal companies now own that. They now own my child's security in her own bed. [Pauses.] And how can they expect me as a mother to look over that? How is it, what if I done this to their kids? What if I created terror in their children's lives? And that is what it has done to my children.
>
> After all of this had taken place, in order for me to be a mother, and in order for me to keep my children safe, and ensure my children's future as free American citizens, I've had—it's not an option—I've had to stand up and fight for our rights.

While the motherhood identity is a significant motivating force among many of the women I interviewed, this identity was discussed in ways that emphasize a protector duty or role. For instance, in her reflection on why women tend to be the ones on the front lines of the environmental justice movement, the late Judy Bonds stated, "women are the protectors, the mother figure. They protect their children, they want to protect their grandchildren, and they want to protect their communities." Likewise, Maria Lambert told me, "It's the need to protect, that need inside of most women, and I would say probably 99.9 percent of the women have that need to protect somebody, whether it's a husband, a child, a parent, a neighbor, an animal, whoever." Lorelei Scarboro further explained that her drive to protect extends beyond protecting individual people to also include "the environment and the wildlife and the vegetation."

The interviews I have conducted suggest that it is not simply a "motherhood identity" that drives the activism of many Central Appalachian women; rather, it is more accurate to describe their activism as stemming from a broader "protector identity." These women understand the moral authority for their activism emanating not only from a calling to protect their children and grandchildren not only from irresponsible mining practices, but also from an obligation to protect their communities, their mountains, their heritage, their family homeplace, and their way of life.

Each of the women interviewed has a deep connection to the people in her community and to the physical place that she calls home. Being motivated to activism to protect "home" is a strong theme throughout these interviews. One example is the case of Mary Miller and Pauline Canterberry of Sylvester, West

Virginia, who became involved in the environmental justice movement after a coal preparation plant adjacent to their town began covering their homes in coal dust. Because of the coal dust, their homes lost 90 percent of their resale value. As Pauline relates, "I was mad, because, I mean, I worked hard for my home. I worked under a lot of hard conditions for my home. And I didn't think anybody had the right to destroy it."

Activist Lorelei Scarboro also cites the threat to her home as one of the primary reasons she was spurred to action. As she relates, Massey Energy's Eagle 2 mine permit includes a portion of Coal River Mountain that is directly behind her house: "My home's threatened. The family cemetery is threatened. The stream that runs by my house, the deer that I sit there and watch leap across the fence—everything where I am, because of Eagle 2 [mine], is now threatened. So I really don't have a choice [except to fight]."

A question these women are often asked is, "If things are so bad, why don't you just move?" While moving may seem a reasonable solution to those from outside the region, for many local residents—even those who could afford to move—leaving is not an option they are willing to consider. The attachment to home and community is so strong that they feel compelled to fight back. Lorelei Scarboro expresses the intensity of this connection to place: "It's difficult to explain the attachment, the sense of place that Appalachians have. It's a connectedness to the land, to your surroundings. It's not the value of the house; it's not the price of the ten acres. It's the memories. It's what you have there. It's where you've been. It's the life you share with the people you love."

The place attachment that Lorelei describes is a bond that connects individuals to their environment. This bond is not simply a relationship with the physical landscape; it is also composed of interpersonal, community, and social relationships. As Judy Bonds expressed, "It's my soul . . . it's not just these mountains—it's our culture and our heritage." Thus, just as important as the physical landscape (or perhaps more important) are the intangibles—culture, history, and community—that the land represents.

A number of the activists in my study explained that their place attachment and drive to protect the land is part of their identity as "Appalachians." As Debbie Jarrell relates, "We are Appalachian women, and . . . our roots run so deep, you can't distinguish us from the earth we live on. It's just a part of us." Maria Gunnoe further describes the connection she sees between being an "Appalachian woman" and fighting the injustices of the coal industry: "As mothers of future generations of Appalachian boys and girls, we can't allow them to steal this from our children—it's too precious. And it can't be replaced."

Despite the fact that the existence of an "Appalachian identity" is contested among some Appalachian scholars, claiming this identity may, in fact, be a mobilizing and empowering act for some, as it reinforces place attachment (Bell 2013).

Scholar-activist Steve Fisher (2010) attests to this possibility, stating, "I've witnessed local social justice struggles transformed as participants have come to see themselves as Appalachians." Indeed, the women I have interviewed draw on their attachment to the place of Appalachia and their Appalachian identity as sources of strength and as a motivating force for their activism. They not only seek to protect their children, families, and communities, but they also are driven to protect those aspects of their lives and sense-of-self that are connected to their physical surroundings, family histories, and cultural traditions (including, sometimes, religious frameworks, as discussed in other examples in this chapter).

Challenges to Indigenous Social Movements in Extraction-Oriented Postneoliberal Regimes in the Andes

The first part of this section on indigenous movements in the Andes is by Carmen Martínez Novo, and the second part is by Luis Alberto Tuaza Castro; they have worked together as activist researchers in Ecuador, through FLACSO, the Latin American Faculty for the Social Sciences. Martínez Novo has conducted traditional and collaborative research in Ecuador on the relations between indigenous movements and their nonindigenous allies since 2002. Tuaza Castro is an indigenous Kichwa scholar with a PhD from FLACSO who teaches at Universidad Nacional de Chimborazo and FLACSO. He collaborates on a daily basis with indigenous communities in Chimborazo as a researcher and spiritual leader.

Geographical and Historical Background

The Andes are the longest mountain range in the world. With an average height of more than two miles above sea level, they form a continual range of highlands along the western coast of South America. The formation of the mountain range dates back to approximately 20 million years ago, when the ocean crust dipped under the South American tectonic plate, pushing the land up dramatically. The Andean mountain range runs through seven South American countries (Venezuela, Colombia, Ecuador, Peru, Bolivia, Chile, and Argentina), north to south. The Andean highlands are rich in natural resources: on the eastern side, they contain hydrocarbons; copper and other resources are found on both sides of the mountain range. Salars (salt-encrusted depressions) that were produced by the dry climate in the southern Andes contain large deposits of lithium. Gold and silver have been mined in the Andes for centuries.

The Andes have been home to many indigenous cultures. In the fifteenth century, the Incas consolidated an empire that covered most of this mountain range and incorporated or subdued many preexisting groups. The language of the Inca Empire was Quechua, which is still spoken in several Andean countries. The Ecuadorian dialect of Quechua is Kichwa, a name that is also applied to the people who speak it. Another important native language in the region is Aymara.

In the sixteenth century, the Spaniards conquered the Inca Empire with the help of native groups who resented Inca domination. During the colonial period, instead of exterminating native peoples, the Spaniards taxed them and used them as forced laborers and serfs in mines and large agricultural units called *haciendas*. In the second half of the twentieth century, a number of Andean countries carried out agrarian and political reforms that liberated native peoples from serfdom and granted them some land as well as full citizenship. However, the legacy of colonialism is still alive in the Andes in the form of racism and discrimination against native peoples and the descendants of African slaves. To fight for land, economic inclusion, and cultural rights, native Andean peoples have organized powerful social movements since roughly the 1970s.

Turn to the Left and Extraction in the Andes in the Twenty-First Century

A number of governments that reject neoliberalism were elected in the Andean Region in the first decade of the twenty-first century (French 2009; Oxhorn 2009; Weyland 2009; Cameron and Hershberg 2010). The most radical among them were the governments of Hugo Chavez (1999–2013) of Venezuela, Evo Morales (2006–present) of Bolivia, and Rafael Correa (2007–2017) of Ecuador (Weyland 2009). These governments self-identified as leftist, twenty-first century socialist, or postneoliberal. Evo Morales was reelected for the third time in 2014, and Chávez was replaced by his vice-president Nicolás Maduro when Chávez died of cancer in 2013. Correa has also been replaced by his vice-president Lenin Moreno in elections in 2017. Although the turn to the left is over in several Latin American countries where the right is currently governing, the self-identified postneoliberal left is still in power in Venezuela, Bolivia, and Ecuador. What does this mean for the social movements of the Andean countries?

Neoliberal reforms were forced upon Latin American nations starting in the early 1980s by US-led international financial institutions such as the International Monetary Fund and the World Bank as a way to solve the debt crisis of the region. Following international and US guidelines, Latin American governments reduced social services and subsidies, privatized state enterprises, and discontinued agrarian reforms and other projects of social inclusion that had started in earlier historical periods and were characterized by nationalist welfare state approaches (Harvey 2005; Skidmore, Smith, and Green 2010, 368–375). Neoliberal reforms caused a great deal of suffering and triggered a number of social protests and uprisings in Andean countries (Hylton, Thomson, and Gilly 2007; López Maya 2003; Zamosc 1994; Coronil and Skurski 1991). The election of nationalist and anti-imperialist regimes in the first decade of the twenty-first century signaled the reaction of the population against neoliberalism, and represented the political manifestation of the deeper process of social movement–building described above.

Although some critics claim that these governments continued being neoliberal but with more extensive social policies, the governments of Chavez, Morales, and Correa reversed some key neoliberal trends: They sought to build stronger states,[7] sought a greater role for the state in the economy, opposed free trade and protected their internal markets against it, controlled financial flows, reversed neoliberal labor regimes, increased the redistribution of public moneys to the poor, and rejected US hegemony (Escobar 2010, Martínez Novo 2016). For these reasons these governments self-identified and were identified by some scholars as postneoliberal. There is a debate that falls outside the scope of this chapter on whether these governments would like to return to an earlier period of stronger nationalist states with social policies that characterized Latin America from the 1930s to the 1970s (French 2009), or whether they would like to build different socialist states (López Maya 2009). In fact, both Keynesian welfare state and socialist tendencies were present in these governments because they were eclectic, made up of different tendencies and currents (Postero 2010a; Martínez Novo 2013).

Postneoliberal Andean regimes were able to engage in bold politics, some state formation, redistribution, and establishment of relative independence from the United States because they possess abundant nonrenewable natural resources such as oil (Venezuela and Ecuador), natural gas (Bolivia), copper (Venezuela, Ecuador, Bolivia), gold (Venezuela, Ecuador, Bolivia), and lithium (Bolivia) and because the price of these commodities was very high during the 2000s (Weyland 2009). Oil and natural gas are strategic sources of energy, copper and lithium are central to the booming electronics industry, and copper is also a key resource for construction and transportation. The price of gold has skyrocketed in the context of a global economic crisis that has encouraged investment in precious metals. The budgets of these three Andean countries are heavily dependent on the exploitation of natural resources because of the long tradition in Latin America of dependence on the export of raw materials and agrarian products, the poverty of the majority of the population, and the relative absence of assertive and progressive taxation systems.[8] However, when the price of oil plunged in 2014, the revenues and redistributive capacity of Venezuela and Ecuador suffered greatly. Faced with that situation, these countries turned aggressively toward mining as an alternative source of income.

Social participation and the inclusion of the proposals of social movements were purportedly an important part of the agenda of postneoliberal governments because they originated in antineoliberal feelings and movements, and because their participants self-identified as part of the political left (Escobar 2010). The latest constitutions of Venezuela (1999), Bolivia (2009), and Ecuador (2008) include articles on indigenous rights and autonomy, emphasize decolonization (particularly in Bolivia), and, in the case of Bolivia and Ecuador, highlight the

Andean concept of "good living" (*sumak kawsay* in Kichwa or *suma qamaña* in Aymara), which is to be applied to government development plans (Centellas 2013; Martínez Novo 2013). The Ecuadorian Constitution of 2008 was the first in the world to recognize the rights of nature.

Despite good intentions, these governments clashed with indigenous social movements in frontier areas because of government dependence on the extraction of nonrenewable natural resources (Postero 2010b; Martínez Novo 2013). As is well known, extractive activities pollute water sources and the environment, divert huge amounts of water from peasant agriculture, and bring disruptions and displacement to local people. In addition, the centralizing tendencies of these governments led them to perceive the autonomy of social movements as a threat.

Neoliberalism, Extraction-Oriented Postneoliberalism, and Challenges to the Indigenous Social Movement in Ecuador

The indigenous movement in Ecuador has been considered the strongest in Latin America during the 1990s (Yashar 2005). Unlike many other indigenous movements in Latin America, the Ecuadorian movement developed in the fight for land and cultural rights for indigenous peoples was able to achieve a national-level organization that joined together in collaboration communities, associations of communities, provincial, regional, and national organizations (Zamosc 2007; Lucero 2008). It also led massive uprisings that paralyzed the country every other year during the 1990s and early 2000s and was able to halt implementation of the neoliberal agenda in Ecuador. Furthermore, Ecuador's indigenous movement contributed to the ousting of two presidents: Abdala Bucaram in 1997 and Jamil Mahuad in 2000 (Zamosc 2007).

Despite its strength, the indigenous movement in Ecuador has faced many challenges in both the neoliberal and post-neoliberal periods. The neoliberal strategies of governments and international organizations in large part debilitated the indigenous movement throughout the decade of the 1990s. For example, because of this movement's ability to contribute to ousting presidents, or to legitimate their ousting by other forces like Congress or the military, different presidents have carried out redistribution of resources in indigenous communities while trying to bypass the leadership. Another strategy has been to ally with smaller indigenous organizations with the intention of weakening and dividing this social movement (Zamosc 2007, Martínez Novo 2014). The World Bank, for its part, created its first ethnically focused development program in Ecuador to target a movement that opposed its policies of neoliberal restructuring. This program, called PRODEPINE (Program for the Development of the Indigenous and Black Peoples of Ecuador), encouraged the indigenous (and the Afro-Ecuadorian) movements to focus on short-term development goals instead of pushing a long-term political agenda, and privileged a younger leadership of development technocrats (Bretón 2005). Finally, the neoliberal policies of recognition of indigenous peoples, based on tokenism, provided a few jobs for indigenous leaders while precluding the deeper structural transformations that these communities desperately needed. This process widened the gap between the leadership and the grassroots, and produced resentment within the grassroots.

Not all challenges to the indigenous movement have been external; some have been internal, such as the ill-conceived alliance of CONAIE (Confederation of Indigenous Nationalities of Ecuador) and its political branch Pachakutik with Colonel Lucio Gutierrez in 2000 to conduct a coup d'état and remove an elected incumbent. Two years after the coup, Gutierrez was elected president in alliance with Pachakutik. After a year in power, the alliance broke up and President Gutierrez' policies sought to further weaken the indigenous movement (Zamosc 2007).

Thus, the government of Rafael Correa encountered a debilitated indigenous movement when he came to power in 2006. Although Correa first tried to ally with the indigenous movement to win the elections, Pachakutik's decision to run with its own indigenous candidate initiated the antagonism between Correa and organized indigenous people. The power of the indigenous movement to resist governments and policies, as well as the dispute that started later between Correa and indigenous organizations regarding control of natural resources and development strategies for indigenous people have deepened this mutual hostility.

The rise of Correa's radical option further debilitated the indigenous movement, which was no longer the only organization able to put a hold on neoliberal policies in the eyes of the population. Many urban *mestizos* (non-Indians) who up to then had supported the indigenous movement because of its ability to oppose neoliberalism, and even indigenous people who did not profit from the targeted recognition of the neoliberal period, sided with Correa. Moreover, the government of Correa continued the practice of previous governments of distributing jobs, public works, and cash transfers directly to the indigenous people, bypassing and delegitimizing the historic leadership of the indigenous movement.

The government of Correa bases its legitimacy on being of the left, even a decolonial avant-garde. Yet the Correa government's heavy dependence on natural resources to finance itself and its fear of the power of the indigenous movement to oppose extraction and challenge the centralization of decision making has produced tensions and contradictions in law, policy, and government practice.

Some of these contradictions can be found in the 2008 Ecuadorian Constitution. Indigenous peoples are granted rights, but these are made difficult to obtain in other sections of the Constitution and in follow-up statutory legislation. For example, the Constitution states that Ecuador is plurinational, a concept associated with autonomy, self-government, and equality of different cultures and groups. However, the Constitution emphasizes the unity of the state, Kichwa is not accepted as an official language with equal status to Spanish, and nonrenewable resources belong to the central state. Indigenous communities should be consulted when their territories or rights are affected by the extraction of natural resources, but consultation is not binding. Another example of a contradiction is that indigenous territories are included in the constitutional text but are not part of the regular organization of the state. To create an indigenous territory, petitions and referenda should be based on the current organization of the state, which is based on the distribution of the *mestizo* (non-Indian) population, making it very difficult to achieve the creation of new indigenous territories. Furthermore, the smallest autonomous unit acknowledged in the follow-up Law of Territorial Organization is the parish,[9] which tends to be a *mestizo* enclave, not the surrounding indigenous communities.

Another source of confusion is that the state appropriates the agenda of the indigenous movement and then waters down its meaning. For example, intercultural bilingual education (based on Spanish and Native American languages and cultures) was a political project of the indigenous movement, and the education system for indigenous people has been relatively autonomous since its official approval in 1988. Although the central government still controlled the finances of the system, indigenous organizations could manage education, decide on the curriculum, and make hiring choices. The Correa government discontinued this autonomy in 2009: now the executive controls policy, curriculum, and particularly hiring. Taking into account that the bilingual education system is one of the few careers, if not the only career, open to indigenous professionals in a very discriminatory labor market, this decision gives great power to the executive over the employment opportunities for educated and professional indigenous strata. Once the executive controlled the indigenous education system, it called the whole education system (for both non-Indians and indigenous citizens) "intercultural," instead of using this name exclusively for the system that educates indigenous citizens. Meanwhile, the government has blurred the meaning of interculturalism. The new education law[10] defines interculturalism as "interactions between any cultures in the world" as opposed to a specific project of liberation for colonized indigenous peoples in Ecuador. In addition, protest by teachers is prosecuted and criminalized by education law.

The ambiguities of the Correa government's stance toward indigenous people can also be perceived in public events when the president has addressed this population. For example, Correa chose an indigenous community for his first investiture in January 2007. However, community members were not allowed in the main square of their own town, close to the newly elected president, because this space was reserved for important guests who were mostly nonindigenous. At this event, local indigenous peoples were not treated as equals and actors, only as background for the indigenism of the government and as recipients of its ideas and policies.

Some government policies have not been ambiguous, but openly aggressive toward indigenous peoples. In January 2009, the National Assembly of Ecuador approved a new mining law despite the protests of indigenous people. This law allows for the expansion of large-scale mining. Indigenous people were not formally consulted in the creation of a law that affects their territory and rights as required by the 2008 Constitution. The mining law allows companies to carry out prospecting and extraction in exchange for a fee in indigenous territories that, according to the 2008 Constitution, are indivisible and should be protected for customary use. The mining law also allows for the repression and criminalization of those who oppose mining activities.

Indigenous leaders have been insulted and stigmatized by the president and other high authorities because they have opposed laws promoting extraction in their territories or restricting their autonomy (like the new education law that abolishes educational autonomy for indigenous peoples). Correa has called indigenous leaders "golden ponchos"[11] (referring to their indigenous but elite status), troglodyte (because they allegedly oppose development and represent the past), and stone throwers and terrorists (because they resist government policies). Other high-level authorities like the secretary of culture have accused the indigenous movement of being allied with the political right and with the United States and even of being supported by the CIA (Quintero Lopez and Sylva Charvet 2010). According to a report by Amnesty International (2012), this aggressive campaign of stigmatization has caused an increase in societal prejudice against indigenous peoples and has legitimized private violence against its leaders and followers.

Amnesty International (2012) has also demonstrated how the legal system has been used against indigenous and other social leaders. Public prosecutors have accused leaders of protests against mining and for indigenous control of natural resources of crimes such as terrorism, sabotage, and obstruction of public roads. These processes have been time-consuming and expensive for indigenous leaders and have had the effect of spreading fear and discouraging participants in the movement from protesting. In July 2013, Shuar leader José Acacho was found guilty of terrorism for leading the protest of Amazonian indigenous people against the mining, water, and education laws of the Correa government. More recently, communities have been displaced from mining areas that have been militarized through the use of the state of exception.

The Correa government weakened indigenous organizations through co-optation, division, and repression. The government created confusion by adopting the vocabulary of social movements while creating difficulties for the implementation of their agenda. We ask the following questions: How should indigenous social movements react to these strategies of cooptation, confusion, and repression by governments that depict themselves as progressive, pro-social movement, and indigenous friendly but that are ultimately authoritarian, and that rely heavily on the extraction of natural resources that displaces indigenous people and hinder their livelihoods? How can the social movements in the Andes protect themselves from division, stigmatization, ambivalence, and confusion in such a situation?

Survival and Resistance Strategies in Indigenous Communities in the Ecuadorian Andes

Indigenous communities of the Andes have demonstrated resistance to capitalist exploitation for centuries. (Luis Alberto Tuaza Castro has contributed this part of the discussion that focuses on indigenous communities' current strategies of survival and resistance.)

Mining

In the past, the indigenous communities of the mountains of Ecuador confronted the hacienda system, a system of large landholdings that for more than four hundred years subjected indigenous Andeans to virtual slavery. Indigenous peoples of the Andes struggled for freedom and organization. Later, they fought for the recognition of their ethnic diversity, for intercultural bilingual education in Spanish and the Kichwa native language, for their visibility in the social and political arena, and against the implementation of neoliberal policies. Today, they are focusing their struggles on mining, water, and the defense of their land. The Ecuadorian Constitution of 2008, as mentioned above, recognized the rights of nature, but one of the priorities of the Ecuadoran government has been open pit mining, and the concession of this activity to transnational mining companies, the majority of which come from Canada and China. For this reason, there are permanent confrontations between the government and indigenous organizations, particularly in the Amazon and in the Azuay province of Ecuador.

In the province of Azuay, gold, copper, and silver deposits have been found in Camilo Ponce Enríquez, Santa Isabel, and Girón Counties, and in the following parishes of Cuenca County: Tarqui, Victoria del Portete, Chaucha, and Molleturo. In Victoria del Portete, the Ecuadorian government has granted the rights of exploitation of the Qimsacocha site to the Canadian company Iamgold. The communities of Tarqui and Victoria del Portete have unanimously rejected this concession and have strengthened their irrigation organizations (*juntas de riego*) to resist this governmental decision. Irrigation organizations have asked the government that this transnational company leave the region immediately. According to the irrigation organizations, mining will drain their water sources, pollute the environment, and endanger their standard of living. The members of the irrigation organizations of these parishes have joined demonstrations and have generated a series of debates within the province of Azuay as well as throughout

Ecuador. Other social organizations that are also confronting the government because of mining in the provinces of Imbabura and Zamora Chinchipe have shown their solidarity with this struggle.

In October 2011, the communities of Victoria del Portete celebrated a prior consultation required by the 2008 Ecuadorian Constitution and the International Labor Organization Convention 169 signed by Ecuador in 1998 regarding this mining concession. Ninety-two percent of the population of these parishes rejected future mining activity in Quimsacocha. However, the government argued that the consultation is not binding because the Ecuadorian state is the only owner of those mines. So far, mining extraction in this region has stalled.

Expansion of the Agrarian Frontier

It was assumed in Ecuador that the two agrarian reforms, carried out in 1964 and 1973, would solve the problem of land tenure. Indigenous peoples were expected to overcome poverty and to achieve sufficient income once granted land, but, it turns out, they are not enjoying better days. The productive lands of the valleys are still concentrated in a few hands. Meanwhile, indigenous people only received low-quality land located in mountain slopes at high altitudes. For this reason, indigenous peoples have had to expand the cultivation of land to 4,000 to 4,200 meters above sea level. At this altitude, there are ecosystems dominated by straw fields that provide water throughout the year (the so-called Andean *páramo*). To stop the expansion of the agrarian frontier over needed water sources, the government is giving a bonus of US$30 per hectare of Andean *páramo* preserved. Communities have not accepted this offer because, according to the leaders of organizations like ECUARUNARI,[12] this is a government strategy to control the indigenous population and to achieve popular support. However, the communities are aware of the need to preserve the *páramo*. In the meetings in indigenous communities there are discussions about the importance of nature and what it means for indigenous people. Indigenous peoples are cultivating native species of plants and have reintroduced llamas and alpacas. The communities in the slopes of the Chimborazo volcano are promoting community tourism to control the expansion of the agrarian frontier. Communities are also prioritizing community management of water. In Guamote County there is a corporation called Jatun Pampa, made up of 35 communities, that manages the drinking water service without municipal or state control by the National Secretary of Water. Initiatives to promote organic agriculture are growing. There are communities that grow and produce potatoes and other organic products without the help of chemical fertilizers or pesticides.

Poverty

Poverty is still pervasive in indigenous communities. The organization of community banks and community savings and credit unions, as well as the continuation of ancestral practices of cooperation such as the *minga* (collective work on public infrastructure) help alleviate poverty. Several savings and credit unions have been created throughout Ecuador. An example is the indigenous savings and credit union Mushuk Runa ("New Man" in the native Kichwa language). This financial institution serving the whole country provides credit to small producers up to US$5,000 with little paperwork or bureaucratic hassle.

Communities are also requesting and building irrigation canals. The irrigation project of the Ozogoche River is the number one priority in Guamote County. This irrigation project will increase agrarian production and will radically transform the living standards in more than 73 communities of the Palmira and La Matriz parishes, which are located in low quality, dry lands.

Indigenous Organization

During recent years, the indigenous movement of Ecuador has suffered a decline. There are several explanations for this, including the failure of the alliance of the indigenous movement with the government of ex-President Lucio Gutierrez, the separation between national and provincial leaders and the grassroots of the indigenous movement, and the multiplication of organizations caused by the intervention of nongovernmental organizations. An additional explanation is the application of participatory budgets by municipal governments.

Politically, the indigenous movement has been organized in an authoritarian fashion, and the same leaders have been in the same position for many years. In a research project that I carried out with Víctor Bretón in Colta and Guamote counties on the dissolution of Haciendas Llinllín and Totorillas, we discovered that although these haciendas disappeared from the land 35 years ago during the period of agrarian reform, their legacy is still alive in everyday issues. The children and grandchildren of the old *kipus* (indigenous overseers) still control political, economic, and religious power in the communities that were once part of these two haciendas. The *kipus* were indigenous people with qualities of leadership that controlled the indigenous population, defended the interests of hacienda masters and *mestizo* overseers, and maintained relationships with the *mestizos* (non-Indians) of the county and parish centers who oppressed indigenous peoples. Once the old haciendas were dissolved, these *kipus* became the leaders of indigenous communities. Later, when development agents arrived in these communities, these ex-*kipus* became brokers in the world of international development and cooperation. When groups of communities formed second-level indigenous organizations, and, later, when regional indigenous organizations like ECUARUNARI were created, these ex-*kipus* became the national leaders. The children and grandchildren of *kipus* also became the evangelical pastors who control power in the community and participate in its management.

What is being done to transform this situation? Communities in the area of Baldalupaxi in Columbe Parish are reinforcing the *cabildo* (parish government) that had been displaced and had lost its authority due to the growth and multiplication of organizations. In the same area, indigenous inhabitants are trying to consolidate in one community the five communities that had been created to capture funds from the participatory budget of the Municipal Government of Colta. The members of the communities of Llinllín and Chismaute Telán are still united despite requests by some leaders who would like to divide them into three communities.

Yet the Indigenous Movement of Chimborazo is regaining the strength it enjoyed during its foundational years and during the 1990s. In this organization's Third Congress, which took place August 24–25, 2012, Delia Caguana, a recognized and respected indigenous leader, was elected president. Delia's election broke up the patrimonial control of COMICH (the Confederation of the Indigenous Movement of Ecuador) by one person and his family. "We would like new people to direct our organization" and "We are tired of being ruled by only one person" were the slogans that some members repeated during the congress. The communities and the older leaders trust Delia's leadership. Six hundred people were present at the ceremony in which Delia assumed the staff of office and started in her position as president of COMICH. By the end of September 117 communities and 25 second-tier federations of communities had affiliated with the indigenous movement of Chimborazo.

Racism and Discrimination

Racism and discrimination continue to be realities that deeply affect indigenous people. According to Article 1 of the 2008 Constitution, Ecuador is a plurinational, intercultural, and multiethnic society. According to Article 11 of the Constitution, discrimination for ethnic reasons is forbidden. This is not implemented in practice; racism is flourishing in Ecuador.

Racism and discrimination are also present within the Catholic Church. After the Second Vatican Council, with the development of liberation theology, the Catholic Church in Latin America favored the poor and worked for the liberation of indigenous peoples. I am a witness to the pastoral compromise of Monsignor Leonidas Proaño, called the Bishop of the Indians. Proaño worked for social transformation and for the dignity of indigenous people. However, when the Catholic Church turned towards the political right through the influence of Opus Dei, there was no space in the church for indigenous people. The Catholic Church still wanted to have indigenous priests as well as an indigenous pastoral presence but wanted them to conform to the interests of Rome and of those who had power within the Catholic Church. I was an indigenous priest at the time, and witnessed with grief the impossibility of creating the kind of Indian church that Bishop Proaño had dreamed of. But what did people in Chimborazo do? A group of 25 catechists, and two indigenous priests, and the older priests who were friends of Monsignor Proaño created the Indigenous Pastoral Monsignor Leonidas Proaño for the purpose of creating a church that could walk with two feet: living church and popular organization. This pastoral organization now serves more than forty communities in Colta, Guamote, and Riobamba counties. It has also created missions for indigenous migrants in Riobamba, Quito, and Yaruquí. It is led by a group of lay members and seeks to be a bridge to unite indigenous Catholics and evangelicals.

Migration

In the last few years, several indigenous families have had to leave their homes and their communities. Academic studies perceive this situation as a threat to the preservation of their culture. However, the indigenous community has also organized in the spaces of migration. It is not unusual to find indigenous communities from Chimborazo in Quito, Santo Domingo, Machala, Ambato, Riobamba, Guayaquil, the Santa Elena peninsula, Medellin, Caracas, and New York. We could say that some urban spaces have become "indigenized." The pillars that make possible the creation and reinforcement of indigenous communities in large cities are the preservation of culture, the rescue of historical memory, the collective celebration of faith, and the creation of solidarity networks.

Finally, organization continues to be a permanent challenge for indigenous people, but I believe it is important to continue to work on it, since there is no other strategy apart from organization that can be a tool to negotiate with the government, the state, and development institutions. The Constitution of Ecuador recognizes collective rights, and indigenous peoples are visible in social and political domains because of organization and collective action. Mama Transito Amaguaña, a historic indigenous leader used to say: "without organization we are like the quinoa grain. When the wind arrives, it can push the grain far away. However, if we are organized we are like quinoa grains within a sack. The wind may arrive, but it will not be able to destroy us." Similarly, Tayta Manuel Agualsaca, a leader of the struggle for the land in Columbe, used to say: "when there is no justice, when there is no freedom, when there is no life, when we are sad, then, is when we need organization the most."

Conclusion

All of the mountain regions and natural reserves discussed in this chapter, the Himalayas and the state of Odisha in India, Appalachia, and the Andes, are rich in natural resources. Channa described the use of hydraulic energy and the introduction of cash crops such as apple farming in the Himalayas. Pandey focused on bauxite mining in the beautiful and sacred natural landscape of tribal Odisha. Bell discussed the importance of coal for the economy of Appalachia. Oil, copper, lithium, gold, and silver are some of the strategic resources extracted from the

Andes. These resources have been used by the nations that contain these regions and by private transnational companies in the context of internal colonialism. Whereas nations and companies have profited, local populations have suffered the negative environmental effects of extractive and development activities. This has been possible because the populations of these three mountain regions have been dominated on the basis of ethnicity and class. For nations and corporations to justify the domination of indigenous and mountain populations, those communities have been described as primitive, and as being opposed to progress and modernity. Thus, the wealth of these regions has been siphoned off for the benefit of national and international elites through processes of economic domination and discursive stigmatization. The concept of internal colonialism cannot technically be applied to Appalachia because the Appalachian population is not in its entirety an indigenous colonized group (although it has indigenous and Afro-descendant residents), but the majority of the group has its origins in settler colonialism. However, this population has also been ethnicized and stigmatized in ways that in some respects parallel the experiences of the indigenous peoples of India or the Andes.

In the Himalayas and Odisha, the implementation of neoliberal policies by the Indian government has meant a focus on mining, cash crops, and the production of energy that has negatively affected the traditional livelihood of the local population. In Appalachia, economic processes associated with the extraction of coal have increased the aggressiveness of extraction techniques while lowering the number of jobs and benefits offered by this industry to Appalachian communities. In the case of the Andes, both neoliberalism and governments that call themselves postneoliberal have continued to increase pressure on the environment, exploiting natural resources on which their national budgets depend, regardless of their political bent. Perhaps so-called postneoliberal governments have been even more aggressive because of their need for resources for state formation and redistribution. Despite their decolonizing discourses, postneoliberal governments have kept an internal colonialism approach, sacrificing local mountain populations to the needs of the nation. The kinds of environmental degradation suffered by the Himalayas, Odisha, Appalachia, and the Andes have been considerable: landslides, deforestation, and pollution of water, air, and vegetation in the Himalayas and Odisha; landslides, floods, pollution, and structural damage to the landscape in Appalachia; and the draining and contamination of water, pollution, and displacement of populations in the Andes. The authors described how environmental degradation has severely affected the health and economic survival of indigenous and mountain peoples.

To confront this situation, local populations in all four cases have emphasized their attachment to the natural environment. They have also reinforced their local identities to increase the cohesiveness and organization of their group.

In the case of the Himalayas and Odisha, religion has provided a language and organizational structure to protect the natural environment and traditional lifestyles. Religion is also central to the organization of social movements in the Andes. In the case of Appalachia, Shannon Elizabeth Bell highlights the important role played by working-class women who have adopted protector roles that extend from their families to the community and the natural landscape. Economic development and mining have severely affected the human rights of women in Odisha as described by Annapurna Devi Pandey. Similar to what Bell discusses in Appalachia, Kondh women have formed organizations in Odisha to defend their rights and those of their children and to fight aggressive forms of economic development such as mining.

In the case of the Himalayas, Odisha, and Appalachia, this chapter discussed the creation of environmental movements. In the case of the Andes, both Carmen Martínez Novo and Luis Alberto Tuaza Castro described a longer trajectory in which powerful social movements have had to confront serious challenges posed by neoliberal and postneoliberal institutions. The suffering triggered by the imposition of neoliberalism in Latin America promoted the early formation of social movements. However, neoliberal funding by the World Bank and nongovernmental organizations contributed to cooptation and division within these organizations. The greater control over state and society sought by postneoliberal governments poses an even more important and complex challenge to these movements. Tuaza Castro also posed that whereas social movements can be important tools for liberation, they also need to be evaluated in terms of their internal democracy for their constituencies to feel included and served. Despite this pessimistic evaluation, Tuaza Castro narrates the reconstitution of social movements through a return to the community, a renewal of the membership, and alternative forms of organization around water or religion.

Mountain populations have proposed alternatives for development to those imposed by nations and transnational companies. These strategies seek to enhance instead of destroying the livelihoods of native groups as well as the natural environment. In the case of the Himalayas, Channa highlights the construction of nature as sacred and the activism of local religious specialists. In the case of Appalachia, Bell explained the reinforcement of community to challenge the use of the environment as disposable. In the case of the Andes, Tuaza Castro discussed community alternatives for development like raising native species, organic agriculture, credit cooperatives, local control of water, and community led tourism. Interestingly, tourism appears as an environmentally and community friendly alternative in the Andes and Appalachia (Kingsolver 2011), but less so in the Himalayas, unless linked to religious pilgrimage. As discussed by Subhadra Mitra Channa, local populations in the Himalayas oppose tourism that would damage the environment. If controlled by communities, or used for their benefit, tourism may be advantageous. If controlled by outsiders it could be another aggressive strategy for development that does not take into account the welfare of locals. There are some interesting contrasts among our contributions regarding the role of migration: while Bell argued that migration is seen as deleterious to local culture for an Appalachian population deeply attached to their region, Tuaza Castro argued that migration is an important strategy for survival in the Andes that does not necessarily dissolve communities, since they are reconstituted in new locations.

The Global Mountain Regions Conference allowed the authors to realize that indigenous and mountain populations throughout the world are similarly marginalized and suffer parallel processes of extraction and development that are threatening their natural environment and their livelihoods. They are using different concepts and tools to organize against environmental destruction—drawing on religion, motherhood, gender, community, and local identity—sometimes in powerful and successful collective actions. The movements are also vulnerable to outside attempts to coopt and divide them, and they learn from their mistakes. An ongoing dialogue on how to respond to these challenges and how to strengthen oppositional strategies and local organizations would be very beneficial to these groups.

CARMEN MARTÍNEZ NOVO is Associate Professor of Anthropology at the University of Kentucky. She is the author of *Who Defines Indigenous?* and editor of *Repensando los movimientos indígenas*. Her work focuses on indigenous rights and identities in Mexico and Ecuador.

SHANNON ELIZABETH BELL is Associate Professor of Sociology at Virginia Polytechnic Institute and State University. Her books include *Fighting King Coal: The Challenges to Micromobilization in Central Appalachia* and *Our Roots Run Deep as Ironweed: Appalachian Women and the Fight for Environmental Justice*.

SUBHADRA MITRA CHANNA is Professor Emerita, Department of Anthropology, Delhi University. She has published four books, received a number of international scholarly awards, and has lectured in many countries. Much of her work has focused on gender and ecology in the Himalayas.

ANNAPURNA DEVI PANDEY teaches cultural anthropology at the University of California, Santa Cruz. Her research foci include women's activism, leadership, and empowerment in rural and tribal India, and women's identity making in the Odia Diaspora in California. She has served as a Senior Fulbright Scholar in India, as president of the Orissa Society of the Americas, and as a collaborator on several film projects in addition to her own publications.

LUIS ALBERTO TUAZA CASTRO is Professor and researcher at the National University of Chimborazo and adjunct Professor at FLACSO, Ecuador. He is an indigenous Kichwa scholar. His books include *Etnicidad, política y religiosidad en los Andes centrales del Ecuador* and *Crisis del movimiento indígena ecuatoriano.*

Notes

1. They are also known as *Adivasis* (indigenous people or Scheduled Tribes) (Shah 2010).

2. Keeping in view the independent lifestyle, culture, and lack of acculturation of some of the tribal groups, they have been treated as a separate group and were termed Primitive Tribal Group in the Fifth Plan (1974–1978) period. To avoid the word *primitive* they have been redesignated as Particularly Vulnerable Tribal Groups (PVTGs). Odisha houses 13 Primitive Tribal Groups out of total 75 Primitive Tribal Groups in India, the highest in number. For reference, see http://Odisha.gov.in/e-magazine/Odishareview/2010/December/engpdf/203–206.pdf.

3. The following areas are under Schedule V in Odisha: Mayurbhanj, Sundargarh, Koraput, Rayagada, Nabarangpur, and Malkangiri districts in whole, Kuchinda tahasil of Sambalpur district, Keonjhar, Telkoi, Champua, Barbil tahasils of Keonjhar district, Khondamal, Balliguda and G.Udayagiri tahasil of Khondamal district, R.Udyagiri tahasil, Gumma and Rayagada block of Parlekhemundi tahasil in Parlakhemundi sub-division and Suruda tahasil of Ghumsur sub-division in Ganjam District, Thuamul Rampur and Lanjigarh blocks of Kalahandi District and Nilagiri block of Balasore District. The total area of the scheduled areas contains almost 70 percent of the forest areas of Odisha even though they form only 44 percent of the state area (Kumar and Choudhary 2005, 13).

4. Government of Odisha Annual Plan 2011–2012.

5. The district has a high percentage of tribal population, which is 44.5 percent of the total population. The literacy rate among the tribal people of the district is 40.3 percent, out of which Standard Tribe (ST) male literacy is 38.01 percent and ST female literacy rate is 25.97 percent (Shahoo 2011). For further reading related to this section of the chapter, see Bhushan, Hazra and Banarjee (2008), Mohanty (2013), Nayak (2010), Pandey (2002), Prucha (1988), and Singh (2011).

6. The mainstream environmental movement is characterized by conservation and preservation efforts, while environmental justice movements seek social justice for people who live, work, play, and learn in polluted environments (Cole and Foster 2001).

7. "Stronger states" here refers to states that have greater control over their societies, more participation in the national economy, and increased international projection. In the case of Ecuador there is also a significant effort at strengthening infrastructure, production, and the educational system. This may not be the case in Venezuela, which started as a more developed country, but whose infrastructure, educational system, and productive capacities seem to be deteriorating (López Maya 2013).

8. Part of the state formation efforts in Ecuador are directed towards fighting tax evasion, making income taxation more efficient, and increasing indirect taxes, particularly of luxury products. However, the budget remains dependent on natural resource extraction.

9. COOTAD, Código de Organización Territorial, de Autonomía y Descentralización, Law of Territorial Organization, Autonomy and Decentralization. This law was officially approved in 2010.

10. LOEI, Ley orgánica de educación intercultural, Organic Law of Intercultural Education, approved in 2011.

11. Outer garment designed to keep the body warm typical of the Andes.

12. ECUARUNARI is a regional indigenous organization of the Ecuadorian highlands that is part of CONAIE (Confederation of Indigenous Nationalities of Ecuador), the largest indigenous organization in the country.

References for the Section on the Himalayas

Channa, Subhadra Mitra. 2010a. "Wilderness of the Civilization: Knowledge and Perception of the Jad Pastoral Community." In *Nature, Culture and Religion at the Crossroads of Asia*, edited by Marie Lecomte-Tilouine, 222–243. New Delhi: Social Science.

———. 2010b. "A Ritual Transfer: From the High to the Low in Hindu-Tibetan Himalayan Communities." In *Transfer and Spaces,* edited by Gita Dharampal-Frick, Robert Langer (section 1), and Nils Holger Peterson (section 11), 43–64. Wiesbaden, Germany: Harrassowitz.

Galey, Jean Claude. 1994. "Hindu Kingship in Its Ritual Realm: The Garhwali Configuration." In *Himalaya Past and Present,* edited by Maheshwar P. Joshi, Allen C. Forger, and Charles W. Brown, 173–237. Almora, Uttarakhand, India: Shree Almora Book Depot.

Geertz, Clifford. 1973. *The Interpretation of Cultures.* New York: Basic.

Guha, Ramachandra. 1989. *The Unquiet Woods: Ecological Change and Peasant Resistance in the Himalayas.* Delhi: Oxford University Press.

Guha, Sumit. 1999. *Environment and Ethnicity in India, 1200–1991.* Cambridge: Cambridge University Press.

Mazumdar, Lipika. 1998. *Sacred Confluence, Worship, History and Politics of Change in a Himalayan Village.* PhD diss., University of Pittsburgh.

Sax, William. 2002. *Dancing the Self: Personhood and Performance in the Pandava Lila of Garhwal.* Oxford: Oxford University Press.

Unnithan-Kumar, Maya. 1997. *Identity, Gender and Poverty: New Perspectives on Caste and Tribe in Rajasthan.* Oxford, UK: Berghahn.

References for the Section on Odisha, India

Bailey, F. G. 1957. *Caste and the Economic Frontier: A Village in Highland Odisha.* Manchester: Manchester University Press.

———. 1960. *Tribe, Caste, and Nation: A Study of Political Activity and Political Change in Highland Odisha.* Manchester: Manchester University Press.

———. 1969. *Stratagems and Spoils: A Social Anthropology of Politics.* Oxford: Basil Blackwell.

Berry, Kim. 2003. "Developing Women: The Traffic in Ideas about Women and Their Needs in Kangra, India." In *Regional Modernities: The Cultural Politics of Development in India,* edited by K. Sivaramakrishnan and Arun Agrawal, 75–98. Stanford, CA: Stanford University Press.

Bhushan, Chandra, with Monali Zeya Hazra and Souparno Banarjee. 2008. *Rich Lands Poor People: Is "Sustainable" Mining Possible?* Delhi: Centre for Science and Environment.Elwin, Verrier. 1936. *Leaves from the Jungle.* London: John Murray.

Government of Odisha. *Budget Plan Link 2011–2012,* http://finance.odisha.gov.in/Budgets/2011-12/Budget_Plan_Link_2011_12.pdf.

Kumar, Kundan, and Pranab Ranjan Choudhary. 2005. *A Socio-Economic and Legal Study of Scheduled Tribes' Land in Odisha.* Bhubaneswar, India: World Bank.

Mishra, Mamata. 2001. "Ghumusar Mahila Sangathan: Tribal Women United against Oppression and for Social Justice." *Connect*, August 20.

Mohanty, Meera. 2013. "Mining Leads to Poverty: Jairam Ramesh to Tribals." *Economic Times*, January 14.

Nayak, Abhaya Narayan. 2010. "Primitive Tribal Groups of Odisha: An Evaluation of Census Data." *Odisha Review*, Census Special, December, 202–205.

Padel, Felix. 2010. *Sacrificing People: Invasions of a Tribal Landscape*. Delhi: Orient BlackSwan.

Padel, Felix, and Samarendra Das. 2010. *Out of This Earth: East India Adivasis and the Aluminium Cartel*. Delhi: Orient BlackSwan.

Padhi, Sakti, and Nilakantha Panigrahi. 2011. *Tribal Movements and Livelihoods: Recent Developments in Odisha*. CPRC-IIPA (working paper no. 51). New Delhi: Indian Institute of Public Administration.

Pandey, Triloki Nath. 2002. "Some Thoughts on Marginalization and Marginalized Communities." *Journal of Anthropological Survey of India*, no. 51, 1–7.

Prucha, Francis Paul. 1988. *The Indians in American Society*. Cambridge, MA: Quantum.

Sahoo, Laxman Kumar. 2011. "Socio-Economic Profile of Tribal Populations in Mayurbhanj and Keonjhar Districts," *Odisha Review*, May, 63–68, http://Odisha.gov.in/e-magazine/Odishareview/2011/may/engpdf/63–68.pdf.

Shah, Alpa. 2007. "The Dark Side of Indigeneity? Indigenous People, Rights, and Development in India." *History Compass* 5(6):1806–1832.

———. 2013. *In the Shadows of the State: Indigenous Politics, Environmentalism, and Insurgency in Jharkhand, India*. Durham: Duke University Press.

Singh, Satbir. 2011. "'Why We Fight': Policy & Planning in India's Tribal Areas and the Search for 'Inclusive Growth.'" MSc diss., University of London.

Sivaramakrishnan, K., and Arun Agrawal, eds. 2003. *Regional Modernities: The Cultural Politics of Development in India*. Stanford, CA: Stanford University Press.

Vedanta Resources, PLC. 2012. *Annual Report and Accounts*, http://ar2012.vedantaresources.com/files/2012_AR.pdf.

References for the Section on Appalachia

Ahern, Melissa M., and Michael Hendryx. 2008. "Health Disparities and Environmental Competence: A Case Study of Appalachian Coal Mining." *Environmental Justice* 1 (2): 81–86.

Bell, Shannon Elizabeth. 2010. "Fighting King Coal: The Barriers to Grassroots Environmental Justice Movement Participation in Central Appalachia." PhD diss., University of Oregon.

———. *Our Roots Run Deep as Ironweed: Appalachian Women and the Fight for Environmental Justice*. Champaign: University of Illinois Press.

Bell, Shannon Elizabeth, and Richard York. 2010. "Community Economic Identity: The Coal Industry and Ideology Construction in West Virginia." *Rural Sociology* 75 (1): 111–43.

Bell, Shannon Elizabeth, and Yvonne A. Braun. 2010. "Coal, Identity, and the Gendering of Environmental Justice Activism in Central Appalachia." *Gender & Society* 24 (6): 794–813.

Brown, P., and F. I. T. Ferguson. 1995. "'Making a Big Stink': Women's Work, Women's Relationships, and Toxic Waste Activism." *Gender & Society* 9 (2): 145–172.

Cable, Sherry. 1992. "Women's Social Movement Involvement: The Role of Structural Availability in Recruitment and Participation Processes." *Sociological Quarterly* 33 (1): 35–50.

Cole, Luke W., and Sheila R. Foster. 2001. *From the Ground Up: Environmental Racism and the Rise of the Environmental Justice Movement.* New York: New York University Press.

Culley, M. R., and H. L. Angelique. 2003. "Women's Gendered Experiences as Long-Term Three Mile Island Activists." *Gender & Society* 17 (3): 445–461.

Epstein, B. 1995. "Grassroots Environmentalism and Strategies for Change." *New Political Science,* no. 32, 1–24.

Erikson, Kai T. 1976. *Everything in Its Path: Destruction of Community in the Buffalo Creek Flood.* New York: Simon and Schuster.

Fisher, Steve. 2010. "Claiming Appalachia—and the Questions That Go with It." Appalachian Identity: A Roundtable Discussion. *Appalachian Journal* 38 (1): 58–61.

Flood Advisory Technical Taskforce. 2002. "Runoff Analyses of Seng, Scrabble, and Sycamore Creeks, Part I." Division of Mining and Reclamation, Department of Environmental Protection. Accessed October 8, 2007, http://www.wvdep.org/Docs/1593_Part%20I.pdf.

Geredien, Ross. 2009. "Assessing the Extent of Mountaintop Removal in Appalachia: An Analysis Using Vector Data." Technical Report for Appalachian Voices. Boone, NC. Accessed May 20, 2010. http://ilovemountains.org/reclamation-fail/mining-extent2009/Assessing_the_Extent_of_Mountaintop_Removal_in_Appalachia.pdf.

Hendryx, Michael. 2008. "Mortality Rates in Appalachian Coal Mining Counties: 24 Years Behind the Nation." *Environmental Justice* 1 (1): 5–11.

Hendryx, Michael, and Melissa M. Ahern. 2008. "Relations between Health Indicators and Residential Proximity to Coalmining in West Virginia." *American Journal of Public Health,* no. 98, 669–671.

Hendryx, Michael, Melissa M. Ahern, and Timothy R. Nurkiewicz. 2007. "Hospitalization Patterns Associated with Appalachian Coal Mining." *Journal of Toxicology and Environmental Health,* no. 70, 2064–2070.

Kaplan, Temma. 1997. *Crazy for Democracy: Women in Grassroots Movements.* New York: Routledge.

Kingsolver, Ann. 2011. *Tobacco Town Futures: Global Encounters in Rural Kentucky.* Long Grove, IL: Waveland.

Krauss, Celene. 1993. "Women and Toxic Waste Protest: Race, Class, and Gender as Resources of Resistance." *Qualitative Sociology* 16 (3): 247–62.

Naples, Nancy A. 1992. "Activist Mothering: Cross-Generational Continuity in the Community Work of Women from Low-Income Urban Neighborhoods." *Gender & Society,* no. 6, 441–463.

Orem, W. H. 2006. "Coal Slurry: Geochemistry and Impacts on Human Health and Environmental Quality," US Geological Survey, Eastern Energy Resources Team. Presentation to the Coal Slurry Legislative Subcommittee, West Virginia Senate Judiciary Committee, November 15.

Palmer, M. A., et al. 2010. "Mountaintop Mining Consequences." *Science* 327 (5962): 148–149.

Peeples, J. A., and K. M. DeLuca. 2006. "The Truth of the Matter: Motherhood, Community, and Environmental Justice." *Women's Studies in Communication* 29 (1): 59–87.

Scott, Rebecca R. 2010. *Removing Mountains: Extracting Nature and Identity in the Appalachian Coalfields.* Minneapolis: University of Minnesota Press.

Scott, Shauna. 2012. "What Difference Did It Make? The Appalachian Land Ownership Study after Twenty-Five Years." In *Confronting Ecological Crises in Appalachia and the South: University and Community Partnerships,* edited by Stephanie McSpirit, Lynn Faltraco, and Conner Bailey, 39–48. Lexington: University Press of Kentucky.

Scott, Shauna L., Stephanie McSpirit, Sharon Hardesty, and Robert Welch. 2005. "Post-Disaster Interviews with Martin County Citizens: 'Gray Clouds' of Blame and Distrust." *Journal of Appalachian Studies* 11 (1–2): 7–28.

Stewart, Bruce E. 2011. *The Moonshiners and Prohibitionists: The Battle over Alcohol in Southern Appalachia.* Lexington: University of Kentucky Press.

EPA (US Environmental Protection Agency). 2005. "Mountaintop Mining/Valley Fills in Appalachia—Final Programmatic Environmental Impact Statement." Accessed September 28, 2007, http://www.epa.gov.

References for the Section on the Andes and Latin America

Aguirre Beltrán, Gonzalo. 1991 [1967]. *Obra antropológica IX: Regiones de refugio.* Mexico City: Fondo de Cultura Económica.

Amnesty International. 2012."*Para que nadie reclame nada" ¿Criminalización del derecho a la protesta en Ecuador?* London: Amnesty International.

Bretón, Víctor. 2005. *Capital social y etnodesarrollo en los Andes.* Quito: CAAP.

Cameron, Maxwell, and Eric Hershberg. 2010. *Latin America's Left Turns: Politics, Policies, and Trajectories of Change.* Boulder, CO: Lynne Rienner.

Centellas, Miguel. 2013. "Bolivia's New Multicultural Constitution." In *Latin America's Multicultural Movements: The Struggle between Communitarianism, Autonomy, and Human Rights,* edited by Todd Eisenstadt, Michael Danielson, Moisés Bailón, and Carlos Sorroza. Oxford: Oxford University Press.

Coronil, Fernando, and Julie Skurski. 1991. "Dismembering and Remembering the Nation: The Semantics of Political Violence in Venezuela." *Comparative Studies in Society and History* 33 (2): 288–337.

Escobar, Arturo. 2010. "Latin America at a Crossroads: Alternative Modernizations, Post-Liberalism, or Post-Development." *Cultural Studies* 24 (1): 1–65.

French, John. 2009. "Understanding the Politics of Latin America's Plural Lefts (Chavez/Lula): Social Democracy, Populism, and Convergence on the Path to a Post-Neoliberal World." *Third World Quarterly* 30 (2): 349–370.

González Casanova, Pablo. 1969. "El colonialismo interno." In *Sociología de la explotación.* México City: Siglo XXI. Source: Red de bibliotecas virtuales CLACSO.

———. 2006. "Colonialismo interno: Una redefinición." In *La teoría marxista hoy: Problemas y perspectivas,* edited by Sabina González, Javier Amadeo, and Atilio Borón. Buenos Aires: CLACSO. Source: Red de bibliotecas virtuales de Ciencias Sociales en América Latina CLACSO.

Harvey, David. 2005. *A Brief History of Neoliberalism.* Oxford: Oxford University Press.

Hylton, Forrest, Sinclair Thomson, and Adolfo Gilly. 2007. *Revolutionary Horizons: Past and Present in Bolivian Politics.* New York: Verso.

López Maya, Margarita. 2003. "The Venezuelan Caracazo of 1989: Popular Protest and Institutional Weakness." *Journal of Latin American Studies* 35 (1): 117–137.

———. 2009. "El socialismo rentista de Venezuela ante la caída de los precios petroleros internacionales." *Cuadernos del CENDES* 26 (71): 67–87.

———. 2013. "Understanding the Legacy of Chavism." Invited talk, University of Kentucky, March 22.

Lucero, Jose Antonio. 2008. *Struggles of Voice: The Politics of Indigenous Representation in the Andes.* Pittsburgh: University of Pittsburgh Press.

Martínez Novo, Carmen. 2013. "The Backlash against Indigenous Rights in Ecuador's Citizen's Revolution." In *Latin America's Multicultural Movements: The Struggle Between Communitarianism, Autonomy, and Human Rights,* edited by Todd Eisenstadt, Michael Danielson, Moisés Bailón, and Carlos Sorroza. Oxford: Oxford University Press.

———. 2014. "Managing Diversity in Postneoliberal Ecuador." *Journal of Latin American and Caribbean Anthropology* 19 (1): 103–125.

———. 2016. "Authoritarian Ways to Overcome Neoliberalism." *Progress in Human Geography* 41(5), Special Issue, Learning from Post-Neoliberalisms, http://journals.sagepub.com/doi/abs/10.1177/0309132516648539.

Oxhorn, Philip. 2009. "Beyond Neoliberalism? Latin America's New Crossroads." In *Beyond Neoliberalism in Latin America? Societies and Politics at the Crossroads,* edited by John Burdick, Philip Oxhorn, and Kenneth Roberts. New York: Palgrave Macmillan.

Postero, Nancy. 2010a. "Morales's MAS Government: Building Indigenous Popular Hegemony in Bolivia." *Latin American Perspectives* 172 (37): 18–34.

———. 2010b. "After the Revolution: Shifting Notions of Indigeneity in Evo Morales's Bolivia." Paper presented at Repositioning Indigeneity in Latin America conference, Johns Hopkins University, November 5–6.

Quintero Lopez, Rafael, and Erika Sylva Charvet. 2010. "Ecuador: La alianza de la derecha y el corporativismo en el putch del 30 de septiembre de 2010." Partido Socialista Frente Amplio del Ecuador. www.psecuador17.org.

Skidmore, Thomas, Peter Smith, and James Green. 2010. *Modern Latin America.* Oxford: Oxford University Press.

Stavenhagen, Rodolfo. 1970. "Classes, Colonialism, and Acculturation." In *Masses in Latin America,* edited by Irving L. Horowitz. New York: Oxford University Press.

Weyland, Kurt. 2009. "The Rise of Latin America's Two Lefts: Insights From Rentier State Theory." *Comparative Politics* 41 (2): 145–164.

Yashar, Deborah. 2005. *Contesting Citizenship in Latin America.* Cambridge: Cambridge University Press.

Zamosc, León. 1994. "Agrarian Protest and the Indian Movement in the Ecuadorian Highlands." *Latin American Research Review* 29 (3): 37–68.

———. 2007. "The Indian Movement and Political Democracy in Ecuador." *Latin American Politics and Society* 49 (3): 1–34.

People Like You

Si Kahn

Old fighter, you sure took it on the chin
Where'd you ever get the strength to stand
Never giving up or giving in
You know I just want to shake your hand

Because people like you
Help people like me
Go on, go on,
People like you
Help people like me
Go on, go on

Old battler, with a scar for every town
Thought you were no better than the rest
You wore your colors every way but down
All you ever gave us was your best

But you know that
People like you
Help people like me
Go on, go on
People like you
Help people like me
Go on, go on

Old dreamer, with a world in every thought
Where'd you get the vision to keep on
You sure gave back as good as what you got
I hope that when my time is almost gone

They'll say that
People like me
Helped people like you
Go on, go on
Because people like you
Help people like me
Go on, go on

CHAPTER 8

Rebuilding Mountain Communities after Natural and Human-Made Disasters

Jude L. Fernando, Lina Maria Calandra,
Stephanie McSpirit, Pam Oldfield
Meade, Jeremy Paden, and
Shaunna L. Scott

DESPITE THEIR DIVERSITY, disaster-affected mountain regions around the world share many common experiences. Top-down bureaucratic and technocratic mind-sets continue to dominate understandings of and responses to natural and human-made disasters in these marginalized communities. Consequently, global economic and political powers exploit disaster as an opportunity to dominate the spaces of disaster-affected communities. Critical local pedagogy provides many opportunities to transform the current knowledge-production practices that inform disaster responses. The contributors to this chapter show that the conceptual apparatuses, analytical methods, and representation styles in critical pedagogical practices vary as they are guided by the place-specific commitments of those working together for social and environmental justice.

This chapter brings together the contributions of a group of scholars, activists, and practitioners who share the experience of living or working in mountain regions that have endured earthquakes, tornadoes, and environmental disasters related to the coal industry. Drawing on the scholarship of Brazilian public intellectual Paulo Freire, Jude Fernando's broad outline illustrates the potential application of critical local pedagogy approaches in studies exploring natural and human-made disasters in global mountain regions. The contributors to this chapter employ a variety of styles in telling their stories as they exemplify their commitment to making learning relevant to social and environmental justice.

The contribution by Shaunna Scott and Stephanie McSpirit demonstrates a way to build capacity for survivors of human-made disasters. Scott and McSpirit worked as participants in communities in Martin County who had been affected by the human-made spill of coal slurry that contaminated drinking water and polluted a large watershed. As a part of Scott and McSpirit's endeavor, they have polled residents for over a decade about their attitudes toward science and government and their need for information. Scott and McSpirit demonstrate the critical role of citizens in Martin Country in resolving problems of the environmental pollution that is aggravated by corporate irresponsibility and government failure.

Lina Calandra focuses on the participatory experience in the context of the city of L'Aquila, hit by an earthquake in April 2009. She describes the actions that she and her colleagues took as geographers, when their own community was disrupted by a natural disaster that was exacerbated by a subsequent social disaster—a lack of shared governance in the rebuilding process, which they worked to address. She also reflects on the potential for empowering those affected by natural disasters when the geographical narratives of a natural disaster, elaborated by participatory and community-based research, focus on the intersection of politics, science, and society that are embedded in those narratives.

Creativity and diversity in expression are the hallmark of critical pedagogy. Jeremy Paden exemplifies this in his poem aimed toward empowering Haitian people to rebuild their livelihoods after the earthquake. Pam Oldfield Meade expresses, through words and painting, her understanding of what it means to live in a mountain community, reflecting on her experience of the tornado in March 2012, and showing how her relationship to a natural disaster was shaped by and continues to shape her life in the community of West Liberty, Kentucky.

Jude Fernando's section below provides a broad framework for using critical pedagogy in the interest of promoting social and environmental justice in responding to disasters in mountain regions.

Critical Pedagogy as an Empowering Tool for Rebuilding Mountain Communities

Critical pedagogy can contribute to addressing the growing desire to find effective responses to the issues that natural and human-made disasters create in global mountain regions. It addresses the limitations of the current top-down and prescriptive nature of scholarly and policy responses in understanding and responding to the vulnerability of those affected by disasters. Unlike current approaches, critical pedagogy uses methods that do not separate understanding-based knowledge from action-based knowledge or scholars and policymakers from the survivors of disasters. Additionally, these methods do not privilege one disciplinary method over another.

Our approach to critical pedagogy begins with problematizing the many approaches to learning "as parts of systems of belief and action that have aggregate effects within the power structures of society" (Burbules and Berk 1999, 36). Inquiry might begin with the question of who benefits from systems of belief and actions. That implies that "the primary preoccupation of critical pedagogy is with social injustice and how to transform inequitable, undemocratic, or oppressive institutions and social relations" (Burbules and Berk 1999, 36). Our approach to critical pedagogy differs from critical thinking. The primary aim of critical pedagogy is to develop critical thinking as the basis for constructing counter-hegemonic knowledge and practices, which, according to Giroux (1988), means becoming able to articulate the possible as part of becoming critical.

Production of knowledge in critical pedagogy aims "to raise ambitions, desires, and real hope for those who wish to take seriously the issue of educational struggle and social justice" (Giroux 1988, 177). Referencing Paulo Freire (1970), Burbules and Berk (1999, 25) note that critical pedagogy in the Freirian tradition is not about providing knowledge and skills but addressing "directly the self-contempt and sense of powerlessness that he believed accompanied illiteracy." Freire's commitment to empowering the powerless entails the "development of a sense of confidence and efficacy, especially in collective thought and action; and the desire to change, not only one's self, but the circumstances of one's social group" (Burbules and Berk 1999, 25). The pedagogical method that Freire advocated to promote all of these is dialogue: "cultural action for freedom is characterized by dialogue, and its preeminent purpose is to conscientize the people" (Burbules and Berk, 1999, 26). Conscientization is a process that aims to bring about both the personal and systemic changes that are necessary to achieve meaningful freedom.

Being committed to environmental and social justice, critical pedagogy seeks to address the limitations of knowledge production, in both formal and informal settings, by employing a variety of transdisciplinary approaches—both formal and informal—including those methods used by the victims of disasters that are not considered legitimate approaches in academic or policy circles. In all these efforts, this approach seeks to cultivate an equal, nonhierarchical participation space where scholars, practitioners, and survivors of disasters participate as co-learners committed to the environmental and social well-being of those who live in global mountain regions and beyond.

Critical pedagogy is an intensely political endeavor. It involves uncertainties and risks for all stakeholders, as their aspirations, values, and practices involve directly engaging with oppressive power relations while searching for ways to transform those power relations.

Compared to others, there are some unique ways in which those who live in mountain regions are vulnerable to natural disasters. The terrain in mountain regions isolates the poor and socially marginalized in particular from other locations in terms of transportation infrastructure. Isolation leads to neglect of these areas in the course of disaster-mitigation responses. When disasters do occur in these regions, our understanding of the disaster and the associated disaster response plans is framed by predetermined technocratic narratives that do not consider the history, culture, economy, and politics shaping the vulnerability of these communities to disasters, nor do they consider the local knowledge and practices they employ to build resilience and cope with the impacts of disasters. The primary function of hegemonic post-disaster narratives is to discipline disaster-affected areas—their society, culture, politics, and economy—to function according to highly racialized and oppressive economic and political interests.

Decisions regarding disaster mitigation are purely top-down, as members of mountain communities are hardly able to participate, particularly in places where the local population is viewed as illiterate and thus is excluded from formal systems of governance. The policymakers' responses to disasters are influenced by mainstream development discourse that views these mountain regions as objects of tourism, repositories for extraction of natural resources, and recently protected areas vital for protecting national security or addressing climate change. Understanding the potential for natural disasters and local communities' coping strategies assumes a lower priority; researchers and policymakers are not equipped to understand local systems of communication and do not prioritize space for genuine participation. Disasters in global mountain regions unfairly receive selective global attention, depending on how important they are to global economic and political interests. As time passes, global attention to disasters in geographically and politically isolated mountain regions fades away far more quickly than is the case with disasters in other regions. By then, the local communities—their culture, economy, and society—have already been silenced and subjugated to functioning according to the interests of hegemonic disaster narratives. But the agency, autonomy, and spirit of the local communities are never completely colonized, and pathways for their liberation are not entirely closed. Disasters also bring the residents together and open new opportunities for them to be the primary agents in rebuilding their own communities.

Scholars have a critical role to play in addressing such a predicament, and opportunities for the rebuilding of disaster-affected global mountain regions require a change in the nature of scholarship itself. Critical pedagogy not only critiques but also produces counterhegemonic knowledge and practices. In the process, it provides visibility and empowers those affected by disasters so that they also function as producers of knowledge and action. Critical pedagogy blurs the boundaries between the production of knowledge for policy and for action and between researchers and their subjects, as these researchers are committed to social and environmental justice. Notably, the subjects are as committed as the researchers to social and environmental justice in the process of inquiry and practice. In the process of knowledge production, researchers and their subjects become co-producers of knowledge to the extent that the roles of the researchers and their subjects become indistinguishable. Both are open to change, and they share a great deal of humility in learning from each other. They become subjects of the shared values, aspirations, and practices that guide their commitment to social and environmental justice. Critical pedagogy does not seek final answers for such dynamic issues, with a dramatic once-and-for-all reveal, but rather hopes to facilitate a process of learning hand in hand with democratic and transformative actions. Democracy here is primarily a process of empowering the local community by addressing the unequal power differential among the scholar, the practitioner, and the subjects of their interventions.

The methods in critical pedagogy are not predetermined but evolve through the process of practice—just as a relationship, one that determines vulnerability to natural disasters, evolves between humans and nature. This approach also views the environmental crisis and the risks of and vulnerabilities to disasters as interlinked. Humans can understand and cope with disasters only by understanding and transforming the relationships between themselves and nature as well as understanding how social, economic, and political relations mediate these relationships. The contributors to this chapter share different types of critical pedagogical practices, articulated and represented in a variety of different styles that are not entirely common to mainstream practices.

The approach of Shaunna Scott and Stephanie McSpirit in the following section illustrates the importance of human action and politics in understanding the risks associated with disaster. Basing their narrative on organizing around the coal waste disaster in Martin County, Scott and McSpirit demonstrate the importance of citizen mobilization to harness the social and environmental responsibility of the governmental and private sectors, journalists, and academics.

Martin County Coal Waste Disaster: The Importance of Citizen Action and a Free Press in the Face of Corporate Irresponsibility and Government Failure

Sometime after midnight on October 11, 2000, the 72-acre Big Branch coal waste impoundment owned by Martin County Coal Company ruptured in Martin County, Kentucky. Just over 300 million gallons of coal waste, including water, diesel fuel, heavy metals, and other contaminants leaked through a series of abandoned underground mine tunnels and exited through Coldwater and Wolf Creeks. The black lavalike substance flooded people's homes, temporarily displacing many Coldwater and Wolf Creek residents from their homes. The coal waste from the impoundment flowed down Cold Water and Wolf Creeks, to the Levisa Fork, into the Tug River and proceeded into the Ohio and Mississippi Rivers, and finally into the Gulf of Mexico. It disrupted water services primarily along the Levisa Fork and Tug River. The Martin County coal waste spill was the largest environmental disaster in the southeastern United States, dwarfing the well-known Exxon Valdez disaster spill of 11 million gallons of oil. Fortunately, this disaster did not kill or injure any people, though it did damage property and destroy wildlife and vegetation. The Kentucky Division of Water reported the death of all aquatic life for 60 miles.

In our account, we will share information about the disaster and its aftermath, provide an overview of the research and engagement activities that we have undertaken in Martin County, and discuss the findings from that work. Finally, based on this experience, we will offer suggestions about how to rebuild community after disaster. But, first, let us begin with some contextual information about Martin County and the company that owned the Big Creek Reservoir: Martin County Coal. Martin County, Kentucky, the site of the disaster, is a poor, racially homogenous rural county whose residents have a low (but rising) educational attainment rate and whose economy depends upon coal. The county is a Republican stronghold, though local elections can swing to either party. Mike Duncan, a banker from Martin County, was the chair of the national Republican Party during the 2008 presidential election. Martin County does not have a pro-union class-based history and identity to provide the community with organizational capacity and a tradition of social action, as many other central Appalachian mining communities do.

At the time of the disaster in 2000, Martin County Coal Corporation was a subsidiary of Massey Energy, a corporation established in 1920 and headquartered in Richmond, Virginia. Massey's CEO, Don Blankenship, rose through management ranks by decreasing production costs—his critics would say—through union busting and ignoring safety guidelines. In the early 2000s, Massey was the largest coal producer in Central Appalachia, and in 2010, it was the sixth largest producer in the United States.

Massey has a well-earned reputation for its poor environmental and health and safety record as well as its strong anti-union position. After a fatal mine fire at Aracoma, West Virginia, in 2006, the corporation was forced to pay one of the largest mine death settlements, $4.5 million, because of its repeated violation of coal mine safety rules. It also had to pay $20 million in water pollution fines to the US Environmental Protection Agency (EPA) in 2008. The following year,

2009, Massey was purchased by Alpha Natural Resources for $8.5 billion, with Massey retaining a 46 percent share of the stock. Don Blankenship was forced to resign as a result of the merger. Then, in April 2010, its mine in Upper Big Branch in West Virginia exploded, killing 29 miners. On April 6, 2016, Don Blankenship was sentenced to a year in prison for conspiracy to violate federal mine safety laws, the violation of which resulted in the deaths of 29 men. In short, the company and the CEO responsible for the Martin County disaster of 2000 had a record of putting profit ahead of worker and public safety.

The material that leaked from the Martin County impoundment, called coal slurry or sludge, typically contains a wide range of heavy metals including arsenic, lead, cadmium, chromium, iron, manganese, aluminum, and nickel, all of which pose a danger to human and environmental health. Nevertheless, throughout 2000 and 2001 the local water district, the EPA, and the Kentucky Division of Water (KDOW) consistently maintained that the water was safe to drink. Local residents were highly skeptical, and the local newspapers, the *Martin County Sun* and *Mountain Citizen*, investigated and reported on these concerns. When a federal report that identified several heavy metals and carcinogens in the waste was not shared openly with the residents of the county, people began to believe that the government was more committed to protecting the company's financial interests than safeguarding their health. It certainly did little to allay public fears when the EPA under the Bush administration set up its command headquarters for managing the disaster behind a guarded gate on company property. The EPA claimed that this was a matter of convenience because they could use company office equipment to conduct their work. Later, it emerged that the company was allowed to draft all of the press releases that were issued from the EPA's command post. The fact that the agency relied on the company to collect water samples for safety testing also concerned the public.

Finally, the EPA's decision to capitulate to Massey's request that the agency cede its authority under the Comprehensive Environmental Response Liability and Compensation Act of 1980 (CERLCA, also known as Superfund) meant that the federal government gave up its right to oversee cleanup and recovery and its ability to sue the company as well as collect from the company costs of health impact assessments. Meanwhile, the US Mine Safety and Health Administration (MSHA), the agency that allowed the company to put more waste into an unrepaired reservoir that had already leaked 100 million gallons of slurry in 1994, fined the company $11,000 for two minor violations and declared itself lacking culpability.

Jack Spadaro, an MSHA investigator whose first job was to investigate a 1972 coal waste disaster in West Virginia that had killed 125 people, refused to sign the report and brought his concerns to public attention by resigning from the accident investigation committee in 2001. In 2003, Spadaro was placed on leave and questioned about providing housing to an MSHA instructor with multiple sclerosis, and his office was ransacked and the locks changed.

The KDOW, however, did not cede its right to sue the corporation and in 2002 secured $225,000 to restock the waterways with fish and $150,000 for independent water testing. The state of Kentucky collected $1 million in natural resource damages, $1.75 million in civil penalties, and $500,000 to compensate for state response costs. Two years later, in 2004, they released $150,000 to Eastern Kentucky University (EKU), which, with the oversight of local citizens, conducted independent testing of the public water supply in Martin County. By this time, an election had ushered in an administrative change in local government, which resulted in new water plant management. Public water treatment facilities were improved under the new management. A research team composed of citizens and university researchers found the local water supply to be safe for human consumption in 2005.

Concerned by the lack of evacuation notification in the aftermath of the Martin County disaster, local citizens joined with Kentuckians for the Commonwealth and our research team in a five-year effort (2003–2008) to convince the Kentucky state legislature to follow West Virginia's lead and mandate emergency and evacuation planning to prepare for such events. The Kentucky state legislature ignored public demand for this safety measure.

Over the past decade or so, we have conducted 65 interviews and collected 723 surveys from Martin County and Perry County, Kentucky, a comparison county that also has coal waste reservoirs but was not directly impacted by the disaster in 2000. In addition to the surveys and interviews, we also did participant-observation and newspaper content analysis. And Stephanie coordinated an EKU–citizens' group collaboration with the local water district to test the water. We have worked with Kentuckians for the Commonwealth and the citizens of Martin County to lobby the state of Kentucky to mandate emergency and evacuation planning for high-hazard dams and impoundments.

As a result of this research and community engagement, we have learned both how a disaster can impact community relationships and social trust in the short term and, also, how community and trust can be rebuilt over the long term. In the first two years following the disaster, we observed increased levels of overt conflict and environmental concern in Martin County, particularly focused on the safety of drinking water and the toxicity of coal waste. When compared to Perry County, we found that Martin County residents that in 2001 had less trust in government, mining regulatory agencies, the EPA, scientific experts, and corporations. None of this was surprising, of course. In 2001, we also found that there was strong support both in Martin and Perry Counties for the creation of an independent citizens' committee to monitor and test public water supplies and also strong support for government-mandated emergency and evacuation planning to prepare for similar events that might occur in the future.

As part of our recent analysis of the 2011 Martin County survey data, we created an index that measures social trust through four general survey questions. The first one measured general trust in science and experts. The second measured trust in community, neighbors, and local corporations/businesses. The third question measured general trust in government and government agencies. The fourth question more specifically measured trust in local government.

All four questions were recorded on a Likert-type scale and scaled so that 5 represented the maximum amount of trust and 1 the minimum amount. These four items were summed to create a social trust index with a range from 5 to 20. Higher scores represented higher levels of trust in other individuals and social institutions.

When we compared our Martin County respondents in 2011 to those in 2001, we found that the Martin County's social trust index climbed from 7.7 in 2001 to 8.4 in 2011. However, even in 2011, Martin County still lagged behind Perry County, the control county in our prior research, which had a social trust index of 9.4 in 2001. (Neither of the counties scored particularly high on social trust.) In Martin County, as reported initially, results show that Community Attachment, Perceived Environmental Risk, and Trust in Institutions all improved after 10 years. Statistically speaking, after 10 years people had a greater desire to stay in the county. They also had greater trust in coal companies, local government, and federal mining agencies. In addition, there was also less concern with drinking water quality and coal waste. They were also less likely to not know what to believe.

In Perry County, there was also less concern with drinking water quality and coal waste after 10 years. However, results corresponding to trust in institutions were mixed. Trust in coal companies increased over time, whereas trust in local government and the EPA declined. When comparing changes over 10 years for the two counties, we identified the following significant differences in changes over time:

1. The increase in the desire to stay in Martin County was significantly greater than the increase in the desire to stay in Perry County, from 2001 to 2011.
2. The decrease in concern with drinking water quality and coal waste in Martin County was significantly greater than the decrease in concern in Perry County, from 2001 to 2011.
3. Changes in the trust in local government, the EPA, and federal mining agencies were significantly different for the two counties after the ten intervening years between the surveys.

Even though Martin County has not caught up with Perry County on its trust index score, the levels of trust in Martin County have increased significantly over the 10-year period, while Perry County's have not.

What accounts for this partial rebound? We have identified the following factors that support renewed trust: (1) independent water tests found the public water to be safe in 2005; (2) changes in local public water district management and the new management oversight of improvements at the water plant restored public confidence in water safety; and (3) the election of Barack Obama in 2008 resulted in significant changes in the actions of the EPA toward polluting industries, such as the coal industry.

Unfortunately, there are even more reasons in Martin County not to trust, including (1) MSHA's failure to repair or close the impoundment after the 1994 leak; (2) EPA's capitulation to the company's request to cede its CERCLA (Superfund) authorities; (3) the lack of public oversight of the corporate-led cleanup efforts and the local water board's failure to incorporate citizen-advisors; (4) the Kentucky state legislature's refusal to mandate emergency and evacuation planning for impoundment failures; and (5) the existence of high hazard dams and coal waste impoundments in Kentucky (McSpirit 2002). (High hazard dams are those the failure of which is predicted to result in the loss of human life.)

So even though we consistently found that a vast majority of those surveyed both in Perry and Martin Counties, and in our 2001 and 2011 survey sweeps of Martin, favor state-mandated emergency evacuation planning for high hazard dams, our five-year effort to persuade the Kentucky state legislature to mandate coal waste disaster planning (2003–2008) failed in five legislative sessions. Kentucky still has no plan to provide emergency warning for citizens living downstream from coal waste impoundments in spite of the fact that the state is home to approximately 70 coal waste impoundments, 23 (30 percent) of which are classified as high hazard and pose a significant threat to populations living downstream (Scott, et al. 2012). West Virginia, in contrast, mandated coal waste disaster planning 40 years ago in response to a similar disaster in Buffalo Creek.

In *A New Species of Trouble* (1994), Kai Erikson reflected on this earlier coal waste disaster in the Central Appalachian coal fields, the Buffalo Creek, West Virginia, disaster of 1972: "It can be profoundly painful when the people in charge of a company at the time of a severe mishap deny responsibility. . . . This is not the way of neighbors. . . . It is the way of hostile strangers. . . . The mortar holding human communities together is made up at least in part of trust and respect and decency." (Erikson 1994, 238–239). Our research supports Erikson's contention. We found that the disaster—more specifically, the government's and the corporation's actions both before and after the disaster—did in fact cause the mortar of social trust in Martin County to crumble. After 10 years, however, it has been partially reconstructed.

What we observed in Martin County was corporate and government irresponsibility and collusion, lack of government transparency, and refusal by federal agencies to involve the public in environmental monitoring and recovery.

Investigative journalism by the two local papers and state papers such as the *Lexington Herald-Leader*, as well as the participatory research and water testing that we helped facilitate played a positive role in helping area residents get information and exert some, albeit limited, power in the situation. Citizens require a more reliable and consistent effort across all levels of government to resist corporate domination and to act in a publicly responsible manner. In Appalachia, we have found that this does not occur often, and even then, only when citizens effectively organize to make it happen. Universities and journalists can and should play a positive role in the struggle to hold corporations and governments accountable for public and environmental health and safety.

The central theme of Scott and McSpirit's analysis is the necessity of multistakeholder participatory action anchored in the mobilization of citizens in the disaster-affected areas. Lina Calandra's section below illustrates the diversity and contextual specificity of community-based action research.

Participatory and Community-based Research, Action, and New Forms of Democratic Praxis in L'Aquila, Italy, after an Earthquake in 2009

To illustrate how participatory and community-based research can empower inhabitants and contribute to social and political rebuilding of a territory stricken by a disaster, in this section I focus on the case of the earthquake in my town of L'Aquila on April 6, 2009. After briefly retracing the main stages of the post-earthquake period, I focus in particular on three aspects of geographical participatory action research conducted to change the political dynamics needed for the social reconstruction of the different communities living in the municipality of L'Aquila: (1) how citizens, students, and scientists together involved themselves (from June to September 2010) in community-based and participatory/participating action research (called Communication for Active Listening Initiative, Iniziativa C.As.A.) to elaborate a common interpretation of the territorial context after the earthquake; (2) how the geographical narrative issued from the research was presented publicly to people during the world café meeting called City Laboratory (Laboratorio città—September 10, 2011); and (3) how the engagement of research and researchers has activated a communication process at the political and social level within the municipality of L'Aquila.

The aim of my contribution is to illustrate that the geographical narrative of an event in a territory could mediate between politics, society, and science when this narrative is elaborated in a truly participatory way. In other words, I illustrate how, in the case of L'Aquila, participatory and community-based action research is making it possible to open communication channels between the political, scientific, and social realms to try to restore conditions for democratic decision-making processes and for reconstruction.

Characterized by a long history of destructive earthquakes (Antonini 2010; Clementi and Piroddi 1986), L'Aquila, in the Apennine Mountains, is the regional capital of Abruzzo, and had about 73,000 residents and 25,000 college students in 2009. Within a few seconds of the quake on April 6, L'Aquila lost almost all the buildings of strategic importance and their functions: the prefecture, police headquarters, the hospital, the regional court, and most of the university and school buildings, the churches, the theaters, and so on. The earthquake affected 57 municipalities. Of the 308 victims, the greatest number of them were in the municipality of L'Aquila, where there were 272 victims, most of them in the village of Onna and the area within the medieval walls of the city bordered by Via XX Settembre. It was in this area, which mostly includes buildings from the 1950s and 1960s (Stockel 1988), that 50 percent of the deaths occurred, and many of the dead included young college students. Why? What had happened over the decades in this area of the city, in terms of institutional and individual behavior, that led to such socioterritorial vulnerability? Similarly, why in a district that had been recent urbanized (with buildings mostly from the years 1980 to 1990) such as Pettino (10,000–15,000 inhabitants in 2009), about 40 percent of the buildings suffered severe structural damage?

The problem actually comes from the conditions before the quake, from how territorial planning had been practiced in the past and how individuals defined their own daily behavior and their own relationships with political power.

What is vital is to reconnect the daily lives of people with real possibilities for intervention in democratic life, with the opportunity to have responsibility and to decide on their living spaces. What happened in L'Aquila with the earthquake of April 6, 2009, which directly affected me, my friends, my family, and my whole community, was a revelation that people had lost the ability (cognitively, practically, and organizationally) to govern the city and territory as a whole, to think beyond the individual and in terms of shared public decisions to prevent additional environmental, social, and health risks in the region of L'Aquila.

During the emergency phase (Alexander 2010), the director of command and control (Di.Coma.C) of the National Civil Protection Service declared the historic center of L'Aquila and all other smaller historic centers in the municipality off-limits and this prohibition persists. At first, about 70,000 persons from the municipality of L'Aquila were sheltered in tents and hotels on the Adriatic coast. Then Berlusconi's government decided to build 19 new complexes, the so-called CASE (Antiseismic Sustainable Eco-compatible Complexes), planning to move all the displaced people—actually only about 14,000 to 15,000 of them—especially residents of the historic center of L'Aquila city. The result is a territory that is fractured and fragmented and accentuates the disrupted character of communities and the temporary and nomadic conditions of everyday life.

As soon as Civil Protection left (on January 2010), the citizens realized that they did not have the right to decide what to do about their own land. So it happened that many citizen groups founded after the earthquake organized large demonstrations that have not been covered by the media. For example, on June 2010, 20,000 people from almost all the major municipalities affected by the seismic crater occupied the roadway, and the news did not provide any information about this event. Only the demonstration in Rome, on July 7, where the police became violent, had any resonance in the media. These forms of protest were actually dividing the people inside the Municipality of L'Aquila, and the problem was becoming defined around who was "for Berlusconi" and who was "against Berlusconi." To avoid social division and this manichean and sterile framing of the problem, we had to find a different way of taking action (Kemmis and McTaggart 2000, 2005). That is how the participatory and community-based action research idea came into the the the citizen movements (Reason and Bradbury 2001; Lather 1986; Matthey 2005; Morgan 2007; Pain 2004; van Asselt 2000; van Asselt and Rijkens-Klomp 2002).

The geographical question on which the research had to focus was evident. The earthquake has clearly revealed the importance of places in everyday life, for the psycho-physical health of people and for the welfare of the entire community (Tuan 1977). The loss of places puts attention on the need to develop a geographical narrative capable of expressing the pain, anxiety, anger, and hope around this loss. Furthermore, the earthquake has underlined the link between a lack of democracy and a state of emergency. Emergency has had its origin in a lack of (or a wrong) communication between representative institutions and inhabitants of the represented territory. And now, there is still a lack of political debate and, consequently, a nondemocratic policy-making process around reconstruction (Calandra 2012a). Thus, the research has to be focused on the problems of citizenship and spatial justice (Harvey 1975, 1996, 2000; Jouve and Booth 2004; Laurin, Klein, and Tardif 2001), starting with the importance of places in everyday life.

So the challenge of participatory and community-based action research was to imagine a communication process capable of restoring the legitimacy of representative institutions and transforming the social contract that links politics and citizenship (Blake 2007). With this aim, students, researchers, and citizens of L'Aquila together conducted the Communication for Active Listening Initiative (Iniziativa C.As.A.) from June to September 2010 among displaced people who live now in the new houses of CASE sites. Soon this work began to have a therapeutic effect on everyone involved. At the end, more than 1,000 people answered a questionnaire for the project, and many individual stories were collected through long interviews. What was learned through this project?

The most significant research data is that which refers to the effects of the disaster at a social-regional level: a sudden and violent acceleration of the dispersal and fragmentation of society. Through the pre- and post-earthquake comparison, the survey reveals the changes that have affected the places and behaviors of everyday life (leisure, study, work, shopping, etc.), highlighting post-earthquake social and territorial discomfort and the subsequent disruption of the urban life and the geographical patterns of life, brought on by this new geographical arrangement in L'Aquila and its surroundings. People in the region have experienced disorientation, loneliness, and discomfort, feeling a lack of connection to and through public places. L'Aquila was once a quiet provincial town characterized all in all by a good quality of life. Daily life in L'Aquila is now organized completely around new needs and behaviors. Suddenly, thousands of people were faced with problems accomplishing basic tasks: going to the grocery store, picking up a pension, receiving mail, going to the doctor, going to work, and taking their children to school. Even more than three years after the earthquake, mobility continues to be a major problem, both due to the lack of public services and the disrupted traffic: (a) there are paths, for more or less temporary relocation, but it is basically random and chaotic; (b) varying number of residents are concentrated in specific areas; and (c) increases in travel time, especially because of the congestion on the main roads. Moreover, due to the earthquake it became almost impossible to walk to work, to school, to the grocery, or simply to take a walk because of the disruption of public spaces and paths. It has become necessary to take a car, and to use the few routes that have been open for travel.

Another significant change, which certainly merits closer examination, concerns the habits of L'Aquila residents in relation to purchases, specifically the places where they go shopping. In this regard, one can point out how, in the first year after the earthquake, the number of centers and commercial galleries almost doubled. Even with respect to leisure, there were significant changes in habits. There was an important increase in the percentage of people who spent the day staying at home, highlighting the trend of a turning of individuals in on themselves and on their family environment.

Participatory Action Research as Catalyst of a New Democratic Praxis

And so what could be done with what was learned through the participatory research after the earthquake? What was the research team's responsibility to the many people who had devoted so much time to answering questions, and to the researchers themselves who had devoted so much emotional energy to this project (Agnew 1987; Cahill 2007; Chatterton and Maxey 2009; Cloke et al., 2000; Cutchin 2002; Elias 2006)? All of the team felt a great responsibility to communicate how changing habits were not the result of free choice but of the reconfiguring of the context of life after the earthquake. Those changes were not going in the direction of encouraging a reconstruction of public spaces, public life, and a sense of community, and with them close networks, trust, and solidarity. Instead, spending more time in the car and only being able to move around the area in the car in fact excludes the possibility of meeting people on the street and perhaps getting together for a coffee at the bar. There is more shopping, but it happens in a mall, with more impersonal relationships between customers and merchants. Spending so much free time at home led participants to say they had increased feelings of mistrust, insecurity, discouragement, and depression. Finally, the team felt it important to communicate the finding that the spread and intensification of such attitudes were laying the groundwork for an inability to control our own lives, and that this is rooted in a lack of communication between people, and between people and institutions. It is the loss of communication capital that feeds the inability of individuals and communities to govern cognitively and practically our territory and that, as a consequence, prevents reorienting behavior toward interest in, and care and responsibility for, our living places.

It was important for us to give back to the city the information, the data, and the stories. At the operational level, it was first important to develop the geographical narrative about how individual behaviors and individual relationships to places changed after the earthquake. This was done through visual and cartographic representation, useful to activating and developing communicative processes (Crampton 2001; Dodge, McDerby, and Turner 2008; MacEachren et al. 1992; Polelle 1999). So all the information and data were put in graphic form and put on 40 posters; then those were discussed in a public meeting in September 2011, a public participatory meeting called City Laboratory (*Laboratorio città*), which was attended by citizens, associations, politicians, administrators, some members of the town council and also children in the space of a "Junior" City Laboratory managed by researchers in pedagogical science (Calandra 2012b).

The meeting concluded with a commitment to collaborate with the local administration, and so the research process and the visible and public presentation and discussion of research results were useful to activating praxis at the level of the municipality (Fuller and Kitchin 2004; Funtowicz and Ravetz 1993; Ravetz 2006; Schrag 1986; Schrag and Ramsey 1994). In fact, two main participatory process were conducted by the municipality of L'Aquila with the participation of the team: (1) the first (October–December 2011) to publicly discuss with the different communities of L'Aquila municipality the text of a public participation regulation (approved by the municipality on January 2012); and (2) the second (March 2012) to inform and gather comments on the reconstruction plan.

Then, using the same participatory method, the coalition of political parties supporting Massimo Cialente (the outgoing mayor) decided to elaborate the electoral program and, after elections (in May 2012), also the operational plan for 2012–2017 (approved by the municipality on June 2012). The operational plan was a result of actions of the citizens in mobilizing all stakeholders through effective communication that utilized a variety of place-based methods.

Success of rebuilding post-disaster mountain communities is mainly driven by how people reconnect with each other and with place after a disaster. It is about how people imagine the relationship between themselves and nature in their rebuilding efforts. Imagination, a key to rebuilding, could be harnessed in a variety of different ways, including poetry and art.

In response to a powerful earthquake in Haiti, Jeremy Paden wrote this poem, which complements the work of social scientists in earlier sections of this chapter by conveying in words what Pam Oldfield Meade goes on to express as a painter in the intersections of the verbal and the nonverbal about how communities experience, remember, and reassemble after disaster.

For Haiti

Jeremy Paden

Here is a stand, let us sit for a night
    or two or three in silence before we speak.
    I wish it were a copse of blue-flowering lignum,
    shedding petals that float like butterflies,
    or the ceibas under whose canopies Anacaona
    and Guacanagarix held court, or the guayaba
    and guanábana that fed Guarocuya's rebels,
    even the bushes and shrubs Mackandal
    used for his potions and powders,
    anything but this grove of felled mahogany.

    Where is the poem that will not forget
    that Bolívar forgot Pétion's aid?
    The poem that will remind Charles X
    that Haiti paid for her freedom in blood?
    The poem that will stand before Monroe
    and recite his Doctrine?
    Where is the poem that will escape
    from Fort Dimanche and wander
    through the streets of Port au Prince
    crying out for Papa Doc to remember
    he was the son of a justice of the peace
    and a baker woman, crying out
    that he not forget the wretched of the earth,
    strangled by his Tonton Macoutes?

Let us stay a while in this denuded place
and write a poem that will not forget Haiti.

Haiti, I see you in a t-shirt that says
Phillies 2009 World Series Champs,
bending over a bucket of lard and clay
and salt, making mud pies to sell at market.
I hear you in the laugh of the boy
with whom I played soccer one summer day
on plains made barren from centuries
of slashing and burning sugar cane.

Haiti, there are stories that we keep
under lock and key in a cupboard.
In that cupboard, beside your bananas,
beside the green cane we no longer grind down
to molasses and refine into sugar,
beside your double-pot distilled rum,
we keep you, wasting away on mud pies.
And every once in a while we crack open
the door and yell,
"Stop cutting down your trees for firewood!"
Never mind that you have no electricity.
Never mind that a stove costs more
than you will earn in a lifetime.

Let us write a poem that will haunt us
like Tonton Macoute, even after all
the children have been adopted
and the halls of government have been rebuilt.

Haiti, how many wrongs can one poem right?
Can a poem reforest your hills,
keep tectonic plates from shifting,
undo a dam that forced a valley of people
to leave their fertile fields for slums?
Can a poem resurrect your creole pigs?
Can it redress centuries of misrule?
Can a poem give you a livelihood
where you do not have to peddle
your goods to tourists, squeezing

the last penny out of their vacation funds?
Can it settle in and disrupt our lives
like chagas disease?

Can a poem, like a strangler fig or mangrove,
send down roots from the sky?

There is a fault which runs the length
of the Caribbean and on that fault lies Haiti
and on that fault are we.

Let us write a poem that will change our lives,
a poem strong enough to endure
the pressures of the fault on which it stands.

Artwork for Hope and Healing

Experiences of disasters are highly personal and located in specific places and moments. Pam Oldfield Meade speaks, as an artist, about disaster moving through her home community:

I grew up and still live on a farm in eastern Kentucky, in the foothills of the Appalachian Mountains. It is a beautiful here, both the people and the natural landscape. The area is known for having a strong sense of community among residents, and that can be seen in many ways. Growing up, I spent many days at the little post office in my small community of around two hundred people, White Oak, talking to my neighbors about gardens, weather, and everything that was worth knowing.

As I grew older and began thinking about the ways of the world, I continued to make art that carried themes in it of what I was pondering. Where did we come from and where are we going? How many people have stood in this exact spot by this creek over the years? Where is all the wisdom stored—is it flowing through the waters and embedded in the soil? In the painting called *Watching the Valley* I have words flowing from the woman's hair into the plowed fields and into the water. Her hair, worn in a bun—like some of the wise women I knew growing up—is shaped into a spiral, which I used as a symbol of hope and healing.

Many, like my family, farmed the rich bottomlands along the creeks and rivers. On our farm we raised cattle, sheep, tobacco, strawberries, and other crops. Each year we grew a large garden of vegetables to eat freshly picked and to preserve for the following winter months. My painting *14 Day Icicle Pickles* will remind me for the rest of my life that my mom wanted all her children to be able to grow and preserve their own food; self-sufficiency was important to her. She was very proud of me when I started making the pickles. Lifting the heavy crocks

Fig. 8.1 *Watching the Valley*, 2007. Photo credit: Pam Oldfield Meade

to drain and boil the pickling solution each day had become too big a job for her as she got older. I am thankful to have learned how to make those pickles and how to do so many things from her and the all women in my life. Many people carry on these traditions today.

I first began making art as a child loving to draw and paint. I am still inspired by the things that stirred my creativity when I was younger: a complete fascination with the moon that I could see through my window at night; the green colors of spring; the horses I rode up and down hills and through the fields; and, always, the water flowing in creeks, rivers, and ponds.

My art has continued to reflect the things that first inspired me but also reflects other themes and subject matter that are important to me. My series called Nature's Theatre threads memories from childhood with more serious

Fig. 8.2 *Licking River in October,* 2015. Photo credit: Pam Oldfield Meade

issues. Other pieces have social justice and equality messages. Some deal with personal matters. I didn't set out to create a series of mourning paintings, but over the years, unfortunately, I have painted several: *Funeral Clothes, Cemetery Hill I, Cemetery Hill II, Super Moon over White Oak, Arils / Exit, My Knee Bone's Connected to My Heartstring.* One thing we have in common around the world, we are all going to experience worry, troubles, sorrow, and heartbreak. I have used my paintings to express some of these feelings. My sister-in-law and I were standing again at the cemetery, having lost another beloved family member and each of us was wearing a black outfit we'd worn too many times already that year. She said to me, "I am sick of wearing these funeral clothes." That is how I came to paint the piece that has our shadows wearing funeral clothes and with writing that lists all the people who had died and a little something about them. I try to include a symbol of hope in my art. The painting *Broken World* addresses the opioid epidemic facing our world, which is truly a disaster. There is an addiction story written in the painting and a spiral that represents healing.

A constant motivator that keeps me making my art is the inspiration coming from other people's art. It was through experiencing regional literature, theater, music, and stories—and of course, the diverse visual art—that I genuinely

Fig. 8.3 *Funeral Clothes*, 2004. Photo credit: Pam Oldfield Meade

became proud to be from Appalachia. Although I grew up loving this place, once I learned more about the history of the region, about the brilliant people who had lived and still live here, and developed a deeper understanding of my rich and complicated culture, I valued this place and myself more. The painting *River of Earth*, named and inspired by the novel of the same name by James Still, was the first to speak to this. *Pokeberry Theatre* was created after being at the Seedtime on the Cumberland Festival, experiencing a feast of music, plays, films and art. I began working on this painting before I even got back home. Listening to music, reading books, listening to stories, dancing—all these things show up in my art. I did the cover art for the book *Ancient Creek* by Gurney Norman (Old Cove Press). Aunt Haze is an ancient healer, very connected to nature. She's two or three hundred years old. She's someone that I think about when I need to be healed.

Most every town in eastern Kentucky has regularly scheduled art exhibitions, live music, quilt shows, festivals, and many other activities that are so very important for the health of all communities, especially when disaster hits. The diverse artist community has been a strong part of our mountain community's healing. With the shock of a disaster, the sadness of so much loss

Fig. 8.4 *Ancient Creek*, 2006. Photo credit: Pam Oldfield Meade

is overwhelming, and sometimes art can help people share experiences when words fail us. On March 2, 2012, a devastating EF3 tornado tore through my hometown of West Liberty, Kentucky. Sadly, 7 people lost their lives in our county alone. Forty-five confirmed tornados touched down in the southeast that day, killing 41 people. In Morgan County, hundreds of people lost homes, businesses, belongings, livestock, pets, and other irreplaceable treasured items. Donations and workers poured in from all over the United States to assist in the face of the horrible destruction left behind. Local people worked tirelessly to coordinate and assist efforts to get our town, somehow, back up and running.

Soon after the tornado, local artists began meeting to think about what could be done to help our beloved community. We formed the West Liberty Area Artist Collective and established partnerships to carry out several projects. High school and middle school art teachers led efforts to get their students involved with creating art that could help express the strong emotions that came with so much loss and devastation. They invited local artists to join students in creating banners depicting things they had that had been lost and damaged, along with words of gratitude and encouragement. One banner showed the historic courthouse as a jigsaw puzzle with words that said "Back Together." One large banner depicted a church that was destroyed along with beautiful stained glass windows that residents considered treasured public art. One said "Helping Hands," another said "From the Rubble We Will Rise." Forty-five banners were created—they hung in

Fig. 8.5 *Tornado Tree*, 2012. Photo credit: Pam Oldfield Meade

West Liberty for several months. The Community Art Tent was another project that came out of the meetings.

The Morgan County Sorghum Festival has happened every September in West Liberty since 1971. Featuring delicious locally produced sorghum molasses, it draws thousands of visitors to town for music, arts and crafts, food (country ham and biscuits are a favorite), a parade with marching bands and floats, and many other activities. Residents were happily surprised when town leaders announced that the festival would go on as usual that fall following the tornado. Everyone thought it would be canceled—it lifted everyone's spirits to have another thing return to normal. Plenty of work had to be done to make the town safe—workers had to fence off dangerous areas all over town. It turned out those fences were perfect for displaying the student's banners!

The Community Art Tent allowed us to help artists in both our county and the surrounding counties who also had tornado damage. We decided to have one big tent where people could exhibit and sell their art for the three-day festival, with no booth fees or commissions. The Sorghum Festival committee supported this and provided a tent and displays. The Morgan County Cooperative Extension Service assisted with money for a few expenses and provided a sound system for an open microphone performance by students at the tent. Morgan County Arts and Recreation assisted as well. West Liberty Area Artists Cooperative members took care of sales for the more than 50 artists selling—we had great sales, festival attendance was the largest in years. Many of the artists did demonstrations for festival attendees. We were all excited to make sales and have people view and comment on our art, but looking back it was the fellowship with each other and with the people attending the festival that we remember as most important.

Another art project was the creation of a public sculpture from tornado debris. Art and vocational teachers, students, local artists, along with the local extension service, county government, and others worked together to gather and store debris to create a sculpture that would stand as a symbol of the past, of things lost, but also of the hope and renewed energy that came from both the outpouring of help from people all over (all over West Liberty and Morgan and surrounding counties vans of volunteers were a common sight for months after the tornado) and the coming together of the community to help rebuild. Teachers and students spent months welding and securing items, including stained glass from local churches. A sculpture will be installed soon now that the first phase of the rebuilding has being finished and a site can be selected.

Though much progress has been made to rebuild after tornado, there is more to be done. No doubt, the depressed economy in this area has slowed down the process. A great number of people were forced to move to other towns after losing homes, apartments, and employment—many did not return. Many business owners found it difficult to reopen—hardly anyone had sufficient insurance to rebuild and restock.

Downtown West Liberty is finally free of construction projects for the time being. There are plenty of vacant lots that hopefully will have new buildings and businesses on them before long. Several businesses and churches have rebuilt with attractive buildings. Some of the new structures that were built are using alternative energy supplies such as solar panels. It was recently reported that the geothermal system installed by one of the banks has reduced their energy cost by 45 percent from those of the previous building, which was destroyed. This system also supplies energy to other buildings downtown. The Morgan County Cooperative Extension Service now has an impressive complex that offers many services to farmers and residents.

The old courthouse was able to be restored, as were several more of the older buildings. It is wonderful to have recognizable structures from prior to the tornado since so much has changed. Out in the county there has been progress as well—homes, barns, and businesses have been rebuilt. Artist Dean Hill used lumber from his barn that was blown down to build a beautiful studio and gallery (www.deanhillphotography.com).

Though there are many problems in the process of rebuilding after a disaster, having a strong sense of community elevates the effectiveness of efforts to solve them. Having local artists living and working is an important component as well. We know that art offers new perspectives and gives an emotional release to the artist creating it and to the person viewing, listening, watching, and participating. It helps us remember teachings from our elders, and we are also reminded to respect the wisdom of young people—they are essential. We need art in all our communities as a daily way of life. In rural areas, especially with so many challenges, art is essential. We especially need artists when disasters happen—they help us heal.

Conclusion

Whatever the language each author in this chapter finds most comfortable—mapping, rhyming, painting, or polling—each is attuned to the role that place plays in constituting the social and ways in which that can be undermined (literally, by mountain top removal or earthquakes) by human-made and natural disasters. A comprehensive understanding of the causes of human and nature's vulnerability to disasters requires systematic interrogation of the pedagogical tools and practices employed by the researchers and policy makers. The relationship between humans and environments in mountain communities is a key resource for rebuilding and going on in post-disaster situations. The responsibility of scholars committed to social and environmental justice is to search for ways of exposing oppressive human–nature relations and to be advocates for more just relations.

JUDE L. FERNANDO is Associate Professor of International Development in the Department of International Development, Community, and Environment at Clark University. He researches the comparative roles of governmental and nongovernmental institutions in sustainable development, environment, livelihoods, gender and empowerment, child labor, humanitarian assistance, and governance. He authored *The Political Economy of NGOs: State Formation in Sri Lanka and Bangladesh.*

LINA MARIA CALANDRA is Associate Professor of Geography in the Department of Human Studies, University of L'Aquila (Italy), where she heads the cartographic and GIS laboratory "Cartolab." Her research interests include the geography of colonialism in Africa as well as the relationships between environmental conflicts and local development in Africa and in the Apennine Mountains.

STEPHANIE MCSPIRIT is Professor of Sociology at Eastern Kentucky University. She has worked extensively on community-based research projects in the eastern Kentucky Appalachian region. She co-edited the book *Confronting Ecological Crisis in Appalachia and the South: University and Community Partnerships.*

Pam Oldfield Meade is a visual artist working in paint and mixed-media and a longtime community arts advocate and organizer living and working on the eastern Kentucky farm her great-grandfather established. Her art is inspired by the stories of people and places around her, memories and dreams, current events, and by the natural world of the Appalachian Mountains. Old Cove Press is publishing a book of her work.

Jeremy Paden is Associate Professor of Spanish and Latin American Literature at Transylvania University in Lexington, Kentucky. He is the author of essays on colonial and contemporary Latin American literature and a poet. His most recent collection of poems is *ruina montium*, a collection of poems on the Chilean mining accident of 2010 and a meditation in verse on environmental disasters.

Shaunna L. Scott is Associate Professor of Sociology and Director of Appalachian Studies at the University of Kentucky. She edits the *Journal of Appalachian Studies*. She is author of the ethnography *Two Sides to Everything: The Cultural Construction of Class Consciousness in Harlan County, Kentucky* and coeditor of *Studying Appalachian Studies: Making the Path by Walking*, winner of the 2016 Weatherford Award.

References

Agnew, John. 1987. *Place and Politics: The Geographical Mediation of State and Society.* London: Allen and Unwin.

Alexander, David. 2010. "The L'Aquila Earthquake of 6 April 2009 and Italian Government Policy on Disaster Response." *Journal of Natural Resources Policy Research* 2 (4): 325–342.

Antonini, Orlando. 2010. *I terremoti aquilani.* Todi, Italy: Tau.

Blake, Megan. 2007. "Formality and Friendship: Research Ethics Review and Participatory Action Research." *ACME: An International E-Journal for Critical Geographies* 6 (3): 411–421.

Burbules, N., and R. Berk. 1999. "Critical Thinking and Critical Pedagogy: Relations, Differences, and Limits." In *Critical Theories in Education*, edited by Thomas S. Popkewitz and Lynn Fendler. New York: Routledge. http://faculty.education.illinois.edu/burbules/papers/critical.html.

Cahill, Caitlin. 2007. "Repositioning Ethical Commitments: Participatory Action Research as a Relational Praxis of Social Change." *ACME: An International E-Journal for Critical Geographies* 6 (3): 360–373.

Calandra, Lina. 2012a. "Per una geografia sociale dell'Aquila post-sisma: Comunicazione visuale e nuove forme di democrazia." In *Geografia sociale e democrazia: La sfida della comunicazione*, edited by Claudio Cerreti, Isabelle Dumont, and Tabusi Massimiliano, 287–311. Rome: Aracne.

Calandra, Lina. 2012b. *Territorio e democrazia: Un laboratorio di geografia sociale nel doposisma aquilano.* L'Aquila, Italy: L'Una.

Chatterton, Paul, and Larch Maxey. 2009. "Introduction: Whatever Happened to Ethics and Responsibility in Geography?" *ACME: An International E-Journal for Critical Geographies* 8 (2): 1–11.

Clementi, Alessandro, and Elio Piroddi. 1986. *L'Aquila.* Bari, Italy: Laterza.

Cloke, Paul, Phil Cooke, Jerry Cursons, Paul Milbourne, and Rebekah Widdowfield. 2000. "Ethics, Reflexivity and Research: Encounters with Homeless People." *Ethics, Place and Environment* 3 (2): 133–154.

Crampton, Jeremy. 2001. "Maps as Social Constructions: Power, Communication and Visualization." *Progress in Human Geography* 25 (2): 235–252.

Cutchin, Malcolm. 2002. "Ethics and Geography: Continuity and Emerging Syntheses." *Progress in Human Geography* 26 (5): 656–664.

Dodge, Martin, Mary McDerby, and Martin Turner. 2008. *Geographic Visualization: Concepts, Tools and Applications.* New York: John Wiley & Sons.

Elias, Marlène. 2006. "'Practicing' Geography: Reflections on an Uncommon Encounter between Research and Practice." *Research and Practice in Social Sciences* 1 (2): 156–167.

Erikson, Kai. 1994. *A New Species of Trouble: The Human Experience of Modern Disasters.* New York: W.W. Norton.

Freire, Paulo. 1970. *Pedagogy of the Oppressed.* New York: Seabury Press.

Fuller, Duncan, and Rob Kitchin. 2004. "Radical Theory, Critical Praxis: Making a Difference beyond the Academy?" In *Radical Theory, Critical Praxis: Making a Difference Beyond the Academy,* edited by Fuller and Kitchen, 1–20. E edition. Vernon and Victoria, BC: Praxis.

Funtowicz, Silvio, and Jerome Ravetz. 1990. *Uncertainty and Quality in Science for Policy.* Alphen an den Rinj, The Netherlands: Kluwer Academic.

———. 1993. "Science for the Post-Normal Age." *Futures* 25: 735–755.

Giroux, Henry A.1988. *Teachers as Intellectuals: Toward a Critical Pedagogy of Learning.* South Hadley, Massachusetts: Bergin & Garvey.

Harvey, David. 1975. *Social Justice and the City.* Baltimore: Johns Hopkins University Press.

———. 1996. *Justice, Nature and the Geography of Difference.* Oxford: Blackwell.

———. 2000. *Spaces of Hope.* Berkeley: University of California Press.

Jouve, Bernard, and Philip Booth. 2004. *Démocraties métropolitaines.* Sainte-Foy: Presses de l'Université du Québec.

Kemmis, Stephen, and Robin McTaggart. 2000. "Participatory Action Research." In *Handbook of Qualitative Research,* edited by N. K. Denzin and Y. Lincoln, 567–605. Thousand Oaks, CA: Sage.

Kemmis, Stephen, and Robin McTaggart. 2005. "Participatory Action Research: Communicative Action and the Public Sphere." *Handbook of Qualitative Research,* edited by Denzin and Lincoln, 559–603. Thousand Oaks, CA: Sage.

Lather, Patti. 1986. "Issues of Validity in Openly Ideological Research: Between a Rock and Soft Place." *Interchange* 17 (4): 63–84.

Laurin, Suzanne, Juan-Luis Klein, and Carole Tardif, eds. 2001. *Géographie et société: vers une géographie citoyenne.* Sainte-Foy: Presses de l'Université du Québec.

Lourde, Audre. 1984. "The Master's Tools Will Never Dismantle the Master's House." In *Sister Outsider*, 110–113. Berkeley, CA: Crossing.

MacEachren, Alan, B. Buttenfield, J. Campbell, D. DiBiase, and M. Monmonier. 1992. "Visualization." In *Geography's Inner Worlds: Pervasive Themes in Contemporary American Geography*, edited by Ronald E. Abler, Melvin G. Marcus, and Judy M. Olson, 99–137. New Brunswick, NJ: Rutgers University Press.

Matthey, Laurent. 2005. "Éthique, politique et esthétique du terrain: cinq figures de l'entretien compréhensif." *Cybergeo: European Journal of Geography*. http://cybergeo .revues.org/3426.

McSpirit, Stephanie. 2002. "The Martin County Project: Researching Issues and Building Civic Capacity after an Environmental Disaster." Flex-E-Grant Program, Appalachian Regional Commission. Richmond, Kentucky: Eastern Kentucky University. Accessed September 10, 2017, http://martincounty.eku.edu/sites/mar-tincounty.eku.edu/files/Martin_County_Project_Final_Report.pdf.

Morgan, David. 2007. "Paradigms Lost and Pragmatism Regained: Methodological Implications of Combining Qualitative and Quantitative Methods." *Journal of Mixed Methods Research* 1: 48–76.

Pain, Rachel. 2004. "Social Geography: Participatory, Research, Progress." *Human Geography* 28 (5): 652–663.

Polelle, Mark. 1999. *Raising Cartographic Consciousness: The Social and Foreign Policy Vision of Geopolitics in the Twentieth Century*. Lanham, MD: Lexington.

Ravetz, Jerome. 2006. "Post-Normal Science and the Complexity of Transitions towards Sustainability." *Ecological Complexity* 3: 275–284.

———. 2012. "The Significance of the Hamburg Workshop: Post-Normal Science and the Maturing of Science." *Nature & Culture* 7 (2): 133–150.

Ravetz, Jerome, and Silvio Funtowicz. 1994. "Uncertainty, Complexity and Post-Normal Science." *Environmental Toxicology & Chemistry* 13 (12): 1881.

Reason, Peter, and Bradbury, Hilary, eds. 2001. *Handbook of Action Research: Participative Inquiry and Practice*. London: Sage.

Schrag, Calvin. 1986. *Communicative Praxis and the Space of Subjectivity*. Bloomington: Indiana University Press.

Schrag, Calvin, and Eric Ramsey. 1994. "Method and Phenomenological Research: Humility and Commitment in Interpretation." *Human Studies* 17 (1): 131–137.

Stockel, Giorgio. 1988. *La città dell'Aquila: Il centro storico tra il 1860 e il 1960*. L'Aquila, Italy: Gallo Cedrone.

Tuan, Yi-Fu. 1977. *Space and Place: The Perspective of Experience*. Minneapolis: University of Minnesota Press.

van Asselt, Marjolein. 2000. *Perspectives on Uncertainty and Risk: The Prima Approach to Decision Support*. Dordrecht, The Netherlands: Kluwer Academic.

van Asselt, Marjolein, and Nicole Rijkens-Klomp. 2002. "A Look in the Mirror: Reflection on Participation in Integrated Assessment from a Methodological Perspective." *Global Environmental Change* 12: 167–184.

The Border Line

Si Kahn

For weeks we hid in ditches
For weeks we crawled through fields
For weeks we hid by day and ran by night
We sweated up the mountains
We shivered through the swamps
'Til finally the border came in sight

Across the bloody border
Along the barbed wire fence
The searchlights on the tower turn and shine
Are you keeping freedom in?
Are you keeping freedom out?
With your guns and dogs along the border line

Lying in the bushes my daughter by my side
I watched the searchlights flashing off the guns
Do I tell her to go back when there's nothing left behind?
Do I tell her to close her eyes and run?

Across the bloody border
Along the barbed wire fence
The searchlights on the tower turn and shine
Are you keeping freedom in?
Are you keeping freedom out?
With your guns and dogs along the border line

Now tell me
Who makes the borders?
Who draws the maps?
Who strings barbed wire through the land?
Who buys the bullets?
Who pays the guards?
Who puts the rifles in their hands?

Across the bloody border
Along the barbed wire fence
The searchlights on the tower turn and shine
Are you keeping freedom in?
Are you keeping freedom out?
With your guns and dogs along the border line
With your guns and dogs along the border line

CHAPTER 9

Moving Heaven and Earth behind Mountains

EVERYDAY LIFE FOR DISPLACED MIGRANTS ON THE HAITIAN SIDE OF THE HAITIAN-DOMINICAN BORDER

Daniel Joseph

IN 2015, THOUSANDS of Dominicans of Haitian descent and undocumented Haitian migrants were forced out of the Dominican Republic after the Dominican constitutional court upheld a 2010 constitutional amendment that revoked birthright citizenship from children of undocumented Haitians (Hazel 2014) who had entered the country illegally since 1929 (Andreopoulos and Arat 2014). About 2,203 of these forced migrants arrived in the mountainous border region of Anse-à-Pitres, Haiti, during June to July 2015 where they took up residence in six camps: Parc Cadeau 1 and 2, Tête-à-l'Eau, Fond-Jeanette, Maletchipe, and Savanne Galata (GARR et al. 2016). One year after their arrival, the International Organization for Migration (IOM) relocated about 250 of them into the center of the town Anse-à-Pitres, while the majority continued to live in the camps. This chapter examines how these forced migrants, under precarious conditions, make a living in Anse-à-Pitres—a place previously unknown to most of them.

I arrived in Anse-à-Pitres in early September 2016, exactly one year after the influx of forced migrants to the area, to conduct fieldwork for my doctoral dissertation in anthropology. As a Haitian from the other end of the country,

I was unfamiliar with this city on the border of the Dominican Republic, with the mountainous physical environment, and with the local political institutions and the people; only the shared tropical climate and national identity were familiar to me. Before going to Anse-à-Pitres, I did not know anybody except a worker with the Service Jésuite aux Migrants (SJM), or Jesuit Refugee Service, I had met in Port-au-Prince who works in the area. The SJM helped me enormously in establishing my networks in the area. Serving as a volunteer for this organization put me in contact with the community of forced migrants. I traveled between the city and its rural areas to meet migrants in different places such as the marketplace, the camps, churches, and in private meetings held by the SJM where I did participant observation and took part in activities such as focus groups and orientations organized by the SJM. I went weekly to the camps of Parc Cadeau 1 and 2, Tête-a-l'eau, Fonds-Jeanette and Maletchipe to meet with people. About 250 migrants had been relocated by the IOM in the center of Anse-à-Pitres. I visited the homes of these migrants weekly as well. They founded an organization called ODRA (Organisation pour la Défense des Rappatriées de l'Anse-à-Pitres, or Organization in Support of those Repatriated to Anse-à-Pitres). I participated in an ODRA meeting held every Sunday afternoon. Informal conversations with migrants and formal interviews with long-term residents in the area helped me get a sense of people's way of life in Anse-à-Pitres.

Anse-à-Pitres before and after the Arrival of the Migrants

Anse-à-Pitres is located in the southeast department of Haiti. Anse-à-Pitres has an area of 185.19 square kilometers and a population of about 23,500, as of the 2005 census (Mairie de Anse-à-Pitres 2008). The city itself (downtown) is only 3 square kilometers. Like Ouanaminthe, Belladère, and Fonds-Parisien, Anse-à-Pitres is one of the official crossing points, on land, to the Dominican Republic. Anse-à-Pitres and its Dominican sister city Pedernales are separated by the Pedernales River. The province of Pedernales is about ten times larger than Anse-à-Pitres. People cross a small bridge every Monday and Friday to go to the binational market between the two cities. Wooding and Williams (2004, 55) have documented this weekly movement of Haitian border residents to Dominican markets: thousands of people cross the bridge on the Massacre River between the two countries every Friday and Monday to buy and sell goods in the Dajabon Market in the Dominican Republic. From the mountains in Anse-à-Pitres, one has an almost complete view of Pedernales and its peripheral areas. On the Dominican side, there is Pedernales, where the infrastructure is in good condition and there are fairly decentralized state services. On the Haitian side, Anse-à-Pitres remains isolated from Port-au-Prince, the capital city, because the roads are in bad condition. The population has poor access to electricity and public services. People are directed towards Jacmel, Port-au-Prince, for professional education and for important state services such as issuance of a passport. They are even directed toward Pedernales—outside Haiti—for markets and healthcare services. This is typical of Haiti, where residents of rural areas are forgotten in comparison to those in the capital where the government often concentrates its activities (Mazzeo and Chierici 2013). The condition of infrastructure in Anse-à-Pitres exemplifies the marginal presence of the state in the most remote areas of the country (Schwartz 2009). For example, Mirta—a woman who recently gave birth—makes weekly trips to Pedernales to buy milk for her newborn. While residents of Anse-à-Pitres go to Pedernales for basic services, Dominicans go to Anse-à-Pitres to have a drink or participate in cockfighting. Considered simply as *gwògman* (drinkers), they are allowed through the entry gate even without an identity document.

It is generally said that Haiti is an agricultural country. As such, a great percentage of Haitians in the rural areas dedicate themselves to agricultural activities. However, there are no large-scale agricultural enterprises in Anse-à-Pitres because only 17 percent of the town's mountains and plateaus are humid, allowing residents to produce vegetables and coffee. The rest of the mountains and plateaus in the area are too dry for agriculture. Therefore, the local economy is predominantly based on fishing, commerce, and moto taxi. Commercial activities consist mostly of exchange, including the export of seafood and import of staple foods and second-hand clothes from the Dominican Republic, for which Haiti is the second largest trading partner after the United States (Pauyo 2011). Other industries, in the informal sector, are gambling and cockfighting. These activities attract many Dominicans over the border. With regard to leisure, Anse-à-Pitres is a noisy city with DJs playing music in public areas every day. The music stops around midnight. There is a real cacophony, with bars playing different songs simultaneously. These bars attract many people on weekends—mainly Haitians and a few Dominicans.

The arrival of forced migrants in the summer of 2015 has not been without consequences for the life of the city—especially social and economic changes. The forced migrants have not dramatically changed, reinforced, or increased the scale of agricultural production in Anse-à-Pitres, but over time they have contributed to the local economy. Many forced migrants were or still are agricultural workers in the Dominican Republic. In Anse-à-Pitres, they continue to support the productive force of the Dominican economy. From Anse-à-Pitres, they continue to cross the border secretly and illegally to the Dominican Republic to work the land through agreements with Dominican landowners. According to Lauren Derby (1994, 516), Haitians' labor has produced most of the agricultural goods circulating in the Dominican border provinces. This cannot be good news for the local economy in Anse-à-Pitres, which suffers from a lack of productivity; most migrants say that while they are in the Dominican Republic, they buy their items there once they are paid or sell their products there. This means that little of their money comes to Anse-à-Pitres. Therefore, their economic contribution to the city is very low.

Physically and socially, the migrants do have an impact on the community of Anse-à-Pitres. They have changed its demographics. Even though many migrants have left the city and have been relocated somewhere else since their arrival in 2015, their presence in the camps and in the sites of food distribution cannot go unnoticed. Natives of Anse-à-Pitres are already complaining about the forced migrants, maintaining that they are increasing insecurity in the area and projecting a bad image of the city. Even though certain permanent residents look unfavorably on the forced migrants, the migrants are not proving to be very "invasive" in the city. They are living completely on the margins of the community of Anse-à-Pitres. They form their own enclave, separate from the permanent residents of the city. The fact that most migrants are not from Anse-à-Pitres may explain this. The formation of an enclave of forced migrants does not encourage integration into the larger community of Anse-à-Pitres.

The Settlement of Forced Migrants in the Area

Most migrants in Anse-à-Pitres come from places such as Belle-Anse, Marigot (Jacmel), and Thiotte. This makes the camps look like a multicultural setting. For the most part, the migrants arrived in 2015 and have spread throughout the area, into places such as Fond-Jeanette, Bois d'Ormes, Tête Source, Tête-à-l'Eau, and downtown Anse-à-Pitres. Migrant camps are found in Parc Cadeau, Maletchipe, Tête Source, Tête-à-l'Eau, and Fond-Jeanette, which only has a few resident families remaining. When I arrived in Anse-à-Pitres, many migrants had already left the camps. This changed the physical structure of the camps. The IOM conducted a census of migrants' houses for a relocation program. Many migrants I talked to in Parc-Cadeau, for example, expressed their disappointment about the program, maintaining that they missed the opportunity to participate in it only because they were at work when IOM representatives came by the camps. In some cases, they reported that fellow migrants stole the tarpaulin with their assigned number on it and obtain assistance in their name. Through the IOM program, financial aid was given to the select migrants to relocate to a place of their choice. Some migrants chose to go to their home communities in Haiti. Others, especially Dominicans of Haitian descent who do not have considerable ties in Haiti, returned to the Dominican Republic. Still, many forced migrants—more than 200—stayed in Anse-à-Pitres and have been relocated downtown.

Why did they choose to relocate in Anse-à-Pitres when they were not from this area? Anse-à-Pitres is considered a relatively safe choice for them. Many migrants asserted that there is nothing to live on in their place of origin. Therefore, they stay in Anse-à-Pitres because there is a seemingly more vibrant economic life on the border, with access to the binational market and easier access to Pedernales in the Dominican Republic. They believe that they can more easily cross the border to go to work in the Dominican Republic, despite the mistreatment of Haitians there.

Economic reasons, however, do not fully explain the choice to remain in Anse-à-Pitres. There are migrants who maintain that they stayed in Anse-à-Pitres because they do not have money to go back to their place of origin. For other migrants, it is because the last members of their family in their place of origin died; therefore, all their ties to that place have been cut. And even though some family members may still be living, they are ashamed to go back after such a long time because they did not pay a friendly visit to, or stay in touch with, those left behind. For a small group of forced migrants, they chose to relocate in Anse-à-Pitres because they were encouraged to do so by a friend, who ended up influencing their choice. Finally, a large number of migrants believe that they are more likely to get aid from nongovernmental organizations while they are in Anse-à-Pitres than in other places. For example, in Parc Cadeau #2, one of the migrant camps, I met an old woman who is from Thiotte but who relocated to this camp in order to follow the aid apparatus. This is mostly how migrants chose their place of settlement and how Anse-à-Pitres became a primary location for many of them.

Life on the Backside of the Mountains

Forced migrants arrived in Anse-à-Pitres with almost nothing. Everyone I met complained that everything they had stayed behind: for example, their gardens, their homes, and their cattle. When they were in the Dominican Republic, the mountains were their breadbasket. From their work, they could get a little something to feed their children. Here in Anse-à-Pitres, they have no land to work and are abandoned by the state, which still welcomed them saying: "Haiti is ready to stand up straight to receive with dignity its children, our brothers (Alphonse 2015)." Now unable to feed their families, send their children to school, or get legal documents for themselves and their children, they do not know what to do. *Mwen pa gen rele, mwen pa gen reponn* (I have nobody to call, no one to answer me) is one of the many expressions they use to describe their harrowing experience of life in Anse-à-Pitres. This is what I call "mountains behind life"; it is as though they are carrying the mountains on their backs, every day. I have met people who simply say that they have not eaten for one or two days. Their biggest concern is that there is almost nothing they can do in Anse-à-Pitres to generate a small income. According to them, no one will call them for a day of work. If we look at this in a Marxian sense, all they have is their labor power, but it is difficult to convert this labor power into capital (Marx and Engels 1942, 208–209).

The lack of connection with long-term residents in Anse-à-Pitres does not help the forced migrants. It is difficult for them to establish strategic networks in the community that could bring about openings such as cash for work, food sharing, or other forms of mutual assistance. Some of their biggest supports are the SJM, which works to provide them birth certificates and provides some other forms of assistance; the Catholic Church; and the IOM, which gave about

20,000 gourdes (US$300) to some selected migrants to rent a place for one year after they arrived in Anse-à-Pitres. The IOM also promised to furnish their houses and to continue to provide them with economic assistance beyond the rent. However, the relocated migrants lament the extreme poverty in which they are living, in a house sometimes not comfortable at all (with nothing inside—not even a bed on which to sleep). A man I will call Guillaume describes the terrible situation he is experiencing: "I don't have anything. I am sleeping and eating badly. They [the organizations and the state] forget about us. I am sleeping on the floor. Animals are better off than I am, because someone would take care of the animals." As this shows, the situation of the forced migrants is stressful. To their daily stress, we must add the issue of the rent support that will be ending soon. They do not know what they will do after rent support ends. Some are already thinking of returning to the Dominican Republic while others are thinking of going back to the camps where they lived for a while before they had been relocated to the town.

In the camps, the experience of a difficult life is similar. Hunger, slums built from bits of junk, a hot sun, and dust convey an atmosphere of desolation (Sérant 2015) in the camps. I spoke with a young man who must be in his early twenties; he lives in a slum made of pieces of clothes and wood in the camp of Parc Cadeau #2. The way he explained to me how he is living is heart-rending: "I was born in the Dominican Republic and my mother still lives over there. She has papers. When everyone was leaving the Dominican Republic, I followed my neighbors to Parc Cadeau #2. I could stay here in the camp but there is nothing. We are eating the dust. In order to survive, I bought a cup of salt and I suck a grain every morning."

As this young man says, the place is terribly dusty. I was sitting down with a small group of migrants surrounding me. Each time a child passed by, the child's feet raised the dust, making it a dust bowl. The people who were by my side then shouted at the child. Moreover, when you look at the mountains, you only see small trees and big stones. The land in Parc Cadeau is arid and does not seem conducive to agriculture. However, forced migrants never give up in the face of so many difficulties; they look for alternatives.

Making Ends Meet in Anse-à-Pitres, Haiti: An Unsettled and Unsettling Border-Crossing Experience

Forced migrants say clearly that there is nothing they can do in Anse-à-Pitres to make a living. To them, life can be bleak in this border area and their future is completely uncertain. When standing up in the camps in Parc Cadeau and looking at the mountains that dominate the region, at first glance, one notices the aridity of the region. There is no water. If these mountains have to be used for agricultural production, there has to be human intervention. The migrants have already cleared the place, cutting the trees to make charcoal and build their slums. As an alternative to the uncertainty of life in Anse-à-Pitres, forced migrants from Parc Cadeau, Maletchipe, Fond-Jeanette, and Tête-à-l'Eau continue to cross the border on a daily basis to go to work in the Dominican Republic where they constitute the largest and most vulnerable minority population in the country (Matibag and Downing-Matibag 2011).

Crossing the border has become a way of life for forced migrants despite all the complications that go with it. The legal process for crossing the border involves having at least a Haitian passport to go to the sister city of Pedernales. However, the majority of forced migrants do not have any identity documents at all. Still, they find a way to work in the Dominican Republic. They simply avoid the official entry and sometimes find themselves having to negotiate to pay 25 to 50 pesos to soldiers who are watching the unofficial entry points. Because they lack legal documentation, often times, several migrants told me, they cannot go to harvest their gardens in the Dominican Republic. Soldiers can seize their digging tools and machetes, and refuse them access.

Despite humiliation, forced migrants keep on going to the Dominican Republic to earn a living even though they are subject to arbitrary raids on the bateys, communities, and even on the streets (Simmons 2010). Many of them work on Dominican landowners' property and share the harvest with them. They work according to a system of sharecropping that may vary according to landowners; the majority contends that they give one-fifth of the harvest to the owner and keep four-fifths of it. The majority of forced migrants with whom I spoke told me that if they do not go to the Dominican Republic, they and their children will not eat. For instance, a woman I visited in the camp of Tête-à-l'Eau put it clearly: "We have nothing. The little things that some organizations gave us when we arrived here are over. We are turning towards the Dominican Republic for pieces of wood even though Dominicans chase us."

The forced migrants have few options for strategies to generate income in Anse-à-Pitres. The land is not available to them, as most of them are not from the area. The trees are already cut, which means the migrants cannot make charcoal. They maintain that no one would call them in Anse-à-Pitres to pay them to work for a day. For example, after being relocated to downtown Anse-à-Pitres, a man I will call Marcelin said the following: "In order to survive, I go to the priest because my wife has already sold everything they gave us such as kitchen utensils so that we could eat." Another woman who came to register her children for birth certificates said this about her work options: "I have no occupation except bringing children into the world."

Conclusion

From Anse-à-Pitres, one has a view of the mountains and plateaus of the two sides of the border. On the western (Haitian) side, the mountains of Tête-à-l'Eau, Parc Cadeau, or Fonds-Jeannette are not available to forced migrants for making a living. Yet the forced migrants believe that the state could intervene and assign to them pieces of this land and put in place an irrigation system that would allow them to work and make a decent living in Anse-à-Pitres. Despite the aridity of some of these mountains and plateaus, forced migrants say that, with the intervention of the local state, they could cultivate them. On the eastern (Dominican) side, the mountains and plateaus of the province of Pedernales such as Mencia, Aguas Negras, Altagracia, and Abila can also be seen from Anse-à-Pitres. Forced migrants have already been driven out of these places. However, they still remain their breadbaskets as they do not have any real alternative. As a result, many forced migrants challenge Dominican soldiers' surveillance and take advantage of the porosity of the border to go to work in the Dominican Republic. This porosity was noticed by Martinez (1995), who maintained that historically the border has been porous in another way since, until 1915, the movement of people across the border was not documented. Forced migrants work on the property of Dominican owners with whom they share the crop, to whom they sell their labor, and they make charcoal and collect pieces of wood to sell. They maintain that they do not have such opportunities in Anse-à-Pitres, Haiti, which could at least help them *fè san soti nan wòch*, literally "get blood from stones." It is a usual expression in Haiti used to talk about how people are trying hard to make ends meet where there seems not to be any hope. Through the life experiences of migrants in Anse-à-Pitres, it is possible to really understand the meaning of this expression and why many of them continue to turn toward the mountains on the other side of the border while having their feet in Haitian and Dominican society at the same time.

Acknowledgments

I want to thank the Service Jésuite aux Migrants, the organization with which I am volunteering in Anse-à-Pitres, Haiti, for its support, and the National Science Foundation for a Doctoral Dissertation Research Improvement Grant.

DANIEL JOSEPH is a PhD candidate in anthropology at the University of Kentucky. His research interests include transnationalism, migration, identity, citizenship, social and political exclusion, and the informal economy of the Caribbean region. His current research, supported by a National Science Foundation Doctoral Dissertation Research Improvement Grant, focuses on Dominicans of Haitian origin who were deported by the Dominican Republic and, with other migrants, are now seeking to create livelihoods in the Haitian-Dominican border region.

References

Alphonse, Roberson. 2015. "Martelly: nous recevons nos frères debout dans la dignité." *Haiti le nouvelliste.* June 16. Accessed January 1, 2016. http://lenouvelliste.com/lenouvelliste /article/146187/Martelly-Nous-recevrons-nos-freres-debout-dans-la-dignite.

Andreopoulos, Georges, and Zehra Arat. 2014. *The Uses and Misuses of Human Rights: A Critical Approach to Advocacy.* Basingstoke, Hampshire, England: Palgrave Macmillan.

Derby, Lauren. 1994. "Haitians, Magic and Money: *Raza* and Society in Haitian–Dominican Borderlands, 1900–1937." *Comparative Studies in Society and History,* no. 36, 488–526.

GARR (Groupe d'Appui auz Repatrier et Refugees) et al. 2016. *Human Rights Situation of Families in the Anse-à-Citres Camps.* Investigative Report of Human Rights Organizations. January 3. http://www.ijdh.org/wp-content/uploads/2016/04/GARR-Report-Anse-a-Pitres-2016-ENG.pdf.

Hazel, Yadira Perez. 2014. "Sensing Difference: Whiteness, National Identity, and Belonging in the Dominican Republic." *Transforming Anthropology* 22 (2): 78–91.

Mairie de Anse-à-Pitres. 2008. *Projet de renforcement de la gouvernance locale: schema d'aménagement urbain.* IDCO, PADF, MICT, Port-au-Prince, Haiti.

Martinez, Samuel. 1995. *Peripheral Migrants: Haitians and Dominican Republic Sugar Plantations.* Knoxville: University of Tennessee.

Marx, K., and F. Engels (1942). *Wage-Labour and Capital.* Melbourne: Workers' Literature Bureau.

Matibag, Eugenio, and Teresa Downing-Matibag. 2011. "Sovereignty and Social Justice: The 'Haitian Problem' in the Dominican Republic." *Caribbean Quarterly* 57 (2): 92–117.

Mazzeo, John, and Rose-Marie Chierici. 2013. "Social Foundations for a Community-Based Public Health Cholera Campaign in Borgne, Haiti." *Human Organization* 72 (4): 312–322.

Pauyo, Nicolas. 2011. *Haiti: Re-foundation of a Nation.* AuthorHouse.

Schwartz, Timothy T. 2009. *Fewer Men, More Babies: Sex, Family, and Fertility in Haiti.* Lanham, MD: Lexington.

Simmons, David. 2010. "Structural Violence as Social Practice: Haitian Agricultural Workers, Anti-Haitianism, and Health in the Dominican Republic." *Human Organization* 69 (1): 10–18.

Wooding, Bridget, and Richard David Williams. 2004. *Needed but Unwanted: Haitian Immigrants and Their Descendants in the Dominican Republic.* London: Catholic Institute for International Relations.

Black Gold

Si Kahn

You read in all the history books
The same old story told
How us poor miners all got rich
Digging that old black gold
But you know the company got the gold
You know the miners' lungs got black
You know the company got the gold
You know the miners' lungs got black

I went to Detroit city
To see about a job
They said I'd make good money
Working on the loading dock
But you know the boss was always loaded
You know the boys was always docked
You know the boss was always loaded
You know the boys was always docked

The politicians come around
Wearing a big stuffed shirt
We send them off to Washington
And they vote for "right to work"
That means the company's always right
That means the miners do all the work
That means the company's always right
That means the miners do all the work

You can talk about democracy
Well, I just have to laugh
I know I'm gonna end my days
Down in this old coal shaft
But you know the company gets the coal
You know the miner gets the shaft
You know the company gets the coal
You know the miner gets the shaft

CHAPTER 10

Environment, Health, and Justice

TRACING THE CONNECTIONS IN
GLOBAL MOUNTAIN REGIONS

Mary K. Anglin, Gregory V. Button,
and Dolores Molina-Rosales

WRITING IN THE aftermath of apartheid's dissolution and with the ascendance of the African National Congress as South Africa's ruling party, H. K. Heggenhougen (1995) warned against complacency elsewhere in the world, particularly within the Global North, where ongoing practices of marginalization and exploitation constitute a kind of functional apartheid. As Heggenhougen (1995, 281) observed in his editorial for the journal *Social Science and Medicine*, "The epidemiology resulting from the direct and 'hidden' human rights abuses of functional apartheid point to a worldwide epidemic of pandemic proportions—to incredible human suffering and needless death." The task for an ethically engaged medical anthropology, he argued, was to investigate the economic, political, and historical factors fostering social inequalities and disparities in health—as first steps in their dismantling and towards the restoration of human rights.

Heggenhougen's call resonates with more recent work exploring the relationship between late twentieth- and twenty-first century capitalisms and articulations of a "global color line" (Marable and Agard-Jones 2008; Harrison 2008; Mullings 2005); approaches that consider global configurations of gender in conjunction with "shifting demarcations of class, race, color, ethnicity, case, age, and regional location, and the heightened marginality these confer" (Gunewardena and Kingsolver 2007, 10; Hankivsky et al. 2010); and an activist turn in anthropology that situates well-being and health as matters of social justice (Briggs and Mantini-Briggs 2003; Farmer 2006; Lane et al. 2004; Nguyen and Peschard 2003; Rylko-Bauer, Whiteford, and Farmer 2009; Sargent and Larchanché 2011; Schulz and Mullings 2006; Susser 2009). This chapter continues in that vein by examining connections between current economic policies, specific practices of environmental degradation (and, at times, remediation), and the positioning of particular constituencies directly in harm's way.

Our approach to disparities in health thus draws on the framework of environmental justice to highlight the disproportionate burdens of environmental contamination and health risks borne by low income, racial and ethnic minority, and indigenous communities. At the same time, an environmental justice framework emphasizes the potential of grassroots efforts for achieving social justice and, as a consequence, of accruing greater knowledge about specific aspects of discrimination (Brulle and Pellow 2006; Bullard et al. 2007; Checker 2005; EJRC 1991; Mohai, Pellow, and Roberts 2009; Singer 2009; Weber and Messias 2012; Wilson 2010). We are likewise influenced by "social determinants of health" perspectives that investigate multiple pathways in the production of health and disease, while addressing the specific means through which vulnerable populations come to "embody inequality" and experience "incredible human suffering" (Krieger 2001; Krieger and Davey Smith 2004; Levins and Lewontin 1985; Susser and Susser 1996).

In the spirit of the conversation initiated at the Global Mountain Regions Conference in October 2012, the following sections provide our individual voices and interests in the areas of environment (Gregory Button), health (Dolores Molina-Rosales) and environmental in/justice (Mary Anglin). Gregory Button and Mary Anglin describe environmental problems—at times, outright crises—transpiring in different regions within Appalachia from the vantage points of federal policy and grassroots activism, respectively. Dolores Molina-Rosales draws upon her prior research with indigenous women in Chiapas, Mexico, to consider broader questions about access to health care.

Environment—Disastrous Effects of the Coal Industry in Appalachia

> They are doing to us what they are doing to the mountains.
> —Marie Gunnoe[1]

On February 11, 1994, William Jefferson Clinton, President of the United States), issued Executive Order 12898 establishing environmental justice as a national priority. The executive order directed federal attention to racial minorities and low-income individuals, populations known to bear a disproportionate risk of living near, and thereby being exposed to, hazardous waste and other environmental pollutants. In issuing this executive order, President Clinton was assuring that all communities in the United States would have the right to a safe and healthy environment. The impetus for this order came from a growing body of literature on environmental justice research (Bullard 1990; United Church of Christ 1987; US General Accounting Office 1983) documenting disturbing environmental inequities.

When it comes to economic justice, perhaps no region of the United States has been more overlooked than Appalachia. Despite mid-century "War on Poverty" efforts like Robert Kennedy's 1968 tour of the region in which he held hearings in Kentucky on hunger and poverty, the inequities experienced by residents of Appalachia have not featured strongly in the nation's consciousness. Over the past several decades, however, a series of tragic events has at least temporarily seized the nation's attention. One of those was the Buffalo Creek flood in 1972, the result of the sudden rupture of the Pittston Coal Company's slurry impoundments at the site. Over 125 people were killed and some 4,000 people were displaced by this event (Erikson 1978). National attention returned temporarily to the region's environmental hazards in 2000 when a Massey Energy coal slurry impoundment pond burst, releasing 306 million gallons of toxic sludge into two tributaries of the Tug River and contaminating the water of 27,000 residents (McSpirit et al. 2007). This region was in the national news again in 2008 when the Tennessee Valley Authority's Kingston coal plant's coal ash impoundment imploded, spewing 1.1 billion gallons of coal ash over 300 hundred acres and into the Emory and Clinch Rivers and damaging nearby homes (Button 2010). In 2010, the explosion in Massey Energy's Upper Branch Coal Mine in West Virginia left 29 miners dead. A federal investigation concluded that the disaster occurred because of flagrant safety violations (Tavernise 2011). While these dramatic events have helped underscore the environmental hazards in the region, there have been scores of similar human-caused disasters over the past century and more.

Today, most of the severely economically distressed regions in Appalachia are in areas where mountaintop removal mining is occurring (Hendryx, Fredorko, and Anesetti-Rothermel 2010). As of 2017, it is estimated that this extractive process has destroyed over 500 mountaintops in Central Appalachia (see ilovemountains.org). Increasingly robust campaigns by regional environmental organizations including the Ohio Valley Environmental Coalition, Appalachian Voices, Kentuckians for the Commonwealth, and Coal River Mountain Watch, along with numerous others, have helped bring great attention to the continuing harm to communities and the environment in the region caused by this practice. The Sierra Club and many other environmental organizations, including those mentioned above, have called for accountability to Clinton's executive order on environmental justice by the US Environmental Protection Agency (EPA) and those under its jurisdiction.

The ruinous practice of mountaintop removal mining (MTR) has long brought attention to environmental damage, but in recent years harm to human health has become an increasing source of concern for those in and beyond the region. There are a growing number of studies that document and support long-standing claims by residents. David Holzman (2011), for example, published an informative overview of some of the harmful effects of MTR. In one study, Ahern et al. (2011) found significantly higher birth defect rates in MTR areas, increasing with the prevalence of the mining practice. Another study published in the *Journal of Community Health* (Hendryx et al. 2012) claimed that cancer rates were twice as high in communities exposed to MTR compared to communities where MTR was not practiced. These studies have, of course, been challenged aggressively by the mining industry in the United States. The body of literature documenting the negative health effects of mountain top removal mining continues to grow, however, and many researchers call for recognition of the strong links between economic, health, and environmental disparities in Appalachia (Hendryx 2013).

Similar warnings about high cancer rates and birth defects emerged in the early 1980s in the controversy surrounding toxic waste disposal in Love Canal, New York. Unfortunately, the health establishment ignored these early warnings and warnings in other communities for an inexcusably long period of time (Button 2010). We cannot afford to ignore sobering warnings about the negative health effects experienced by those displaced by and living with mountain top removal mining.

Health—Marginalization and Health Inequalities: "A Space of Vulnerability" among Women in the Chiapas Highlands

In 1995, participants in the United Nations' Fourth World Conference on Women, in Beijing concluded that inequality—in all its forms—is the major barrier to women having access to adequate health care. In Mexico, over 20 years later, poor or indigenous women still deal with inequitable access to care.

The availability of health services in the Chiapas Highlands varies according to where the sick person lives and the person's economic situation. In urban areas, many have access to employment-related health insurance, and they can go to private or state clinics to use those benefits. Urban residents without steady jobs can go to public clinics where the payment is minimal. In rural and marginal areas, people have free access to health care centers, which may be attended sometimes by a doctor, by a nurse, or by local people who have received first aid training and can prescribe some medications. The centers, however, do not have an operating room. In cases of serious illness or complications, patients must take an ambulance, if available, to the regional hospital.

People living in rural areas, then, must often travel to the closest urban center to address their health problems. Patients usually leave the town accompanied by a family member. They need to use their own money for transportation and for lodging and meals in the city. Dealing with an emergency can be very complicated because someone with access to a vehicle needs to be found at the time that the emergency arises. This can be difficult—when, for example, the emergency occurs in the middle of the night. Moreover, patients who are living in the mountains have to travel on twisty roads, which can be both uncomfortable and dangerous.

In highland Chiapas, it is common to consult practitioners in both the traditional Mayan and the allopathic biomedical health systems. Patients may go to local healers like midwives, people who give massages or herbs, or those who help the sick with prayers or through following the pulse as a diagnostic process (Hatala and Waldram 2017). Sometimes, when the patient or the patient's family believes that the health problem cannot be addressed adequately through these means, they may seek alternative care in regional or urban biomedical clinics.

In Chiapas, 26 percent of childbirths are attended by midwives (Berrío Palomo 2015). However, when a complication arises, it may be the same midwife who suggests moving the patient to a clinic. But in emergencies the decision about when to leave the village may depend on relatives of the woman in labor. Power dynamics in the household, then, may constitute another of the obstacles to women's access to adequate care, not only the lack of adequate medical infrastructure or bad road conditions.

I have documented some of these health access issues experienced by women in the Chiapas Mountains. The women who shared their stories with me were living in marginal conditions. They identified ethnically as *ladino,* Tzeltal, or Tzotzil. This region has one of the highest rates of maternal mortality in Mexico. When I started this research, as a Mexican scholar with long-term ties in indigenous communities I was part of the Committee for Risk-Free and Voluntary Motherhood. Many physicians in regional clinics had said that women from the marginalized areas were too "ignorant" to seek prenatal care and to arrive at the hospital early enough during pregnancy crises for effective clinical intervention. So I designed a study focusing on marginalized women's perspectives on why they prefer a particular kind of care during their deliveries, since some women use both the traditional Mayan health system and the allopathic one.

In that study, I learned that women who preferred to have their births at home did not identify any risk with home birth; instead, they saw it as the normal and expected means of delivery. By contrast, women who chose to give birth in the hospital often felt stigmatized. According to interviews with these women and their relatives, regardless of the circumstances, the decision to go to the hospital was seen as proof that the woman was not strong enough to deliver her child at home. They related that childbirth was considered an event requiring strength to live through what they could expect to be a painful experience. That may contribute to a family's decision to avoid transferring a woman to the hospital, even if the midwife has signaled that the birth has turned into a medical crisis for the woman. There are several factors, explained earlier, compromising the woman's autonomy in making decisions in this situation—she cannot, for example, simply pick up the telephone and call for an ambulance.

During childbirth, traditional medical practices, cultural views, gender roles, and socioeconomic status can shape the mother's and her family's evaluation of risk during delivery. How risk is perceived by marginalized women and their families in highland Chiapas may determine the time it takes to decide to seek allopathic medical attention, and that, in turn, can affect the doctor's options and the clinic's "success rate," which may in turn have consequences for the clinic. Problems of health and disease must be interpreted in terms of local realities, not simply through a biomedical framework. Economic and social marginalization, environmental conditions, lack of local access to emergency obstetric services, and social and gender inequalities combine to make women more vulnerable when coping with circumstances that are already complicated or dangerous.

The situation of women in the Chiapas Highlands exemplifies how local-level realities are shaped by environmental contexts and social inequalities, but above all demonstrates what some authors call a "space of vulnerability," which combines "1) the risk of exposure to stress; 2) the risk of inadequate capacities to cope; and 3) the risk of severe consequences from stress, crisis and shocks" (Leatherman 2005, 51). In this case, in the mountains of Chiapas, a woman's delay in seeking emergency treatment during a complicated delivery can mean her death.

Inequalities in health are related to other forms of inequity. Policy makers and public administrators in Mexico need to work on improving local infrastructure as well as the availability of health care resources for everyone, including those who live in rural and economically marginalized areas. Equitable processes need to be a goal, not only in the public sphere, but also within family contexts, to promote women's well-being.

Justice—Local Histories of a Global Struggle: Examples from the Blue Ridge Mountains

A defining and oft-cited moment in the US environmental justice movement was the protracted struggle (1978–2003) of Warren County, North Carolina, residents against a rural landfill poorly equipped to contain polychlorinated biphenyl or PCB (NC PCB Archives, n.d.; Bullard 1990). Those efforts addressed not just the activities of corporate polluters who had dumped the hazardous chemicals along country roads rather than comply with environmental guidelines, but equally state and federal policies that prioritized a "quick fix" approach to environmental problems over democratic practice or the well-being of low income and minority communities. More than a decade after the initial Warren County protests, the first People of Color Environmental Leadership Summit met in Washington, DC, to discuss the experiences of US grassroots environmental organizations and minority communities in developing a globally focused, broad-based approach. The principles of environmental justice formulated during the 1991 summit comprise "a multi-dimensional social justice framework for capacity-building, political mobilization, policy development, and environmental reform" (Wilson 2010, 21–22). Their influence, I contend, is still at work today.

For example, the espousal of "political, economic, cultural, and environmental self-determination" in Environmental Justice (EJ) Principle 5 offers a means to examine environmental injustices in places like Appalachia, where such problems derive from state or national economic priorities and their implications for local land use. The net results are, of course, experienced as profitability on the part of corporate and governmental stakeholders—albeit with decreased quality of life or poor health for workers and surrounding communities (EJRC 1991). In what follows, I describe two examples from the late twentieth- and early twenty-first centuries to talk about the conjoining of economic factors with environmental and health concerns, and local histories of struggle in the Blue Ridge Mountains of North Carolina.

As with Warren County's PCB landfill, efforts in the late 1970s and 80s to site hazardous waste incineration in or along the western Carolina mountains (Mitchell and Caldwell Counties, respectively) hinged upon their near invisibility to the state's largely urban population and the clout of a government bent on promoting a lucrative, if toxic, industry. Thus, complaints by residents and workers in Mitchell County about odors and 50-foot flames emanating from the incinerator's smokestacks and chemical compounds discharged into streams led to inspection and citations from the North Carolina Department of Natural Resources and Community Development but little else.[2] Crops failed and wildlife deserted the regions near the facility; workers watched safety equipment melt on contact with the toxic soup they were forced to handle daily and voiced concerns about their increased risk of cancer as well as other health problems.[3] At the same time, the owner of this facility was appointed by Governor James G. Martin to head a committee overseeing the containment of hazardous waste statewide.

What changed this situation from one in which the incinerators operated with near impunity to their sudden closure in the late 1980s was the emergence of grassroots activism: the forming of a chapter of the Western North Carolina Alliance (WNCA) in Mitchell County and, later, the Caldwell County Citizens for a Clean Environment (4CE).[4] As one journalist reported, "Without the steadily building local pressure and the increasing litany of evidence, the state would probably have issued a compromise permit that left the economic health of Mitchell Systems intact and the community's safety permanently at risk" (Buchanan 1988, 89). And the precedent set in Mitchell County paved the way for the successful campaigns of 4CE.

The Mitchell County chapter no longer exists, and the Western North Carolina Alliance has become part of a larger coalition, Mountain True. In place of the Mitchell County Chapter is another locally focused grassroots group, the

Toe River Valley Watershed Partnership, which, along with state and regional organizations, has championed a range of environmental concerns. Still, the millennium's defining issue has been county and state budget deficits, as well as the swelling ranks of the unemployed and their impact on the viability of households and communities.

Accordingly, the multinational corporations that mine and process minerals in western North Carolina for a global market, including the computer industry, operate with little oversight or expectations of accountability. For example, a suspicious fire that burned one industrial plant to the ground in 2008—with the night watchman unexpectedly absent—necessitated the evacuation of neighboring communities but resulted in only a two-day investigation by the North Carolina Bureau of Investigation and the Federal Bureau of Alcohol, Tobacco, Firearms, and Explosives (Brown 2008). Greater attention was given the unemployment of workers during the rebuilding of that facility, whose smokestacks now reach as high as the ridges nearby, but no information was ever provided about the chemicals or particulate matter released through the fire (Brown 2008; Wachter 2008).

How do we compare this incident with the prior effort to rid the county of a hazardous waste facility? Is it possible to address "externalized costs of production"—for example, the blasting of ridges to remove (and later process) commercially valued minerals, with harm to local ecologies and human health—in a region long tied to extractive industry (Epstein et al. 2011; Reid 2009)? What roles should activists (or journalists and researchers, for that matter) take in discussions about environmental contaminants, the links of those contaminants to specific industries, and potential threats for health, given the power of continued economic recession?

Even so, recent protests and partial victories for Mitchell County, North Carolina, include the refusal in 2012 to allow a fluoride processing plant (repurposing a locally available mineral) within one township, as well as a newly launched effort in 2013 to document levels and types of sedimentation in local waterways and, ultimately, the impact of mining. Moreover, regionally focused organizations including Clean Water for North Carolina, Appalachian Voices, the Watauga Riverkeeper and other members of the Waterkeeper Alliance, Mountain True, and the Alliance of Carolinians Against Coal Ash respond to, and foster, community-based advocacy in western North Carolina and elsewhere. As stated by Appalachian Voices, coalition efforts such as these have a "common purpose of protecting our beloved mountains and rivers, our forests and farmland, and our children's future."[5] Even in these challenging times, there may be ways to unite locally framed concerns about economic and cultural self-determination with "the fundamental right to clean air, land, water, and food" (EJ Principle 4, EJRC 1991). Appalachia's future depends on this, as does the well-being of populations residing along global chains of production and hazardous waste dispersal.

Conclusions

One thread connecting these short essays is a concern for how the privileging of economic forces and technological rationalities has been used to promote environmentally devastating productive processes, as well as undermine the health and well-being of communities in global mountain regions. The absence of empirical data about particular pollutants and their implications for human health, especially when combined with the indeterminacy of scientific methods, has at times served as rationale for assertions that no real harm is being done through environmental exposures, that particular technologies of containment are effective, or that additional oversight is unwarranted and disruptive of economic profitability (Checker 2012; Russell, Lewis, and Keating 1992).

In 2012, environmental justice advocates in the Global North, including Appalachia, focused on holding institutions such as the EPA accountable for insufficiently characterizing and responding to risks posed by synthetic chemicals, extractive industries, and the byproducts of industrial processes. In 2017, however, US-based environmental activists, researchers, community members, and bureaucrats alike "march[ed] *for* science"[6] and for government repositories of scientific data, drawing attention to the need to retain the EPA and other agencies in the wake of the federal government's antienvironmental "reforms" (Davenport 2017). While the US march was planned as a protest of emerging federal policy, it also served to recognize new kinds of alliances for the public good.

Western biomedicine's reluctance to account for alternative approaches to health and disease—as repositories of knowledge, not simply culturally informed systems of "belief"—has meant that the expressed needs and practical strategies of vulnerable populations are all too frequently overridden or ignored. Thus, when issues such as maternal health (and the prevention of maternal or neonatal mortality) are identified as priority areas by national health care programs and international agencies including the World Health Organization, technological medicine is construed as the remedy—irrespective of accessibility, effectiveness, or cost. Informal systems of medicine and traditional healers, including midwives, may themselves be discredited as "risky," with the result that young indigenous women seeking responsive, locally available care are doubly marginalized (Cosminsky 2016; Miranda 2017).

Nevertheless, community-focused organizations such as the Chiapas-based Committee for Risk-Free and Voluntary Motherhood advocate for health equity and indigenous rights over the authoritative stance of biomedicine. Scientific studies document and legitimate residents' claims about the toxic exposures produced by mountaintop removal mining practices. Grassroots knowledge and local activism combine—as in the case of the Mitchell County Chapter of WNCA and the 4CE, and the regional alliances that follow in their wake—to protect natural resources and promote community health. As these essays illustrate, whether through "democratized" science (Anglin 1998, Brown et al. 2004, McCormick et al. 2004) or participatory action research or knowledge communicated through informal channels (Bullard et al. 2007; Checker 2005, 2012; Ottinger and Cohen 2011), oppositional claims are made and acted upon in the name of health as a fundamental human right.

MARY ANGLIN is Associate Professor in, and past chair of, the Department of Anthropology at the University of Kentucky. Her research interests coalesce around questions of health, environment, livelihoods, and activism in North America, as well as the practical applications of anthropological knowledge to struggles for social justice. Her writings include the book *Women, Power, and Dissent in the Hills of Carolina*.

GREGORY BUTTON, PhD, has researched disasters and public health crises globally for more than twenty-five years as a journalist, anthropologist, and public health professional. He is the author of *Disaster Culture: Knowledge and Uncertainty in the Wake of Human and Environmental Catastrophe* and has coedited other volumes.

DOLORES MOLINA-ROSALES is an Anthropologist at ECOSUR (El Colegio de la Frontera Sur), a research center in southern Mexico. Her interests are in the intersection between gender and environment, and she focuses especially on social inequality and environmental vulnerability. She has worked in coastal, mountain, and rainforest ecosystems, much of her work being in the Chiapas Highlands, and in coastal areas on gendered responses to hurricanes and floods.

Notes

1. Maria Gunnoe, lifelong resident of West Virginia and 2009 winner of the Goldman Environmental Prize, was commenting on the impact of mountaintop removal.

2. Soil and water tests conducted by one NRDC (National Resource Defense Council) scientist, showing organic and heavy metal contamination, were disregarded by other state agencies (Buchanan 1988).

3. Toxicity studies were conducted in 1990 by the National Institute of Occupational Safety and Health (NIOSH), and in 1990–1991, with public comment in 1994, by the Agency for Toxic Substances and Disease Registry (ATSDR) of the Centers for Disease Control and Prevention (CDC). The ATSDR concluded that the Caldwell County incinerator was a significant "public health threat," while the NIOSH study showed neurologic damage in workers from both facilities (ATSDR 2010; Kawamoto 1992).

4. Community activists monitored truck deliveries (and frequently the absence of truck manifests or required HAZMAT inventories), workers and activists documented plant operations, and county officials refused requests for assistance by the owner and plant managers, while legal teams and other experts talked with regulators at state and federal levels.

One landowner sued the facility for violation of state discharge permits and for "trespass" on private property (*Biddix v. Henredon Furniture Industries Inc.* 1985).

5. This quote is from the website of Appalachian Voices, http://appvoices.org/about/, accessed May 15, 2017.

6. This site provides more information on the March for Science: https://satellites .marchforscience.com/, accessed May 15, 2017

References

ATSDR (Agency for Toxic Substances and Disease Registry). 2010. Petitioned Public Health Assessment: Caldwell Systems Incorporated, Lenoir, Caldwell County, North Carolina. Atlanta: US Department of Health and Human Services (1994/2010). Electronic document: http://www.atsdr.cdc.gov/hac/pha/pha.asp?docid=1072&pg=1, accessed June 24, 2013.

Ahern, M. M., M. Hendryx, J. Conley, E. Fedorko, A. Ducatman, and K. J. Zullig. 2011. "The Association between Mountaintop Mining and Birth Defects among Live Births in Central Appalachia, 1996–2003."*Environmental Research* 111 (6): 838–846.

Anglin, Mary K. 1998. "Dismantling the Master's House: Cancer Activists, Discourses of Prevention, and Environmental Justice." *Identities: Global Studies in Culture and Power,* no. 5, 183–218.

Berrío Palomo, Lina Rosa. 2015. "Diversidad de atención durante el embarazo y parto: Reflexiones sobre los saberes locales de mujeres indígenas." Centro Nacional de Equidad de Género y Salud Reproductiva.

Biddix v. Henredon Furniture Industries Inc. 1985. No. 8424SC1245. Court of Appeals of North Carolina, July 16, 1985. Accessed March 2, 2016. http://law.justia.com/cases /north-carolina/court-of-appeals/1985/8424sc1245-1.htm.

Briggs, Charles L., and Clara Mantini-Briggs. 2003. *Stories in Time of Cholera: Racial Profiling during a Medical Nightmare.* Berkeley: University of California Press.

Brown, Phil, Stephen Zavestoski, Sabrina McCormick, Brian Mayer, Rachel Morello-Frosch, and Rebecca Gasior Altman. 2004. "Embodied Health Movements: New Approaches to Social Movements in Health." *Sociology of Health & Illness* 26 (1): 50–80.

Brown, Wesley. 2008. "Unimin Fire Cause Unknown." *Mitchell News-Journal,* December 10. Accessed June 24, 2013. http://www.mitchellnews.com/articles/2008/12/10/news /news01.txt.

Brulle, Robert J., and David N. Pellow. 2006. "Environmental Justice: Human Health and Environmental Inequalities." *Annual Review of Public Health,* no. 27, 103–124.

Buchanan, Millie. 1988. "No Safe Haven for Mr. Foushee's Incinerator." In *Environmental Politics: Lessons from the Grassroots,* edited by Bob Hall. Durham, NC: Institute for Southern Studies.

Bullard, R. D. 1990. "Ecological Inequities and the New South: Black Communities under Siege." *Journal of Ethnic Studies* 17 (Winter): 101–115.

Bullard, Robert D., Paul Mohai, Robin Saha, and Beverly Wright. 2007. *Toxic Wastes and Race at Twenty 1987–2007: Grassroots Struggles to Dismantle Environmental Racism in the United States.* Cleveland, OH: United Church of Christ Justice and Witness Ministry.

Button, Gregory V. 2010. *Disaster Culture: Knowledge and Uncertainty in the Wake of Human and Environmental Catastrophe.* London: Routledge.

Checker, Melissa. 2005. *Polluted Promises: Environmental Racism and the Search for Justice in a Southern Town.* New York: NYU Press.

———. 2012. "But I Know It's True': Environmental Risk Assessment, Justice, and Anthropology." *Human Organization,* no. 66, 112–124.

Cosminsky, Sheila. 2016. *Midwives and Mothers: The Medicalization of Childbirth on a Guatemalan Plantation.* Austin: University of Texas Press.

Davenport, Coral. 2017. "Trump Plans to Begin EPA Rollback with Order on Clean Water." *New York Times,* February 28. Accessed May 13, 2017.https://www.nytimes .com/2017/02/28/us/politics/trump-epa-clean-water-climate-change.html?_r=1.

EJRC. 1991. Washington, DC. "Principles of Environmental Justice." Adopted October 27. Accessed June 24, 2013. http://www.ejrc.cau.edu/princej.html.

Epstein, Paul R., Jonathan J. Buonocore, Kevin Eckerle, Michael Hendryx, Benjamin M. Stout III, Richard Heinberg, Richard W. Clapp, Beverly May, Nancy L. Reinhart, Melissa M. Ahern, Samir K. Doshi, and Leslie Glustrom. 2011. "Full Cost Accounting for the Life Cycle of Coal." *Annals of the New York Academy of Sciences* 1219 (1): 73–98.

Erikson, Kai T. 1978. *Everything in Its Path: Destruction of Community in the Buffalo Creek Flood.* New York: Simon and Schuster.

Farmer, Paul. 2006. *AIDS and Accusation: Haiti and the Geography of Blame.* Berkeley: University of California Press.

Gunewardena, Nandini, and Ann Kingsolver, eds. 2007. *The Gender of Globalization: Women Navigating Cultural and Economic Marginalities.* Santa Fe, NM: School for Advanced Research.

Hankivsky, Olena, Colleen Reid, Renee Cormier, Colleen Varcoe, Natalie Clark, Cecilia Benoit, and Shari Brotman. 2010. "Exploring the Promises of Intersectionality for Advancing Women's Health Research." *International Journal for Equity in Health* 9 (5): 1–15.

Harrison, Faye V. 2008. *Outsider Within: Reworking Anthropology in the Global Age.* Champaign: University of Illinois Press.

Hatala, Andrew R., and James B. Waldram. 2017. "Diagnostic Emplotment in Q´eqchi´Maya Medicine." *Medical Anthropology* 36 (3): 273–286.

Heggenhougen, H. K.1995. "The Epidemiology of Functional Apartheid and Human Rights Abuses." Editorial. *Social Science and Medicine* 40 (3): 281–284.

Hendryx, Michael. 2013. "Personal and Family Health in Rural Areas of Kentucky with and without Mountaintop Coal Mining." *Journal of Rural Health* 29 (s1): s79–s88.

Hendryx, M., E. Fedorko, and A. Anesetti-Rothermel. 2010. "A Geographical Information System-Based Analysis of Cancer Mortality and Population Exposure to Coal Mining Activities in West Virginia, United States of America." *Geospatial Health* 4 (2): 243–256.

Hendryx, Michael, Leah Wolf, Juhua Luo, and Bo Webb. 2012. Self-Reported Cancer Rates in Two Rural Areas of West Virginia with and without Mountaintop Coal Mining. *Journal of Community Health* 37 (2): 320–327.

Holzman, David C. 2011. "Mountaintop Removal Mining: Digging into Community Health Concerns." *Environmental Health Perspectives* 119 (11): a47-6-a483.

Kawamoto, Melody M. 1992. *NIOSH Health Hazard Evaluation Report.* HETA 90–240-2259: The Caldwell Group, North Carolina. Washington, DC: US Department of Health and Human Services, Public Health Service, Centers for Disease Control and Prevention, National Institute for Occupational Safety and Health.

Krieger, Nancy. 2001. "Theories for Social Epidemiology in the 21st Century: An Ecosocial Perspective." *International Journal of Epidemiology* 30 (4): 668–677.

Krieger, Nancy, and George Davey Smith. 2004. "'Bodies Count' and Body Counts: Social Epidemiology and Embodying Inequality." *Epidemiologic Reviews* 26 (1): 92–103.

Lane, Sandra D., Robert A. Rubinstein, Robert H. Keefe, Noah Webster, Donald A. Cibula, Alan Rosenthal, and Jesse Dowdell. 2004. "Structural Violence and Racial Disparity in HIV Transmission." *Journal of Health Care for the Poor and Underserved* 15 (3): 319–335.

Leatherman, Thomas. 2005. "A Space of Vulnerability in Poverty and Health: Political-Ecology and Biocultural Analysis." *Ethos* 33 (1): 46–70.

Levins, Richard, and Richard Lewontin. 1985. *The Dialectical Biologist*. Cambridge, MA: Harvard University Press.

Marable, Manning, and Vanessa Agard-Jones, eds. 2008. *Transnational Blackness: Navigating the Global Color Line*. New York: Palgrave Macmillan.

McCormick, Sabrina, Julia Brody, Phil Brown, and R. Polk. 2004. "Public Involvement in Breast Cancer Research: An Analysis and Model for Future Research." *International Journal of Health Services* 34: 625–646.

McSpirit, Stephanie, Shaunna L. Scott, Duane Gill, Sharon Hardesty, and Dewayne Sims. 2007. "Risk Perceptions after a Coal Waste Impoundment Failure: A Survey Assessment." *Southern Rural Sociology* 22 (2): 83–110.

Miranda, Veronica. 2017. *Reproducing Childbirth: Negotiated Maternal Health Practices in Rural Yucatan*. PhD diss., University of Kentucky.

Mohai, Paul, David Pellow, and J. Timmons Roberts. 2009. "Environmental Justice." *Annual Review of Environmental Resources* 34: 405–430.

Mullings, Leith. 2005. "Interrogating Racism: Toward an Antiracist Anthropology." *Annual Review of Anthropology* 34: 667–693.

NC PCB Archives. n.d. "Birth of a Movement: Environmental Justice and Pollution Prevention." Accessed June 24, 2013.http://www.ncpcbarchives.com/.

Nguyen, Vinh-Kim, and Karine Peschard. 2003. "Anthropology, Inequality, and Disease: A Review." *Annual Review of Anthropology* 32: 447–474.

Ottinger, Gwen, and Benjamin R. Cohen, eds. 2011. *Technoscience and Environmental Justice: Expert Cultures in a Grassroots Movement*. Cambridge, MA: MIT Press.

Reid, Jeffrey C. 2009. "The Mineral Industry of North Carolina." In *USGS 2006 Minerals Yearbook*. Washington, D.C.: US Department of the Interior/United States Geological Survey.

Russell, Dick, Sanford Lewis, and Russell Keating. 1992. *Inconclusive by Design: Waste, Fraud, and Abuse in Federal Environmental Health Research; An Investigative Study by the Environmental Health Network and the National Toxics Campaign Fund*. Accessed February 1, 2014. https://archive.org/details/Inconclusive ByDesignWasteFraudAndAbuseInFederalEnvironmentalHealth.

Rylko-Bauer, Barbara, Linda M. Whiteford, and Paul Farmer, eds. 2009. *Global Health in Times of Violence*. Santa Fe, NM: School for Advanced Research.

Sargent, Carolyn, and Stéphanie Larchanché. 2011. "Transnational Migration and Global Health: The Production and Management of Risk, Illness, and Access to Care." *Annual Review of Anthropology*, no. 40, 345–361.

Schulz, Amy, and Leith Mullings, eds. 2006. *Gender, Race, Class and Health: Intersectional Approaches*. San Francisco: Jossey-Bass.

Singer, Merrill. 2009. "Beyond Global Warming: Interacting Ecocrises and the Critical Anthropology of Health." *Anthropological Quarterly* 82 (3): 795–820.

Susser, Ida. 2009. *AIDS, Sex, and Culture: Global Politics and Survival in Southern Africa*. New York: Wiley-Blackwell.

Susser, Mervyn, and Ezra Susser. 1996. "Choosing a Future for Epidemiology II: From Black Boxes to Chinese Boxes and Eco-epidemiology." *American Journal of Pubic Health* 86: 674–677.

Tavernise, Sabrina. 2011. "Report Faults Mine Owner for Explosion That Killed 29." *New York Times*. May 19.

United Church of Christ Commission for Racial Justice. 1987. *Toxic Wastes and Race in the United States: A National Report on the Racial and Socio-economic Characteristics of Communities with Hazardous Waste Sites*. New York: United Church of Christ.

US General Accounting Office. 1983. *Siting of Hazardous Waste Landfills and Their Correlation with Racial and Economic Status of Surrounding Communities*. RCED 83–168. Washington, DC: GAO.

Wachter, Dana. 2008. Overnight Fire at the Unimin Plant in Spruce Pine, North Carolina. TriCities.com. Accessed June 24, 2013. http://www.tricities.com/news /article_45e72a02-2b57-55f8-835f-0e40446ed413.html.

Weber, Lynn, and DeAnne K. H. Messias. 2012. "Mississippi Front-Line Recovery Work after Hurricane Katrina: An Analysis of the Intersections of Gender, Race and Class in Advocacy, Power Relations and Health." *Social Science and Medicine,* no. 74, 1833–1841.

Wilson, Sacoby M. 2010. "Environmental Justice Movement: A Review of History, Research, and Public Health Issues." *Journal of Public Management and Social Policy,* no. 16, 19–50.

When the Morning Breaks

Si Kahn

This place is so flat
You can watch the sun go down
And follow it until it fades from sight
The smoke from the paper mill
Covers up the town
It's gonna be a long and lonesome night
But watch the sun and sky

When the morning breaks
Heading for the mountains of our home
I'd rather be here
In a strange place with you
Than the most familiar
Place I've ever known

Back in the mountains
The winter's coming on
The garden has all gone to weed and seed
The dogs and the neighbors
Must wonder why we've gone
Or what we'd hope to find here that we'd need

When the morning breaks
Heading for the mountains of our home
I'd rather be here
In a strange place with you
Than the most familiar
Place I've ever known

The old house is empty
The lights have all gone out
Upon a home we built with work and care
And sometimes I stare
Through the spaces of the night
Wondering what the hell we're doing here

When the morning breaks
Heading for the mountains of our home
I'd rather be here
In a strange place with you
Than the most familiar
Place I've ever known

CHAPTER 11

Circulating News in Rural China and Appalachia

Al Cross and You You

A RURAL MOUNTAIN village in China and a rural mountain community in the Appalachian region of the United States are very different, and so are the social and political systems of the two countries. But with the help of a US academic institute dedicated to helping rural journalists, a Chinese scholar explored the contrasts and similarities with the Chinese community she has studied and a Kentucky community that also gets characterized as suffering from isolation and poverty.

You You is an associate professor in the Department of Journalism in the Film School at Shanghai University. She was born in Jiangsu Province in southeast China, near Shanghai, and received a doctor of sociology degree from the university in 2006. She has focused her research on the relationship among politics, culture, and communication in Chinese rural areas, with particular attention to the consequences of mass media reform during China's comprehensive social transformation since 1978. In 2011, she published two books in China, *The Transformation of Mass Media in Chinese Rural Areas* and *Social Role of Mass Media in Chinese Rural Areas during the Social Transformation*.

During 2012–2013, You You was a visiting scholar at the University of Kentucky, working with its Institute for Rural Journalism and Community Issues to explore the social role of a local newspaper in a mountain community in Kentucky and to make comparisons with rural news media in China.

Al Cross is an associate professor and director of the Institute for Rural Journalism and Community Issues in the School of Journalism and Media at the University of Kentucky. He was born in Knoxville, Tennessee, grew up in southern Kentucky, and received a bachelor's degree in mass communications from Western Kentucky University in 1978. He was an editor and manager of rural weekly newspapers in Kentucky, then worked 26 years for the state's largest newspaper, The (Louisville) *Courier-Journal*, the last 15-1/2 as its chief political writer. He was president of the Society of Professional Journalists in 2001–2002.

In 2004, he joined the institute as interim director and was named director in 2005. His faculty appointment is in the Extension Title series, reflecting the fact that most of his work is directed off campus. One-fifth of his time is devoted to teaching, and in his community journalism classes he has offered an Appalachian option, in which students can do reporting and research in the region.

While the institute is focused on helping American journalists cover rural issues, its associates have worked in Zambia and Botswana for freedom of information and coverage of HIV and AIDS, and have traveled to India to explore a relationship with a nongovernmental organization in one of India's most rural states to promote news coverage of issues by journalists and citizens. The institute frequently hosts visiting journalists from other countries. You You learned of the institute through one of the University of Kentucky scholars visiting Shanghai University in an ongoing exchange. She arrived in Lexington, Kentucky, to affiliate with the institute as a visiting scholar in August 2012.

Through consultation with the institute, You You, along with Mary Chellis Austin, a student in Al Cross's community journalism course, chose to learn more about rural journalism by focusing on one particular newspaper and its readership in eastern Kentucky. They were oriented to the region by Edmund Shelby, then-editor of the *Manchester Enterprise* in Clay County, and Anne Shelby, a noted Appalachian author and storyteller. Some of what You learned was from ongoing visits to the area. The *Manchester Enterprise* also conducted a survey of its subscribers, and You drew on that information in her comparison for Shanghai University of news media use in rural mountain regions of the United States and China.

The Institute for Rural Journalism and Community Issues and Its Work in Appalachia

In 1998, retired weekly newspaper chain owner Al Smith heard strong concerns about rural mountain communities in eastern Kentucky from his friend, lawyer Steve Cawood. Smith had been federal co-chair of the Appalachian Regional Commission, a national development agency begun in the 1960s' War on Poverty to focus on the well-being of the Appalachian region, which crosses 13 states. Cawood was from Pineville, Kentucky, where the Cumberland River cuts through

Pine Mountain, the northwesternmost of the great ridges of the Appalachian Mountains that run from southwest to northeast.

Cawood told Smith his concerns for the future of his county, in Kentucky's southeastern corner: prescription drug abuse, increasing health problems, and underresourced schools. He said that the easy-to-mine coal was running out, and there were few good local job options for the students who made it through high school. Smith knew about these problems because of his work with the Appalachian Regional Commission, his previous ownership of a large weekly newspaper in nearby London, Kentucky, and as host of a weekly political discussion program on statewide television, but this first-person account from the heart of the coalfield stuck with him.

Smith tried to interest the Lexington and Louisville newspapers, which had reporters stationed in Eastern Kentucky, in a major reporting effort on the problems Cawood had outlined. They covered problems as they arose, but no special effort seemed forthcoming. Smith shared his concerns with his friend Rudy Abramson (Institute for Rural Journalism and Community Issues 2008), a native of Appalachian northern Alabama who had retired as a Washington correspondent for the *Los Angeles Times* and was coediting the *Encyclopedia of Appalachia* (University of Tennessee Press 2006).

Abramson said he thought he could get a reporting fellowship from the Alicia Patterson Foundation to conduct reporting in Appalachia and write a long-form account, with photographs (Abramson 2011). He did, and when he returned from reporting, he told Smith that few small-town newspapers in the region were holding corporate and public officials accountable, and they included little reporting on the national and global forces that were affecting their communities.

Smith and Abramson thought Appalachia needed some sort of organization to help its local media and provide news stories and commentary on broader issues with local impact. Their idea became the Institute for Rural Journalism and Community Issues, based in the School of Journalism and Media, part of the College of Communication and Information at the University of Kentucky. Beginning as a pilot project with some small grants and then, in 2004, large grants from the John S. and James L. Knight Foundation and the Ford Foundation, the institute was able to employ its first full-time staff member, a director (this writer, Al Cross), who also teaches community journalism in the journalism school.

The mission of the institute, now with the support of an endowment and state funding, is to help nonmetropolitan news media define the public agenda in their communities through strong reporting and commentary, especially on issues that have a local impact but lack good local sources. One of the best examples of that is surface coal mining in Central Appalachia, often mountaintop removal mines that raise multiple environmental issues. One of the institute's first workshops, Covering Coal, at South Charleston, West Virginia, in 2005, was the first to bring journalists, industry representatives and experts, environmentalists, mine-safety and environmental regulators, and citizens' groups into the same room in the Central Appalachian coalfield to discuss issues in the industry and specifically how to cover them in the news (Institute for Rural Journalism and Community Issues 2005a). Covering Coal prompted a follow-up, Coal-Media Roundtable, in 2006 in Pikeville, Kentucky, where journalists and industry representatives, in approximately equal number, discussed issues and coverage, and aired their grievances about each other.

The institute also exists to help all journalists with coverage of issues that affect rural America—education, local economies, the environment, and health care—and to encourage journalism that holds local officials and institutions accountable.[1] Each year it presents the Tom and Pat Gish Award for courage, integrity, and tenacity in rural journalism, named for a couple who published the *Mountain Eagle* in Whitesburg, Kentucky, in Central Appalachia (Institute for Rural Journalism and Community Issues 2005b).

While the institute has a national mission and has done international work, it does most of its work in Appalachia and Kentucky. It publishes *The Rural Blog*, a daily digest of events, trends, issues, ideas, and journalism from and about rural America; the director has often observed that if *The Rural Blog* were a printed newspaper, Appalachia would be the focus of its second section—more specifically Central Appalachia (the coal mining region that comprises eastern Kentucky, southern West Virginia, southwest Virginia, and the Cumberland Plateau of East Tennessee), much of which is labeled by the Appalachian Regional Commission as "economically distressed."

The institute is needed because most rural news media staff lack the resources required to conduct in-depth reporting on accountability and to insulate themselves from the pressure that may come from advertisers, officials, and others influential in the community. Many rural news media, including approximately 60 percent of weekly newspapers in the United States, are now owned by chains that may provide some financial insulation and support but have as their first priority return on investment, not community service. Many of these chains are publicly traded corporations, whose first obligation is a legal one to their stockholders.

In Kentucky and Central Appalachia, almost every county has its own newspaper, but the institute's research has shown that most of them:

- fail to adequately cover county government (for content analysis of Appalachian Kentucky papers' coverage of county budgets and statewide audit of county jails, see Cross 2006);
- do not publish local editorials, even broadly defined, and may even lack an editorial page (for content analysis of Kentucky weekly newspapers, see Cross and Hansen 2008);

- have been slow to embrace the internet, and many ignore it (for research in three Eastern Kentucky counties and work with newspapers in those counties, see Cross and Hansen 2010);
- fail to reach even half the local households and are dependent on single-copy sales, opening doors to competition and sensational approaches (for statistical analysis of circulation patterns of weekly newspapers in Kentucky and West Virginia, see Cross, Bissett, and Arrowsmith 2011); and
- rarely provide adequate coverage of public health problems, which are some of the worst in the nation (for content and statistical analysis of rural Kentucky newspapers, see Cross and Vos 2011).

For example, Kentucky is ranked 1st among the states in deaths from cancer and lung cancer and in preventable hospitalizations; 2nd in smoking and poor health days in the last month; 6th in obesity; and 44th of the 50 states in overall health status. It is also home to 54 of the 220 counties that the US Centers for Disease Control and Prevention have identified as most vulnerable to outbreaks of HIV and hepatitis C from intravenous drug use. All of these problems are concentrated in Appalachian Kentucky.

The institute's first workshop for journalists, in 2005, was Covering Health Care and Health in Central Appalachia, held at Hazard, Kentucky (Gross 2005). It attracted more than 50 participants and spurred more coverage of the issues by the region's news outlets. To encourage more coverage of health issues in Kentucky newspapers, the institute has received six grants from the Foundation for a Healthy Kentucky to publish Kentucky Health News (KHN), an online digest of health-related news that pertains to the state, supplemented by original reporting on Kentucky health topics (Cross and Vos 2011). The effort appears to be encouraging more health coverage, including special newspaper sections on health, using much KHN material. In November 2016 the institute conducted a health journalism workshop in Appalachian Kentucky.

The institute has also promoted the use of advanced reporting techniques in Appalachia, with the help of Daniel Gilbert, who won a Pulitzer Prize for his computer-assisted reporting at the *Bristol* (Virginia) *Herald Courier* on the mismanagement of mineral royalties by energy companies and the Commonwealth of Virginia in the Appalachian section of the state. With a grant from the Ethics and Excellence in Journalism Foundation, Investigative Reporters and Editors, the institute held two Rural Computer-Assisted Reporting Mini Boot Camps in Johnson City, Tennessee, and Lexington, Kentucky, in 2011 and 2012. Almost all the participants were from news media in Appalachia. The foundation approached Gilbert, now an energy reporter for the *Wall Street Journal*, about support for such work after he created the Rural Computer-Assisted Reporting Fund at the institute with the prize money he received for winning the community journalism award from the Scripps Howard Foundation. The foundation matched his donation, and the state of Kentucky matched both, enabling the institute to fund two annual fellowships for attendance at the Computer-Assisted Reporting Boot Camp of Investigative Reporters and Editors, the workshop where Gilbert learned the skills that enabled him to do his prize-winning work.

With funding from the John S. and James L. Knight Foundation, the institute held the National Summit on Journalism in Rural America in 2007 (Shafer 2007). The event attracted participants from 18 states, several in Appalachia, and featured release of the institute's research on training backgrounds and needs at rural newspapers (Cross et al. 2007). The institute regularly produces research that is presented at the annual conventions of the National Newspaper Association. Most of that research is mentioned in the bullet points above.

In 2014, the institute reported for Appalachian Kentucky news media on the organization and development of Shaping Our Appalachian Region, a bipartisan effort by state and federal officials focusing on increasing economic investment and innovation in Appalachian Kentucky, with funding from the Rural Policy Research Institute. As the institute's director, I was part of a focus group that the Appalachian Regional Commission (ARC) held on the ARC and its work in Kentucky. In 2015, I won the James Madison Award for Service to the First Amendment from the Scripps Howard First Amendment Center at the University of Kentucky. The Institute for Rural Journalism and Community Issues, along with other organizations in the region, will continue finding ways to support coverage of challenging issues in the local news media in Appalachia.

The Transformation of Mass Media in Chinese Rural Areas: A Case Study in Sanjia Village

I (You You) conducted sociological research in a rural Chinese village against the backdrop of the comprehensive social and market transformation in early twenty-first century China, looking at the influence of mass media in a rural community through survey and interview methods.

The Village

Sanjia Village is 1,000 miles from the capital of Beijing, 820 miles from China's biggest city, Shanghai, and less than 500 miles from Guangzhou, in the middle of Hunan province, in the middle southern part of China. Its landscape is crisscrossed by gentle, low hills, much like the Appalachian region but at a little lower elevation. The village has just over 1,000 residents in about 300 households, nearly all of them with small-scale agricultural livelihoods. It is similar in those respects to many rural communities in middle and western China.

Despite a great increase in China's GDP, poverty is still a primary issue in the central and western rural areas of China. Sanjia is no exception: the per capita disposable income of residents is less than half of that of urban residents, and the economic gap is widening.

The economic and social reforms since 1978 have greatly transformed life in Sanjia, as in other similar villages. The overwhelming majority of the labor force migrates from the village to work in cities, only coming back, like seasonal birds, for festivals, leaving mostly elders and children as full-time residents in the village. Such large-scale migration of the young and educated is a kind of economic and social blood transfusion to cities that foreshadows a wider gap between rural and urban areas in the future.

The media structure in Sanjia reflects that of most of rural China. The village gets 11 different newspapers, but only subscribes to 19 copies in all, and receives negligible radio broadcasts. Television is the primary mass medium that audiences can access cheaply and easily, though internet access has advanced over the past five years.

Instrumental Role before Comprehensive Social Transformation

Before social transformation, the government controlled almost all national resources, reflecting a distinct characteristic of Chinese politics in the twentieth century. This is widely known as "totalism"[2] (named by Dang Zhou, professor at the University of Chicago), which means the government has nearly infinite power over politics, economics, culture, ideology, and social life—even over the opportunity for people to exist and develop.

Using totalism, the government built up the mass media system all over the nation, including in rural areas. Therefore, mass media played an instrumental role in promoting through propaganda the Chinese Communist Party's guidelines, policy, and ideology. That is to say this is mainly a one-way communication system, from the top to the bottom. In Sanjia, radio programs and films produced outside the community were the main media to which people had access, for the area had no TV at that time, and few residents could read newspapers. The emphasis was on media content, not audiences' responses.

Nevertheless, this one-way system, to some extent, made sense to the Sanjia residents I interviewed. First of all, because of the relatively equal distribution of media, most people, as they listened to the radio or watched films, thought they were treated fairly and equally by the media. Second, the most important news and state-promoted virtues such as austerity, self-reliance, modesty, and honesty in those days were broadcast by radio to innumerable villages like Sanjia. Third, most Sanjia people got great pleasure from the free movies: not the notions, concepts, logic, and morality that the government hoped to deliver, but the stories, love, beauty and music that people really enjoyed.

It should be noted that the mass media system was only supplementary at that time, secondary to conferences that connected the government and Sanjia residents. Face-to-face communication was obviously more effective.

The Transformation of Mass Media in Sanjia Village since the Reform

Since 1978, a market economy has gradually been supplanting the planned economy in China, and the mass media system has also changed. In Sanjia, with the end of government maintenance of existing media, radio, and free movies—popular for 30 years—quickly became history. Most of the paper radio boxes, installed freely into everyone's home in the 1950s, had already been damaged by 1970 because of weak materials. The village's four public loudspeakers stopped working by 1976, and the government stopped showing free movies to Sanjia peasants by the 1980s. The marketplace became the only path for residents to access those media.

While the political system of totalism gradually became more limited, the government still dominated the most important national resources so it still may be called an authoritarian government. Under the new circumstances, the government set up a television system instead of radio throughout the nation. Television quickly replaced radio and movies as the leading mass media. Consequently, cable TV service was also placed in rural communities. Television could reach all people, regardless of whether they were educated, unlike the case with paper-based media, which requires literacy. The first TV set came to Sanjia in 1983. From then until the mid-1990s, households purchased TV sets one after another with great enthusiasm.

At the beginning, there were many difficulties watching TV in Sanjia: power failure, voltage instability, unstable signals, expensive but low-quality TV sets, and lack of TV programs. However, comparing the present to the past without TV, at present, many Sanjia residents expressed nostalgia for the very early period of getting TVs. The crucial policy that had made that time a good one for many was the Distribution of Land to Farmers for a Certain Term in Villages. It clarified that peasants had the right to keep a part of their income after paying a certain proportion to the government and to the local collective. To Sanjia residents, TV sets represented their most prized private property as proud market participants during the initial stage of economic reform.

When I did field research in Sanjia, residents were in another situation entirely. Owing to the cable TV installed by the government in the 1990s, most early difficulties with TV had been solved. However, the one-way communication system was mostly retained. Watching TV became part of Sanjia residents' daily life, consuming three to four hours per day. A TV set may have initially been a symbol of wealth, but entertainment is now the most common motive for watching TV, and variety shows and TV plays were for the most part welcomed by Sanjia viewers. News stories and advertisements were too far from their local community for residents to relate to readily. They had more enthusiasm for favorite local entertainments such as mahjong and religious events than TV programs.

In the past, many Sanjia residents thought radio represented the will of the state or found beautiful things in movies or regarded TV as a symbol of wealth. When surveyed about that time, a majority of them expressed a positive outlook and an eagerness to engage with the outside world through mass media. Since the mid-1990s, as the focus of the reform moved from the rural areas to the cities and the urban-rural economic gap has widened. Rural residents—especially those in middle and western China—have felt a sense of relative deprivation and of greater limitations to development. Sanjia residents surveyed expressed uncertainty about their future and, consequently, about the use of mass media only for entertainment.

What I learned about rural consumption of market-based mass media from the residents of Sanjia was that this media made them feel like their area was insignificant, or backward, while they had not felt that way in state media representations. It increased a sense of alienation and reduced their sense of self-worth to how much wealth they had. The growing use of the internet for direct contact with others, though, is increasing a sense of agency in relation to media in rural areas.

The internet and new media having come onto the stage in Sanjia over the last five years has quite dramatically affected Sanjia residents, and largely ruined the one-way communication system. Although much fewer than half the households in Sanjia have computers, most (especially children) have mobile phones, making internet access common. No longer must they passively accept traditional media constructed by the government; they have a way to connect to the outside world, express ideas, and produce content of their own for the first time, through social media. It arouses their passion for life and again creates visions of various possibilities. But as their children grow up, all or most will leave for cities and the local community will still be abandoned.

The *Manchester Enterprise* in the Oneida Community

During my (You You) affiliation with the Institute for Rural Journalism and Community Issues, residents of Oneida, Kentucky, a rural community in the same county in which the *Manchester Enterprise* is published, taught me about rural media reception so that I could think comparatively about what I learned from the residents of Sanjia, China.

The Oneida Community

Oneida is an unincorporated community in the northeast of Clay County, Kentucky, with its post office 16 miles from the county seat of Manchester. The county was known in the 1800s for salt-making, in the 1900s for coal mining, timbering, and marijuana growing, and in the 2000s for being one of the most economically distressed counties in the United States. The small mountain community of

Oneida, 100 miles from Lexington, Kentucky, mostly along winding mountain roads, can be breathtakingly beautiful. It is around the same size as Sanjia.

Compared with Sanjia, Oneida's economic figures are much greater in terms of absolute value, but they are similar in terms of relative value. The 2010 US Census (US Bureau of the Census, n.d.) found Clay County to be the poorest county in the United States in per-capita income and second lowest in median household income. The real values of earnings in Sanjia and Oneida are almost equal, and meeting vital household needs with the median income is challenging.

There are other similarities. The majority of working age adults in Oneida are unemployed, while their counterparts in Sanjia are away from the community working in cities. In both communities, it is difficult to find employment locally, and minimum wage work is supplemented through hunting and fishing. Many more adults of working age stay in Oneida than in Sanjia, so there is a more vibrant system of social support.

The Manchester Enterprise in Oneida

The residents of Oneida have access to several types of media, which unquestionably plays an important role in the community, for better or worse. The similarity with residents of Sanjia is that most media time is spent with TV. People mainly watch game shows and soap operas to relax, secondarily getting national news. Internet use did not appear to be widespread among older people, but is much used by young people who have access to it.

My goal was to learn some things about comparable media use in rural Kentucky. The *Manchester Enterprise*, with the assistance of the institute, had sent out a survey to subscribers. That anonymous information enabled me to learn the following about how the *Manchester Enterprise* is used by its readers.

This newspaper serves residents with a clear local emphasis in its coverage of news, features, sports, and advertising, and has proven successful in American newspaper terms. About half the households in Clay County subscribe to the newspaper or, more commonly, regularly buy single copies. The actual readership is larger because subscribers and regular buyers share the newspaper with relatives and neighbors.

Most Chinese newspapers, which circulate in much wider areas, would consider this a miracle beyond their reach; in the United States, such community newspapers are a major source of news about what is going on in the community. The daily *Herald–Leader* in Lexington, Kentucky (a regional urban center) has some circulation in Clay County but rarely covers news there. As in China, rural news consumers do not see much of a reflection of themselves in urban media. In the local newspaper, however, the survey of Oneida readers showed that people gravitated toward sections that were meaningful to them in local terms, such as the sports or arts news, and that the middle class was most engaged with the newspaper.

The strategy of such a community news outlet is often to focus its attention on the everyday lives of ordinary people. It is a successful tactic, winning high market share and social acceptance. Its owner and employees get profits and wages, respectively, and residents have the opportunity to know their local environment and participate in community affairs. The *Manchester Enterprise* makes a great effort to include the small community of Oneida, for example, in its coverage of the broader community of Clay County. Because of its long-term service and attendant reputation, whether people read the newspaper or not, residents expressed more trust in the information in the newspaper than what they heard by word of mouth. The newspaper, for Oneida residents, seems to represent more community spirit than a force for social change (the newspaper, for example, has no editorial page).

In summary, the *Manchester Enterprise* covers ordinary people's lives and helps reinforce a sense of local identity through media representation. This contrasts with the media experience of residents of Sanjia, China, who see little representation of local identity and issues in the media market available to them, mostly TV.

Conclusion

We believe our comparison shows the potential for increasing mutual under-standing between rural mountain residents across national boundaries by having more communication about the relationship between social, political, and media systems. The *Manchester Enterprise*'s role in the Oneida community, operating in the US system of an independent news media, offers Chinese readers insights that could reduce the alienation between the country's national-dominated news media and rural residents who lack their own media outlets. The internet is being used to address that gap in part, but it is not widely accessible. The role of the Institute for Rural Journalism and Community Issues in helping rural news media grasp the local impact of national events, trends, and issues may also pro-vide a paradigm for assistance to rural media's service to their readers, viewers, and listeners. In China, the tradition of more regional conversations could be leveraged to organize rural-urban dialogues like those facilitated by the Institute for Rural Journalism and Community Issues to build more possibilities for criti-cal rural media production.

AL CROSS is director of the Institute for Rural Journalism and Community Issues and associate extension Professor of Journalism at the University of Kentucky. He publishes *Kentucky Health News*, the *Midway Messenger*, and *The Rural Blog*.

YOU YOU is Associate Professor of Communications in the Department of Journalism at Shanghai University. Her research focuses on the relation between media and the social environment. She has written books about the social roles of mass media during the Chinese social transformation and urban community media and the construction of urban community itself.

Notes

1. For more information on the institute, see www.RuralJournalism.org.
2. Tang Tsou, *Er shi shi ji Zhongguo zheng zhi: cong hong guan li shi yu wei guan xing dong de jiao du kan* (Hong Kong: Niujin da xue chu ban she), 1994, 3.

References

Abramson, Rudy. 2011. "A Judge in Coal Country." Alicia Patterson Foundation. Accessed April 14, 2017. http://aliciapatterson.org/stories/judge-coal-country.

Cross, Al. 2006. "Coverage of Public-Policy Issues at Newspapers in Eastern Kentucky and Central Appalachia Is Lacking," March. Accessed April 14, 2017. http://www.uky.edu/CommInfoStudies/IRJCI/publicpolicycoverage.html.

Cross, Al, Bill Bissett, and Heather Arrowsmith. 2011. "Circulation Patterns of Weekly Newspapers in Central Appalachia and Kentucky." Newspapers and Community Building Symposium, Albuquerque, NM, September 23. Accessed April 14, 2017. http://www.uky.edu/CommInfoStudies/IRJCI/NNA paper 2011.pdf.

Cross, Al, Vaughan Fielder, C. T. Tigas, and Beth Barnes. 2007. *A Survey of Training Backgrounds and Needs at Rural Newspapers in the United States.* Accessed April 14, 2017. http://www.uky.edu/CommInfoStudies/IRJCI/survey2007.doc.

Cross, Al, and Elizabeth Hansen. 2008. "Keeping Quiet or Taking the Lead? A Study of Editorial Pages in Kentucky Newspapers." Accessed April 14. 2017. http://www.uky.edu/CommInforStudies/IRJCI/KyEditorialpages.pdf. .

Cross, Al, and Elizabeth K. Hansen. 2010. "Discerning a Train Coming Down the Track: Three Rural Weekly Newspapers and the Internet." Paper presented to the National Newspaper Association Convention, St. Paul, MN, September 26, 2008. Accessed April 14, 2017. http://www.uky.edu/CommInfoStudies/IRJCI/NNApaper2010.pdf.

Cross, Al, and Sarah Vos. 2011. *Reporting Health: Rural Newspaper Coverage of Health in Kentucky.* Report to the Foundation for a Healthy Kentucky.

Gross, David. 2005. "Conference Explores How to Cover, Boost Rural Health." Institute for Rural Journalism and Community Issues, March. Accessed April 14, 2017. http://www.uky.edu/CommInfoStudies/IRJCI/reportsford.html.

Institute for Rural Journalism and Community Issues. 2005a. "Conference Provides Advice for Citizens, Story Ideas for Journalists." Accessed April 14, 2017. http://www.uky.edu/CommInfoStudies/IRJCI/coalreport.htm.

Institute for Rural Journalism and Community Issues. 2005b. "Publishers of Mountain Eagle Get Award Named for Them." Accessed April 14, 2017. http://www.uky.edu/CommInfoStudies/IRJCI/gish.html.

Institute for Rural Journalism and Community Issues. 2008. "Rudy Abramson, Acclaimed Author and Co-founder of Institute for Rural Journalism, Passes Away." Accessed April 14, 2017. http://www.uky.edu/CommInfoStudies/IRJCI/AbramsonObit.htm.

Kentucky Health News, http://kyhealthnews.blogspot.com.

Shafer, Mary Jo. 2007. "National Summit [on Journalism in Rural America] Focuses on Future of Rural Journalism." Accessed April 14, 2017. http://www.uky.edu /CommInfoStudies/IRJCI/summitoverview.htm.

Tsou, Tang. 1994. *Er shi shi ji Zhongguo zheng zhi: cong hong guan li shi yu wei guan xing dong de jiao du kan.* Hong Kong: Niujin da xue chu ban she.

US Bureau of the Census. n.d. Accessed April 14, 2017. http://factfinder2.census.gov /faces/tableservices/jsf/pages/productview.xhtml?pid=ACS_11_5YR_DP03.

CHAPTER 12

Thinking about the Future

GLOBAL MOUNTAIN STUDENTS AND EDUCATIONAL CHOICES

Jane Jensen, Marco Pitzalis, Mir Afzal Tajik, and Alan J. DeYoung

THIS CHAPTER DISCUSSES the movement of students from one level of schooling to the next, leading to educational attainment. In our discussion we consider the structure of school, the agency of the student, the values of his or her family and community, as well as the influence of the political economy on the social value of educational credentials. Our discussion focuses on three mountain regions: the rural villages of Sardinia, Italy, the coal-mining region of eastern Kentucky in the United States, and the highlands of northern Pakistan. In this comparative essay, we consider why individuals choose to continue (or not continue) their education after compulsory schooling, why they choose particular educational pathways, and how the exchange value of educational credentials is understood in these economically marginalized communities.

In many rural mountain regions across the globe, improving educational attainment is a primary goal for policy makers. Social and economic wealth depends on the capacity to increase educational attainment and grow "human capital." Such growth, however, increases tensions around equity of access to and through educational pathways and conflicts surrounding the public subsidy of private ambitions, aspirations that may take successful students, especially those going to university, away from their mountain homes. In the mountains of northern Pakistan, educational attainment also involves basic questions of literacy, social justice, gender and ethnicity, as well as the common dilemmas of "brain drain" and equity of access. All three regions face complex questions of how education serves local needs for development and sustainability as well as individual aspirations for success in a modern global marketplace.

In Sardinia, Italy, the structure of the school system, which includes universal elementary education and secondary education pathways, highlights the decisions students and their families make after the eighth grade or around the age of 14. Physical access to different secondary education options and cultural values regarding different types of education play a role in these decisions. In Appalachian Kentucky, the structure of the American school system from kindergarten to twelfth grade is uniform and compulsory but includes choices of curriculum, whether to continue to postsecondary education, and what to study. Appalachian educational decision making also reflects structural considerations of access and cultural values regarding types of educational credentials.

The education system in northern areas of Pakistan is even more complicated by the existence of three parallel school systems in the country (the national curriculum and Matric examination, a *Madressah* education,[1] and overseas systems such as 'O' and 'A' levels of the Cambridge Examination System).[2] Despite the constitutional obligation to provide free and compulsory education to children 5 to 16 years old, about 30 percent of Pakistani children aged 6 to 16 (23 percent in rural areas and 7 percent in urban areas) are out of school. The country ranks second in the world in the number of out-of-school children. Girls lag behind boys by one-third in the rural areas. However, there are success stories of community-based schools that provide access and better quality education to children, particularly girls, in the northern areas of Pakistan.

This chapter explores these considerations in these three mountain regions to highlight the ways that educational decision making is culturally produced and ways that educational outcomes often reflect the reproduction of social inequalities.

Sardinia, Italy

Sardinia is an island in the west of the Mediterranean Sea. Its economy has been characterized by an old industrial tradition of coal and metal extraction and by a traditional pastoral economy. The extraction activity has entered its last stage of life; the coal mines that are still operating are on the verge of closing. Modern Sardinia is characterized by the crisis of an old economy and by a difficult transition toward new economies of tourism and the digital marketplace. The current economic crisis is hitting both agriculture and industry, and the most pressing problems in Sardinia are unemployment and the loss of jobs in all sectors. In Sardinia most of the population is concentrated in a few towns near the coast, while hundreds of villages in the interior and isolated mountain regions are experiencing a profound demographic crisis. Nevertheless, the countryside is essential for the island's economy and as a source of identity.

Although Sardinia is traditionally considered a region of southern Italy, for a number of reasons, several of Sardinia's social and cultural characteristics distinguish it from the traditional image of southern Italy. For example, the *Cosa Nostra*, or Italian mafia, does not exist in Sardinia—a fact that has been the object of several sociological studies and debates in an effort to explain this major difference between Sardinia and Sicily. In addition, we find other important differences in cultural, political, and social behavior. For example, the consumption of books, newspapers, and movies is equal to that of the most developed Italian regions. In 1974 Sardinia was the only southern Italian region supporting the national referendum to introduce divorce into Italian law, and Sardinia has one of the highest rates of female contraceptive use in Italy. These examples of a modern approach to marriage and sexuality provide a sense of how modern social behaviors are distant from traditional models of femininity on the island and in contrast to the more traditional culture of Sicily and the rest of Mezzogiorno.

Sardinia retains a mix of traditional and rural ways of life, economic distress, along with cultural openness and modernity. In the last 60 years, Sardinia has changed. Schools and universities have had a central role in this change. Sardinia is no longer an island of cultural distress and widespread illiteracy. Nevertheless, Sardinia has one of the highest secondary school dropout rates in Italy. These rates are even higher among the deindustrializing working class and higher in rural zones than the urban areas. Without continuing to increase educational attainment, Sardinia will not be able to continue its forward trajectory, but at what cost to small rural communities in its mountains?

The Italian Model of Schooling

The Italian school system has a single comprehensive pathway until the age of 14 divided into two segments: primary school (ages 6 to 10) and middle school (ages 11 to 14). Primary and middle school are separate. Even if the school has one administration (called a "comprehensive institute"), where students go to the same school building from kindergarten to middle school, the primary school and middle school are organized separately, and the professional and the pedagogical culture of the teachers is different in each level.

The passage from primary school to middle school in Sardinia is important but not dramatic. Every school furnishes an identical formal program (or curriculum) and students theoretically receive an identical education. Furthermore, schools are fairly well distributed in all the areas and villages. Nevertheless, schools differ in the "social qualities" of their service areas which are then translated in "school qualities." For example, certain schools in certain villages acquire a reputation within the community as "good schools" or "bad schools."

Students have no choice of which school they can attend, as enrollment is based on residency. In middle school, Italian students follow a standard curriculum. There is no individual choice of courses and students are not differentiated by level. The students' peer group also remains the same for three years.

At the age of 14, students encounter their first significant decision. High school (upper secondary) in Italy offers a complex typology of programs, including general, technical, and vocational programs, which are provided by different establishments. These correspond to the symbolic order of social value relative to the current labor market and reproduces old partitions, criticized by Gramsci (1971) as reproducing the old concept of the hierarchy of cultural values established in the mid-nineteenth century, reinforced by the reforms introduced during Fascism, and remaining unchanged during the period of the Italian republic. This three-tier partition of schooling reproduces class divisions and the status of education in relation to Italian society and culture.

The system of *Licei*, with general curriculums preparing students for university study, stands in clear contrast to the technical and vocational programs that prepare students to enter the workforce immediately after high school and obtain a job. It is possible for students from vocational sectors to attend university, but it is very rare. Most of the students that attend the university come from the upper secondary schools that have a general program of study that is further divided into different segments. The general sector or "college prep" is divided in six segments. The highest, in educational and social value, is represented by the curriculum of classical studies centered on the study of ancient languages; the next highest program in status is that of scientific studies. Thus, every sector is differentiated and presents an implicit hierarchy. The choice of programs by students and their families reflects this implicit social hierarchy, with the socioeconomic status of families and the quality of the students' middle school influencing where they go.

In this way, the passage from middle school to high school is the first critical crossroad on the way to university. The choice is charged with consequences because different school programs provide students with different competencies and skills. School programs reinforce existing cultural differences, which are linked to the cultural circumstances of families. In this way, the destiny of the student is largely decided at the age of 14. The choice of school program reproduces social inequalities, but even more problematic is the unequal distribution of opportunities between those students living in urban centers and those in the countryside. We call this the "structure of the offer."

The Structure of the Offer of Sardinian Schooling

In urban areas we find a wide range of possibilities for schooling: all kinds of school programs are available and students enjoy a better chance of enrolling in the school of their choice. In rural zones we often find a very limited offering, nearly a monoculture. The distribution of different school types in the country depends on the economic legacy of each area: thus, in one zone we may only find a school for agriculture or for tourism. In another zone we may only find a school with a general or college prep program. So the individual's school choice is determined by the availability of school programs in the area. Thus, the economic and social histories of the different areas determine the distribution of possibilities.

Moreover, this distribution of school programs changes the way the schools are perceived and the way they perform as a school. Indeed the prestige of a school is directly linked to its social history. There is circularity in the social image of the school and the choice by families. The image justifies the choice and the choice reinforces the image.

So we have to consider that families and students make a choice within the social field of education where the signification of schooling is relational: it can be understood only by considering the collection of positions in the school field and their social meaning. Every family translates the space of school choices realistically available into their social world and into their social history. With increased unemployment and rapidly changing labor markets, however, people from every social group want their children to attend school to be successful. Educational aspirations differ little across social classes and regions. In spite of this, students from different social groups have different school destinies.

In our research, responses from a sample of 18 schools in the Province of Cagliari (southeastern Sardinia) shows that schools are differentiated by their social qualities and for the school qualities of their students. There are two main groups of secondary schools: the urban general schools and the technical and vocational program schools, which are located primarily in the rural zone. (There are some technical schools in the urban zone and one general school in the rural zone.) At the extremes we find the town's most prestigious school and a vocational school, considered by middle class families as a "bad school."

Students and their families choose within two structural conditions: (1) first they choose from among the schools offered in their territory; (2) second, they choose within the structure of school meanings, with its symbolism and social value. Families from rural zones have a limited range of choices. Often they take buses to go to the next upper secondary school. The choice in this case between different programs is linked to the teenager's identity as a student. The identity of the student is the result of a process of construction of his own social identity within the school and in the student's social life.

The results of this differentiated structure of secondary school offerings can be seen in postsecondary enrollments. Sardinia has two universities: the University of Cagliari in the south of Sardinia, founded in 1626, and the smaller University of Sassari, founded in 1617. Almost all of the students at these two universities are from Sardinia; however, competition in the Italian university market pushes

Table 12.01 Comparison of program enrollment in secondary school to University of Cagliari (by percentage of students in program)

Secondary school programs	High school degrees	
	Secondary school	University of Cagliari
Classic and scientific programs	37.6	65.2
Artistic, linguistic, education	14.8	15.4
Technical and vocational	47.6	19.4

Source: University of Cagliari, academic year 2010–2011.

students from wealthy families to enroll in more prestigious Italian universities on the mainland, further stratifying the Italian postsecondary system. Sardinian universities enroll, above all, students from the upper working class and middle classes, which results in these universities experiencing higher dropout rates than those in other areas of Italy. Again, as shown in table 1, university enrollment varies in relation to the choice of secondary school program.

In conclusion, as the offering of school programs is unequally distributed in the region, school segregation is produced both in a structural and in a constructivist way: through the structure of the offer and through the construction of the choice. The match between offer and demand tends to succeed for middle and upper class students choosing academic programs where institutional goals and families' goals meet. For working class students and immigrants assigned to vocational school, the meeting between offer and demand is a failure. Students are at risk of dropping out; teachers are at risk of burnout.

Appalachian Kentucky, United States

Kentucky has one of the lowest levels of postsecondary educational attainment in the United States, and these levels are even lower in the Appalachian region of eastern Kentucky. Within this region, however, there are success stories. A small, but steadily increasing number of students in eastern Kentucky not only finish high school, but also choose to continue on to postsecondary education; however, this is a success story with a twist. Going to college often means leaving behind rural mountain homes or results in a highly vocational treatment of higher education, which may not result in increases in cultural capital or power within the local political economy.

In a research study of the life paths of young people from two high schools in eastern Kentucky initiated in 2006, a clear picture emerges of both relative success and the social reproduction of regional inequalities in Appalachia. The students' postsecondary credential attainment reflects cultural values for labor market potential in the ways they choose where to go to school and what to study. The study looked at two groups of students who grew up in two different communities in the same Appalachian region. One group attended a city school and one attended a rural county school. Both schools were approximately the same size, and families in their service area had the same per capita income. The city school, however, was in the top 10 percent of the state in going to college and the county school was in the bottom 25 percent. The city was home to banking, judicial institutions, and a small university, while the rural community had only a small gas station and a few government buildings. Both communities would be considered rural, with approximately 56,000 residents in total in 2006, and most readers would consider the "city" to be no more than a large village or town. The goal of the research project was to investigate how differences in high school environment and community values with respect to education in the town versus country setting were reflected in individual students' expectations and aspirations.

Eight to 10 students from each school were interviewed, with the majority of the data generated during their last year of secondary school and first year of college. The subsequent choice of college, major program of study, extracurricular activities, and vocational path were tracked through social media messages and alumni data from each student's high school. The students were selected from among those in their senior class for their college aspirations and, as a group, for their representativeness of various economic and educational backgrounds. The students had a variety of postsecondary institutions to choose from within the Appalachian region and across the country. The analysis included understanding students' choices of where to go to college as well as what to study.

The students' college choices reflected the ways they imagined their futures. The county students generally said they did not want to go far away. They did not want to feel "like people were making fun of their accents." They wanted to go where they knew folks. And when asked if they considered themselves "Appalachian," they said, "I'm not sure if I'd say Appalachian, but I'm definitely from the mountains." When asked if they would want to come home after finishing university, they generally (with one clear exception) said, "Yes, maybe after a couple of years away, but yes."

The city students claimed they did not mind leaving the mountains to travel to university. They had classmates (who were not interviewed) going all across the country and they did not find this unusual. They also wanted to go where they knew people, but they already had friends at colleges in the lowlands. They also had multiple choices because of the variety of places they applied for admission: "I don't know if I want to go to U Georgia or UK." When asked about being Appalachian, they replied, "I wouldn't say so" or "I'm from 'the city'" or "I'm from Kentucky." When asked if they would return to their mountain city, they responded, "Maybe. There aren't many jobs here. Maybe someday, but I don't know."

Thus in a superficial examination of the students' first choice—where to go to college—differences between the two groups are dramatic. All but one of the city students interviewed left the mountains to attend university, albeit mostly still in Kentucky, but definitely outside Appalachia. None of the county students left Appalachia and they all attended a university where they knew their classmates.

Once in college the differences were less substantial. Further analysis of subsequent choices—what to study, whether to participate in co-curricular activities, and whether to continue to graduation—did not reveal significant differences between the groups. They studied, played, succeeded, and sometimes failed as most university students do. In fact, despite less exposure to college culture than the city students, the county students were just as involved in university student groups, including social fraternities and sororities, as the city students. Members of both groups worked while in college, and members of both groups achieved or struggled academically at about the same level. One of the city students found his learning disabilities too much to overcome, but most of the successes and failures for those in both groups were the result of individual academic capital and motivation. Differences between the groups emerged again, however, when examining the students' career choices and how they positioned themselves to exchange their university credentials in the labor market.

The differences in postcollegiate outcomes between the two groups were stark. Of the city students who participated in the study, all but the student with severe learning disabilities pursued a graduate degree or professional experience within six years of graduating from high school. Their career trajectories included medicine, law, architecture, and business. In contrast, only four of the county students completed their university degree, with one still taking classes and one finishing a two-year degree instead of her originally planned baccalaureate. The county students' career trajectories include health sciences, education, and retail service. Jobs in nursing, teaching, and health care are available in the region, which may explain their choices. These career paths, however, do not hold the same social status, income potential, or personal autonomy as more professional careers.

The debate over the purposes of education, especially the ways in which education as an institution is a system of social reproduction that reflects the power structures of the political economy, has often returned to the question of whether formal education is intended to provide vocational training or an education supporting the democratic ideal of critical reasoning. As Freire and Macedo (1987) argue, critical literacy is reading both the world and the word. Bourdieu (1986) might call this cultural capital: credentials that can be exchanged for more than just the substance of the "ticket" but for other currencies of social status and power. These students' choices of majors and subsequent life choices may reflect how the structure of their educations has prepared them (or not) to engage in the world following schooling.

This glimpse of two groups of students and their biographies helps us understand that it is not just the educational system that reproduces social status and ambition, but the nested contexts of family, community, and labor market. Why did the county students aspire to such technocratic programs or discontinue their education? Are their choices right for them if they want to stay in their home communities, despite not being marked as successful by the more middle-class economic measures of salary or status? This research is limited by the small number of students studied; however, the biographies of these rural students do reflect educational statistics for the region (McGrew 2013), especially with regard to patterns of vocationalism (choosing a "pink collar" or "blue collar" vocation useful in the region over a "white collar" profession) and of mobility with higher socioeconomic status students venturing further from home for college and subsequently for work.

If the political economy of the coalfields helps explain why the county students followed more vocational career paths, why were the city students who live in the same coalfields so likely to go to graduate school for professional careers? This cannot be explained by parental education or income, as both groups represented the same range of socioeconomic status and parental educational backgrounds. These are small samples, but the outcomes of higher education and the ways that aspirations are constrained and framed by the particulars of where-you-are-from is worth more study. While we need to study postsecondary aspirations and how to encourage students to further their education, we also need to pay attention to where they go and what they dream of. Is their education "further" (vocational) or "higher" (professional), as the British terms are used? And what does this mean to their communities if they stay or leave?

Northern Areas of Pakistan

The northern areas of Pakistan comprise the entire province of Gilgit-Baltistan and the Chitral district of Khyber-Pakhtunkhwa Province. Gilgit-Baltistan spreads over 72,971 square kilometers with an estimated population of 1.8 million people, whereas the Chitral district covers an area of 14,850 square kilometers and is inhabited by nearly half a million people. These rural, mountainous regions of Gilgit-Baltistan and Chitral are home to some of the world's highest mountains, natural lakes, scenic valleys, and unique cultural traditions. According to Mortenson and Relin, about "sixty of the world's tallest mountains lord their severe alpine beauty over a witness-less high altitude wilderness" (2006, 7). Four of the world's highest mountain ranges—the Himalaya, Karakoram, Pamir, and Hindu Kush—meet in these regions. Most communities here are settled at 3,000 meters or above. These regions are usually described by both Pakistani and international travelers as the most beautiful mix of valleys, mountains, and streams anywhere in the natural world. However, recent years have seen faster changes in the landscape of these places due to natural disasters and economic development activities. There are many isolated valleys and villages, most of which lacked access roads and other means of communication until recently. There are still some that do not have all-weather access to other parts of the country. Many valleys and villages remain cut off from the rest of the country for three or four months every year due to harsh winters. So they often lack basic year-round necessities of life, including access to education and health facilities. Local governments are still unable to provide these facilities due to lack of resources and transportation in winter.

The economy in Gilgit-Baltistan and Chitral had been dependent on tourism, which flourished with the construction of the Karakoram Highway between Gilgit-Baltistanand China. However, sectarian tensions and the deterioration of law and order in other parts of Pakistan have now affected these regions as well. Under peaceful conditions these areas would be able to enjoy the benefits of their strategic situation, as Gilgit-Baltistan connects Pakistan with China through the KKH and Chitral provides the shortest land route to Afghanistan and Central Asia. Culturally, people in these regions have a lot in common with people in the Central Asia, particularly Tajikistan.

Meanwhile, Gilgit-Baltistan and Chitral are fortunate to have an array of civil society institutions engaged in supplementing the local governments' efforts towards development of this area. The most prominent of these are the institutions of the Aga Khan Development Network (AKDN), which are the pioneers of development in education, health, environment, culture, and other sectors in Gilgit-Baltistan and Chitral. The AKDN is a group of agencies with mandates that include the environment, health, education, architecture, culture, microfinance, rural development, habitat, disaster reduction, the promotion of private-sector enterprise, and revitalization of historic cities. These agencies include:

1. Aga Khan Academies (AKA)
2. Aga Khan Agency for Microfinance (AKAM)
3. Aga Khan Education Services (AKES)
4. Aga Khan Foundation (AKF)
5. Aga Khan Fund for Economic Development (AKFED)
6. Aga Khan Health Services (AKHS)
7. Aga Khan Planning and Building Services (AKPBS)
8. Aga Khan Trust for Culture (AKTC)
9. Aga Khan University (AKU)
10. Focus Humanitarian Assistance (FOCUS)
11. University of Central Asia (UCA)

The AKDN works to improve the standards of living and prospects of people in the disadvantaged regions in Asia and Africa, as well as in Pakistan and Tajikistan. Operating in more than 25 countries, these agencies follow a philosophy of community-based self-help efforts for development whereby local communities are active participants in their development efforts (Tajik 2004). The development philosophy underpinning the AKDN is that "a humane, sustainable environment must reflect the choices made by people themselves on how they live and wish to improve their prospects in harmony with their environment" (AKDN 2007, 1). Therefore AKDN agencies take a long-term, multiagency, multisectoral input approach to development, which creates the local–international synergy they believe necessary for community development (Tajik 2004).

Education in Northern Areas of Pakistan

There are about 3,000 schools and educational institutions in Gilgit-Baltistan and Chitral, including an international university and subcampuses of two other universities. The government is the largest provider of education in the region; however, an increasing number of private and community-based schools and colleges and *Madressahs* also provide such services. School education is divided into (a) preschool and primary school (kindergarten to grade 5), (b) middle school (grades 6 to 8), (c) high school (grades 9 and 10), and (d) higher secondary school (grades 11 and 12). All students in the public sector schools have to study the same subjects from kindergarten to grade 8. After grade 8, students can choose to study sciences, arts, or commerce. After grade 10, students can have further choices within these disciplines; for example, within the sciences, they can either choose medicine or engineering. Similarly, within the arts, they can select law or political science or Islamic Studies or linguistics, and so on. The decision regarding what a student chooses to study is usually taken by parents or teachers. However, this trend is gradually changing as students, particularly in the private schools, get career counseling and sometimes decide to pursue other subjects.

In Gilgit-Baltistan, the subject of Islamiyat (Islamic Studies) has been a bone of contention between the two main sects of Islam, the *Sunnis* and the *Shiis*, each fighting for including its own interpretations and theological position. There have been many sectarian clashes and violence here concerning the school Islamic curriculum, which has led to closure of schools for months and the loss of lives in the streets, mainly over content of the Islamiyat. However, the government is trying to neutralize the controversy by including only Islamic themes and topics common to both *Sunnis* and *Shiis*.

The Karakoram International University in Gilgit-Baltistan is a relatively new regional university with high academic goals and aspirations. This university can play a pivotal role in bringing about positive reforms in education and, by implication, in the local society. It seeks to connect with universities in other mountainous societies to learn how to develop and deliver a rural curriculum, which could cater to the diverse needs of rural communities. However, the subcampuses of the other two universities in Chitral are operating in modest buildings with limited resources. These two university campuses do not have the capacity to offer any viable program that could fuel a positive change in the local education landscape.

Nonetheless, the Aga Khan University has established professional development centers (PDCs) in both Gilgit-Baltistan and Chitral, and these centers develop and implement high-quality professional education programs and school improvement models by drawing upon international best practices and local wisdom. Thousands of teachers, school principals, educators, and education managers have benefited from the capacity-building programs offered by these centers. Located in Karachi (to the south), the Aga Khan University's Institute for Educational Development (AKU-IED) has developed more than 300 teacher educators and education managers from Gilgit-Baltistan and Chitral through its PhD, masters of education, and advanced diploma programs. These graduates are now working as leaders and change agents in these regions.

Generally, the progress of education in the northern areas of Pakistan has been remarkable, with a literacy rate much higher than those of other provinces of Pakistan. Much of the credit for this improved education standards goes to the Aga Khan Education Service Pakistan (AKES,P), which is among the largest private networks of education institutions in Pakistan. Beginning with its very first school opened in 1905 in Gwadar, Balochistan (now a province of Pakistan), AKES,P has been providing quality education for over a hundred years in some of the most remote areas of Pakistan. It is a direct provider of education for students from preprimary to higher secondary school and facilitates access to tertiary education through provision of scholarships, hostels, career counseling, and other educational support services. Table 12.2 below provides data about the number of schools and the population served by the schools. Most of these schools are for girls—many of whom only three decades ago had no formal schooling. For example, the female literacy rate in Chitral district was 10 percent just before AKDN opened a chain of girls' schools in the 1980s (Tajik 2004). Now the literacy rate for females in the district is around 58 percent.

AKES,P concentrates its energy and resources on improving educational practice; leadership, and management in diverse and challenging contexts; female education; active learning and child-centered teaching methods; use of information technology; school-based teacher development programs; and working in partnership with the local government and communities. As active partners in education, the local communities provide free land, local materials, and unskilled labor to construct school buildings, while AKES,P provides nonlocal materials, skilled labor, and technical support for construction work. Similarly, the local communities elect school management committees (SMCs) to closely work with AKES,P management in the day-to-day management and operations of schools. AKES,P provides academic and technical support, including hiring and training teachers, paying teachers' salaries, and funding other school operations related

Table 12.02 AKES,P Schools in GB and Chitral at a glance

	Primary	Middle	High	Higher Secondary	Total
No. of schools managed directly by AKES,P	69	40	36	6	151
No. of schools managed by local communities in partnership with AKES,P (community-based schools)		200			200
Total					351

Students enrollment, by gender and school type

	Female	Male	Total
AKES,P managed schools	15,690	15,514	31,204
Community-based schools	16,583	7,107	23,690
Total			54,894

Staff and Volunteers

Teachers	1,800
Other staff	700
Volunteers	2,000
Total	4,500

to curriculum and assessment. Students pay tuition (subsidized by AKES,P) to contribute to the overall costs of school operations (AKESP 1997).

To increase the local communities' ownership of these schools, AKES,P is gradually delegating more responsibility for managing them to the local communities. For example, AKES,P provided matching grants to those communities that had both financial and management capacity to gradually take over the overall management of their schools. The grants were deposited in the school account, and the accruing interest was used to pay the teacher salaries. Some communities in far-flung villages have taken over the management of their schools and upgraded them to college level, thereby enabling young women in local villages to receive education from preprimary to grade 14 at their doorstep. The girls who, a few decades back, were denied from education are now encouraged to explore various fields of education, including natural sciences, social sciences, and liberal arts.

In some parts of Pakistan, girls are still discouraged from going to school, and even if some of them do get education, they are restricted to more stereo-typical occupations such as teaching or nursing. However, girls in most parts of the Northern Pakistan can now choose from many career paths, based on their qualifications and interests. Girls have also begun to participate in many activities previously the purview of boys and men, such as mountaineering and other outdoor sports. For example, Samina Baig, a 23-year-old girl from a remote village in Gilgit-Baltistan, on May 19, 2013, became the first Pakistani woman to climb Mount Everest. Another young girl from Chitral, Sifat Gul, won the Best National Micro-Entrepreneur Award Female by the Pakistan Poverty Alleviation Fund in 2007 (http://www.akdn.org/press-release/first-microfinance-banks-client-wins-best-micro-entrepreneur-award). Similarly, an increasing number of qualified women are in leadership positions in the public and private sector and civil society institutions (Tajik et al. 2015).

The AKDN agencies' work is guided by the philosophy that socioeconomic development in the rural, mountainous areas will not be sustainable unless both men and women are actively engaged in the development process. There-fore, women's empowerment is another underlying principle in the work of each AKDN agency.

The AKDN believes their community-based education system still has a number of challenges, but that it works better than most other private and pub-lic sector school improvement models because the local communities own the schools and thus invest their time, energy, wisdom, and resources in the schools. This model follows the principles of "school as a learning community," where parents learn how to run and manage a school even as children learn the school curriculum and co-curriculum schemes. Teachers learn not only how to teach but also how to develop the dual role of community development activist and education reformer. Similarly, AKES,P continuously learns how it can better mobilize local communities towards education at the same time they learn how to improve the quality of education in the school.

What is more intriguing than the increase in literacy rate is the transforma-tion of local communities that were once dead-set against girls' education. Many local community schools now work as active and effective partners in the man-agement of schools, colleges, and hostels for girls. There once was a time when this region sorely lacked qualified human resources to lead education and school-ing. Now the region exports leadership to educational institutions in other parts of the country. While most development has traveled from urban cities to the rural areas, the lesson of how organized communities can work to improve their lives has traveled from the northern areas to the rest of Pakistan (Tajik 2004).

The interventions of the AKDN agencies in this region have not only contrib-uted to the socioeconomic development of the local communities, but they have also led to a positive change in education policy, with the government actively encouraging a much greater role for local communities in education as well as other development sectors. The present educational landscape of Gilgit-Baltistan and Chitral has been described as a comprehensive process of change in recent decades, having positive impact on the educational, socioeconomic, political, and cultural conditions of these regions (Benz 2014).

As a result, the northern areas of Pakistan present a contextually relevant model and a community-based approach to development in all fields, especially in education. This model of development and education is worth exploring, and the AKDN believes it is replicable in many other mountainous societies.

From Mountain to Mountain

These three examples raise important questions for policy makers interested in increasing human capital in mountain communities. The choices that students and their families make are not without constraint. School policy and location influence and shape those choices. Furthermore, educational decisions are strongly influenced by cultural values, which are, in turn, products of cultural interpretations and negotiations of local political economies. And, finally, the educational choices available for the children of mountain communities often mask a persistent and unequal partitioning of schooling into vocational and professional career pathways that can result in the social reproduction of inequalities within the seemingly successful story of succeeding in school.

JANE JENSEN is Associate Professor and director of graduate studies in the Department of Educational Policy Studies and Evaluation, and a Chellgren Professor for Undergraduate Excellence at the University of Kentucky. She is the author of *Post-Secondary Education on the Edge: Self-Improvement and Community Development in a Cape Breton Coal Town* and coauthor of *Piecing It Together: A Guide to Student Academic Success.*

MARCO PITZALIS is director of the Inter-University Center for Educational Research and a faculty member in the Department of Social Sciences at the University of Cagliari, Italy, among other affiliations. Some of his recent publications focus on cultural capital and education and the technological turn. He has also done research on the political mobilization of shepherds in Sardinia, Italy.

MIR AFZAL TAJIK is Associate Professor at the Nazarbayev University Graduate School of Education (NUGSE). Before joining NUGSE in September 2016, Dr. Tajik worked as an Associate Professor and held leadership positions including interim director, associate director, head of graduate programs, and head of Outreach Centres and Education Development programs at Aga Khan University Institute for Educational Development.

ALAN J. DEYOUNG is Professor emeritus of Sociology and Education at the University of Kentucky. He focuses on educational reform in post–Soviet Central Asia and South Asia. He has been a Fulbright Scholar in Kazakhstan, Kyrgyzstan, and Turkmenistan. He has written or edited six books on education and higher education reform in Appalachia and in Central Asia.

Notes

1. *Madressahs* are schools established by religious organizations that offer free but predominantly religious education.
2. The 'O' and 'A' level education is provided by private sector schools only, mostly the elite private schools.

References

Aga Khan Development Network (AKDN). 2007. An Ethical Framework. http://www.ismailimail.wordpress.com/2007/02/24/aga-khan-development-network-akdn-an-ethical-framework/2/.

Aga Khan education service, Pakistan (AKESP). 1997. *Northern Areas & Chitral Program Description*, Gilgit.http://www.agakhanschools.org/brochures/akes.pdf.

Benz, Andreas. 2014. *Education for Development in the Northern Pakistan: Opportunities and Constraints for Rural Households*. Karachi: Oxford University Press.

Bourdieu, P. 1986. The forms of capital. In J. Richardson (Ed.) *Handbook of Theory and Research for the Sociology of Education* (New York, Greenwood), 241–258.

Freire, P., & Macedo, D.P. 1987. *Literacy: Reading the Word & the World*. London: Routledge.

IIS and AKDN. 1999. *Social Norms and Social Exclusion Reaching the Poor: Progress programmes of the Aga Khan Development Network. Values, Norms, and Poverty*. A Consultation on WDR 2000/1: Poverty and Development. Johannesburg, South Africa, January 12–14.

Gramsci, Antonio. 1971. *Selections from the Prison Notebooks*. International Publishers.

McGrew, C. 2013. *Education Policies and Migration Realities: Utilizing a State Longitudinal Data System to Understand the Dynamics of Migration Choices for College Graduates from Appalachian Kentucky*. Unpublished doctoral dissertation. University of Kentucky, Lexington, KY.

Mortenson, Greg and Relin, David Oliver. 2006. *Three Cups of Tea: One Man's Mission to Promote Peace—One School at a Time*. London: Penguin.

Tajik, Mir Afzal. 2004. *From Educational Reformers to Community Developers: The Changing Roles of Field Education Officers . . . in Chitral, Pakistan*. PhD Dissertation, University of Toronto, Canada.

Tajik, Mir A., Nawab Ali, and Khan, A.W. 2015. *The Role of Civil Society Institutions in Promoting Cultural Diversity and Pluralism in District Chitral*. Unpublished research report, AKU-IED, Karachi.

CHAPTER 13

Jirga

EVERYDAY PEACE-BUILDING IN RURAL
MOUNTAIN COMMUNITIES OF PAKISTAN

Sajjad Ahmad Jan

PASHTUNS ARE A Muslim ethnic group living in patrilineal clans and villages in the mountain regions of Pakistan. The 30 million or so Pashtun residents of Pakistan belong to 400 different tribal groups. Pashtuns are not only marginalized in material terms, they are also denied equal access to the government services provided to other regions of the country. The tribal regions of Pakistan do not have a strong presence of public institutions, and, for that reason, people in the region often feel they are being treated as second-class citizens by the state. In the state's absence, local people have created their own institutions through tribal and clan affiliations and identities. In this chapter, I argue that even though these village-level organizations cannot completely replace the work of public institutions, these small, informal organizations—their collective aspects, at least—can serve as examples for other mountain residents working to sustain their communities in the absence of state and public services. I am writing as a Pashtun from the rural mountains of Pakistan who is now living and teaching at a university in Peshawar, an urban center within the region. There are gendered and generational critiques of the villages' informal institutions, and young people who are participating both in their village communities and in urban university life often see these informal institutions as too conservative because they are dominated by male elders and allow for little participation by women, for example. These young people are organizing their own small-scale informal institutions to promote human rights, share their musical heritage, and put forward other efforts they find meaningful, while maintaining connections to their villages. Traditional village-level informal institutions do not have adequate resources to address every single issue that villagers face, but when it comes to resolving local disputes and keeping the peace at the village level, they play a key role. Acknowledging the critiques of gendered dimensions of these decision-making systems, this chapter describes some of the benefits of small-scale collective decision-making and action at the village level, in which it matters that villagers know one another well throughout their lives and support one another through reciprocity. Residents of this region grow tired of being stereotyped in the international press as living in a site characterized by constant violence; I describe here everyday peace-building at the village level that has a lot to contribute to global discussions.

British colonial administrators once labeled the northwestern part of Pakistan "Sarzameene-Be-Aaeen," which means a land without any rule of law or coverage by a state. The northwestern parts of Pakistan are predominantly inhabited by the Pashtuns. The Pashtuns' homeland stretches between Afghanistan on its western side and Pakistani Punjab on its eastern side. It is broadly called the province of Pakhtunkhwa—which means the area where Pashtuns are located. It is one of the four provinces of Pakistan and can be divided into three broader subregions: the Central Pakhtunkhwa, the Northern Pakhtunkhwa, and the Southern Pakhtunkhwa. The Central Pakhtunkhwa, also known as the Peshawar Valley, has fertile plains suitable to support subsistence as well as large-scale agriculture and industrial activities. It has the highest population concentration among all the three subregions of the province. The capital city of Peshawar is also situated in this subregion. The Northern Pakhtunkhwa is predominantly mountainous and is home to some of the most famous mountain ranges in the world, like the Himalayas and the Hindu Kush.

The Southern Pakhtunkhwa is home to arid and dry plains as well as minor mountain ranges. Administratively, the province is comprised of 25 districts and 7 tribal regions that are stretched along Afghanistan's border. These tribal regions, commonly known as "agencies," have recently been merged in the province. Pashtuns in this region continue to live without adequate support and services from government institutions. The people of this peripheral mountain region address most of their issues through traditional institutions. The most important of these informal arrangements is the *jirga*, an assembly of elders working to resolve disputes between individuals as well as groups. Other matters such as conducting weddings and funerals, harvesting crops, building homes, and coping with natural and manmade disasters are also taken care of through informal arrangements at the clan or village level. These informal arrangements are based on the principle of reciprocity: that is, you help me and I will help you.

In the Pashtuns' language and culture, *Kalai Ulas* and *Gham Khadi* are terms that show the strength of networking ties between people. The literal meaning of Kalai Ulas is "Village People" and of that Gham Khadi is "Grief Happiness." They simply explain the spirit of people motivated to take care of the village and the support of the people living there for one another in both grief and happiness.

Pashtun tribal leaders try to fill the vacuum created by the negligence of the state in establishing institutions equivalent to social security and other services.

Kalai Ulas and Gham Khadi are the manifestations of those informal arrangements that Pashtuns adopt at the village or community level to survive and cope with expected and unexpected events, including disease, disability, death, floods, harvesting, and construction needs. Ashar in the Central and Northern Pakhtunkhwa and Palandra in the tribal area of Khyber Agency are two important instances of the Pashtuns working to help each other in the harvesting of crops and home building. In both cases, people of a single village (in some cases, people of more than one village) gather and harvest crops or build a home for a person. This is done for all who are in need and who contribute to harvesting crops and building the homes of other people. This has the advantage of specialization: when many people are available for a task, different subtasks are assigned to different people and no single person needs to do all the different tasks. This enhances the skills and productivity of a person in doing a particular task, as the person becomes more efficient at doing that particular task. If we take the example of cutting and threshing wheat, we can say that some people would cut the wheat, others would collect and bind the wheat, while still others would take it to the thresher. This is the case with other tasks requiring the work of many, like building a home for someone. This collective action economizes on money and material, as well as time, and those with the fewest resources benefit the most from these sorts of collective actions. Other instances of informal arrangements at the village and societal level through collective action are the holding of weddings and funerals.

Both weddings and funerals are costly for the people in the Pashtuns' region, and they deal with this through informal collective arrangements at the community and village levels. Wedding costs include providing to the wedding couple a house or a room, jewelry, home appliances, and utensils, and preparing and serving meals to the entire village and community. These requirements for a wedding are fulfilled through collective informal arrangements under the principle of reciprocity. People from the village and community help the groom build a house or a room, and they also contribute cash gifts so that the bride and groom may arrange for all that is necessary for a new life. They make all the arrangements for serving the guests invited by the couple and their families. Other villagers work as cooks to prepare the meals and serve as waiters to present the meals to the guests. This greatly minimizes the costs for the families of the bride and groom, for fulfilling a task that has immense social value in the local culture.

The other important, and unexpected, event in which this arrangement applies is the death of someone in the village. The family that bears the grief of the death of a family member also has to bear the costs of fulfilling rituals, which have great importance in local culture and tradition. The costs range from those for preparing the grave to purchasing a coffin for the deceased to serving the people who came to participate in the rituals. Young people from the village take their tools and go to the graveyard to prepare a grave for the deceased. Others make arrangements for the people who will come to participate in the rituals. They are served tea and water, and sometimes meals. The cost of the coffin and other costs are borne by people of the village. Fellow villagers provide food and meals for the family of the deceased and the guests. The family of the deceased is not encouraged to prepare meals for themselves or for their guests for three days—others do that for them. Both for weddings and for funerals, tents, crockery, and other tools are owned and purchased by a whole Pashtun village. The family conducting a wedding or facing a funeral is provided with all of these materials without cost. Informal arrangements in the form of collective action at the village and community level also help resolve conflicts between individuals and clans through *jirga*.

Resolving disputes and feuds through jirga between individuals, families, and clans is the established norm in the Pashtun region. The literal meaning of jirga is "congregation or assembly of people," and it evolved over centuries in Pashtun villages. It is a Pashtun version of the Punjabi *Punchayat*. *Jirga* is a simple and informal way to resolve disputes between people. It is less costly than appealing to the nonexistent or overburdened and less efficient judiciary. In jirga, people from a village or clan gather and sit to discuss and decide on any dispute between the people. The people gathering for jirga do not need chairs and tables and sofas to sit on. They do not even need stationery to write up the proceedings or decisions of the jirga. What they need is a piece of land to sit on, and they often draw lines on the ground to calculate the costs and compensations to the parties in the dispute. Sometimes jirga is comprised of elders from different Pashtun clans and tribes; that jirga is known as *Loya jirga*. The literal meaning of Loya jirga is "Grand Congregation" or "Grand Assembly." That group deals with issues faced by the Pashtuns at large, like the effects of terrorism. The most important feature of jirga is that everyone (if allowed to participate in the jirga) has an equal right to speak and vote, regardless of age. This shows the collective aspect of Pashtun informal institutions described earlier. If any party to a dispute violates the ruling or decision of the jirga, the jirga has the right to confiscate the securities submitted to the jirga before it is convened, from the concerned party. This way of resolving disputes between the Pashtuns is less costly and is readily available. Though not a perfect substitute for the more formal governmental judicial system, even the poorest residents have access to jirga and can resolve any issue pertaining to them through jirga with minimal cost in time and resources compared to the government judiciary, where cases may go on for decades.

Rather than being seen as "lawless," tribal areas in the mountains of Pakistan, some aspects of Pashtun villagers' collective institutions provide examples of peace-building and problem-solving for larger organizations and states facing their own economic and political challenges.

SAJJAD AHMAD JAN is Assistant Professor in the Department of Economics, University of Peshawar, Pakistan. His recent research interests and projects focus on socioeconomic issues in Pakistan including social exclusion, vulnerability to poverty, socioeconomic marginalization, and formal and informal social security mechanisms.

CHAPTER 14

Mapping and Measuring Digital Divides in Mountain Regions

GLOBAL AND LOCAL KNOWLEDGE AND SILENCES

Stanley D. Brunn and Maria Paradiso

GEOGRAPHERS ARE AMONG those social and policy scientists interested not only in the information produced and knowledge about places and regions, but also the impacts of information and communication technologies (ICTs) on economies and cultures at global and local scales. Geographers incorporate much of their writing about these subjects in discussing the diffusion of ICTs, the diversity and density of ICT innovations on cities and rural areas, and the relationship of these issues to social well-being. In this chapter we explore these issues especially as they help us understand mountain regions and cultures. The discussion is divided into two major sections; the first looks at what we know (and, correspondingly, what we do not know) about mountain regions on a global scale, and the second examines what the impacts are of ICTs on one specific rural mountain region, namely, southern Italy, among young and older populations.

We begin our discussion by looking at two concepts: the geographies of knowledge and the geographies of silences. They are used to examine the differential knowledge bases about major mountain regions. We map and graph some of the unevenness that exists. Following this discussion, we look at an example of local knowledge geographies, in this case, three mountain communities in southern Italy. Here we explore place attachment and retention as they relate to potential mobility, broadband use, and the presence of digital divides.

Geographies of Knowledge and Silences

As human/environmental geographers interested in mountain cultures, economic justice, and environments, there are two concepts that help us understand some important and neglected geographies, especially as they relate to information and technology. The first is the "geographies of knowledge and silence" and the second, related to it, is the "cartographies of silence" (Brunn and Wilson, 2012).

In the past decade geographers having been investigating "knowledge" questions within the context of "what we know about any subject"—not only addressing the question of *what* we know, but also *how much* do we know about a given subject (Livingstone 2010). The question of the *quantity* of knowledge, or what we know, can be addressed by using a number of sources, including materials in libraries, museums, archives, and collections where textual and cartographic materials are housed. While we tend to think of these familiar sources for finding out how much we know about a given subject, a more recent research database and source has entered the scene: the Google search engine; it is a virtual storehouse of electronic information about almost any subject. To be more specific, the Google hyperlinks or electronic sources (maps, numerical data, visuals) are the major sources used by many current scholars, and especially young scholars (some of whom may see print sources as less reliable and less accessible than sources available online). One could easily make the case that the amount of information on any subject is best discerned by using the Google search engine and that if we want to examine what scholars have produced, we could use the Google Scholar database.

A follow-on question to the above case for Google as a "know all" source of information is how much do we know (about a culture, an economy, a mountain region, or even a food, musical instrument, farming practice, or custom, for example) using this knowledge base, which—as we know—is very uneven. We also would have to acknowledge, with some humility, that our Google-based knowledge base is language biased and culturally biased, and also very strongly Europeanized-world biased.

An examination of major library holdings or Google search engine hyperlinks would reveal that there is much more information available about some cultures, environments, economies, and regions than others. We can think of this "unevenness" conceptually, that is, we know more or have more information available (published) about European mountain cultures than those in East Africa, or we know more about the agricultural economies of the North American Middle West than about the crop and livestock systems in Southeast Asia. The

Google search engine provides one index or barometer of such a knowledge base, biased in the aforementioned ways.

In this study we use English-language entries in the Google search engine, recognizing that the results for any region, country, or, in this case, mountain range, would differ if we used another widely spoken language such as Spanish, French, Chinese, Arabic, Russian, or Hindi. We selected English, as it is recognized as the dominant scholarly language of internet messaging and communication worldwide. We also recognize that the volume of hyperlinks changes regularly. Thus, the results for any mountain region in any language will be different in 2020 than in 2013.

Using the entries in the Google database for the 40 mountain ranges listed in Table 1 shows significant differences in the volume of information. A casual reading shows that the largest volumes were not entirely in English-speaking or even in European countries.

The unevenness in knowledge about major mountain ranges and systems is also clearly apparent in Figure 1.

The next step focused on major categories of information about mountains. We selected 22 different subject categories related to mountain economies, cultures, and societies. The leading categories were Industry (583 million), Ethnicity (576 million); Mining (541 million), Religion (538 million) and Conflict (500 million). The fewest entries were Language (201 million), Culture (200 million), History (198 million), Social Media (131 million) and GIS, or Geographic Information System (114 million).

If we enter the names of the mountain systems below, and the words *history, culture, environment,* and so on, we obtain sharply different numbers. The leading regions for examples of several categories are: *History*: Guiana Highlands (40 million), Alps (26 million), Andes (19 million), Rocky Mountains (15 million), and Brooks Range (9 million); *Culture*: Norway Uplands (44 million), Guiana Highlands (40 million), Andes (12 million), Alps (9 million), and Atlas (8 million); *Environment*: Brazilian Highlands (51 million), Guiana Highlands (39 million), Cascades (20 million), Alps, Atlas, Rocky Mountains, and Andes (11 million each), and Appalachia (9 million); and *Tourism*: Cascades (67 million), Norway Uplands (42 million), Guiana Highlands (35 million), Rocky Mountains (11 million), and Alps (10 million).

We also expanded our knowledge question into a cartographic domain (Crampton 2001; Edney 2009). That is, we can consider features of cultures, economies, and so on that are on maps. We discovered that we (again, here "we" referring now to Google users, with the limitations already discussed) know more about cultures, economies, and environments in some mountain regions than in others. For example, we would know much more about the economies of the Snowy Mountains in Australia than we would about the Andes and much more about the Alps than about the Appalachians. Variations also exist when looking at features of mountain cultures in relation to general or even specific topics

Table 14.1 Volume of hyperlinks to information on major mountain regions

Mountain region	Hyperlinks (millions)
Pyrenees	110
Andes	107
Himalayas	47
Sierra Nevada	41
Alps	26
East African Highlands	19.9
Scottish Highlands	16.8
Brooks Range	16.2
Atlas	12.4
Snowy Mts.	11.2
Norway Uplands	9.4
New Guinea Highlands	8.8
Caucasus	7.7
Rocky Mts.	6.7
Japanese Alps	5.9
Southern Alps	5.0
Annamese Mts.	4.0
Appalachia	3.5
Western Ghats	3.0
Brazilian Highlands	2.9
Tien Shan	2.5
Cascades	2.3
Hindu Kush	2.2
Hejaz	2.2
Urals	1.9
Carpathians	1.5
Pennines	.9
Apennines	.9
Altai	.7
Zagros	.7
Sierra Madre Occidental	.7
Ozarks	.6
Pamirs	.6
Drakensberg Mts.	.5
Ethiopian Highlands	.4
Guiana Highlands	.3

Table 14.1 (Continued)

Mountain region	Hyperlinks (millions)
Dinaric Alps	.3
Sierra Madre Oriental	.2
Tibesti Mts.	.10
Verkhoyansk Range	.03

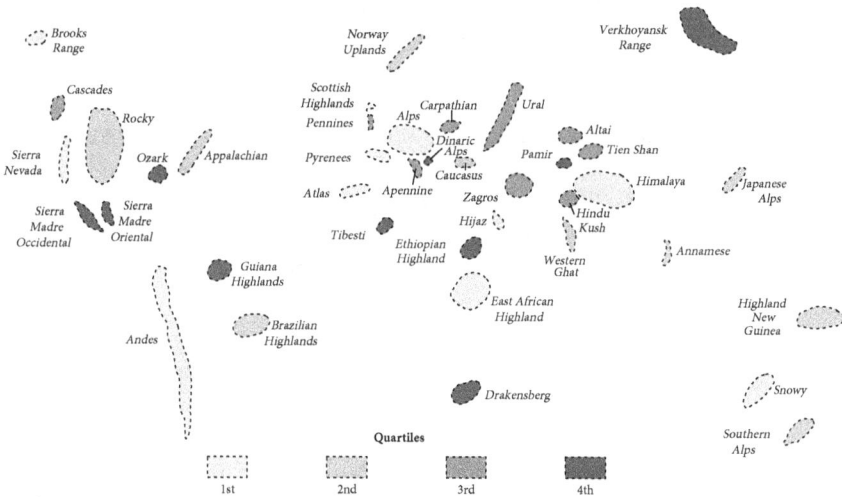

Fig. 14.1 Global Mountain Regions, Google Hyperlinks, June 2013–Total

such as languages, religion, music, endangered languages, childhood diseases, or impacts of globalization. The mountain regions with the most map entries in the Google search engine were Norway Uplands (44 million), Guiana Highlands (39 million), Andes (22 million), and Appalachia (18 million). The fewest map entries were for Dinaric Alps (191,000), Sierra Madre Oriental (112,000), and Tibesti Mountains (only 57,000).

We also wanted to observe any relationships between the total number of hyperlinks and the number of maps for each mountain range. Overall, there was a direct relationship between the two rankings. On the one hand, there were some mountain ranges that ranked high in total number of hyperlinks but had very few maps, such as the Sierra Nevada, Highland New Guinea, and Southern Alps. On the other hand, there were some mountain systems for which there were relatively few hyperlinks, and only a moderate number of maps; these include the Verkhoyansk Range, Guiana Highlands, and Ethiopian Highlands. The ranges with the fewest maps were in Asia, with the highest number of maps being available for Europe or for English-speaking countries. These results might have been different, of course, had our search been in Mandarin or Hindi.

The Geographies and Cartographies of Silences

When we look at the unevenness in published information or information available electronically in English-language searches, we might consider the paucity of information within the context of the "geographies of silence" (Brunn and Wilson 2012). Silences may exist for several reasons. First, those places may not have been the subject of information collected or published. Second, there are likely only a few ways in which the information could or would be disseminated. That is, "information or knowledge gatekeepers" prevent information from being available. These gatekeepers may be government agencies, scholarly presses, private presses, or even official scientific organizations that preclude the release of new knowledge about new places. Third, someone may believe that the new information would be of little use to anyone. "Silent" or silenced information may be about the origins and spread of diseases, genocide, or natural disasters; some with power may consider "no news or reporting" the best policy.

The silences of knowledge production and manipulation also exist with respect to visual images, that is, maps and photographs. It should come as no surprise to scholars or to the general public that there are many silences in the worlds of cartography and photography. Maps and photos, whether in books, in articles, or on the internet, are considered major vehicles for informing readers and viewers about geographic subject matter. In a world that is increasingly hungry for instant information about any subject, the visual is often the primary source of information. Viewers are moved by photos of places, especially those that evoke powerful images of conflicts and destruction.

Returning to the silences related to maps and photos of mountain regions, our database of these sources also reveals much unevenness. We have thousands of maps related to some mountain cultures, economies, and environments and very few about others. The same could be said about photographs of mountain cultures in relation to photos of cities. We have more maps about the Pyrenees than are accessible about the Atlas Mountains, even though both have played important roles in European and European-African history. We know more about the Caucasus Mountains than about the Zagros Mountains, even though both have played major roles in their region's early history. European colonial ventures in Africa, Latin America, and Asia provided opportunities for Europeans to "collect and map" information for colonial acquisitions and hegemony. To "control" a people and place meant you could "prove" or establish your legitimacy by producing maps that showed your claims against a colonial rival. The proof was in the printed map that was disseminated. The map gave control. In a similar vein today, one might consider the internet as a legitimate, legal, and official source to prove a territorial claim or provide an electronic document about ownership.

We do know from historical studies of the mapping of European states and colonial explorations that there were variations in how many maps were produced and what they conveyed. Detailed maps would be constructed on places in and around one's European state; these might show major physical features (rivers, mountains, lakes, etc.), economic livelihood (ports, agricultural regions, forested lands, etc.), as well as legal claims (state boundaries and intrastate political jurisdictions). Colonial maps of distant locations might only show coastal features and important towns, leaving large areas where little was actually known. Thus "cartographic silences" were much in evidence on many colonial maps from the fifteenth to the early twentieth century. There remain "map silences" in many countries today as well as in many mountain economies, environments, and cultures. We would expect to find thousands of detailed maps about property ownership, crop and livestock patterns, glaciers, and church cemeteries in the Swiss and Italian Alps, but few about the mountain regions in the Central Andes, Central Asia, the East African Highlands, and highland Papua New Guinea.

When we consider mountain regions in the United States or elsewhere, there are also vast differences in the amount of information. In August 2013, these were the numbers for major US regions: South 7.7 billion hyperlinks, New England 1.7 billion, Middle West 717 million, Pacific Northwest 110 million, and Appalachia only 3.5 million hyperlinks. There were also differences in the regional knowledge about Appalachia: Northern Appalachia 1.7 million, Central Appalachia 2.3 million, and Southern Appalachia 3.5 million hyperlinks. There is also some unevenness when it comes to maps: Southern Appalachia 7.6 million, Northern Appalachia 5.2 million, and Central Appalachia 5.3 million hyperlinks. One might also conclude that many local and regional officials (law enforcement, fire, police and security, property, health care, and education) are probably lacking accurate, current, and detailed maps. Also there would likely be sharp differences in the quantities and the qualities of maps about major categories documenting human conditions (e.g., poverty, obesity, or access to health care) between Lexington and Knoxville and between southern and northern West Virginia. The reasons behind the sharp "cartographic divides" between the "knowledge-rich" Bluegrass region of Central Kentucky and "knowledge-poor" Eastern Kentucky are similar to the reasons behind the differences in the production of textual knowledge (books, chapters, articles, etc.). That is, reasons related to power and wealth are behind the production and dissemination of regional knowledge, whether it is in the form of detailed maps of property ownership, conditions of poverty, domestic violence, environmental injustice, or community empowerment. Maps are not only vehicles of knowledge but also instruments of power for those who make, manipulate, and use them to exert power.

The Visual Worlds, GIS, and Social Media

Knowledge and cartography questions need to be expanded in today's world to include advances in information technologies, especially the growing importance of the visual. It would be useful to learn the uses of GIS by individuals and groups in mountain regions, whether in Appalachia or the central Andes or highland Central Asia or Southeast Asia. A GIS is itself about the visual presentation of geographic information. Those visuals may be overlays of materials about what is already known. Information from a GIS about any place, just like scholarly articles and books, is itself uneven. Thus we have many more reports, documents, scholarly articles, photos, and maps about some places than others. The mountain ranges with the most English-language GIS references were New Guinea Highlands 15.8 million, Japanese Alps 13.6 million, Brazilian Highlands 13.3 million, Pyrenees 9.7 million and Caucasus 8.5 million. Among those with the fewest visuals were Western Ghats 71,000; Tibesti Mountains and Annamese Mountains had only 8,000.

Cartographic gaps and silences also persist between those who make and those who use GIS maps. There is power in mapping information from ground-based fieldwork or using satellite imagery to study poverty, environmental pollution, inadequate delivery of social systems, and disaster-prone regions. The empowerment of local groups using PPGIS (Public Participation GIS) is just as important as aiding them in the production of base maps about cultural, economic, and environmental settings. Community organizers and activists teaching empowerment skills to rural and urban dwellers recognize not only the importance of the production and consumption of the visual, but also of knowing how to manipulate visual images for effective grassroots purposes.

Complementing the use of GIS and PPGIS is the use of social media to inform supporters and engage in decision-making. The social science literature on the role of Facebook, Twitter, iPads, and so on is slowly emerging (Wilson and Starkweather 2013). Scholars looking at these phenomena recognize that many of the extant theories, models, and concepts used to analyze communities, networks, identities, and associations are of little use in examining the shifting worlds of speed, fluidity, ad hoc geographies, and network geometries. Among the questions that need asking are (a) what social media are being used? (b) how are they used? (c) who uses them? and (d) how effective are they in empowering local groups? One might expect the existence of significant cultural and technological divides between those who use and do not use social media and those who want to but cannot because they are not connected to the internet. Broadband access is not available everywhere on the planet, even in rich countries. Providing data that answers some of these questions would inform us about the likelihood of moving to another location for employment or remaining in place for family reasons or social pressures. We examine next these intersecting questions of knowledge, technology, and mobility by looking at three case studies in a mountain region of southern Italy.

Local Knowledge Geographies: Digital Gaps, Place Attachment, Retention, and Marginalization

Before looking at the three communities in Italy, we discuss briefly three specific concepts related to culture, place, and migration that will help us understand the impacts of digital divides. The first is *place elasticity*, the second is *place attachment*, and the third is *mobility* and its counterpart, *immobility*. This research focused on the concept of place elasticity (Barcus and Brunn 2010), but expanded to investigate how broadband coverage in small rural and mountain villages can reinvigorate or weaken place attachment and thus limit the exodus from, and abandonment of, mountain areas in western countries. The assumption was that place attachment in contemporary society would no longer be based on emotional linkages to places and mediated by a sense of place or kinship. When traditional agricultural job markets, values, cultures, and routines have been disrupted and not adequately replaced, it might be expected that place attachment and ties to communities would be severely eroded. Since belonging is an emotional attachment rather than an official representation or citizenship, identities and engagements need to be reexamined in light of new factors that mediate everyday life and the process of familiarization and rooting (Powell and Risbeth 2012). The hypothesis tested in the following comparison is that the internet is perceived everywhere and along generational lines as a distinctive trait of society that shapes residents' rooting everywhere. It is a main link between citizens and residents to their lifeworlds. Yet the lack of broadband coverage may affect place elasticity and place attachment in declining mountain communities. To address these questions we relied on interviews with residents in three categories (students, heads of families, and elderly residents) in the southern European mountain region of Sannio-Appennines, in Italy. The region is similar culturally to other European mountain regions affected by digital gaps.

In the contemporary Western world, digital isolation and digital gaps challenge the notion stated by Barcus and Brunn (2009, 128) that, "Other characteristics that might influence place attachment include strong or extensive social networks, leadership roles in churches, schools and other organizations, or adherence to a particular culture or cultural value or long-term engagement with a place." These social structures may not be sufficient to allow for place retention for future generations where communities suffer general decline and broadband remoteness and isolation. This gap or perceived gap is likely even more serious for younger generations, especially those living in declining state welfare systems with neoliberal approaches to community services.

If place attachment deteriorates because of the declining quality of life in small villages, then what about the worsened perceived sense of attachment because of digital isolation? Conversely, what do residents have to say about broadband usages vis-à-vis place retention and revitalization? Answers to these questions have many implications for community activism, improved quality of life, and local communities' revitalization. In a contemporary world, Web 2.0 users are more likely to be active builders and users of e-content for digital interactions with the economic, social, and political lifeworlds, and also those associated with business and institutional initiatives.

Our objective is to expand thinking beyond such familiar factors such as age, sex, education, occupation, marital status, family status, home ownership, race, and ethnic origin (Shaw 1975). Although these factors may predispose some residents to migrate while others are more likely to remain in place (Barcus and Brunn 2009), we want to consider the role of a digital divide and place retention, mobility, and immobility, which may be especially important categories for young people and college students in mountain areas.

With regard to mobility, Barcus and Brunn (2009, 26) state that, "The idea that an individual's propensity to move or not to move over their lifetime is in some way linked to their sense of place attachment is often overlooked in the migration and mobility literature." Less attention has been paid to individuals who choose not to move away from a rural place, which here we refer to as "immobile" (see Barcus and Brunn 2009). Whether one chooses to leave a region or stay in it (although the possibility of choice may not always be assumed) may or may not have to do with place attachment. Those who leave may continue to maintain strong connections to community via the internet, if that is possible. We use *place elasticity* to refer to the possibility that strong connections to community may be maintained virtually, not only by residence in the community. Considerations of place satisfaction need to include the significance of the personal, the domestic, and the local as spaces infused with political possibilities (Bondi, Smith, and Davidson 2005; Lister 2003; Dyck 2005). That is why we inquire into interactions between citizen institutions and local politics, and citizens' perceptions of the commitment of local politicians to support community well-being. This perspective highlights the significance and intersections of characteristics that relate to personal identity, place attachment, and elasticity, all ideas related to active citizenship, belonging, needs, and lifeworlds. All of these are also played out through emotions (Bronwyn 2013) and result in satisfaction and place attachment. Digital access and literacy can be related to maintaining connections to place for those who have left, and also to facilitating place-based global engagement for those who choose to stay.

Local Examples: The Mountain Regions of the Sannio Appennines

We investigated the above issues in the "Sannio" Appennines. In the Benevento region, the field research was based on interviews with young people, elderly residents, and heads of families living in small villages and small cities (up to 10,000 inhabitants). The province has a dispersed rural population with Benevento as the capital. There are many rural schools scattered in an area that has experienced population decline as well as declines in tobacco production. The area is also affected by declines in the state welfare system and public debt containment, which is also linked to the European Union's binding requirements for member states. Primary services have been severely cut. Besides a deterioration of citizens' access to services and opportunities, poor broadband access is common with minimal access to high-speed internet connections. There is a lack of coverage in many remote and mountain villages. Social networks and even an individual's sense of "home," traditionally often rooted in their identity with a "home county" ("il mio paese" my village, "I paesani" my village residents) may be diluted and possibly dissolved through these reconfiguring economic and social conditions. Brunn and Barcus (2009, 31) have written about similar changes in Central Appalachia. As Gaventa (1980, 31) writes about Appalachia, "there is a strong importance attached to personal relations, personal interaction, and to the social organizations of kin, neighbour and church." Likewise, in Sannio, family, coffee shop, the village square(s) sports, the village's annual party, friends, and "Pro Loco," local agencies for heritage preservation, help perpetuate place attachment, but they do not seem to be strong enough to keep some people from leaving. Family reunions are likely to survive and help keep ties to place if young families will stay in sufficient numbers, especially in villages, after the older generation passes on.

Sannio Research

This project included interviews with 65 residents in three sample areas. The first was Sant' Arcangeo Trimonte, which has 500 residents. It is considered a "white area," that is, there is no broadband coverage; 15 people were interviewed. Limatola, which has 4,000 residents, is considered a "gray" area in that there is some broadband, but it is not extensive; 28 residents were interviewed. Guardia Sanframondi, a small city of 5,592 inhabitants, is considered a "black" area because broadband has been fully developed; 20 citizens were interviewed here. The semi-structured interview was administered to three groups: older residents, breadwinners, and young people, especially students. The sample was chosen in the context of exploratory research methodology (Yin 2013). This research method was chosen because of the pioneering nature of the topic; it is thus tacit knowledge, not based on a sample meant for statistical testing. This method allows us to ask why, how, and when a topic is new and data are difficult to collect. Our discussion aims to generate a hypothesis on if and why broadband coverage and digital interactions help ameliorate challenging living conditions in mountains or more isolated areas. Twenty years of previous fieldwork and research experience in the area and membership in a Research Centre of Excellence on the Information Society provided us with in-depth knowledge of the region and related subject matter. The exploratory sample analyzed three different situations: an area with no broadband coverage, a medium-access area, and an area with full and extensive use.

A first major research question or assumption we sought to answer is whether place attachment is linked to place genealogy (Bronwyn 2013, Barcus and Brunn 2010); the second question was about young people's attachment/roots and their internet use. A series of questions were asked about personal data, satisfaction with local services, and public services, local institutions, and local politics. We identified for each category the factors of place and place attachment and retention, and mobility or immobility, to understand the influence that broadband use may have, or not have, in their daily life. Specific questions were asked about the attachment to his or her territory and the level of attachment or nonattachment, and the second set of questions were about the different stages of internet access (with none, some, and widespread broadband availability, that is, the white, gray and black areas mentioned above). Those interviewed were asked about their satisfaction with broadband availability and uses, especially the web, what devices they used, how satisfaction and services might be improved, how it has or might improve living and working conditions, and also about their relationships with local administration.

The Sannio region offers a number of opportunities to study these questions and observations about community participation and empowerment and spatial justice issues that arise from broadband inclusion and internet geoweb uses in rural mountain villages. In cases where no broadband access gap existed, we still wanted to look at the geographies and geometries of social media (cell phones, iPads, iPods, etc.) and how these are impacting youth and elderly, "smart" economies and networks, and so on. We expected that many of these social worlds and networks could be a mix of local and global, and those with high or low levels of digital literacy.

Narratives about the living conditions of residents and imagined changes in their lives and attachment to their territories were attributed to the adoption of broadband. Or if no broadband would be introduced, how would that situation affect the sustainability and livelihoods of small communities? The issues of quality internet adoption and "appropriation" are also the platforms for advanced community action and participation through participatory GIS (PPGIS) or geoblog. All issues of adoption and appropriation via user-generated contents represent ways to alleviate spatial justice (urban-rural, plain-mountain) and social justice issues, that is, improving the chances or opportunities for youth in their future, whether in rural or metropolitan areas. Broadband use can contribute positively to living conditions, especially where people are simply tied to a place or are in a situation of unwanted immobility. For comparison, Barcus and Brunn (2009, 2010) identified three groups in studying place mobility in rural eastern Kentucky: those who were rooted in place, tied to place, and mobile with strong place attachments. For Sannio the third category is most applicable, but we would add "unwanted immobility" as a new category.

Since social networks are often subtly intertwined with individuals' sense of attachment in rural areas, we asked individuals to estimate the role of

Sant' Arcangelo Trimonte (village, semi-mountain)
Limatola (small city, rural)
Guardia Sanframondi (small city, mountain)

No broadband; No place attachment

No broadband; Yes place attachment

Yes broadband; No place attachment

Yes broadband; Yes place attachment

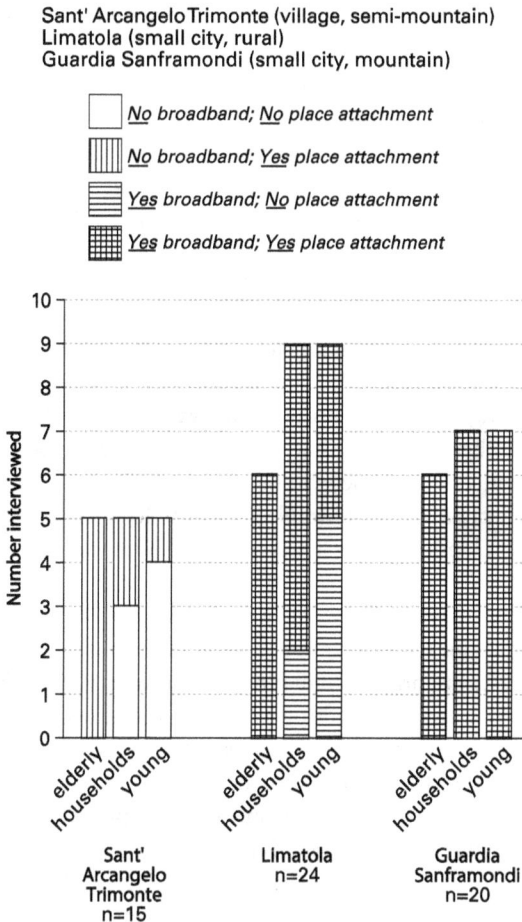

Fig. 14.2 Broadband Usage in Three Rural Southern Italian Communities

technology-based social networks and social media as well cyberspace at a higher level, that is, as relates to place attachment and spatial justice. The results are shown in Figure 2.

Sant'Arcangelo Trimonti

Lack of broadband must be included among the many challenges in this village. In the sample of elderly residents, no one knew what broadband meant, but everyone was familiar with the internet because they had heard about it on TV or from their children or grandchildren. The only exception was a woman of 76, who not only knew the internet, but also used it: "slowly, not to get bored in my daily life, I learned to watch the news on the internet: it's great fun!" However, after learning what is meant by broadband, all responded that the presence of broadband does not in any way affect their relationship with their village; they said that it may improve the area, helping those who need a computer for work or study. The elderly also considered that broadband could, perhaps, "keep in place" young people, who, increasingly, are abandoning the village.

For this category, then, broadband would be a factor in place retention for future generations. All householders, however, warned about the absence of broadband, with the sole exception of one interviewee, who did not like technology and was not even being forced to use it because of a job. Broadband, according to all respondents, would certainly contribute to improving the lives of the country by (a) making it easier to access information and some services, (b) reducing travel to obtain needed supplies and services (with the ability to buy online too; traveling for many family needs was considered stressful and was impeding job searches for female householders in several cases); (c) facilitating the lives of students and of those who use it, especially for work; and (d) aiding local producers by creating, for example, a website for direct sales of their products. In the householders category it emerged as a source for innovative ideas and business ideas.

One of the interviewees, particularly active in the area, believed that "thanks to the internet, you can try to attract people in other ways. Since, in the village, most of the activities are organized during the summer, you might think how to entice tourists to visit the place, taking advantage of the occasion, booking their rooms too, maybe just making them available by locals. By doing so, you have changed the country and also earned something."

A different idea is that expressed by one of the women who claimed to be very dissatisfied with what the area offers. She prepared desserts for private events and, she stated, if she had a website, that she might be able to start up a business with potential contacts accessing that website. A third citizen highlighted the possibility of having easier access to health services, being able to receive via email, the results of tests ordered by the doctor, thus having a diagnosis.

As for the increase of broadband links within the territory, four of the five respondents said it would help them to live better, but would not improve their relationship with the territory; two of the three respondents claimed not to be tied to the country where they live. For them, broadband access would not be a factor in place retention.

Young people, more than any other demographic, responded that they experienced much more, and more deeply, the lack of connection compared to the previous categories. They also all agreed that broadband would certainly improve the place for living. In addition to making it easier to access information, broadband could allow the development of local products and improve the quality of life for the elderly. In fact, one respondent proposed the organization of a shopping service for the elderly: "with a group of guys you may fill up the shopping lists and send an email to the nearest supermarket, which could provide for the delivery." Even for young people, as for the elderly, there emerges a factor of improvement through reduction of travel and ability to purchase online or establish a service business.

With reference to the impact of broadband on the link with the territory, we found that of those interviewed who already had strong attachment to his or her territory, broadband had no effect on ties to the village. But it allowed them to live a better life; with respect to the young people interviewed, all believed that broadband availability would probably strengthen their ties to place. Ultimately, all inhabitants believed that broadband would improve the area and could be a factor in place retention, especially for future generations. It could offer new opportunities to the village and be a means to implement major positive changes.

Limatola

At the outset it needs to be stated that there is no perfect correspondence between subjects who do not have broadband (4 of 28) and nonuse of the internet (6 of 28). Also some subjects, while not using the internet, have signed an ADSL contract to allow for their children's and relatives' use. The problem of the digital divide is illustrated, not surprisingly, in the fact that all young people use the internet, but for different purposes and with different intensity. More mature adults and the elderly have difficulty using the internet and need help to access the web.

In general, it is possible to identify within the sample interviewed five typical categories: (1) those who signed a broadband contract (only 2 of 28); (2) those who are aware of the medium and its importance (5 of 28); (3) those who make use of it through a third party (5 of 28)—typically middle-aged people who are not familiar with the personal computer (PC) but are interested in the services offered by the internet; (4) those who have already mastered the medium but are not using it often (7 of 28)—there are various reasons for this, including the limited free time or disaffection, more or less pronounced, with the PC; and (5) those with a full mastery of the medium (10 of 28). Even among those in the latter category, network usage typically occurs only in the manner of consumer users— only in one case was the use active and productive (e.g., creation of his or her own website or creation of a microbusiness).

In assessing the impact of broadband on improving residents' relationship with their own city, the only significant impact was for those residents who stated that it enhanced and facilitated socialization through extensive use of social networks (10 of 28 subjects use them) and that it was perceived as an essential tool to manage commercial communication (for 6 of the 28 subjects). Other possible uses such as the provision of services or the creation of online commerce were not mentioned in the group we interviewed. One individual in the manufacturing sector boasted of being online to set up e-procurement for someone and promote that person's products.

Finally, we found we are far from use of the web for e-government: only one person mentioned it, and only because it is required because of his profession (public servant). The reasons for this phenomenon are primarily because tools required for implementation of e-government and the reluctance of individuals to make use of them.

For several years, Limatola has been enjoying good broadband coverage that, thanks to the intervention of private operators, has addressed problems of internet connection even in the peripheral semi-rural neighborhoods. Despite this, the great potential of the internet seems to be unrealized. The city is well situated and does not look like a place in decline, except that the younger generation are potentially mobile because of the shortage of jobs.

Guardia Sanframondi

It is surprising to discover the very strong place attachment of young people to this small city. They want to stay away from the chaotic world associated with a big city; they consider their place a "little paradise." Their desire to stay in the place in which they live indicates a wished-for immobility, even for the many young people for whom there will not be enough job opportunities. Only one student said that he was not particularly fond of the place, and, rather than suffer any further shortcomings it offers young people, he was ready to abandon it. In short, he was potentially mobile.

The emotional ties that are common to place attachment fall into three categories. For both householders and young people the quietness of the place is very important. The connection to the land, understood here as ties to one's real estate, one's property ("I have my land") is very strong for the elderly, who seem to almost feel indebted to the very fields that have allowed them to live their lives in dignity. Finally, Guardis is famous for wine production and was the first village to develop a local cooperative of wine producers.

Of the three communities, Guardia Sanframondi is the one where nearly all the inhabitants felt there was a cohesive community and a strong place attachment. There was also a positive feeling about the services and about the quality and commitment of the local institutions. There were only two complaints about city hall. One householder accused the local government of showing favoritism; the second claimed to have had a very good relationship with the city councilors.

Citizens feel "bound" to their territory; 20 respondents out of 20 said they were happy to live in Guardia. In other municipalities there was anger and disappointment with local politics because of the economic decline that led to citizen disaffection and dissatisfaction. Regarding place attachment, this small city's ability to satisfy the public seemed to be considerable; there is no particular shortage of services. The city is "in the black" on the National Digital Plan, that is, it is fully equipped with broadband.

The data clearly show strong consumer use of the web. This statement is supported by several observations. None of the elderly respondents used the computer; only one elderly woman knew what broadband meant. Another elderly person knew that broadband "is something that has to do with the internet" because he had heard about it but had no further knowledge; another four respondents did not know about the broadband, but did know about the internet. Broadband had no effect on their relationship with the territory and daily life for any of the seniors who received the questionnaire. There were, however, some differences among the heads of households. One respondent claimed not to use the internet and had a bad relationship with the web. Another acknowledged that he used the internet very little, except he spent much time in front of the PC listening to music, his passion. Another five used the internet to search for jobs and news about their professions. Three heads of households stated that broadband did not affect their place "rootedness" or decision to stay in place, but they did acknowledge that this innovation saved them money and time. One of the interviewees, despite claims that he had no special need for it, stated that it did permit him to expand his export market and increase his visibility and more easily manage communication with customers and suppliers. For young people, however, the broadband had a major impact on their social life. They use the internet, as might be expected, for study and research, leisure and entertainment, news and culture, making extensive use of social networks, especially Facebook, reading newspapers and magazines online, and engaging in various kinds of communication and consultation. Only one of the respondents, whose age was more "advanced" than others (28 years) and had a higher level of education (master's degree), made purchases online.

Five of seven respondents stated that broadband improved their ties to their territory, especially in regards to social connections and service delivery. One respondent expressed strong scepticism about using the web and expressed a preference for face-to-face relationships. The question remains unanswered as to why this pattern exists. In regards to devices used, 6 out of 7 had a desktop computer; 5 had a laptop; 2 students had a smartphone; and 1 fellow had a notebook. Young people have benefited from broadband; all acknowledged that they could make better use of it in the future. In the light of the above results, we conclude that Guardia Sanframondi does not exploit fully the potential of broadband. Among the main complaints about its use were that there are few employment opportunities for young people; however, no one proposed alternative forms of work using the web. The majority of respondents noted the lack of a doctor, but they did not think of telemedicine. Therefore, they lacked innovative ideas and perspectives that could have a significant impact on their territory, improving and enhancing it. The mindset of the place seems to be closed to this type of initiative, which may be critical to preventing the unwanted migration of young people and to making known the beauty of a country rich in history and tradition. The broadband had no effect on the relationship with the territory and daily life for any of the seniors who received the questionnaire.

Conclusion

We have demonstrated through English-language Google search engine data and survey results among mountain communities in southern Italy that knowledge about mountain systems and the uses of broadband technology for empowerment are very uneven. That unevenness is illustrated in the case of Google by the volume of hyperlinks about mountain systems and about topics including maps, culture, religion, language, and economy. The Google analysis is couched within the context of two concepts: the geographies of knowledge and the geographies of silences, the former indicating the amount of information available on the internet and the latter the absence of information. A legitimate follow-up set of research inquiries might focus on the variations in knowledge or Google hyperlinks in other widely spoken world languages such as Spanish, French, Arabic, and Chinese. How different the tabular results and resulting maps of the volume of entries in other languages about mountain systems would be constitutes a fascinating question, as does the question as how the volume of entries for a region change over time. An additional valuable research question could focus on the major topics or websites of each mountain region. Are the majority of those sites about history or culture, about tourism and development, or about environmental and human/environmental conditions, for example?

Variations at another scale, i.e., the individuals surveyed about broadband use in three small rural Italian communities revealed some differences in the digital divides. Disparities existed not only in knowledge or lack of knowledge about broadband and internet use, but more directly in ties to communities and local governments. Elderly and youth populations were included in the samples. Some were knowledgeable and connected, whereas others had limited knowledge and are poorly connected. We discovered cases where some individuals had little knowledge about information technology and had strong place attachments; they were often reluctant to move. Others had internet knowledge and access and faced limited employment locally, but were reluctant to move because of strong place ties.

The basic findings at both the local and global scale reveal that disparities and irregularities in knowledge bases raise the need for further comparative research about issues of spatial justice. Mapping the geographic and social gaps that exist and persist at local, regional, and continental levels are sufficient reasons in themselves for social and policy scientists and community members to devise, plan, and implement steps to document the disparities that exist in order to address them.

Acknowledgments

The Sannio researchers (Maria Paradiso and two students, Olimpio Romaniello and Valentina Iacoviello) appreciate the clarity and insights of local citizens in answering questions about how digital interactions affect mountain life. Their voices and contributions to the surveys were so empowering in many cases that community advocacy planners may use them in developing a "digital plan" to serve community needs and orientation, to improve spatial justice, and to fight the declining quality of life and job markets and support social justice since the urban-rural gap is increasing, even as social justice in metropolitan areas in Europe itself is worsening. We also thank Richard Gilbreath, Director of the Gyula Pauer Cartography Laboratory in the Department of Geography at the University of Kentucky for preparing the high-quality graphics used in this chapter.

STANLEY D. BRUNN is Professor Emeritus in the Department of Geography of the University of Kentucky. He has authored many books, traveled in one hundred countries, and taught in more than twenty. He writes a weekly poem that reflects his concerns about justice, human welfare, and environmental awareness.

MARIA PARADISO serves as chair of the International Geographical Union's (IGU) Commission on the Mediterranean Basin and as vice-chair of the IGU's Commission on the Geography of the Global Information Society. She has founded and chaired several national professional research groups on the geography of the information society in Italy and is active internationally. She is associate editor of *NETCOM—Networks and Communications Studies Journal*.

References

Barcus, H. R., and S. D. Brunn. 2009. "Towards a Typology of Mobility and Place Attachment in Rural America." *Journal of Appalachian Studies* 15 (1–2): 26–48.

Barcus, H. R., and Stanley D. Brunn. 2010. "Place Elasticity: Exploring a New Conceptualization of Mobility and Place Attachment In Rural America." *Geografiska Annaler B* 92 (4): 281–295.

Bondi, L., M. Smith, and J. D. Davidson. 2005. *Emotional Geographies*. Aldershot, UK: Ashgate.

Bronwyn, E. W. 2013. "Young People's Emotional Geographies of Citizenship Participation: Spatial and Relational Insights." *Emotion, Space and Society* 9 (November): 50–58, http://dx.doi.org/10.1016/j.emospa.2013.02.004.

Brunn, S. D., and M. W. Wilson. 2012. "Cape Town's Million Plus Black Township of Khayelitsha: Terrae Incognitae and the Geographies and Cartographies of Silence." *Habitat International*, no. 30, 1–11.

Crampton, J. S. 2001. "Maps as Social Constructions: Power, Communication and Visualization." *Progress in Human Geography,* no. 11, 57–66.

Dyck, I. 2005. "Feminist Geography, the 'Everyday' and Local–Global Relations: Hidden Spaces of Place-making." *Canadian Geographer* 49 (3): 233–243.

Edney, M. H. 2009. "The Irony of Imperial Mapping." In *The Imperial Map: Cartography and the Mastery of Empire,* edited by J. R. Akerman, 11–45. Chicago: University of Chicago Press.

Gaventa, J. 1980. *Power and Powerlessness: Quiescence and Rebellion in an Appalachian Valley.* Chicago: University of Illinois Press.

Lister, R. 2003. *Citizenship: Feminist Perspectives.* New York: New York University Press.

Livingstone, D. N. 2010. "Landscapes of Knowledge." In *Geographies of Science,* edited by P. Meusburger, D. N. Livingstone, and H. Jöns., 3–22. Dordrecht, The Netherlands: Springer.

Powell, M., and C. Rishbeth. 2012. "Flexibility in Place and Meanings of Place by First Generation Migrants." *Tijdschrift voor Economische en Sociale Geografie* 103 (1): 69–84.

Shaw, R. 1975. *Migration Theory and Fact: A Review and Bibliography of Current Literature.* Philadelphia: Regional Science Institute.

Wilson, M. W., and S. Starkweather. 2013. "Web Presence of Academic Geographers: A Generational Divide." *Professional Geographer.* Accessed May 13, 2017. http://dx.doi.org/10.1080/00330124.2013.765290.

Yin, R. 2013 *Case Study Research: Design and Methods.* 5th ed. Thousand Oaks, CA: SAGE.

My Old Times

Si Kahn

Have you ever been like some lost child
Wandering through this world so all alone
Have you ever felt just like a stranger
Trying to make your way back home
Trying to get back where you started
Where they know your people and your past
Have you ever stopped, stood and wondered
If you'll ever find that place at last

I have dreamed beyond the Delta
Past this world of black and white
Known the truth behind the pictures
Photographed in wrong and right
Felt the power that can shake us
Miles past the lives we've found
Seen the unexpected flower
From old roots beneath the ground
So my old times are not forgotten
They shine like childhood in the light
Old memories sleep beside the cotton
And dreams stand still on the river tonight

I have seen the future running
Like this dirt between my hands
I have seen a new day rising

For the people and the land
Like my daddy preached before me
Let me stand for what is right
Hallelujah for the union!
Praise the Lord—and bless this strike.

So my old times are not forgotten
They shine like childhood in the light
Old memories sleep beside the cotton
And dreams stand still on the river tonight
On the river tonight

CHAPTER 15

Artifacts of Home

THE LANDSCAPE SPEAKS

Saakshi Joshi

I HAVE LONG been in conversation with the mountainous region of Garhwal, nestled within the Himalayas. In the early twentieth century, my grandparents started their life-journeys outward from here to the plains of colonial India. Although I was born and raised in Delhi, the mountains have been another place to which I have continuously belonged—through surname (indicator of caste, region, religion), photographs, family functions, and vernaculars. The mountains are alive and stirring within the family as geographical markers of ancestry, through annual trips to the region, as repertoires of memories, and as the foundation on which varied family narratives rest.

A submerged town in the central Himalayan landscape was the premise of my doctoral research. It explored the lives of people displaced by the Tehri Dam in the Tehri Garhwal district of Uttarakhand state, India. The dam was conceived in 1949 and completed in 2005 on the Bhagirathi and Bhilangana, tributaries of the Ganges. At 260.5 meters, the tallest dam in Asia drowned the town of Tehri and affected 125 villages. With its completion, more than 100,000 people were uprooted, becoming the Tehri Dam *visthapit* (ousted). Their resettlement forked into urban or rural, based on where they previously lived (Tehri town or the village). The resettlement was spread across Uttarakhand: in the plains, the valley, the semihilly tracts, and the mountains. New Tehri is the urban resettlement closest to the dam, within a distance less than 20 kilometers. It is situated between altitudes of 1,350 to 1,850 meters, overlooking the dam reservoir, which is spread across 55 sqare kilometers of the Bhagirathi–Bhilangana valley. The town of Tehri was a former capital of the Parmar dynasty in Garhwal, before merging with an independent India in 1949. It was situated en route to some of the most revered Hindu shrines like Kedarnath and Badrinath, which made it a significant transit point for travelers, tourists, and traders. Before the submergence, Tehri was home to roughly 6,000 families.

Although my work involves the Tehri Dam, it is not just about that. It includes apprehensions about the Himalayas as sites of catastrophes, and how far-reaching the consequences of a disaster here can be. Closer still are the intentions that drive us to live through each day. Definitely not thinking about the next earthquake or landslide, but about matters that matter to us in more direct, personal, and contiguous ways. Elements that create our daily lives: livelihood, education, transport, medical facilities to tend to a loved one, food in the belly, water in our taps, view from our windows, sounds which wake us up and lull us to sleep, places we dwell in, neighbors who surround us, a home that will always take us in.[1] Being forcibly removed and then reconfiguring your life—to be able to think about these things like one used to is no simple task.

In the spring of 2013, Professor Ann Kingsolver, then director of the Appalachian Center at the University of Kentucky in the United States was a visiting faculty member in our department.[2] Conversations with her opened my eyes to how people from as far apart as the Himalayas in Northern India and the Appalachian range in the United States can be subjected to similar processes of marginalization, environmental degradation, and resource extraction. These young and old mountain communities faced common anxieties like alienation and internal displacement, linking loss of land with the loss of social and symbolic capital. It made me realize how local experiences, which are products of actions closer to home, find resonance in distant areas. That they are part of larger, interconnected networks. Our exchanges on the parallels between the Appalachians and the Himalayas led me to formulate a research plan involving the two regions, and my consequent application for a Fulbright fellowship. On selection, I was associated with the Appalachian Center for two semesters from September 2014 till June 2015. Along with immersion in academic and nonacademic activities, I was able to frequent eastern Kentucky for social events and short stays. These instances and interactions with community members helped create a vibrant image of life in this Appalachian region, adding to my own experiences and research in the Garhwal Himalayas.

If there were people explaining mountaintop removal (MTR)[3] and its impact to a novice me in a Kentucky home, there were oustees reconstructing the last days before their homes went underwater in Tehri. With over 12,000 kilometers between them, people shared frustrations and fears about displaced lives and landscapes, as well as worries about and hopes for uncertain futures.

Whether picking greens for dinner along a creek in Knott County, Kentucky, or taking an evening stroll in New Tehri, the present always found a way into the past. Each moment would pave the way for snippets of recollections. Be it a verandah in Garhwal or a Knott county living room halfway across the world, a family anecdote in Hindi, Garhwali, or English, the way memories (experiential and material) were summoned always possessed me. If I was shown a miner's beloved carbide headlamp, I was also witness to photographs of protests against the dam. If a friend in Kentucky showed me the open grass field where she had learned cycling, an oustee remembered the playgrounds in Tehri. If a mother of three showed me fossilized shell and leaf imprints her father had salvaged from the coal mines, elderly in New Tehri let me see century-old antlers from hunting, wooden bowls, and records of land holdings from the Tehri king's reign. These memories were a means for people to both accentuate their loss, and to come to terms with it. These became points of reference around which certain instances could be woven. They were also relics, often stowed away in boxes or put on display, or events to be recalled occasionally, as people busied themselves with the present, paving ways for future journeys. Where these concrete memories had sentimental value, they also spoke of the social, economic, ecological, and political life of the family or individual they represented.

In New Tehri, people often used "After Tehri's death" or "When Tehri was alive" during our conversations. I came to understand how anthropomorphizing the town was one of the ways to talk about it and to accept the absence of return. It was an attempt to recreate what had drowned but could be continued, as human lives continue after death through their memorialization. Such interactions influenced me when I saw the door in the spring of 2014. It acted as a passage for its owner to discuss the past, as well as a metaphor for the transformations encountered since displacement and resettlement. Here in the new town it was a door lying in the alley. I had thought it to be a pile of leftover wood from construction work. But once it had been an entrance. Meanings and purposes of the same object had altered. I saw the door eventually as a gateway between the lives before displacement and after it.

Objects have the ability to transport us in time, to trigger specific memories quite abruptly and in a nonlinear fashion. They make the past tangible by their existence, which becomes a validation of the bygone. Although the text builds itself around one particular material memory, every so often, in countless ways, we have been hoarders of our pasts—especially when an eventual return is difficult or nonexistent. This prose is about all the people and places who let me in. Because I now know how unpleasant unburdening oneself can be. This is to their spirit and strength, and the hope that they are. This is to the doors, the frames, the rivers, the creeks, the mountains, visible or gone—reminders of enforced silences and feisty resistances that color our existence, that make us, *us*. This is also to the girl who misses her contra dancing Fridays in Lexington.

In a new town barely a decade old, I met you. It was a little after noon on a spring day in 2014. I was wrapped in my shawl, a pair of thick socks in a bag. It was cold in spots where the sun could not reach. At a height of around 1,600 meters from the sea level, I was struggling with the "shortcut" stairs. They reduced travel time by taking you through the middle of the town, but were strenuous. I preferred the curving roads skirting the new town, overlooking the dam reservoir where the old town lay.

My reason for panting was a phone call in the morning. Mister G wanted me to come over to his house instead of meeting near the playground. A septuagenarian, he was one of the landowners who had actively resisted the dam construction. He lived in a town sector where several three-room and two-room flats had been allocated to the oustees.

While the old town was comprised of different *mohallas* (neighborhoods) that grew over the years, the new town was divided into numeric sectors. The apex of the slope had the collectorate area, with all the government offices and housing for their employees. Going downhill towards the middle of the slope were the independent houses and flats. The sectors here were a mix of residential houses and an area designated as a commercial zone, with hotels, eateries, a market, and the town bus stand. Scattered across this concrete landscape were several temples of varying sizes, one large *gurudwara* built on a mound and two mosques. Further down from this density were one-room flats and tin sheds located at the vertical margins of the resettlement region. These shared boundaries with the agricultural lands of adjacent villages. After crossing a few villages, the base of the slope was the location of offices and accommodations concerned with the dam and its employees.

I was somewhere in the middle, surrounded by pink-colored multistoried structures turning moldy, seepage patterns splashed across their walls. Among the displaced, these flats housed some landowners and several tenants from the old town.

There I paused to see a door in the alley. I knew of engraved wooden doors from the old town being used as temple entrances in the new town. Some were also gifted to high-ranking officials. But this one did not appear to be an entrance or a gift. With dust and cobwebs for company, it appeared apathetic. A few steps to the left of the door was the house number I was given. I pressed the doorbell to find Mister G on the other side. After a customary polite exchange the first thing I asked was, "Does this belong to you?" The septuagenarian nodded. Questions popped in my head as he went past me into the alley.

I see you emerge from the shadow of the staircase, steps halting, phone to ear. You are a new face. You pause briefly for me before ascending the stairs to the white door touched by rust, pressing that clamoring doorbell. *Ting tong* the sounds come. I am yet to grasp the rhythms, pulses, and beats of these bells. Some even make high-pitched copies of the songs of birds. *Tak tak tak,* the absence of wooden taps and knocks that echoed weighs loudly on me.

Old man emerges, squinting behind the screen. With a labored screech, the entrance opens. A glimmer of recognition passes across the door. You glance back at me. Moments later, I see the old man approaching me as you follow him.

I begin to take notice. His feet appear less firm, his gait unsteady. Unlike our early days here, I was not surrounded on all sides then. The sun shone on me longer, the harsh winds slapped me stronger. There were fewer humans. Faces changed frequently. Sometimes I was up against walls, their dust coming off on me. At other times I was cushioned by the earth. Old man would often sit next to me or lean beside me on the wall. Sometimes I would find him squatting near me, speaking or silent or crying. Becoming a broken tree branch.

Through the sun and the rains and the little snow I mostly slept. Old man began keeping to his house more, within his new white door. Outside, my views and interactions became limited to the immediate walls around me, the leaking water, and the *huufff* and the *haaii* of residents. Smaller humans with louder sounds began using me as their jumping board, before one of them tickled a splintered edge of mine. I have not seen them since.

I dwell on these changes as the old man's words continue filling the space around. *Well, some people think I am crazy. That this, this here is occupying unnecessary space.* He moves closer for what feels like an inspection, long overdue. And decides to squat beside me. *Some say I should sell it. This wood has much value. I wasted all those years I could work, fighting. So now at least I can bring in money.* He inches close to the ground to dab at the water around my edges.

Where did this water come from? You look around, searching for a source. *The sewer pipe burst some weeks back. This is not the first time. We've already written to the authorities. Now we wait.* His dabbing is not mild anymore. *Isn't that what we always do? Wait. Curse under our breaths, but wait.* Lightly, his hand brushes my upper edges. *This bit of leak won't scratch this jerk.* His face beams while shifting some of his weight onto me. *It has been around since before me. Before my father. People tell me I should put it to use, any use. But for me, its presence here* is the use. *This, this is home.* And he breaks to pat me lightly.

Do you ever go to your village? We were still outside, talking near the door. My connection to the region was apparent during all introductions, through my surname. I was used to people exclaiming, *Aha! So you are basically from around here* . . . asking the name of my father's village a few sentences after our greetings. The place I had known only through my *dadi's*[4] stories, I finally reached in November 2013. *I actually went there a few months back, for the first time.* In my head I was back in front of the locked room where my father was born in the 1950s. *Nobody is living in the house anymore. It is locked.* On both sides of my family, relatives had moved away from the mountain villages, some farther than the others. *But the place is still there, is it not? The village. . . .* Mister G's words brought me back to where I stood.

Yes.

I heard a sigh. *This is a bit of home I carried along. This is my return.* Getting up from his place near the door, he faced his flat. *Would you like to come inside now? It is starting to get cold.*

Old man's invitation makes your fingers curl up. *Is it okay if I hang around it a bit more?*

Alright. Suit yourself.

Your fingers relax.

We are now a company of two. You caress my edges, probing for approval. *You're quite the heirloom, aren't you?* Your glances turn me into an exhibit on display. Mostly people walk by or pause for a few minutes of rest. The steep stairs on our new sloped town gets them this way. I am clueless as to what you want from me. You stare at me sitting, then you walk around, then you let out soft hums. They sound better than the bells. Then you are back to staring again. I do not mind at all. Running your finger through my dust, you pick on a cobweb tucked away in one of my corners, blowing it away. As you trace my splintered silhouette, I hurt. Your touch is gentle. Especially over the gap where you just lingered. That's where I was forcibly torn apart from my hinges. Your long shadows fall on those gaps in me. The sun is now lazy, relaxing its hold over us.

The screen door screeches to interrupt.

Old man has his hands behind his back. He does not move, probably waiting for you to turn over from me to him. You search for something in your bag and bring out a pair of socks. *Getting cold?* Old man begins a conversation. *My feet are beginning to get cold!* you sit on my edge to wear your socks, and slip on your chappals again. Before you get up, he hands over a photograph to you.

Ahhh, my eyes widened. *When was this?*

Mister G began scratching a bald patch on the head. *Sometime in October 2003? When tunnels 3 and 4 of the dam were shut down. . . .* He closed his eyes for a moment before resuming. *Yes, this was late October. It took around two months for the town to go under. That happened towards November end. When the other two dam tunnels were shut down as well. The water filled up the town swiftly after that.*

My eyebrows furrowed deep as I searched the photograph. An upturned chair, a half open almirah, things thrown around in a hurry rather than props to pose against. I was distracted by Mister G's shaking head. *We were some seventy families left till the end. Still protesting. Crazy people. You know, it never hit us. Even with the water. It was not really happening, was it?*

That photograph showed a mustached man in a pale blue sweater, resting his weight against a door he is holding firmly by its waist. The lean figure was different from the portly belly in front of me, but the moustaches had not wilted. There they stood, man and door, against a backdrop of homely rubble. I flipped it backwards in hopes of any dates or names or message scribbled over.

Who took this photograph? I wanted the story as the memento went back into the safety of his palms.

I see them, lost in words, forgetting me. I glance around. The houses here, bathed in cement and mortar. I cannot make one out from the other. Gated and closed, with doorbells on the side. My home was near the town bazaar. I enjoyed the town's hustle from my place above the cattle shed, whiffs of milk, cow dung, and fodder seeping into my wooden odor. On our street, the sounds of *tick tock tick* echoed from our home.

Day in and day out, year after year, same and similar faces crossed me. But now, year in and year out, it is not the same neighbors. Old man has met many new people, but I often catch known voices. Sometimes, in a hurry, they huddle near me. Now I hear *we will not pay the water bill!* or about a walk against *wild pigs who are destroying our land.* The sounds of wind are louder than the bustle of this town. I suppose they have been harsh on all of us alike.

The people here are the people who let me face the mountains, who leaned against me for a quick chat with neighbors, or sat cross legged, peeling vegetables and discussing rumors, local elections, or the health of their beloved cattle. They are the same, but increasingly forgetful.

Old man looks over at me before turning to you, *Alright! Should we get inside the house now? Look at me, such a bad host! I've kept you out here long enough . . .*

And with that, I am back in oblivion.

SAAKSHI JOSHI earned her PhD in anthropology from the University of Delhi, India, researching the lives of people displaced by the Tehri Dam in the central Himalayan state of Uttarakhand. She was a Fulbright-Nehru Doctoral Researcher in the University of Kentucky Appalachian Center. Her current interests are in ways of belonging, nonlocal projects' impact on local ecosystems, and combining research with writing and storytelling.

Notes

1. Paraphrasing Robert Frost's line from the poem "The Death of the Hired Man."
2. Department of Anthropology, University of Delhi, India.
3. MTR is a surface mining technique involving the removal of 500 feet or more of the mountain summit to reach the buried coal seams ("What Is Mountaintop Removal Coal Mining?" n.d.). Surface mining caused the leveling of thousands of acres of mountaintops, altering landscapes.
4. Father's mother.

Reference

"What Is Mountaintop Removal Coal Mining?" n.d. ILoveMountains, Boone, NC. Accessed August 12, 2015. http://ilovemountains.org/resources.

CHAPTER 16

Resonating with the Trees

TRACKING MUSICAL INSTRUMENT TONEWOOD BETWEEN APPALACHIAN AND CARPATHIAN FOREST ENVIRONMENTS

Jasper Waugh-Quasebarth

I SAT WITH John and Catalin around the small table in the shop office, converted into a small apartment for Catalin's trip through the autumn mountains, where the leaves of hardwoods lie uponthe ridges like piles of loose rolling tobacco and the highest peaks are covered with spruce tops of the eponymous tree. I was interviewing Catalin, a musical tonewood producer from Romania, about some of the similarities and differences between the production, forests, and regulation of the timber industry between the mountain regions. I asked Catalin if there were any sayings in Romanian about making instruments, and he replied that instruments should wake (*trebui trezit*) the wood inside and a successful instrument should sing (*trebui cantata*). John excitedly followed that he uses similar sayings to speak of the musical tonewood that he produces in his small shop in the shadows of the Allegheny Mountains in West Virginia.

He is not alone in suggesting so. In ethnographic interviews conducted across West Virginia, I have found that makers often describe their instruments and component wood as living and breathing occupants of their shops and homes. The craft is a process of enlivening an instrument and its component wood with the optimal tone, a musical voice that speaks to the subjective aesthetics and desires of the craftsperson. One maker, speaking of his tonewood and instruments, said, "You can make a tree sing, that's the magic!" after reciting a favorite phrase in Latin "*Dum vixi tacui, Mortva dulce cano*—In life I stood silent, and in death I sweetly sing. Isn't that beautiful?"

Despite the apparent differences in desired musical tone, there are specific material properties and preparation techniques that establish which wood becomes suitable *tone*wood. First, instrument production traditions coupled with material properties of resonance, density, and grain structure often dictate a specific species of wood for specific instruments and instrument parts; for example, guitars are typically crafted with tropical hardwoods such as rosewoods (*Dalbergia* sp.) and mahoganies (*Swietenia* sp.), and violins are crafted with spruces (*Picea* sp.) and maples (*Acer* sp.). Trees of the required species should grow straight, without twist; evenly; and with minimal defects such as insect boring holes, fungal growth, knots, and pitch pockets where the tree has filled past gaps in growth. In some species, specific growth patterns or genetic defects are selected for aesthetics, such as a satiny, ribbon effect in maple known as curl or the shining raylike patterns raked across spruce grain known as bear claw. The wood must then be split or quarter-sawn, so that the grain runs as straight as possible through the resulting piece of wood, or "blank," making the wood as strong as possible in thin configurations and enabling sound waves to pass uninhibited through the length of the blank. At this point, wood is graded into a series of letters from A to C, with a master class of wood reserved for wood that comes closest to aesthetic perfection. Finally, it must be dried over the course of years in a process of seasoning that allows moisture to pass slowly from the wood, ensuring its stability and clarity through its transformation into a viable instrument.

After all of these processes, it is common to see makers going through stock wood, encircling defects with pencil lines, tracing patterns of common instrument shapes to avoid such spots, and even testing the edges with pocket knives to determine if the grain runs straight through the wood or runs out at an angle. Yet there are makers who resist some of the aesthetic restrictions. One West Virginian guitar maker spoke of ideals as prejudices, appreciating the artistic elements of selecting wood that may have otherwise undesirable qualities, such as a slightly darker stripe of grain through the board. Going a step further, a violin maker suggested that having not perfect wood is simply a part of violin craft. "Strad[ivarius] didn't always have perfect wood," he told me, adding that it is the skill of the craftsperson in working with the same pieces of wood repetitively that is the key to creating a successful instrument.

Nevertheless, aesthetic and nonarbitrary constrictions persist, and finding suitable trees that once felled, opened, sawn, and dried will yield the wood required for the tops, backs, and necks of guitars, violins, cellos, mandolins, basses, banjos, dulcimers, and a litany of acoustic instruments is not assured. Old-growth wood is the standard of quality where growing conditions have allowed trees to grow large enough to yield instrument parts with even, regular, and tight growth lines. Once, while preparing a guitar top, I counted the rings on the piece of West Virginia red spruce cut about forty feet from the guitar maker's shop. The rings counted up to 218, not including wood closer the heart and bark that had been cut out. The guitar maker was excited to have wood that dated back to "Revolutionary times," and indeed the tree may have started growing around when the 1763 Proclamation Line observing Native American land rights was voided and West Virginia's forests were open to exploitation. Throughout that tree's life, clear cutting by timber companies made old-growth forests disappear in the late eighteenth and early twentieth centuries and modern forestry practices felled trees on a regular cycle before they would be viable for instrument craft. We later visited the place in the forest where the guitar maker had been given permission by the National Forest Service to take trees. We found the large stumps of the aged spruces, among smaller trees, indicating that in the twenty years since he had cut, others had been invited to cut spruce in the same spot. Days earlier, I had heard that other tonewood makers from a bordering state had been up on the mountain searching through the forests for spruces that had survived years of clear cutting and extractive forestry.

The absence of regular supplies of musical-quality wood in West Virginia led John to Romania where he linked with Catalin, who had recently begun to cut musical tonewood for European instrument construction companies. He helped Catalin learn what to search for in selecting maple and spruce from the Carpathian Mountains, which sustain some of the last stands of old-growth forest in Europe. Though Catalin still sells tonewood to makers across Europe and the world, John continues to travel to Romania multiple times a year to select from the harvested trees, pulling out stacks of tonewood that will be loaded into a shipping container and begin their long transatlantic voyage to his shop in West Virginia. The business has made fast friends of the two, and when I visited Catalin's shop, his foreman, Mihai, suggested that his kids had been raised with John, who has become part of the family through his frequent visits.

In West Virginia, John has also trained foresters working for the major timber producer in the area (one of the world's largest) on how to select West Virginian spruce and curly maple logs for him to buy, rather than shipping them for potential export to markets for hardwood in manufacturing in Asia. Peering under tarps and breaking the "cookies," or slices of tree trunk, to reveal the grain structure within, John chats with the foresters and laborers employed on massive, desolate timber yards and keeps his finger on the pulse of local forestry. They speak about where the companies are cutting and meeting impossible quotas of board feet set by those in absentee boardrooms while workers move and sort 40-foot logs with large mechanical harvesters, manipulating the machines' arms as if limbs of their own bodies. Nevertheless, the majority of his stock is Romanian and consists of species of hard and soft woods analogous to those found in West Virginia that have suitable qualities, such as sycamore maple

(A. pseudoplatinus) and European spruce (P. abes) instead of West Virginian varieties of maple (A. rubrum and A. saccarhum) or spruce (P. rubens). All of the wood, Carpathian and Appalachian, is finally processed in the shop and spends years drying together on an enclosed porch until the moisture content assures that it is ready to work. This wood is given a final grade and sold to individual makers, small instrument factories, and instrument supply companies across the United States and throughout the world.

While John sources West Virginian trees from private land timber cuts, where many regulations stop at the property boundary, according to John and Catalin Romanian trees and wood are subject to greater scrutiny and regulation by the Romanian state and the European Union. Catalin joked that he could not cut down a tree in his yard in Bucharest without approval from the local council, and said that all the trees cut by his company in the Carpathian Mountains must be approved by a local board and are tagged so as be to tracked through the entire process of becoming tonewood. This contrasts starkly with timbering on West Virginia private land, where companies and their foresters may cut any tree they choose and keep loose account of trees that are not of the highest value. Wood from the same tree may stay together through the process; when I needed a new back while making a violin, John was able to select a replacement to match from the same tree. He then told me about other memorable trees, including the "Smuggler's Tree." Romanian foresters had sold him a maple log after they found that the tree had been cut and a large section removed to be sold illegally. John was able to get violin parts from the remainder of the tree and named it after how it had been procured. Despite some government protections, illegal harvesting in Romanian forests is a looming and serious threat, and privatization and reorganization of forest stewardship have been increasing, following the collapse of the communist regime and total state ownership.

The absence of appropriate wood drives West Virginians to purchase imported wood from Romania and other countries, and, whether directly through importers like John or through luthier supply catalogs, many instrument makers are curious about Carpathian wood and have begun to work with it in violins, guitars, and mandolins. At a guitar maker's shop in Virginia that also figures as a major gathering place for instrument makers and musicians, several men looked at a 1930s, "golden age" C.F. Martin & Company factory-produced guitar. They speculated about using Carpathian spruce to replace the top of this unique instrument, referring to it synecdochically as "Carpathian." A glimpse into the makers' shop showed that among an enormous variety and volume of local, tropical, and sometimes vividly colored tonewood, spruce stamped with John's logo sat perched on the shelf. While we draw comparisons among global mountain regions, the flow of commodities such as tonewood draws attention to inequalities that exist amongst global mountain regions and serve as a caution against equating all mountain communities and effacing inequalities and diversity. Romanian forests provide a large share of timber to Western Europe, and legal and illegal trade of timber products takes advantage of the open borders. While at Catalin's mill in Rașnov, Romania, I noticed that the share of tonewood bound for West Virginia was minimal compared to the stacks of wood bound for instrument makers in Germany, Greece, and Spain.

In an apprenticeship with a nearby West Virginian violin maker, Paolo Marks, I built a violin of my own, using the Romanian spruce and maple imported by John. I selected from John's stock pieces of nearly perfectly quarter-sawn wood with a nice curl in the maple and straight, tight grain in the spruce. John and Paolo considered whether I should use the Romanian maple (*A. pseudoplatinus*), which was easier to work, or the West Virginia red maple (*A. rubrum*), which I felt would be better suited to signifying my year of work in a forested region that has been home to generations of my family. I ultimately chose the Romanian maple, and though the hard maple chipped and flaked away and the soft spruce pulled in tools and splintered along the summer growth, the wood finished finely. While working it, I felt that it was more plastic and predictable than the West Virginian maple that Paolo was using in a simultaneous project. When it turned out that my violin design was larger than predicted, and I needed new wood for the back of the instrument, John took time to find wood from the same tree in his storeroom and opened the wood blocks into two pieces that would be joined for the back to find where the grain best approximated the original back.

Paolo's mastery of the material (working with the same pieces of wood through different projects is a hallmark of his craft) meant that the wood was perfectly finished, though he revealed some defects in his wood as he carved away at the red maple that was not perfectly quarter-sawn. He said that it is not only about the wood, but also about his skill as a craft laborer and making an imperfect piece of wood a viable instrument. It is between the material properties of the wood and the skill of the craftsperson that this wood becomes something greater than a measure of board feet, cubic feet, or tonnage. However, he also says that the first thing his clients often ask is whether the wood is from West Virginia, though they are more often drawn to the wood of the tailpiece, tuning pegs, and fingerboard, which are made of tropical ebony species. Nevertheless, the symbolic import of using local wood in craft entrenched in a forest environment cannot be overlooked.

While I was in Romania with John, he claimed that it is his ability as a craftsperson and a maker of instruments that adds value to the wood that he selects and imports, marking a difference between his tonewood and other tonewood produced in the Carpathians. Looking at wood split or sawed into large pieces known as billets, he can spot material properties and project how the wood will work and sound as a finished instrument. Driving through back country roads in rural Romania with some of his business partners, it became clear to me from the storytelling that filled the car with laughs that his knowledge and affability with his Romanian colleagues enables his access to wood that may be otherwise bought by European companies that dominate the export market from Romania.

Tonewood connects communities of craft and mountain forest environ-ments in the Appalachians and the Carpathians, and reveals stark contrasts and diversity in resource exploitation and extraction on local and global scales. Yet the question of skill employed by the crafters and makers that transforms the material raises other questions about the exploitation of labor and the nature of the work. Romania has factory-like towns devoted to the craft of instruments and exploitative systems of patronage that stand in contrast to the West Virginia makers, who control the means of their production. Following the production of tonewood shows how human activity is bound inexorably to nonarbitrary mate-rials in mutually influential relationships. Drawing attention to this example of the diverse relationships to the material world and our lived environments enables us to better examine the often overcommoditized lifeworlds of mountain communities to draw comparisons and seek insightful and unique solutions.

JASPER WAUGH-QUASEBARTH is a PhD candidate in Anthropology at the University of Kentucky. He focuses on material culture and cultural representations in mountain communities, particularly around heritage, music, and craft. His work with musical instrument makers in the Allegheny Mountains of West Virginia is supported by a Wenner-Gren dissertation fieldwork grant.

Traveler

Si Kahn

The flowers on the mountainside
Have spread their purple stain
The wind comes from the borderlands
And brings the evening rain
Oh traveler won't you rest a while
Lay down lay down your load
The longer that the journey takes
The further down the road

Come rest yourself by springs that lie
Among the trees and ferns
For sure the road is hard to climb
With bends and twists and turns
What dangers lie beyond the hills
There's none of us may know
The longer that the journey takes
The further down the road

But you have given the finest gift
That traveler ever found
To see the road you're traveling on
And know where you are bound
Come meet me at the turning place
Together we will go
The longer that the journey takes
The further down the road

CHAPTER 17

Appalachian and Carpathian Exchanges

TWO ESSAYS

Jessica Murray and Iryna Galuschchak

THESE ESSAYS ARE reflections on our first-hand experiences during brief visits to one another's mountain regions through a scholarly and cultural exchange associated with the annual Carpathian-Appalachian conference; they resonate with the book's focus on ways to compare notes directly across mountain regions, and on the role of the mountains themselves in the relationships built through such conversations.

Jessica Murray's Visit to the Carpathian Mountains

The scene of scarf-clad women guiding cows down the pothole-laden road looked so foreign to me, yet I felt strangely at home as we traveled through the villages of the Carpathian Mountains. Was it simply the familiarity of soft-peaked, blue-toned mountains, or did this scene resonate with former times in Appalachia? These questions lingered in my mind as I found myself in the midst of a completely new landscape and a completely new culture, 5,000 miles from my home in the mountains of Southern Appalachia.

I flew into Lviv, Ukraine, where I connected with other Appalachian scholars attending the Carpathians–Appalachians International Conference: Human and Community Development in Highland Regions. In Lviv, thirteenth-century buildings reflect a synthesis of Polish, Austrian, and Soviet influences. Walking through the city center, a UNESCO World Heritage Site, surrounded by medieval architecture, my senses were delighted at the sound of a new language, the smell of fresh coffee and baked goods, and the sight of people wandering around the colorful city.

We attended the conference in the city of Ivano-Frankivsk, an industrial city that hosts the annual International Blacksmith Festival (Sviato Kovaliv). Lilya, a student at Precarpathian University, guided us through the city streets. We admired the intricate ironwork found everywhere in the form of gates and sculptures. We entered breathtaking cathedrals and explored the city market. Lilya was about my age, kind and eager to spend time with us and show us her city. She said she could always recognize Americans because we dress so "comfortably." With my jeans, sandals, and fleece jacket, I was the quintessential American amid a sea of business-casual Ukranian urbanites.

Though we attended the conference in the city, we stayed in a tongue-and-groove wooden lodge outside the mountain town of Yaremche. On days we did not commute to the conference, we traveled through the mountains to local villages. We met the students and teachers of two small village schools, one of about 160 students, the other with fewer than 10. At first, the students were unsure about our presence; due to the language barrier, most of us could not communicate with them. However, we found quickly that a game of "keep the ball in the air" connected us through the universal language of laughter.

As soon as we departed the city center of Lviv on our second day, I immediately noticed that the majority of homes we passed had very large gardens. Not only were they rich with squashes and greens, but vibrant flowers decorated their yards. Apple trees were abundant in the cities and villages alike. In the market in Ivano-Frankivsk, we saw people selling apples and other produce. We met mushroom foragers who could identify the fungus and tell us exactly where they found it and under what species of tree. We met beekeepers in the market with honey of every shade of amber and gold. We visited an apiary with numerous hives, including "bee gums," recognized by the beekeeper in our American cohort to be similar to those once used in Appalachia. My favorite experience on this trip was hiking up a mountain in the village of Krivnoryvna to the home of the late Paraska Plytka-Horytsvit, an artist and activist whose life works are poorly preserved and largely unknown. Hiking up the mountain that this woman must have frequently traversed, we passed a herd of unfenced cows, apple trees, flowerbeds, and a man working in his garden. He was saving the excess plant material from the garden in hopes that his livestock would accept it as fodder.

This experience of foodways in Karpaty connected with my own journey in Appalachian studies. Having participated in research for the Heirloom Seedkeepers and Stories project, I have seen a fierce independence and resilience in gardening Appalachians. I have met passionate beekeepers, mushroom enthusiasts, flower gardeners, and heirloom seedkeepers. These people represent a culture of self-reliance and connection with the earth, a culture far more sustainable than the commercial system of agriculture that currently dominates foodways

Fig. 17.1 Farmstead in a Carpathian valley.
Photo credit: Jessica Murray

for most Americans. I saw this same independence and resilience in the Carpathian people. I could perceive the love they had for their flowers, for their vegetables, and for their self-governed foodways. In villages such as Krivnoryvna, I saw farming communities reminiscent of preindustrial Appalachia. As if peering through a window that transcended time, I felt as though I had a better understanding of what Appalachia was like when subsistence agriculture was the primary way of life.

Through heirloom seed research in my Appalachian community, we have found that heirloom seed saving and gardening is in steady decline (Winskie and Murray 2013). With the convenience of Walmarts and hybrid seeds, autonomy through the cultivation of food is now a rarity. The village of Krivnoryvna had no Walmart or grocery stores. The practice of growing food for subsistence persists in the villages of Karpaty. I do not doubt that this independence is accompanied by struggle, but we, as Americans and Appalachians, may be able gather inspiration from the Carpathian mountain culture to regain our food autonomy through comparative study of foodways, and perhaps we can relearn our own Appalachian food heritage and exchange ideas in sustainably efficient agriculture.

As a discipline, Appalachian studies is not merely an anthropological account of an isolated region. It is a comprehensive exploration of geography, people, history, and culture. However, these dynamic aspects of the region cannot be fully understood without a context. We may place Appalachia in a national context, a historical context, or an ethnographic context, so why not an international context? My own journey in Appalachian studies as an undergraduate taught me not only about Appalachia and the Carpathian mountain region, but also about how to engage with a community and culture through immersion. Though my visit to Ukraine was brief, I had the opportunity to experience an entirely new culture, orient my Appalachian studies journey in an international context, and develop a deeper understanding of intercultural discourse. The perspective I gained from this experience empowered and motivated me to spend two years living in a rural mountain community in Central America and pursue a career in tropical ecology. In the years since visiting Ukraine, I have crossed new language and cultural bridges to engage in discussions related to food security, conservation, and ecology. As a scientist and conservationist working in a country and culture different than my own, my ability to communicate complex concepts with a diverse audience is critical. However, the most remarkable conversations I had in Ukraine were those centered on common ground, on topics such as beekeeping, or mushroom hunting, or playing ball. I have found that these simple, honest interactions are fundamental to intercultural discourse and cooperation. While I recommend international studies to anyone, anywhere, I am partial to the mountains. There is solidarity in the humility one feels as a mere human among mountains.

Iryna Galuschchak's Visit to the Appalachian Mountains

I want to make a brief comment on the differences between the Carpathian and Appalachian Mountains. Both are beautiful, and both have similar problems with deforestation and floods for those of us who live there. But when I visited the Appalachian Mountains for the first time from the Ukraine to attend the Appalachian Studies Association Conference, I learned of very great differences between the two mountain regions. First, I saw a lot of traffic signs warning of "falling rocks" and came to understand that here this is a huge problem because the Appalachian Mountains are older than the Carpathians. I asked my colleague from the United States who was driving the car to stop by a beautiful field so that I could go and pick some flowers and walk up the mountain to see if the same kinds of mushrooms grow in Appalachia as we find in the Carpathians. But I was told that it was impossible to stop and get out and walk in the mountains there because it was private property. This is not something you would hear in the Carpathian Mountains—where the mountains belong to everyone, and they are not held as private property. It is a real privilege to walk in the mountains. It gives you a sense of freedom and comfort, being in harmony both with nature and with yourself.

Mountains have a strange power. If my husband wants to find answers for himself to something personal, he goes to the forest to think. The forest gives him energy and inspiration. In the Ukraine, everyone can go onto mountain land. When I was younger I would go backpacking. My friends and I prepared food over the fire, played the guitar, and sang songs about our lives and how about how much we loved the mountains. In this way we became more connected to nature.

My family often packs a picnic and goes to the mountains to look for mushrooms. The mountains feed us and heal us. Everyone has a garden, and we do not need to go to the pharmacy and the grocery store for everything. We make tea from the forest and many other products, also we eat from the farms, such as cheese and fruit, to keep us healthy. Organic food is what we all have in the Ukraine. The mountains give us our life and maintain our well-being.

We believe that everything in nature has its own spirit—mountains and trees and forests—and that some families are able to communicate directly with those spirits. There are old people, for example, who can speak with the clouds about the weather or calm animals. My husband's family has this connection. For example, one day we were on a picnic with my daughter and a hedgehog came to join us. Some people live as hermits in the mountains and are connected with their spirits. The mountains give us life.

This is why I did not understand, when in the United States, where they say that you are free, why it was not possible to get out and take a walk up the mountainside. How can you have a connection with the mountains and forests when you have to ask permission to visit them?

Another difference for me was that roads in Ukraine are in very bad condition, which sometimes prevents enjoyment of the beautiful views from the Carpathians because you have always think about how to safely reach your destination. I know that is not good for rural tourism. I hope in the future, something changes.

The Appalachian Mountains for me are very special because looking at them I feel the spirit of the Carpathian Mountains. My second visit to Appalachia was thanks to Professor Ann Kingsolver, who invited me as a scholar to the University of Kentucky's Appalachian Center. There I had the chance, as a visiting researcher, to work with magazines, newspapers, and books dedicated to Appalachian life. I had the great opportunity to meet Ann's family and to learn new and interesting things about the culture and the way of life in Appalachia. Ann invited me to her seminar on global Appalachia. We discussed a huge problem in Appalachia: flooding. Some of the reasons for the flooding are deforestation and the impact of the extractive industries. The students and I saw and discussed documentary films about flooding due to coal slurry impoundments breaking. It was the first time I understood how severe the problem was for people that live in Appalachia.

I am glad that I was able to attend the Mildred Haun Conference on Appalachian studies in Morristown, Tennessee. There I heard interesting information about the way of life, food, culture, and music. When I attended the Lexington Old-Time Music Gathering and listened to Appalachian music, my heart was opened, and in some way I understood how deep the music is and how close it is to my native sounds, the sounds of the Carpathians. While I was in the United States, I visited a number of cities, but somehow I felt closer to the communities in the mountains; there was a warm connection that reminded me of the Ukraine. It does not matter in what country you live, mountains seem to have an invisible force on people.

JESSICA MURRAY has done research on heirloom seed-keeping in northern Georgia and in tropical ecology in Costa Rica, where she worked as a naturalist in a rural mountain community. She is currently doing doctoral work at the University of Utah, studying soil microbial ecology in the tropics.

IRYNA GALUSHCHAK is Associate Professor of Economics at Precarpathian National University, Ukraine. She is the author of over thirty-five scientific papers published in the Ukraine and abroad on the problems of regional development. She has participated in several exchange programs in Appalachia, in the United States.

Reference

Winskie, Jonathan, and Jessica Murray. 2013. "Heirloom Seed & Story Keepers: Growing Community and Sustainability through Arts-Based Research." *Papers and Publications: Interdisciplinary Journal of Undergraduate Research*, vol. 2, no. 1. http://digitalcommons.northgeorgia.edu/papersandpubs/vol2/iss1/10.

CHAPTER 18

Appalachian and Columbian Connections through Cerulean Warbler Migration

A STUDENT PEN-PAL PROJECT

Regina Donour

As a transplant to the hills of Letcher County, Kentucky, I have come to build a life and develop a love for this area. The sheer natural beauty, the strong family ties, and even the exploitation of the coal industry have had lasting effects on me. I came to this part of Appalachia some 34 years ago, raised a family, and 20 years ago began a career as a high school science teacher. My role as a teacher set in motion my commitment to this area as I try to build an informed and concerned community from among the youth of the area.

To teach my students the importance of understanding the world through evidence-based science, I have incorporated various opportunities for them to participate in community service projects. I have also tried to teach my students that it is important to give back to their communities and that solutions to all our problems must come from members of the community. I teach my students that they must take ownership of their communities and work towards making them better places for themselves and others. All of my community service projects have been aimed at improving the environment by addressing the improvement of water quality whether through water testing, garbage pickup, or planting trees on abandoned mine lands.

Addressing water quality issues in Letcher County provides a foundation for appreciating the connections between science, the environment, and the relationship of Letcher County to the rest of the world. Since water is an essential resource for all species and Letcher County has ample sources of water and is at the headwaters of three major rivers, which are a part of the Mississippi River watershed, this presents significant opportunities for learning. The water that flows through Letcher County comes from the sky, which means all of the pollutants in our water came from some action within the county. The real issue is that every drop of water enters our county pure, but by the time it leaves the county it has become too polluted to drink or in most cases even touch.

Young people have the drive to change the world, and those in Letcher County are no different. I share with them the concept "think globally but act locally." My students have such strong ties to the area, but the future economic opportunities are limited for them, which increases the possibility of a "brain drain" from the area. I encourage my students to be involved in improving their community, and—with the increased availability of technology—perhaps the opportunities to remain in the area for employment will be significantly improved. I support students in looking to themselves for the ways to improve their community, explaining that when you are pointing at someone else to blame, three fingers are pointing back at you.

The diversity of Letcher County is limited in that most of my students come from Euro-American, Christian backgrounds and have little experience with the different cultures of the world. There is much isolation in the community. Most students cannot see a connection to the other parts of the world, and they view the problems of their community as unique to the area.

Cerulean Warbler Exchange

One of the community service projects with the Appalachian Regional Reforestation Initiative provided my students the opportunity to reach beyond their mountains to connect with others in a different part of the world. When the US Department of the Interior's Office of Surface Mining Reclamation and Enforcement, the Appalachian Regional Reforestation Initiative, ProAves, and the Cerulean Warbler Technical Group invited project proposals from high school science and Spanish teachers to participate in a pen-pal program to link students in the coalfields of the Appalachia students with the coffee-producing region of the Andean mountains of Colombia, we applied. The cerulean warbler, "a neotropical migratory songbird that needs the help of people young and old to conserve habitat in both its core breeding area (the coal fields of Appalachia) and wintering grounds (which includes the Andean Mountains of Colombia)" was chosen to be the "ambassador" between the two cultures. The expected outcome of the project was that "students who participate in this program have the potential to learn valuable lessons in the conservation of wildlife, reforestation of surface coal mines, shade-grown versus sun-grown coffee plantations, foreign language, world geography, and cultural diversity" (Angel 2008).

My students planted native trees on abandoned mine sites with the desire to restore these areas to the large growth forest that was once a part of the area. With the partners I made during this community service project, I became aware of the lifecycle of the cerulean warbler, a small songbird that lives, reproduces, and spends the summer months in the deciduous forest of eastern Kentucky. As my knowledge of the life of this tiny songbird increased, I learned how the bird migrated to the mountainous regions of South America (Colombia, specifically), where the bird's winter habitat was also being destroyed, due to agricultural development.

I shared with my students this new information regarding the lifecycle of the cerulean warbler and how the actions in Letcher County had a profound effect on the bird's ability to survive and reproduce. As my students began to have an appreciation for how their actions affect other species, the connection that our region had to this small songbird became much more evident. We became aware of how this bird's migration pattern also included the mountains of Colombia, which is also a small, remote area in the world. Students began to realize those connections that our community could have with another small mountainous community.

Both the forests of eastern Kentucky and the shaded coffee plantations of Colombia are facing destruction due to economic development and thereby damaging this small songbird's habitat. I saw this as an excellent opportunity for my students to reach beyond their community and build relationships that allowed them to not only act locally but globally as well. The supporters of the reforestation initiative were able to connect my students at Letcher County Central High School to students in a small school in the mountainous region of Columbia. This was a teaching opportunity as my students could go outside of their community and correspond with students from a different culture—and have some sense of their commonality in the face of economic development and its environmental impacts. The endangered life of the cerulean warbler became a link between these two groups of young adults from very diverse regions.

Spanish language is taught in our school, and the Spanish teacher was very supportive of developing a pen-pal exchange so that her students could practice their language and cultural skills with native speakers. Our high school students were thrilled to have the opportunity to connect with students in Colombia, not only through email but also through social media. The initial pen-pal exchange was organized in 2009, but some seven years later, some of these former high school students (now college graduates) have maintained these initial contacts through social media (Facebook). The life-changing opportunity offered to students of this remote area to reach out and make lasting contacts and friends from an entirely different culture and part of the world has developed in them both confidence and awareness of the connections shared by many regions of the world. This activity enhanced students' understanding of how, as communities and cultures, there are many more similarities than there are differences. It is this type of thinking that supports the acceptance of different people and cultures.

In the pen-pal exchange, the Colombian students wrote in Spanish to the students of Letcher County Central High School, and a college student helped with the translation. The students in Letcher County wrote back to the Colombian students in Spanish to begin the dialogue between two mountainous areas with similar environmental issues. My goal was for the students in my school to not only gain an appreciation for a different culture but also to realize the similarities that exist in areas of limited economic opportunities and environmental degradation. It allowed my students to understand that their lives and their problems are not so very different from those of other young people in other rural areas.

Students' experience with this project opened up their eyes to the possibilities of making contacts in other parts of the world. I encourage students to look beyond their experiences in the community to the possibility of developing relationships outside their own boundaries. I have witnessed from students a real sense of comfort in connecting with others beyond their community, something that in the past has been very challenging for many of our young people to consider. This project built support for students to go beyond their comfort zones and meet those from different cultures and communities. My students have gone on to further their education and seek jobs in various locations, and these types of cultural experiences have enhanced their confidence, supporting them in engaging in the adult world.

Educational Exchanges between the Appalachian U.S. and Germany

As I have continued to build the connections between what my students learn in school and how that is applied in life, I think back on my own education and how travel opened so many doors for me. As an undergraduate, along with studying science I studied German and had the opportunity to visit Germany for 10 days—both West Germany (the Federal Republic of Germany) and East Germany (the German Democratic Republic). It was those 10 days that made a lasting impression on me because for me, visiting a divided Germany was like stepping back into the time I had read about just after World War II.

In 2009, I participated in a summer Fulbright program in Germany. The Fulbright was to observe the German educational system and learn the similarities and differences between the German and American systems. I was assigned a school in Zwickau, Saxony, which was a part of the former East Germany. My visit there (some thirty years after my earlier visit) gave me the opportunity to make comparisons. There had been many changes since reunification, but East Germany was still less advanced than in the western part of Germany, and the attitude of those living in the east was that their living standards were not equal to those in the west. The educational system in the west was also considered superior, the wages were higher, and job opportunities were much greater.

I discovered there were many whose homes and families were in the eastern part of Germany, yet they worked in the west. They would stay at their jobs during the week and drive back to Zwickau on the weekends. The attitude of eastern (Germans), of feeling inferior to those in the western part of Germany, gave me the greatest basis for comparison; I felt the same type of attitude existed in my community of Letcher County when the residents there compared themselves to those in areas such as Lexington. One of the best analogies I heard was when a German businessman from the west doing business in the east remarked, "Well, most people in the east consider me a carpetbagger." It was this comparison to the post–Civil War era that rang a bell with me in comparing my community to that of Zwickau, in Germany.

There were similarities between Letcher County and this former coal-mining region of eastern Germany, and I saw an opportunity to form an exchange between students in my school and the students of Käthe Köllwitz Gymnasium (in Zwickau).

In the summer of 2011, I took eight Letcher County High Schools students for two weeks to live with and attend school with host German students, and, in October, the German students came to Letcher County to live with and attend school with their American host families. All of the German students spoke very good English, but many of their parents never learned English because Russian was the second language taught in Zwickau during the Cold War years, during the years of their formal education.

In 2013, I continued this exchange, taking 10 Letcher County students to Zwickau in June for two weeks. Then in October, 15 German students came to Whitesburg for two weeks. This exchange enhanced my students' appreciation for another culture. This appreciation was not limited to the students who traveled to Germany, but extended as well to the entire student body when the German students visited our school. I continued the German exchange in 2015 and am planning an additional student exchange in 2017.

My students and the German students have continued their relationships via social media, but one of the greatest accomplishments has been the fact that those students participating in the exchange feel they can make these types of trips on their own. The fear of the unknown no longer seems to be a barrier to travel. One of the Letcher County students from the exchange in 2011 traveled to South Africa last summer to vacation with her German host family.

Education is my passion, and education does not only occur in the classroom. I consider travel to be one of the greatest educational experiences I can offer my students. Experiencing different cultures and regions of the world supports my students' learning. As a teacher, I have supported community service projects and organized exchanges between the students of Letcher County and distant communities my students might never have experienced. The ability to expand the opportunities for Letcher County students beyond this small region of Appalachia has been one of my greatest rewards as a teacher. It is the lifelong learning educator in me who is always looking for new experiences that I can share with my students to enhance their learning.

REGINA DONOUR worked as a quality control chemist in private industry and then at home raising her sons. She entered the teaching profession in her early forties and obtained two advanced degrees (secondary education and chemistry) as well as her National Board Certification. For twenty years, she has taught chemistry and biology in a rural Appalachian high school, while pursuing her other interest, traveling internationally.

Reference

Angel, Patrick N. 2008. Flyer announcing The Cerulean Warbler Conservation Pen-Pal Program. London, Kentucky: U.S. Department of the Interior Office of Surface Mining Reclamation and Enforcement, Appalachian Regional Office.

CHAPTER 19

Experience and Expertise

CONFRONTING CLIMATE CHANGE IN THE ANDES

Lisa B. Markowitz

EARLY IN 2016, while doing fieldwork in the southern Peruvian city of Arequipa, I caught up with a long-time acquaintance, Daniel Torres, a veterinarian who for nearly three decades has worked with smallholding ranchers in the Peruvian Highlands. Our conversation quickly turned to the situation of alpaca producers, the *alpaqueros*, who tend their herds in pastures and along rolling ridges at elevations surpassing 4,000 meters above sea level. As we discussed the rapid retreat of mountain glaciers, that quite literally overarching threat to Andean livelihoods, Daniel remarked that without the *alpaqueros*, the high-altitude steppes, the *puna*, would turn into a desert. The herders, he explained, by harvesting and managing water, support the soils and grasses and maintain the wild plants and wildlife. Preventing desiccation of the high-elevation grasslands protects watersheds, crops, and populations lying far below.

In the rural Andes, as in other potential "sacrifice zones" (Klein 2014) across the planet, we see one of the ironies of climate change: those who have least contributed to the climate crisis and rarely enjoy the trappings of fossil-fuel-based affluence are now placed most at risk by rising temperatures. At the same time, the work of the *alpaqueros* in conserving the *puna* (e.g., Palacios Rios 1977; Verzijl and Guerrero Quispe 2013) suggests a second paradox: that the "low tech" agricultural knowledge and practices developed in those same zones have much to offer in coping with the inevitable climate challenges. After a quick introduction to the mountains and their social history, in this chapter I elaborate on the

Fig. 19.1 Newly sheared alpacas.
Photo credit: L. B. Markowitz

potential of Andean agriculture with reference to the current rediscovery of its bounty.

An Overview of the Andes

The Andes are a vast young mountain chain that covers a large swath of western South America. The largest tropical mountain range as well as the longest continental range on the planet, it stretches from Chile and Argentina in the south up through Colombia and Venezuela in the northeast. Comprising much of the topography of the central Andes are the countries of Ecuador, Peru, and Bolivia. The mountains extend over 2.5 million square kilometers and contain a population of about 85 million, or 45 percent of the countries' total populations (Devenish and Gianella 2012, iv). In addition, some 20 million residents of large cities along the Pacific coast rely on mountain resources and ecosystem services, notably irrigation and hydroelectric power (Devenish and Gianella 2012, iv).

In the century before the Spanish invasion, the Andes were home to one of the great Native American empires, the Inca, and, well before their rise in the 15th century, to a series of sophisticated, complex societies. Despite the obvious challenges of the physical environment, Andean peoples carried out impressive engineering and logistical projects. For example, the Incas connected their disparate multi-ethnic population through a road system, created vast state-maintained systems of food storage, and filled those storehouses with surplus food. While potatoes and corn counted as key staple and ceremonial foods, highland producers cultivated a wide variety of tubers as well different grains, including quinoa and amaranth. *The Lost Crops of the Incas* (the pointed title of a National Research Council [1989] compilation) also include numerous fruits and vegetables. And we should not forget the animals domesticated—guinea pigs, alpacas, and llama—furnishing wool and portage along with meat.

One need not romanticize life under the notoriously contentious Inca rulers to observe that the arrival of the Spanish ushered in centuries of hardship and atrocity. Thanks to the combined impacts of colonial warfare and disease, forced labor and relocation, expropriation of lands, resource extortion, endemic racism, and feudal systems that lingered into the 1950s (Bolivia), 1960s (Ecuador), and 1970s (Peru), in those same high mountain regions where sophisticated farming systems were once developed, rural people—predominantly of indigenous heritage—have suffered some of the worst poverty in the hemisphere. The particular configuration varies by country, but in many Andean zones, especially in Peru, and until very recently Bolivia, we find widespread hunger or malnutrition; high rates of illiteracy; lack of essential services such as education and electrical power; contested rights to land, forests, and water; and poor transportation infrastructure and marketing systems. Some figures illustrating the ongoing disenfranchisement of highland residents come from Peru, which, for much of the past decade or so, has had one of the world's fastest growing economies, thanks largely to mineral exports. Although nationwide monetary poverty rates fell by about half, rural poverty rates are three times those of urban areas, and living conditions in the highlands remain far below those in the coast. A speaker of a native language such as Quechua or Aymara is twice as likely to be poor as a Peruvian whose first language is Spanish (Nava 2015, 5, 6). In fact, in some Andean provinces, poverty rates have increased (INEI 2010). In Bolivia and Ecuador, especially, the "red or pink tide" of electoral change and associated indigenous social movements are rectifying certain economic and social disparities. But the residents of these regions remain subject to many forms of structural inequality.

Climate Change

In the Andean Highlands, rising temperatures threaten the already precarious livelihoods of many rural people. There, in contrast to many parts of the world, climate change has been visible for decades. In the Peruvian Department of Cuzco, a community elder described the disappearance of nearby glaciers: "Our *Apus* (sacred mountain deities) have always had sparkling white ponchos. Now some of their ponchos have brown stripes. Other peaks have shed their ponchos altogether" (Bolin 2009, 228). The Andes contain more than 99 percent of the world's glaciers located in the tropical latitudes. With the increase in global temperature between 0.3 and 0.5 degrees per decade from 1901 to 2005 (Chevallier et al. 2011), glaciers are retreating across all the Andean countries—and this rate of retreat has increased since the late 1970s (Rabatel et al. 2013). For reasons having to do with seasonality, tropical glaciers are particularly sensitive to climate varia-tion. The demise of Bolivia's Chacaltaya ski resort near the capital city, La Paz, offers a visually dramatic case in point: once the site of the highest ski lift in the world, the glacial slopes where the national Olympic team trained in the 1980s are now just exposed boulders (Romero 2007).

Although the repercussions of localized climate change extend well beyond athletic disappointments, the particular risks and consequences across this com-plex mountain range will vary; moreover, predicting future change is complicated by information gaps and the paths of future El Niño events, which strongly affect rainfall (Devenish and Gianella 2012, 20). That said, according to projections, warming will likely continue to reduce the area of glaciers, resulting initially in higher discharges of water as glaciers melt, followed by long-lasting decreases in river flows, affecting water availability on the western side of the Andes and along the Pacific coast. Changes in precipitation patterns, in some areas already evident (e.g., Bolin 2009; Postigo 2014; Skarbø and VanderMolen 2014; Valdivia et al. 2010) are expected to include regionally specific increases and decreases in the amount of rain, more intensive downpours, and longer dry periods (Deve-nish and Gianella 2012, 12). Shifts in temperature and hydrology are also affect-ing biotic communities: for instance, Postigo (2014) reports that the expanding habitats of mosquitos and other pests jeopardize the crops and livestock of south-ern Peruvian peasants. Cumulatively, these environmental changes pose serious challenges to cash-poor farmers and ranchers, now faced with recalibrating and reconfiguring their production strategies. Diminishing water flows and supplies will also imperil large-scale agriculture along the Pacific coasts along with the well-being of urban populations reliant on highland-sourced drinking water.

Andean Responses

A head-spinning number of insightful and creative proposals and strategies have been put forth for assessing, confronting, managing, and adapting to cli-mate change in different regions at multiple levels of scale, specificity, practice, and organization. In the remainder of this essay, I want to highlight just one theme that emerges from this body of recommendations: that of promoting agricultural production in mountain areas by building on local knowledge and native products, while improving food security and protecting biodiversity. I draw from a landmark document of global agriculture, the International Assess-ment of Agricultural Knowledge, Science and Technology for Development (IAASTD), sponsored by the World Bank and the United Nations (McIntyre et al. 2009). The multidisciplinary group of analysts highlighted the multiple envi-ronmental benefits of sustainable agricultural practices, as embodied variously in peasant farming systems and in the paradigm of agroecology (Nivia et al. 2009, 52–54). Among other practices, smallholders tend to sequester carbon by recycling nutrients, support biodiversity with mosaic-style land use, and reduce contamination with limited-to-null use of chemical inputs. Also, in contrast to productivist or conventional agriculture, more varieties of more crops are grown, offering additional biohabitats while averting risk from weather or plagues. The knowledge and skills of the people who cultivate these complex and rich fields are precious. Andean producers, historically, are accustomed to dealing with the challenges posed by the high altitudes and low latitudes of tropical mountains— irregular precipitation, a short frost-free season, high levels of solar radiation, and multiple distinct microenvironments. Farmers and ranchers have hard-won experience dealing with climatic perturbations and buffering shocks to their livelihoods through the diversification of production. During the 1990s, as part of a research team in the village of San José Llanga on the Bolivian altiplano, I saw that experience in action. As in many Andean communities, residents raise both livestock and crops. Unlike conventional agriculture in which these activities are separated, the cattle and sheep graze fallow potato, quinoa, and barley plots, fertilizing as they munch. Later on, the hungry ovines will be rewarded with delicious crop residues from the multiple varieties of potatoes planted— some frost resistant, some pest resistant, some better for frying, and some for freeze-drying. The farmers, familiar with the different varieties, stagger sowing times according to experience and the forecast based on local biophysical indicators (Coppock and Valdivia 2001). With the uncertainties of climate change, the need to make such micro adjustments and judgments increase, as do the stakes.

The IAASTD document offers an important general point regarding the sorts of responses to environmental perturbations Andean farmers make regularly. The measures involved in adapting to at least the early stages of climate change correspond to those for reducing carbon emissions. Agricultural win-win opportunities include land restoration—think of the *alpaqueros* protecting the *puna,* and "effective manure management"—think of those Bolivian sheep (McIntyre et al. 2009, 50).

Today, international bodies recognize the contributions of peasant farmers and ranchers. After many decades of racially tinged dismissal of Andean cropping practices and crops and promotion of exogenous Green Revolution–style agricultural technologies and priorities, the past two decades have seen growing national awareness of the value of Andean production systems and products. In Peru, interestingly, this has coincided with the current gastronomic boom that celebrates the newly discovered (by urban chefs) formerly disparaged peasant foods.

Let me conclude with some examples of the ways the expertise of highland producers is spilling to lower elevations, deliciously, with a couple of examples of efforts to improve livelihood via supporting native crops and, not incidentally, to bolster high-altitude ecosystems.

The first, called Papa Andina, was sponsored by the International Potato Center, based in Lima, and numerous institutional partners. Close to 3,000 potato varieties have been cultivated in Peru; however, most shoppers are familiar with no more than 5 varieties (International Potato Center 2007). Papa Andina sought to preserve the tremendous biodiversity of Andean potato cultivation by helping Andean farmers find new markets and better prices for their ancestral crops. The staff worked collaboratively with producers in the central highlands and with food processors, including Pepsico and retailers, to identify market possibilities and develop products appropriate for upscale supermarkets. These have included bags of fresh potatoes and delicious native potato chips. This particular large and well-funded project has had success in creating demand for and recognition of neglected potato varieties, thus supporting biodiversity, and generating additional income for highland farmers (Devaux et al. 2010).

A second initiative, with far less institutional backing, concerns alpaca meat, a staple for rural families of the high-herding zones. Considered a dirty and diseased "Indian food," its consumption was unimaginable by most urbanites until recent decades, and the prejudice persists. Nonetheless, interest in indigenous foodways spurred by the gastronomic boom has widened market prospects. Accordingly, in one southern Peruvian province, herders and processors have endeavored to elaborate and sell products that appeal to chefs and shoppers in the city of Arequipa, and even in Lima, a challenging undertaking, since in effect they must create these markets themselves. One young butcher buys and trims his meat in his provincial hometown, and then hauls it to Arequipa, where he sells fine cuts to restaurants and burgers at the Saturday farmers' market (*bioferia*). He has also found clients in Lima but secure refrigerated transport remains a barrier. He has shared his butchering skills with a group of herding families, who collaborated to sell fresh meat and process cold cuts and jerky in solar dryers supplied by an NGO. Finding markets for these value-added products is daunting; the ranchers must personally contact restauranteurs and rely on help from an NGO-based volunteer in locating supermarket outlets. Despite such obstacles, an expansion of the market for alpaca meat would afford producers an important income stream (Markowitz 2012) and support their efforts to conserve those critical high-altitude pastures in the face of melting glaciers.

Currently, efforts by producers' groups, state agencies, and NGOs to promote other Andean crops such as maca, tarwi, and quinoa, to name but a few, abound. Such projects can lead to increased incomes for peasant farmers and contribute to greater mainstream recognition and appreciation of the productive capacity and environmental significance of highlands spaces and livelihoods. To end on a more speculative note, I also think, based on the stories told to me by many community activists and farmers, that the skills acquired in building markets for these once disparaged foods are some of the same skills that empower people to engage politically and to advocate for their own interests. Given the unfortunate specter of expanding climate-linked resource conflicts, such experience may be even more valuable than technical expertise.

LISA B. MARKOWITZ is in the Department of Anthropology, University of Louisville, where she also served as chair. As a cultural anthropologist interested in agrifood systems at multiple scales and popular efforts to transform them, her long-term research has been in Andean South America with foci on rural livelihood, food security, and value chains. She coedited *U.S. Food Policy: Anthropology and Advocacy in the Public Interest.*

References

Bolin, Inge. 2009. "The Glaciers of the Andes Are Melting: Indigenous and Anthropological Knowledge Merge in Restoring Water Resources." In *Anthropology and Climate Change: From Encounters to Actions*, edited by Mark Nuttal and Susan A. Crate, 228–239. Walnut Creek, CA: Left Coast.

Chevallier, Pierre, Bernard Pouyaud, Wilson Suarez, and Thomas Condom. 2011. "Climate Change Threats to Environment in the Tropical Andes: Glaciers and Water Resources." *Regional Environmental Change* 11 (1): 179–187.

Coppock, David Layne, and Corinne Valdivia, eds. 2001. *Sustaining Agropastoralism on the Bolivian Altiplano: The Case of San José Llanga*. Logan, UT: Department of Rangeland Resources, Utah State University.

Devaux, A., J. Andrade-Piedra, D. Horton, M. Ordinola, G. Thiele, A. Thomann, and C. Velasco. 2010. *Brokering Innovation for Sustainable Development: The Papa Andina Case*. ILAC, working paper no. 12. Rome: Institutional Learning and Change Initiative.

Devenish, Christian, and Cecilia Gianella, eds. 2012. "Years of Sustainable Mountain Development in the Andes—From Rio 1992 to 2012 and Beyond." Lima: CODESAN.

INEI (Instituto Nacional de Estadística e Informática Perú). 2010. "Perú: Ingreso promedio mensual por trabajo, según quintiles y área de residencia, 2001–2009." In *Evolución de los indicadores de empleo e ingresos por departamentos, 2001–2009*, Table 6.20. Lima.

International Potato Center. 2007. *T'ikapapa: Linking Urban Consumers and Small-Scale Andean Producers with Potato Biodiversity*. Lima: International Potato Center.

Klein, Naomi. 2014. *This Changes Everything: Capitalism vs. the Climate*. New York: Simon and Schuster.

Markowitz, Lisa. 2012. "Highland Haute Cuisine: The Transformation of Alpaca Meat." In *Re-Imagining Marginalized Foods: Global Processes, Local Places*, edited by Elizabeth Finnis, 34–48. Tucson: University of Arizona Press.

McIntyre, B. D., H. R. Herren, J. Wakhungu, and R. T. Watson, eds. 2009. *Agriculture at a Crossroads. Synthesis Report. A Synthesis of the Global and Sub-Global IAASTD Reports*. Washington DC: Island.

National Research Council. 1989. *Lost Crops of the Incas: Little-Known Plants of the Andes with Promise for Worldwide Cultivation*. Washington, DC: National Academy.

Nava, Armando M. 2015. "Inequality in Peru: Reality and Risks. OXFAM, working paper Peru no. 1. https://peru.oxfam.org/sites/peru.oxfam.org/files/file _attachments/Inequality%20in%20Peru.%20Reality%20and%20Risks.pdf. Accessed April 20, 2017.

Nivia, E., I. Perfecto, M. Ahumada, K. Luz, R. Pérez, and J. Santamaría. 2009. "Agriculture in Latin America and the Caribbean: Context, Evolution and Current Situation." *International Assessment of Agricultural Knowledge, Science and Technology for Development: LAC Report*. Washington DC: Island.

Palacios Rios, F. 1977. "Pastizales de regadío para alpacas." In *Pastores de puna: Uywamichiq Punarunakuna*, edited by J. A. Flores Ochoa, 155–170. Lima: Instituto de Estudios Peruanos.

Postigo, Julio C. 2014. "Perception and Resilience of Andean Populations Facing Climate Change." *Journal of Ethnobiology* 34 (3): 383–400.

Rabatel, A., B. Francou, A. Soruco, J. Gomez, B. Cáceres, J. L. Ceballos, R. Basantes, M. Vuille, J. E. Sicart, C. Huggel, M. Scheel, Y. Lejeune, Y. Arnaud, M. Collet, T. Condom, G. Consoli, V. Favier, V. Jomelli, R. Galarraga, and P. Ginot. 2013. "Current State of Glaciers in the Tropical Andes: A Multi-Century Perspective on Glacier Evolution and Climate Change." *Cryosphere* 7 (1): 81–102. http://dx.doi.org/10.5194 /tc-7-81-2013.

Romero, Simon. 2007. "Bolivia's Only Ski Resort Is Facing a Snowless Future." *New York Times,* February 2. Accessed April 20, 2017. http://www.nytimes.com/2007/02/02 /world/americas/02bolivia.html

Skarbø, Kristine, and Kristin VanderMolen. 2014. "Irrigation Access and Vulnerability to Climate-Induced Hydrological Change in the Ecuadorian Andes." *CAFE* 36 (1): 28–44.

Valdivia, Corinne, Anji Seth, Jere L. Gilles, Magali García, Elizabeth Jiménez, Jorge Cusicanqui, Fredy Navia, and Edwin Yucra. 2010. "Adapting to Climate Change in Andean Ecosystems: Landscapes, Capitals, and Perceptions Shaping Rural Livelihood Strategies and Linking Knowledge Systems." *Annals of the Association of American Geographers* 100 (4): 818–834.

Verzijl, Andres, and Silvano Guerrero Quispe. 2013. "The System Nobody Sees: Irrigated Wetland Management and Alpaca Herding in the Peruvian Andes." *Mountain Research and Development* 33 (3): 280–293. http://dx.doi.org/10.1080/00045608.20 10.500198.

CHAPTER 20

Sustainable Livelihoods in Extreme Lands

Dipak R. Pant

MY PROFESSIONAL INVOLVEMENT with marginal human habitats began in Nepal when I was teaching anthropology at Tribhuvan University (Kathmandu) from 1987 to 1991. High-altitude Himalayan rural areas, historically inhabited but remote and tough terrains ("extreme lands"), became my concern in Nepal where I found opportunities to serve as a field surveyor and planning advisor for rural development projects. Later from my European base, I found some opportunities to conduct field surveys (and, in a few cases, also to serve as development planner) in many other extreme lands: the Alps and Apennines (Italy); central and northern tropical Andes (Peru, Venezuela); southern Caucasus (Armenia); South American coastal desert (Peru-Chile); tropical savannahs of western Africa (Sierra Leone) and South America (Brazil); Kalahari Desert and arid savannahs of southern Africa (Botswana, South Africa); deserts, steppes, taiga, and highlands in the northern and central areas of Asia (Siberian region of Russia, China, and Mongolia).

Between 2007 and 2012, opportunities to conduct field surveys and experimental projects were found in Mongolia and China. First, I served as the scientific advisor for a European Union–funded project on management capacity building of local officials and entrepreneurs in Mongolia and Inner Mongolia, an autonomous region of China.[1] Later, I had the opportunity to coordinate a Mongolian and European team that implemented another small experimental project[2] designed for local empowerment, targeting the nomadic herding families, the traditional

273

inhabitants of Mongolia's remote steppes (*Thal*), conifer forests (*Taiga*), mountains (*Nuruu*), and desert (*Gobi*). Mongolia's ever-decreasing nomadic herding communities represent one of the last remaining human groups that has changed little in lifestyle and work patterns, probably because of their extremely remote and marginal habitat. Mongolia's nomadic herders are resilient human groups who have been dwelling and wandering around in the extreme lands for centuries, generating interesting organizational and cultural forms in the course of their adaption to adverse physical and climatic conditions. They live and work in difficult terrains, ranging from the grassy rolling hills under the high crests covered by sub-Arctic conifer forests (*Taiga*) in the north to the arid and rugged stretches of dry rangelands merging in the vast desert (*Gobi*) of south and west, intersected by high mountain ranges (Altai and Khangai ranges). In addition to the difficulty of terrain, these lands are also characterized by long and harsh winters, short summers, very little rain, frequent snow blizzards and violent sand storms. The Mongolian herders' habitats are among the most sparsely populated and least developed areas in the world in terms of infrastructures and services. Repeated fieldwork in Mongolia's extreme lands have provided me an understanding of life and livelihoods in the extreme lands.

Currently, I am engaged in a long-term consultation that aims to check demographic decline and to promote economic revival in the remote rural municipalities in Italy's western Alps. The historical inhabitants of the remote western Italian Alps belong to a particular cultural subcontext of Western Europe's continental heartland that spreads across the Alpine regions comprising the mountains and hills of northwestern Italy, southwestern Switzerland, and southeastern France. The remotest Italian Alpine villages are *cul-de sac* settlements, bordering no-man's-land made up by high-altitude forests and shrubs, stony slopes, and ice-covered crests and peaks. A few decades ago, most of the natives of such marginal Alpine areas were traditionally active in agro-silvo-pastoral activities and related craft works as well as in some commodity trading. Now, many are gone because economic opportunities in their localities are scarce; living and working conditions are hard; and many residents express a sense of isolation related to the remoteness of these marginal habitats.

Extreme Lands and Marginality

Attention to the sustainable economy in the world's marginal human habitats (extreme lands) is required for several reasons. They represent the ultimate human outposts on the rurality-wilderness interface. The residing communities play a vital role in preserving the ecosystems and managing the landscapes by maintaining their presidium (as ecological sentinels) in difficult terrains. The world can benefit from observing the traditional adaptive strategies deployed by local populations. These areas are often reservoirs in which one finds concentrated remnants of biodiversity. The local communities' knowledge base includes the native inventory of local biodiversity as well as native resource management principles and practices derived from centuries of ecological sentinel functions and experiments for adaptive strategy and survival in their harsh surroundings. Extreme lands are a good place to learn traditional ecological knowledge, resource management skills, adaptive strategies, resilience, ethics, and solidarity—and to learn about sustainability through local traditions and know-how.

With gradual replacement of local institutions by the modern government charge (bureaucratic encroachment) and with the increasing ramifications of the global market, remote and marginal contexts have been undergoing profound changes, mostly disruptive to their lifestyles and to their livelihoods. Marginal human habitats are vulnerable and, if not properly supported, their residents are likely to leave (it has been happening in the past decades), and no one will be left to protect the valuable resources that remain or to maintain the traditional know-how, cultures and ethnodiversity.

Peace and prosperity in these areas are strategically important for international security and stable interstate relations because these areas usually fall outside the national sociocultural and political mainstreams, are mostly populated by ethnic minorities, and are often straddled across the borders between nation-states.

Extreme lands are characterized by their "marginality": territories that are out of sight and out of mind, far from the development trajectory and mass media mainstream. Many studies on marginality tend to focus on such territories as the politically or administratively neglected realities resulting from a process of regional economic disparity and social marginalization. There seems to be a tendency to consider marginality as well-defined pockets of relative distress where marginality is more the result of a socioeconomic process of exclusion rather than a structural precondition (Sommers, Mehretu, and Pigozzi 1999). More recent studies seem to focus on the multiple dimensions of marginality by taking into consideration geopolitics, culture, society, economic process, and environment (Leimgruber 1994; Leimgruber, Majoral, and Chul-Woo 2003). The spatial marginality is usually referred to in terms of the geographical distance of an area from major economic centers and the difficulty in access and transit due to the lack of infrastructure and, therefore, isolation from the economic development mainstream (Brodwin 2001; Müller-Böker et al. 2004). However, the spatial dimension of marginality is considered to be a relative concept. Regional disparities are said to persist at different scales (national, regional, and global) regardless of the geographical remoteness (Jussila, Majoral, and Mutambirwa 1999; Müller-Böker et al. 2004). Spatial marginality is said to be linked with the regional disparities in living standards between communities in the mainland of economic activity and those in the remote areas, or in the periphery, with a poor resource base (Leimgruber 2004), where marginality primarily manifests as a result of spatial disadvantages (Massey 1994; Sommers, Mehretu, and Pigozzi 1999). Market forces are said to produce inequalities in competitiveness due to distance and physical limitations (Mehta 1995). In most of the studies the concept of marginality has a more pronounced socioeconomic (and political) connotation even when the geophysical aspects are duly considered (Mehretu, Pigozzi, and Sommers 2000; Gurung and Kollmair 2005). The marginal areas are viewed as somehow a temporary state of economic and cultural irrelevance, resulting from a process of exclusion and marginalization. In other words, marginality is often seen as a phase in a process (flux reality), and not as a permanent condition (structural reality).

From a broad geophysical perspective, all surfaces of the planet Earth, including the extreme lands, are undergoing some process of change (flux). From the anthropological perspective, combining spatial (geophysical) conditions with socioeconomic considerations, the extreme lands are structural realities; their marginality is in-built, a permanent condition. Most extreme lands are economically and politically marginalized even in the relatively developed countries (e.g., Appalachia in the United States; Alps and Apennines in Italy; Pyrenees in Spain and France; Urals, Altai, and Siberia in Russia; Xinkiang and Tibet-Qinghai in China).

Not all marginalized contexts are extreme. Economic marginalization occurs also in the relatively mild terrains of the plains or coast (e.g., the urban slums or poor villages). But their marginal status is inherently transitional; it changes by urban regeneration or rural development. A few extreme lands are not so marginalized from an economic point of view. The tourist hotspots in the Alps or the highland resorts in the Rockies are anything but marginalized, thanks to tourism-induced wealth and accessibility (good infrastructure). But physical distance and topographical ruggedness make them permanently different, and socially and politically marginal despite their wealth and accessibility. For a land to be considered extreme, economic marginality is necessary, but not sufficient. The most defining trait of an extreme land is being at the edge of the anthroposphere, bordering the inhospitable spaces and wilderness. Extreme lands are the buffer zones between the "no-man's-land," the (immense) Nature without humans, and the humanized world (anthroposphere and technosphere) where humanity presides over the (subdued) Nature. Extreme lands constitute the human edge in the rural-wilderness interface. Physical hardships and the distance from the mainstream make the inhabitants of the extreme lands politically and economically marginal, but also culturally unique—and, as in the modern times, quite vulnerable. On the whole, the remote marginal human habitats are extreme lands primarily for their geophysical marginality, and for their frontier position (edge, *limes*).

Extreme lands tend to be at the edge (*limes*) also in political terms. As witnessed by the maps of both ancient empires and modern nation-states, the centers and core-settlement zones of the states and empires are located around comfortable and viable zones. Harsh and tough terrains are positioned in the peripheries. Such historical peripheral positioning has put most of the extreme lands on the borders between states, empires, and civilizations, thus on the fault lines in terms of geopolitics and culture areas. This may partially explain some of the protracted interstate border disputes, ethnic tensions, and conflicts on certain extreme borderlands.[3] The extreme borderlands usually fall outside the national political and economic mainstreams of their respective countries and are, mostly, inhabited by the ethnic minorities who transcend the mainstream national identity and modern administrative confinements.[4] Therefore, long-term peace and sustainable prosperity in the extreme lands are strategically important for national (and international) security and for stable interstate relations.

For being "out of sight and out of mind," the remote and marginal areas are of great strategic importance for the governments and corporations as these areas are often rich in natural resources (minerals, timber, water, etc.). The extreme lands serve a variety of programs that are better conducted outside the watch of mainstream media and public opinion: for example, open pit mining, hazardous waste deposit, military experiments, and other dangerous experiments and dumps. Everywhere, the native inhabitants of extreme lands are too small in number and often politically and culturally weak to oppose the exploitation of their habitat or to raise their voices against the hazardous actions in their surroundings. Politically and economically, the native communities of the marginal areas are treated as peripheral elements in the countries to which they belong. The national mainstream and mass media ignore them as negligible "outer" reality.

From the viewpoint of the world-system (the global economy, mass media, political mainstream), extreme lands may seem marginal and peripheral. But from the viewpoint of the Earth-system, they constitute the inner core. The sparsely populated extreme lands are mostly located in the interior of the island, peninsula, and continental landmass. They constitute the *heartland*, the inner core. Even in the small islands in world's mild climate zones (e.g., the Mediterranean or East China Sea) the historically inhabited inner core tends to be relatively harsh and inaccessible terrain and culturally a world apart from the lowlands and coastal areas. The inner core zones are extreme within their contexts and are unique for their ethnicity and sociocultural identity (e.g., the central mountainous zones of Taiwan in East China Sea, interior of Sardinia and Sicily in Italy, and the inner areas of Corsica in France). Everywhere, the most densely populated, urbanized, and developed regions are usually in the mild and moderate zones (for terrain and climate), usually along the coastline or closer to the seafront or water lanes (rivers); they constitute the outer edge of the continental landmasses, the *rimland*. The rural backyards that lie just behind the rimland constitute the *hinterland*. The hinterland supplies food, timber and other natural resources (as well as migrant labour force) to the urban and developed rimland, and also serves as the dumping ground for the wastes generated in and discarded by the rimland. Farther deep inside there is the *heartland*, the most "inner" zones of continental landmass and islands, characterized by tough and harsh terrains with very few inhabitants, far from urban centers and business corridors, that is, the extreme lands.

Lately, more than half of the world's human population has been concentrated in the urban areas (rimland), for the first time in Earth's history.[5] There seems to be an inexorable migratory movement towards the rimland from inner zones. The rimland is increasingly under heavy pressure to accommodate new waves of migrants seeking opportunities, jobs, income and services. The hinterland (rural agrarian backyards) is suffering the loss of human capital (drainage to the rimland) and the pressure of more intensive exploitation of its space, crops, soil, water, vegetation, and so on as it constitutes the supply zone and dumping site for the rimland. The outbound migration and consequent loss of human capital have even more severe consequences in the heartland (the extreme lands) as it is already sparsely populated. The heartland is also facing increasing pressure from the extractive industries (such as mining and timber logging) with serious environmental and economic implications (adverse impact) that are beyond the control of the native residents. The natives of heartland (extreme lands) are vulnerable to both hazards, natural (typical of their extreme habitats) and man-made such as environmental safety and health risks due to mining, waste dumping, and other hazardous activities. Historically, the extreme lands' natives represent the only human presidium in very harsh terrains, as the ecological sentinel and as the depository of ethnodiversity. They always have faced huge challenges due to their material hardships. Now they are facing new challenges stemming from a new subaltern position and identity crisis (and also an inferiority complex vis-à-vis comfortable and glittering urbanity) thanks to ever-pervading urbo-centered, modernity-biased public policies, officialdom, global market encroachment, and mainstream mass media.

Residents of extreme lands deserve serious attention. Because their needs are uncommon, citizen demand and accountability are pretty weak, and markets do not function well there. If not properly supported, the human presidium and ecological sentinel functions in extreme lands may weaken or even disappear; this may cause irreversible loss in human knowledge and environments. Migration from the extreme lands exerts pressure on the rimland's infrastructures and services, and the immigrants risk being further marginalized (in socioeconomic terms) and falling into squalor (slums) and illegality in the rimland.

Extreme Lands as Metaphor of Sustainability and New Strategy for Local Development

The extreme lands constitute a metaphor of global sustainability as they lie at the edge of the anthroposphere, in the rural-wilderness interface. The rural-wilderness continuum is the most explicit and frontal situation of human-Nature interface. These contexts are likely to reflect more acutely the local impacts of global environmental changes (climate uncertainty) as well as the economic transition. The extreme lands provide us unique opportunity to learn about adaptive strategy, resilience, and sustainability. They also challenge us to design and implement innovative and pragmatic local development programs. The challenges posed by the extreme human habitats demand a holistic approach. The holistic approach will lead to rethinking our strategic postures regarding economic development:

- Outward posture: how to reduce human vulnerability, risks, and threats to habitat and population; recover resources and energy from locally available materials (and waste) as much as possible.
- Forward posture: which innovative solutions are needed in integrated management of landscape and infrastructures (e.g., intermodal multiform mobility); resource-*cum*-waste management: less input for high-value output (resource efficiency), more waste dissipation by reuse in the local/live circuits prior to final disposal (circular economy).
- Inward posture: which economic and social policies are appropriate to promote wellness and dematerialized wealth creation; well-being (disposable income, employment, security, health, fitness, comfort, culture, arts, leisure, and recreation) instead of "well-having" (artifacts, material possessions).

The combination of global economic volatility and the urgency of the environmental problems demands strong leadership from governments, business communities, and civil society. The priorities should be the reduction of human vulnerability and the lessening of the pressure on ecosystems. Therefore, the socioeconomic progress of local communities should be measured by a human vulnerability–centered balance score as well as by measuring the decoupling of the volume of total material flow (inputs, instruments, artefacts, waste) from the net value in terms of employment, income, and premium price for the products and services. There are two possible new parameters that we may use to measure the sustainable economic progress of communities in the marginal habitats (perhaps also in the nonmarginal areas), which, once scientifically established and institutionally implemented, may eventually accomplish a paradigm shift in economic thinking and may enable us to move forward toward global sustainability.

- Human vulnerability assessment score: a new way of ranking societies/regions, based on the threats to security, public health, livelihoods, rights and dignity.

- Place-brand value index: measuring the prestige and attractiveness (to visitors, investors) of a place-system for its "quality of context" (quality of environmental resources, landscape, social order, peace and tranquillity, cultural richness, public health, infrastructures, services, and waste management).

These are analytical tools that I suggest as a way to further discussions of sustainable livelihoods in practical ways across mountain regions.

A Way Forward

Development as understood in terms of quantitative growth in gross local output may mislead policy-makers and planners; I suggest using the term *upliftment* instead. Upliftment is concerned with improvement in the socioeconomic conditions and quality of life of communities, with a strong commitment to the preservation and promotion of human capital (reducing vulnerabilities, fostering resilience and capabilities) and natural ecosystems. Upliftment is about the quality of context (place-brand value) through the promotion of local ethos, identity assets, beauty of natural and built environment, and local specialities (*genius loci*). Upliftment is a vertically oriented economic development approach that progressively affirms the decoupling of "value" from "volume," and creates a prestigious place-brand.

Upliftment strives for quality of local products and services, quality of infrastructures and environment (and landscape), and quality of social relations (identity, trust, exchange) through a coherent collaboration among all those concerned with the "overground" resources. The over-ground resources are represented by all sorts of crops, food, agro products, livestock, animal products, forest products, landscapes, environmental resources, aesthetic relevance of natural and built environments, touristic attractions, and so on. The economy based on the "under-ground" resources (mining) and extractive business (timber logging) can provide only limited benefit in terms of local employment and revenues. Mountain regions and other extreme lands can be uplifted by a strong partnership of all those local stakeholders who are concerned with the over-ground resources (farmers, forest workers, herders, beekeepers, fishermen, gardeners, traders, hoteliers, caterers, tour operators, service providers etc.). The "over-ground resource alliance" is necessary for the upliftment. Such an alliance is likely to mobilize a good quantity of resources from within the localities as well as outsiders' investments and tourism. Even without any significant quantitative improvement in the investments and tourist visits from outside, the local inhabitants will have mobilized their own resources and energies and will be able to create for themselves a more attractive and safer place to live and work. Upliftment, leading to a distinctive place-brand, is a win-win strategy for those in marginal and remote human terrains, and perhaps for other places, too.

DIPAK R. PANT is an experienced field anthropologist and an (accidental) economist. He heads the Interdisciplinary Unit for Sustainable Economy and is a senior faculty member of the School of Economics & Management at Università Carlo Cattaneo. He has helped develop environmentally sustainable and socially sound economic policy and development planning guidelines for governmental, industrial, commercial, and nongovernmental organizations in many regions of the world.

Notes

1. EU-TransMongolia Partnership for Sustainable Tourism and Related Businesses Development (2007–2010): a local capacity development project funded by European Commission's Asia-Invest program in collaboration with the Government of Mongolia, the regional administration of Inner Mongolia Autonomous Region (People's Republic of China), the Rural Investment Support Centre (a Mongolian NGO), and the Università Carlo Cattaneo(LIUC, Italy).

2. Mobile Community Training Project (2010–2012): planning and implementation of an itinerant adult training caravan for local empowerment of the nomadic herding communities in the steppes and taiga in the region of Arkhangai, in collaboration with the Rural Investment Support Center (NGO, Ulan Bator), the provincial administration (*Soum*) of Ulziit, and the regional administration (*Aimag*) of Arkhangai, Mongolia. In 2008, preliminary field surveys were conducted and proper contacts were established thanks to an earlier European Union–supported project for which our team served as scientific partner. A comprehensive video report on the Mobile Community Training Project has been available since 2013 (official documentary trailer: http://www.youtube.com/watch?v=MXD2p-ZAuHE).

3. Examples include Pakhtunistan's and Baluchistan's arid highlands across Pakistan-Afghanistan-Iran borders, a theater of violent conflicts for decades; the disputed Himalayan borderlands of Laddakh and Arunachal Pradesh on India-China frontiers; the disputed areas of Jammu and Kashmir on India-Pakistan borders in the Himalaya-Karakorum region; the tensions across the Taklamakan-Dzungarian desert basins and around the Tian-Shan-Tengri Tagh Mountains near China's borders with Kazakhstan and Kyrghizistan; the Chechen, Ingush, and Daghestani unrest in the northern Caucasus on Russia's southern flanks; the Nagorno-Karabakh conflict across Armenia-Azerbaijan borders in the southern Caucasus; the armed struggle in Kurdistan in the rough mountainous area across Turkey-Syria-Iraq-Iran borders; the Polisario-Morocco conflict in the desert of western Sahara; the Darfur conflict in western Sudan's arid mountains and deserts on the borders with Chad; and, recently, the conflict in Mali in the southern fringes of the Sahara Desert.

4. Examples include the *Tuareg* in Sahel (Mauritania, Mali, Chad, Niger); the *Pashtun* across Afghanistan-Pakistan borders; the *Baloch* across Iran-Pakistan borders; the *Kazakh* across Mongolia-Kazakhstan borders; the *Buryat* and the *Dukkha* across Mongolia-Siberia (Russian Federation) borders; the ethnic *Mongol* across Mongolia-China borders; the *Uyghur* across China's borders with Kirghizstan and Kazakhstan; Tibetan ethnic groups (*Bhotiya*) across China's borders with India, Nepal and Bhutan; and numerous ethnic minorities across China's southwestern borders with Myanmar (Burma), Thailand, Laos, and Vietnam.

5. According to the United Nations (2008), for the first time, more than half the world's population is said to be living in cities and towns. The urban percentage of the world's

population is projected to reach 60 percent by 2030. The urban share is likely to rise from 75 percent to 81 percent in more developed countries between 2007 and 2030, and from 44 percent to 56 percent in less developed countries.

References

Brodwin, P. 2001. "Marginality and Cultural Intimacy in a Trans-national Haitian Community," occasional paper no. 91. Department of Anthropology, University of Wisconsin-Milwaukee.

Gurung, G.S., and M. Kollmair. 2005. *Marginality: Concepts and their Limitations*, IP6 working paper no. 4, Swiss National Centre of Competence in Research (NCCR) and Department of Geography, University of Zurich (Switzerland).

Jussila, H., R. Majoral, and C. C. Mutambirwa. 1999. *Marginality in Space—Past, Present and Future: Theoretical and Methodological Aspects of Cultural, Social and Economical Parameters of Marginal and Critical Regions*. Aldershot, UK: Ashgate.

Leimgruber, W. 1994. "Marginality and Marginal Regions: Problems of Definition." In *Marginality and Development Issues in Marginal Regions*, edited by Chang-Yi, D.Ch. Taipei: National Taiwan University.

Leimgruber, W. 2004. *Between Global and Local: Marginality and Marginal Regions in the Context of Globalization and Deregulation*. Aldershot, UK: Ashgate.

Leimgruber, W., R. Majoral, and L. Chul-Woo, eds. 2003. *Policies and Strategies in Marginal Regions*. Aldershot, UK: Ashgate.

Massey, D. 1994. *Space, Place and Gender*. Minneapolis: University of Minnesota Press.

Mehretu, A., Bruce W. Pigozzi, and L. M. Sommers. 2000. "Concepts in Social and Spatial Marginality." In *Geografiska Annaler* B (2), 89–10.

Mehta, M. 1995. *Cultural Diversity in the Mountains: Issues of Integration and Marginality in Sustainable Development*. Paper prepared for Consultation on the Mountain Agenda, Lima (Peru), February 22–27.

Müller-Böker, U., D. Geiger, U. Geiser, V. B. S. Kansakar,M. Kollmair, K. Molesworth, and A. Suleri. 2004. "Sustainable Development in Marginal Regions of South Asia," 225–261. In *Research for Mitigating Syndromes of Global Change: A Trans-Disciplinary Appraisal of Selected Regions of the World to Prepare Development-Oriented Research Partnerships*, edited by H. Hurni, U. Wiesmann, and R. Schertenleib. Berne, Switzerland: NCCR North-South.

Sommers, L. M., A. Mehretu, and Bruce W. M. Pigozzi. 1999. "Towards Typologies of Socio-Economic Marginality: North/South Comparisons." In *Marginality in Space—Past, Present and Future: Theoretical and Methodological Aspects of Cultural, Social and Economical Parameters of Marginal and Critical Regions*, edited by H. Jussila, H., R. Majoral, and C. C. Mutambirwa. Aldershot, UK: Ashgate.

Aragon Mill

Si Kahn

At the east end of town
At the foot of the hill
There's a chimney so tall
It says Aragon Mill

But there's no smoke at all
Coming out of the stack
For the mill has shut down
And it's never coming back

And the only tune I hear
Is the sound of the wind
As it blows through the town
Weave and spin,
Weave and spin

There's no children at all
In the narrow, empty streets
All the looms have shut down
It's so quiet, I can't sleep

The mill has shut down
'Twas the only life I know
Tell me where will I go
Tell me where will I go

And the only tune I hear
Is the sound of the wind
As it blows through the town
Weave and spin,
Weave and spin

Now I'm too old to work
And I'm too young to die
Tell me where will I go now
My family and I
For the mill has shut down
It's the only life I know
Tell me where will I go,
Tell me where will I go

And the only tune I hear
Is the sound of the wind
As it blows through the town
Weave and spin,
Weave and spin

Comparing Rural Livelihood Transitions in the Catalan and Sardinian Regions of Europe and the Appalachian Region of the United States

Domenica Farinella, Ann Kingsolver,
Ismael Vaccaro, and Oriol Beltran

THIS CHAPTER DRAWS from comparative research on the role of regional governance and policy in reimagining rural livelihoods after deindustrialization in three mountain regions, two of which—Sardinia and Appalachia—are highly marginalized within their national contexts. The three examples show the results of very different levels of public investment in rural livelihoods after deindustrialization. Domenica Farinella and Ann Kingsolver have been collaborating in an ongoing comparative research project between Sardinia, Italy, and Appalachian

Kentucky in the United States, both of which have a long history with extractive industries and are transitioning to more locally integrated and sustainable regional economies. Ismael Vaccaro and his long-term collaborator Oriol Beltran joined the comparative project in 2014 because of similarities in conditions of deindustrialization in the three mountain regions. In the Catalan section of the Pyrenees, however, there is not quite the same level of economic precarity as in Appalachia and Sardinia. We include the Pyrenees as an example of what strategies are possible in mountain regions with more capitalization and state support (although the burst of the "housing bubble" led to some disinvestment in sustainable regional development initiatives in the Pyrenees).

Residents of all three reperipheralized regions have been attempting to organize agricultural diversity and strong regional linkages for developing agrotourism and ecotourism with a new focus on experience economies. Our research methods have included discourse analysis, analysis of aggregate data, and qualitative interviewing. Territorial organization of the economy is strongest in the Pyrenees, which already has a recent history of national and regional governmental support, and secondly in Sardinia, where European Union (EU) policies support, however problematically, a regional approach to sustainable development. In Appalachia, there is little coordination between relatively small county-level political and economic entities and little state-level support for development that is focused on regionally integrated economies.

Grounds for Comparison

Sardinia is a large island in the Mediterranean Sea to the west of mainland Italy, just south of French-controlled Corsica. It has experienced foreign occupation and control from the Phoenician and Roman eras through much more recent Spanish occupation to incorporation into the Italian state since the nineteenth century. Always, some residents went inland into the mountain region, escaping coastally concentrated colonization; Nuragic ruins (conical towers of huge dry-laid stones) are a symbol of pride in Sardinia and the current focus of rural experience economy development efforts.

The Appalachian Mountains run north-south in eastern North America and constitute the oldest mountain range on the earth. They were once the size of the Himalayan ranges, but have been worn down over time. Although the mountains defy any political borders, in the 1960s, due to anti-poverty policies explained in this chapter, the United States began recognizing the Appalachian Regional Commission as a political entity spanning 13 states. The only state that is completely within the Appalachian region is West Virginia (which is why that state figures prominently in Appalachian examples in this volume). In Kentucky, 54 of the state's 120 counties—constituting Kentucky's eastern half—are considered to be within the Appalachian region. That region is the focus of the US example in this chapter.

In both Sardinia and Appalachia, the main economic and social indicators are worse than the national averages and demonstrate a persistent economic crisis: depopulation, low population density, lower formal education rates, low income, and high unemployment and poverty rates. According to recent census figures, for example, the unemployment rates (60 percent of the labor force in Sardinia and 40 percent in Appalachian Kentucky) are double their national averages, as are the percentages of those leaving secondary school without a degree (which happens to be 26 percent in both Sardinia and Appalachia). The persistence of these indicators has been used to represent these regions in national discussions as "backward" and "underdeveloped."

Sardinia, Italy, and the central Appalachian region of the United States have parallel histories in that they have been the sites of extractive economies for centuries. The natural resources and residents' precarious labor have supported national and global economic development while there has been little capital reinvestment in these marginalized regions. Paradoxically, as Frank (1966) and Wolf (1982) have noted for other regions, Sardinia and Appalachia have long been powerfully engaged with the global economy through natural resource and social contributions but have been stereotyped as "isolated" and "backward" in national and international imaginations (c.f. Ortu 1988; Batteau 1990; and Pitzalis 2012). The extraction of coal shaped the social context and infrastructural development of both Sardinia and Appalachia, with the importation of workers from other regions as a mining labor force and the establishment of railroads to take the coal to ports for exportation. The coal from Sardinia fueled the industrialization of northern Italy, and bituminous coal from Appalachia contributed to the industrialization concentrated in the northeastern United States and has also been exported to Italy and India and many other nations to fuel coal-burning power plants and steel production.

Lumber, salt, copper, oil, tobacco, and coal booms in Appalachia have fueled global capitalist development (Straw and Blethen 2004). Far from being isolated from the global market, Appalachian territory has been majority absentee-owned, mostly by foreign capitalists, since the United States became a nation in the 1700s. After each phase of deindustrialization, the residents are left to reimagine their landscape and livelihoods (see Kingsolver 2016).

Both Sardinia and Appalachia have represented the undeveloped "other" for state experiments with modernization in the past century. For example, in 1933, under very different governmental regimes (the Keynesian New Deal policies of the United States and the fascist policies of Italy), idealized communities were set up by the Roosevelt administration in West Virginia (Arthurdale) and the Mussolini administration in Sardinia (Carbonia and Fertilia) to demonstrate the positive effects of modernized landscapes and people to a national public.

The Sardinian region was annexed in 1720 by the Kingdom of Savoy from the Piedmont as the first part of what would become the Italian state, created in 1861. During the 1800s, many new policies used Sardinia as an internal colony to exploit for the national interests of the rising Kingdom of Italy and Piedmont capitalism. In particular, there was the privatization and enclosure of common lands and the abolishment of the *ademprivi*, the rights of the local peasants and shepherds to use the land close to the village for agriculture, pasture, firewood, acorns, and plants. The introduction of a new tax on land also caused the peasantry to be displaced through debt and the creation of a parasitic class of new landowners.

In the Pyrenees, the remote areas were more integrated into the state administration and national and international markets in the nineteenth century. As in Appalachia and Sardinia, the resources of the more socially and economically marginalized communities contributed to national industrialization: especially hydropower, which brought electricity, factory production, coal mining, and also milk production.

In the twentieth century in both Sardinia and Appalachian Kentucky, which had both already been largely deforested by foreign capitalists to make lumber for railways, laws enabled ownership of the land and the subsoil to be separated so that surface land use rights could be superseded by mining interests. This changed the landscape even more dramatically. The majority of land in Appalachia has been absentee owned since the 1700s (Dunaway 1996), and in the twentieth century large mining corporations introduced mountain top removal mining, a technique that leaves anyone who may still be able to live in these zones with too few natural resources to even begin to reimagine a sustainable livelihood.

In the nineteenth century, the Italian state used Sardinia as a site of extraction to fuel industrial development. Foreign companies invested in Sardinian lead, silver, zinc, and coal mines and then abandoned the land when these resources were exhausted, leaving pollution behind. During the fascist period, Mussolini made a project of "internal colonization"; his idea was to create new cities with new populations from other parts of Italy that would help the local inhabitants to modernize. The Mussolini regime wanted also to show the power of fascism to transform the land, demonstrating that it could control what it saw as wild land, draining it and building new towns and laying out fields for cultivation in Fertilia and Mussolinia, the two new rural model towns of Sardinia. The fascist internal colonization only reinforced the stereotype of Sardinia as a wild territory with a lot of uninhabited natural space and a primitive population needing to be modernized.

The residents of Sardinia and Appalachia, although diverse in their backgrounds and linked through migration to many regions, have continually been reinscribed in stereotypes as isolated and backwards through schools of literature, painting, photography, and film. For example, Local Color writers in the United

States after the Civil War (e.g., Fox Jr. 1908) represented simultaneously noble and backward mountain people, and in Italy, Grazia Deledda (1913) wrote about the poverty and superstitions of mountain people stuck in time in Sardinia. Wright's 1916 *National Geographic* article on Sardinia, with photos, emphasized the island's isolation and banditry much as feuding has been emphasized in media representations of Appalachia. Accompanying (and justifying) strong modernization policies of the mid-twentieth century were schools of photography and film portraying the seemingly desperate lives of rural mountain people. A film based on a novel by Ledda (1975) portrayed bestiality among shepherds in Sardinia. There was a series of state-financed films in Italy representing the lives of shepherds living in poverty and in need of modernization, and in the United States, the Office of Economic Opportunity in 1965 financed a documentary called *Christmas in Appalachia* that featured coal-mining families' extreme and seemingly permanent poverty in contrast to the majority US population, assumed to be the audience for the televised report.

Looking toward Sustainable Futures with or without State Support: Experiments with Experience Economies

This past year marked the fiftieth anniversary of the founding of the Appalachian Regional Commission, an agency created as part of the "War on Poverty" in the 1960s that was meant to foster collaboration between federal, state, and local governmental partners in regional economic development (see maps and reports at arc.gov). The Appalachian Regional Commission, with joint federal and state leadership in the 13-state Appalachian region, continues into the twenty-first century to prioritize infrastructural development for transnationally controlled extractive economic activity. This investment in infrastructure does not, however, empower local residents. The region's transportation infrastructure is designed to get resources out of the region instead of connecting communities within the region, and there is little internet connectivity. Development funds tend to go to large absentee employers to create low-wage service jobs—for maximum security prisons built on mountain top removal mining sites, for example, for which prisoners have to be imported to Appalachian Kentucky from New Jersey.

Kentucky counties are small and do not tend to collaborate. There is no state-level coordination or support for such collaboration, especially for sustainable economic development. Agricultural production, long dominated by tobacco and cattle, is geared toward shipping primary products out of the region rather than any vertical integration in the region; for a regional economy, agricultural processing and marketing needs to be strengthened, but governmental programs do not tend to foster such regional integration since a low-wage labor force is the most marketable resource under those development policies. Young people (in Stay Together Appalachian Youth, or STAY, for example) tend to work across county and state lines, organizing their own sustainable development ventures, including experience-based agro- and ecotourism ventures. They are making selective use of some neoliberal policies, but are mainly working through the informal sector without reliance on regional economic development investment programs.

Paralleling the US War on Poverty, in Italy, after the Second World War, there were two big public programs to modernize and develop Sardinia: the national Cassa per il Mezzogiorno and the regional Piano Rinascita (Rebirth Plan). The aim was to modernize the "rural region," import "urban civilization," and stimulate economic growth with "industrialization." The investments focused on basic industries (mines, steel, chemical, and oil) have been a failure: the new industries are highly polluting, do not generate jobs, and are not developing a local market because they supply materials for industries in northern Italy. The most publicized symbol of that failure is the petrochemical industry in Ottana, in the rural center of Sardinia.

In the 1950s, in Sardinia, the Common Agricultural Policy caused abandonment of rural and mountain regions, where industrial agricultural techniques could not be introduced. Sardinia lost a great deal of diversity in its agricultural landscape and production knowledge and practices. In the 1980s, to resolve the problem of overproduction, the European Economic Community gave incentives to destroy the means of agricultural production, for example, definitively eradicating the cultivation of grapevines. Many farmers removed their plants. In 2000 the acreage of grapevines was one-third of what it was in 1980. Many cultivars specific to Sardinia became at risk of extinction. Many people in the agricultural sector had developed specialized knowledge in obtaining EU subsidies—for example, the slaughter of pigs thought to have swine flu. European Union policies provided incentives to producers to export *pecorino romano* (romano cheese, made from sheep's milk), and the price was artificially high because of those incentives. When the incentives were stopped recently, there was a huge crisis in the dairy sector—a main sector for the island. Sardinian government policies can also be counterproductive and discount local knowledge, as in the cork forests where biodiversity policies ban the burning of undergrowth, which can lead to fires in the forest killing all of the cork trees.

At the beginning of the twentieth century, some Roman entrepreneurs imported industrial techniques of production of *pecorino romano* into Sardinia. This is large-scale production for export to the global market, mainly in the United States, where it is used as "mixed cheese" to improve the taste of junk food and school pizza. The shepherds stopped traditional cheese making and started selling milk to the *pecorino romano* industry, becoming dependent on the market price of milk, which is very volatile in the global market.

The postwar struggles in the herding sector in Sardinia were not expressions of an archaic, violent, wild culture, but an expression of the emerging new structure of the global market in which the shepherds became subaltern to the interests of the industrial sector and to the uncertainty of milk prices in the global market.

The new EU policies on community-led local development are stimulating a change in local agriculture toward multifunctional farms. The shepherds, for example, stopped selling milk and went back to producing cheese directly, paying attention to the organic quality and innovative techniques of production. Farms have become multifunctional, with natural breeding, forage production, cheese production, agrotourism, educational farming, and energy production. And in the wine sector, young people are restoring traditional varieties of grapes and small-scale, high-quality production linked to agrotourism and countryside management.

In a parallel set of resistance activities in Sardinia, there is empowerment of local communities through spontaneous local committees that struggle against land grabbing. Sardinia has 60 percent of the military zones in Italy, and local communities are contesting military occupation of that land. They also are protesting the overuse of EU incentives for renewable energy development, which has led to speculation in solar and wind farms that are larger than the communities they surround and are not even connected to any grid.

In the Pyrenees, the twentieth-century construction of dams brought a period of localized increases in population and salaries. In the Pallars Sobirà district all construction was over between the late 1950s and the 1960s, and villages that had gained hundreds of citizens lost them all at once. The process in the Valley of Lillet (Berguedà district) with mines and factories (concrete and textile) was similar—cheaper coal could be bought elsewhere, and preference was given to locating factories near cities and cheap energy—so they closed during the 1970s. The golden era of milk specialization also ended with the entry into the European Union. The European limitation of quota production eliminated many farms in the late 1980s. This was the industrialization era in many areas of the Pyrenees (the valleys that did not experience them lost their population even earlier).

In the Pyrenees, the villages connected to roads and main valleys have been able to maintain economic stability. It is the more marginalized higher altitude communities with little infrastructural connection that have experienced the rapid depopulation and economic decline just mentioned. Although the ski industry started to develop in the 1970s, it was only after the year 2000, that there was a consolidation of a certain economic recovery and sustainable livelihood options for those living in higher mountain zones through state (and private) investment in the leisure economy: skiing, parks, ecotourism, and cultural tourisma patrimonial economy. Ranching has not disappeared, but its economic and political weight has become less relevant vis à vis tourism. It is, however, still an important social trope (as ecotourism has also used it as an asset).

At some point in the late 1990s tourism (and public jobs) become the main economic sectors in the Pyrenees. The state through its local institutions promotes all sorts of patrimonial initiatives (often in combination with private entrepreneurs, locals, and neorurals). The consolidation of a wide variety of options—skiing, protected areas, mountain sports, museums, rehabilitated historical infrastructures (churches, castles, forges, mills, etc.), hiking networks, gastronomic tourism (traditional and organic), and street fairs—brings people to, and consolidates them on, the territory. This has happened at the same time that Spanish urban society has fully joined mass consumption and environmentally friendly values.

The Catalan High Pyrenees, where a robust patrimonial leisure industry has been developing for the past thirty years (Vaccaro and Beltran 2007), encompasses the four districts of Vall d'Aran, Pallars Sobirà, Pallars Jussà, and Alta Ribagorça. Combined, these districts host 20 tourist offices, 176 certified rural bed and breakfast facilities, 35 museums, a myriad of restaurants and hotels, two large protected areas, two state-managed hunting reserves, dozens of officially recognized food artisans elaborating hundreds of certified local or traditional products, and dozens of "cultural itineraries" designed to introduce the visitor to the forest, trees of singular relevance, or historical or archaeological sites (Institute for the Development of the Upper Pyrenees and Aran 2010).

In 2006–2008, the Spanish real estate bubble popped and the crisis ensued. Construction and speculation in the Pyrenees (often correlated with ski resorts) stopped completely, and public funds shrank to next to nothing. Many museums closed (or started to be open part time), and some parks became paper parks. Museums started to invest energy in creating economies of scale by creating networks of services and collaboration. The Ecomuseu de les Valls d'Aneu, for instance, is part of a Passport network (14 museums across six Catalan districts) and the Patrim network (eight museums in three regions of two countries), and has started to give guided tours within the rural region, valorizing local resources for visitors more than in the past.

Conclusion

In Sardinia and Appalachia, ironically, regional economies are actually undermined by state and trans-state policies promoted as strengthening regional economic development. The well-being of residents is not improving demonstrably under these anti-poverty policies, but we do see examples of collective agency to address household economic precarity in the construction of regional networks for sustainable development.

The Pyrenees could never compete agriculturally with the lowlands, where intensification is much easier; agroranching has always been the best land use strategy, and it is part of the postindustrial regional livelihood strategy as well. Keeping the traditional Bosa cattle and the extensive breeding of sheep in Sardinia (as opposed to industrial production) and beef cattle finding their own forage in the mountains of Appalachia have also been strong economic strategies. Tying the production of animals into diverse sustainable agricultural and tourism strategies is a growing activity in all three remote regions, along with beekeeping and other ecologically significant activities.

In all three regions, both household precarity and capitalist corporate dominance of the economy are being challenged through collective strategies, with varying degrees of state support or hostility. Regional ecomuseums and training centers that value local and traditional knowledge are serving as sites for counterorganizing a regional sustainable economy that is more inclusive of participation by all members of the community and that values strategies like seed-saving, the use of native plants (for dyes for weaving, for example), and knowledge of traditional artisan patterns and techniques. These obviously cannot compete with goods in global market terms, but they are involving community members in a revalorization of regional identity, knowledge, and reliance on networks of diverse local productive activities and decision-making that can then intersect with global consumers, of eco- and agrotourism, for example, in an experience economy when such an economy is supported by global economic conditions (which render it, in itself, precarious).

It is mainly young people with university degrees who are returning to their home regions to create collective, sometimes very original, strategies for sustainable livelihoods. In Sardinia, for example, three young women formed an experience economy collective to give very specific local tours—of the political murals of Orgosolo, for example; another focused on archaeology and music. In Appalachia, the Appalshop collective is teaching young people media skills to make and distribute their own films about being both very rural and gay, lesbian, or transsexual, for example, or about postmining livelihood options (see ami.appalshop.org). Berea College, in Appalachian Kentucky, has long emphasized as part of its curriculum traditional artisanal and music skills, which young people can then use for the experience economy in Appalachia. In Sardinia, there is a similar collective called the Lifestills Collective with the #Ioresto Project of small films made by young people about resistance and life in rural regions. And in the Pyrenees, young people are significant participants in the ecomuseum strategies. Many are working toward a more inclusive future despite the opposite tendencies of global capitalist logic and practice, but it must be noted that talk of inclusion can itself be silencing of the most marginalized, for example, those who continue to be discriminated against because of their regionally related language or accent, participation in the informal drug economy, or lack of access to higher education.

Domenica Farinella is Lecturer in Environmental Sociology at the University of Cagliari, Italy. Her current research in rural studies includes examining changes for pastoralists in Sardinia, Italy, especially shepherds, and agricultural diversification through multifunctional farms.

ANN KINGSOLVER is Professor of Anthropology and past director of the Appalachian Center and Appalachian Studies Program at the University of Kentucky. Her research in the United States, Mexico, and Sri Lanka has focused on how people make sense of all that gets called "globalization" and act on those understandings. Her books include *NAFTA Stories: Fears and Hopes in Mexico and the United States, Tobacco Town Futures: Global Encounters in Rural Kentucky,* and several edited volumes.

ISMAEL VACCARO is Associate Professor of Anthropology at McGill University. His research, primarily in southern Europe and Mexico, includes foci on environmental anthropology, political ecology, political economy, and territoriality. His coedited books include *Environmental Social Sciences: Methods and Research Design.*

ORIOL BELTRAN is Associate Professor in the Department of Social Anthropology at Universitat de Barcelona. His publications include *Parcs als comunals: La patrimonialització de la muntanya al Pallars Sobirà* and *Social and Ecological History of the Pyrenees: State, Market, and Landscape.*

References

Batteau, A.W. 1990. *The Invention of Appalachia.* Tucson: University of Arizona Press.

Deledda, G. 1913. *Canne al vento.* Milan: Treves.

Dunaway, Wilma. 1996. *The First American Frontier: Transition to Capitalism in Southern Appalachia, 1700–1860.* Chapel Hill: University of North Carolina Press.

Fox, Jr., John. 1908. *The Trail of the Lonesome Pine.* New York: Charles Scribner's Sons.

Frank, Andre Gunder. 1966. "The Development of Underdevelopment." *Monthly Review* 18 (4): 17–31.

Kingsolver, Ann E. 2016. "When the Smoke Clears: Seeing beyond Tobacco and Other Extractive Industries in Rural Appalachian Kentucky." In *The Anthropology of Postindustrialism: Ethnographies of Disconnection,* edited by Ismael Vaccaro, Krista Harper, and Seth Murray, 38–55. New York: Routledge.

Ledda, G. 1975. *Padre padrone.* Milan: Feltrinelli.

Ortu, G. G. 1988. "Transumanza nella storia della Sardegna." *Mélanges de l'École Française de Rome, Moyen-Age, Temps Modernes* 100 (2): 921–838.

Pitzalis, M. 2012. "Gli argonauti del Mediterraneo occidentale: spunti per una lettura sociologica del cinema di finzione in Sardengna." *Studi Culturali* 9 (2): 225–247.

Straw, Richard Alan, and Tyler Blethen. 2004. *High Mountains Rising: Appalachia in Time and Place.* Chicago: University of Illinois Press.

Vaccaro, Ismael, and Oriol Beltran. 2007. "Consuming Space, Nature, and Culture: Patrimonial Discussions in the Hyper-Modern Era." *Journal of Tourism Geographies* 9 (3): 254–274.

Wolf, Eric R. 1982. *Europe and the People without History.* Berkeley: University of California Press.

Wright, H. B. D. 1916. "Little-Known Sardinia." *National Geographic,* vol. 30, no. 2.

Wild Rose of the Mountain

Si Kahn

If I had my life to live
I'd surely live it over
Only walk in brand new shoes
Just lay down in clover
Only work on Christmas Day
All the rest go sporting
Spend my days down at the creek
Every night go courting

Honey from the honeycomb
Water from the fountain
Sugar from the sugar cane
And my wild rose of the mountain

When I think of home sweet home
It makes my eyes go misty
Poppa singing gospel tunes
Momma sipping whiskey
Whiskey from a white oak barrel
Sure does make good liquor
Makes the night seem twice as bright
Days go by much quicker

Honey from the honeycomb
Water from the fountain
Sugar from the sugar cane
And my wild rose of the mountain

If I had a new-made quilt
I'd fill it all with feathers
Take my Rosie by the hand
Lay down there together
Oh the days that we were young
Thoughts that keep returning
Drive the winter right away
Just like a log fire burning

Honey from the honeycomb
Water from the fountain
Sugar from the sugar cane
And my wild rose of the mountain

Honey Corridors in the Nilgiri Biosphere Reserve and Appalachian Coal Production Areas

Tammy Horn Potter and Kunal Sharma

IN A GLOBAL economy that still tends to be dependent on fossil fuels, honeybees and the role they play in pollinating flowers that produce food, the primary fuel for people, tend to be forgotten. This chapter acknowledges the important roles honeybees have played in shaping regional cultures in two different mountain areas (southern India and Appalachia Kentucky), and highlights similar threats facing their honeybees (i.e., deforestation). The authors highlight possible collaborations between beekeepers and coal industries that could minimize threats to bees and support beekeepers and honey hunters.

Honey in the Mountains of India

This section refers to the region in which Kunal Sharma works with honey hunters, in India's southern mountains (the Nilgiris, or the Blue Hills). A parallel section of the chapter discusses Tammy Horn Potter's work with bees and beekeepers in the Appalachian Mountains of the United States.

Fig. 22.1 Kurinji flowers of the Blue Hills. Photo credit: Kunal Sharma

Himalayan Mountains

India was once considered the birthplace of honeybees because of its ecological diversity, originating relatively recently in geological time. When India slowly drifted away from Gondwana, its Deccan volcanoes obliterated any botanical evidence. As the continent moved into Asia during the Cenozoic, scholars use words like *crash, collision,* and *violent* when describing the tectonic event that forced the Himalayan chain of mountains to rise. This mountain chain created numerous rivers. The result was that the "Tibetan plateau as a whole covers less than 5 percent of the world's land, but it is drained by eight of the world's mightiest rivers, including the Ganges, the Brahmaputra, the Indus, the Yangtze, and the Mekong," according to historian Colin Tudge (1996, 70).

This moisture-laden environment is responsible for diverse floral resources. In one region of India, the Blue Hills (or Western Ghats), 4,000 species of flowering plants are known. Of those 4,000 species, 1,500 are endemic to the region. Other authors claim that there are more endemic species. The Keystone Foundation offers the following assessment: "Although the exact number keeps varying with the author and time, what is of interest is that nearly 38% of all species of flowering plants in the Western Ghats are endemic" (Horn 2012, 25). The Kurinji flower, in particular, is a good nectar source. The Blue Hills derives its name from this plant's color when the flower is in bloom. Beekeepers drive many kilometers to be in the Western Ghats when this flower blooms because the honey is distinctive.

Honeybees

Honeybees have evolved according to the various climes that define India: tropics, temperate, and glacial climates. India hosts three types of *Apis mellifera* bees: the giant open-nesting *Apis mellifera dorsata*; the one-combed open nesting *Apis mellifera florea*; and the cavity-nesting *Apis mellifera cerana*, all of which evolved to survive the extremes of India's weather, with its severe winters and ample rainfall. Now India also hosts *Apis mellifera mellifera* (European) because of international nongovernment organizations' influence on its economic and agricultural policies.

Of the four types of bees, the hive bee *A. mellifera cerana* is a smaller bee that stores less honey and maintains a smaller forage field. But it is the bee that people tend to keep in clay pots or log hives (Bradbear 2002, 267). More than a few people still maintain hives in their kitchens, although few make this type of beekeeping a commercial industry because the bees do not make as much honey and the extraction process is time-consuming for the small yield. Those people who sell their honey at market command a good price because buyers believe in the strong medicinal value of honey.

Apis mellifera dorsata and *Apis mellifera florea* nest in the open and, for obvious reasons, prefer the warmer climates. Thriving in a more tropical climate, *Apis mellifera dorsata* builds large colonies outside of rocks and trees and produces prolific amounts of honey, by some estimates as much as 5 to 20 kilogram per colony (Bradbear 2002).

No less of an authority than world bee historian Eva Crane (1999, 154) has affectionately dubbed the *Apis mellifera florea*, "the most user-friendly of the honeybees." The *A. m. florea* bee is smaller and builds nests of only one comb, and in regions where *A. m. dorsata* and *A. m. cerana* coexist, people are likely to overlook *A. m. florea*. Given that *Apis mellifera mellifera* has been introduced, *Apis m. florae* may have more competition as *A. mellifera mellifera* (European) competes for resources and produces larger colonies.

People

Deforestation threatens more than just the land and its habitat. It threatens complex and mutually beneficial social relationships between communities that have been established for hundreds of years. Rock paintings from the Mesolithic show men harvesting honey from *Apis mellifera dorsata*, a tradition that still continues today although threatened by deforestation and the dangers of high wall rock-climbing, tigers, and the stings of the powerful bees (Crane 2001). Just as the Western Ghat region hosts numerous endemic flowering species, it is also home to many different ethnic groups. Approximately two million people identify as belonging to at least thirty different tribal identities. These indigenous communities, called *adivasi*, such as Badaga, Kurumba, Kota, and Toda peoples, still practice traditional honey-gathering techniques. The Kurumbas always leave some of the colonies intact when harvesting honey.

The Toda people, one of the few indigenous vegetarian communities, incorporate the bow and arrow into paternity rites. Traditionally, a man ceremonially gives a bow and arrow to his wife during her seventh month of pregnancy, symbolizing his commitment to protect the child to be born. At the end of this ceremony, his wife is expected to place some symbolic food at the base of the *kaihh(r)sh (Eugenia arnottiana)* tree that includes a piece of honey comb (Nath and Sharma 2007, 258). This is now done subject to availability of the honey comb.

Other *adivasi* people local to the region have become exceptionally skilled artists. The Toda women are known for their embroidery. "One of the oldest motifs is the *Kwudrkorr pukhoor* or the honey comb pattern. This depicts the inside of the honeycomb and is sometimes even embroidered with the brood shown within! Its importance lies in the fact that this was done traditionally only on the cloak of the departed so as to ensure a safe passage to the after world" (Nath and Sharma 2007, 262).

Many Kota women excel in pottery, providing tools and pots to the Badagas and Todas. "Though Kota pottery lacks in embellishments, it has rare grace and poise. The practice of pottery is a collective enterprise in which both women and men participate. However, even though men join in construction of the wheel and help women in digging of the clay and firing, the shaping of the pots on the wheel and paddling is entirely done by the women. Kota women know their clay quite well" (Nath and Sharma 2007, 77).

There are a number of *adivasi* communities, among them Todas, Alu Kurumbas, Badagas, Irulas, Kotas, Paniyas, Betta Kurumbas, Muduvans, Jenu Kurumbas, Mullu, Kasavas, Sholigas, Chettis, Cholanaicken, and Kattunaicken. The indigenous communities of Wynad collect honey as a group. "During the honey season all people of the village go for honey collection—men, women, and the young. Children are strictly monitored as they may eat lots of honey leading to low amounts for sale" (Nath and Sharma 2007, 220).

Green Greed: British Deforestation

The arrival of the British fundamentally changed India beginning in 1799. Perhaps because of their disregard for their own forests in the sixteenth century, the British showed no respect for the Indian cultures who protected their forestlands. When the British began to colonize India, they did so in three main regions, all of which had tremendous forests: "These areas [owed] their existence to rapid accessibility and cheap and efficient transportation links with the wider world . . . three were on the periphery of the Indian Subcontinent: Assam for tea, the Nilgiri Hills and Wynaard Plateau of Kerala for coffee and subsequently for tea, and Sri Lanka (Ceylon) for coffee and tea, the stimulants that were exported for satisfy Europe's continually expanding 'soft drug' culture" (Williams 2002, 362).

Similar to the British settlers who colonized North America, "there was an animosity toward uncultivated land, which was regarded as "waste." Moreover, forests were perceived as the abode of the unruly and disorderly, from the murderous thuggees down to the run-of-the-mill thieves, so that the elimination of the forests would mean an end to lawlessness, as well as unproductive land and population," explains Williams (2002, 366).

During the colonial period, indigenous people were seen by many colonial officials (e.g., medical officers) as having practices that were destructive to the forests and their own well-being, not understanding—as in many parts of the world—the long-term sustainable forest management practices of indigenous residents: "From at least the late 1840s the surgeon-environmentalists saw the 'vagabond habits' of the itinerant *kumri* cultivators in the hills and their torching of the forest as *the* prime cause of forest destruction, decreasing rainfall and increasing dissection, famine, and declining health—not realizing that the regeneration of the timbers they prized so much was dependent on periodic burning," according to Williams (2002, 343). Colonial administrators felt they had to discipline indigenous people in their use of the forest resources, and thus passed the Forest Act of 1865 with that intent.

"One is left with a terrible paradox," Williams summarizes. "An admirable and massive administrative edifice had been constructed for the rational use of the timber resource, which had no parallel in the world at this time or for decades to come . . . it was one of the administrative jewels of the Imperial Crown, a model for the rest of the world. . . . But it was also going to prove to be one of the festering sores in the body of the Indian Subcontinent that has still not been healed. . . . The foresters and their regulations became the face of alien power, which pervaded Indian rural life just as surely as any military, judiciary, or political administrative framework" (Williams 2002, 368–369).

The dilemma created by this paradox remains even today. As a result of the massive deforestation, the British imported Australian eucalyptus trees in 1843 to meet their fuel needs" (Somerville 1998, 218). These trees grow fast and need a lot of water and thus could adapt quite easily to India. Somerville explains that in India, "Eucalypts were planted in the Nilgiri Hills where growth rates of 6–7.5m from seed in only eight months were reported. . . . The major species in India, *E. tereticornis, Eucalyptus resinifera, E. camaldulensis, E. citriodora, E. viminalis,* and *E. robusta,* have also been planted" (219). Still, importing eucalyptus trees could not fill the demand for wood either in the nineteenth or twentieth centuries. According to Williams, "Between 1920 and 1950, in British India, it was official policy to sacrifice forest for crops, even in hilly and mountainous districts, as on the Himalayan slopes and in Orissa Hills, but railways and fuelwood demands continued to take an enormous toll" (Williams 2002, 407).

British colonists transferred *Apis mellifera mellifera* (European) honeybees to India in 1882. In *A Handbook of Beekeeping for India* by British extension specialist J. C. Douglas (1884), the indigenous systems of beekeeping were derided as "barbarous to the bees, less productive, precarious, and not admitting to expansion beyond the limits of an industry to be pursued by the peasantry on a very small scale" (3). Douglas declares that, "Beekeeping in India has before it a great future; as in the other economic arts it is for the European to lead. When the benefits to be derived have been demonstrated, no doubt the natives of India will follow" (6).

Douglas wanted women to participate as much as men: "It is a pursuit in which women readily find pleasure and profitable occupation, many having been very successful in England and America" (135). In addressing the fear of stings, he assures his readers that their awkwardness will subside and there will be fewer stings in time.

A huge challenge to beekeeping was affordability and availability of box hives and extractors. Since India did not have a bee industry as defined by the United States, Douglas advised his readers to adapt the patterns to local Indian customs, "labor being cheaper than machinery" (Douglas 1884, 139). Above all, he advises his readers to appreciate the native bees.

Following in J. C. Douglas's footsteps, contemporary extension specialist Nicola Bradbear suggests that there is still much to be learned among international beekeeping programs (Bradbear and Reddy 1998). For example, in an essay titled "Beekeeping in Bangladesh," M. Nurul Islam (1998, 271), explains: "Efforts to keep bees in wooden hives probably started at the time of the Gandhian self-reliant movement in the 1940s. Prior to this people kept bees in logs, clay pots, or similar methods." And if the records in *Sustainable Beekeeping Development in Karnataka* are to be believed, indigenous honey hunting communities did not fare badly. Bradbear and Reddy write: "An important finding of an analysis of the existing beekeeping situation was that 50–90% of all honey is collected from wild colonies of the rock bee, *Apis mellifera dorsata*. This fact is not revealed in official documents (DIC 1996). Honey-hunters, who collect from the wild, are barely regarded by extension staff as part of the 'apicultural community.' In interviews, honey hunters said they received no assistance from the extension service" (Bradbear and Reddy 1998, 276).

As it turns out, one of the main problems is gaining access to state forests. Even though the political situation has changed, some of paternalistic motives behind the forestry laws passed in the nineteenth century are still in place. Nath and Sharma (2007, 92) quote from the 1998 laws in *Honey Trails in the Blue Mountains:* "The life of the adivasis and other poor people living within and near forests revolves around forests. The rights and concessions enjoyed by them should be fully protected. Their domestic requirements of fuel wood, fodder, minor forest products, and construction timber should be the first charge of forest produce." Although the forestry laws and village forest councils (VFCs) are very good ideas in theory, Nath and Sharma mention that, in practice, *adivasi* people are the first to be disenfranchised by the forestry laws designed to help them. One problem is the lack of funds for the VFCs, designed in the 1970s to give native peoples more governance of the forest in which they live. "So though VFC exists, they are unable to provide for the costs of collection, storage, movement of NTFPs (non-traditional forest products). VFCs lack bargaining power and prices are fixed by the big contractors." In short, Nath and Sharma explain, "the system presently has given rights to the people without the powers to claim them" (96).

Another problem mentioned by Bradbear and Reddy (1998, 267) is the modus operandi involved in the bidding practice: "Auctions are conducted to sell the rights for honey-hunting, and this can make the activity non-economic. It also means that honey-hunters are forced to be secretive." In some ways, then, this practice forces native people to live up to the negative perceptions that British have held for centuries that *adivasi* are thieves, shiftless, and so on.

Honey hunting is still traditionally a male occupation among many tribal people. Frame-hive beekeeping has been promoted in Karnataka within only the last twenty years or so (Bradbear and Reddy 1998, 268). The Directorate of Industries and Commerce (DIC) imported 90 colonies of *A. mellifera mellifera* in March 1996. Some of these have died already, and those that survived were weak (presumably because of varroa mite infestations). None has so far generated honey surpluses greater than can be obtained from *A. m. cerana*. This beekeeping cannot be promoted to farmers until feasibility is established and management methods have been well determined.

In the 1990s, according to Bradbear and Reddy, "there is no strong request arising from beekeepers to introduce *A. m. mellifera.* . . . Some beekeepers have observed that it [*Apis m. mellifera*] does not thrive. They have noticed that during the rainy period it ceases foraging while *A. m. cerana* continues, also that it is more susceptible to predators" (1998, 270).

Bradbear and Reddy articulate some important cultural considerations when it comes to international programs: "It is mainly extension staff who has heard that *A. m. mellifera* is a 'better bee' and quote honey production of 30 kg per colony," they explain. "This is stated without consideration of whether lack of honey production is a limiting factor" (270).

Even though most of traditional honey collection is a male-oriented activity, it would be a mistake to see all tribal residents as patriarchal. The Kurichiars people "are widely considered as one of the earliest inhabitants of the Wynaad hills.

They have a vibrant history and had revolted against the British with the forces of the Pazzhasi Raja. Their reputation as expert archers continues to this day." They are exceptional honey hunters. Furthermore, "They are the only matrilineal society in South India. The women participate in agricultural operations, fishing, animal husbandry, fuel collection, etc. Most land is owned by lineages, whereas there are few individual owners in present times" (Nath and Sharma 2007, 74).

The Badaga people also have deep roots in the Nilgiri region, their language being the lingua franca before the arrival of the British. "They were supposed to have come to the Nilgiris after the breakup of the Vijaynagar Empire in 1565." (75) Information about Badaga myths was written down by medical doctor and botanist Francis Buchanan, who was assigned by Marquess Wellesley, the Governor General, to investigate the state of agriculture and commerce in the dominions of the Rajah of Mysore, acquired by the East India Company (167). His journal began in 1800.

Buchanan referred to the Badagas as "honey and wax gatherers." The primary places were rocks, trees, and cavities. Buchanan did not realize that for a long time prior to the British arrival, the Lingayat priests, for ritual purposes, called the Badagas the *madhura* or *"maanthakula people."*

Buchanan noted that the Badagas had a honey goddess, and her shrine at Sokkanalli in the Sigur plateau is one of seven in the Moyar valley. The Kurumba people even attach maternal privilege to the rocks that provide shelter for *Apis mellifera dorsata*. "They also believe that the rock is their 'mother,' the rope is their 'father' and the tree on top of the cliff is their anna (elder brother). After honey is harvested, they place some on the rocks, and under the tree first, before eating it themselves" (108).

Coal

Into this delicate and time-honored set of social and natural practices come coal companies redefining longstanding community relationships, disturbing cherished and diverse landscapes, and challenging environmental policies. In the *Washington Post* article, "India Confronts Mountain of Coal Problems" (Denyers 2012), the problems identified ranged from an outdated rail system, lack of adequate roads, poor oversight, labor issues, and the simple fact that some of the richest coal seams lie underneath protected forest land.

"Coal-fired plants generate roughly 70 percent of India's power needs," but as Denyer (2012) reported, "coal imports have more than quadrupled since 2001." As of 2012, India imported coal from Kentucky and other places to make up the shortfall that the public-sector mines fail to meet. According to Jack Brammer (2012) of the *Lexington Herald-Leader*, "The deal is for 25 years and involves India's Abhijeet Group and New Jersey-based FJS Energy LLC buying coal from Kentucky and West Virginia through Kentucky-based affiliates FJSE Marshall

Inc. and FJSE River Coal. Under the agreement, Kentucky coal companies will export about 9 million tons of coal each year to the Abhijeet Group, which has been buying coal from Indonesia and Australia."

As the energy needs of India grow rapidly, the country is increasingly looking inwards to meet its expanding needs. What remains to be seen is what the devastation and increasing exploitation of its mineral resource will lead to. Most coal-rich areas are located in the central and eastern highlands, an area considered to be amongst the richest swathes of forest in the country. This region is also home to millions of indigenous communities who depend largely upon the forest for their livelihoods. This poses the most complex dilemma for India's growth planners—whether they can take a long-term view with respect to preservation of forests and its people and fauna or whether they will aim for short-term spikes in coal production that will fundamentally redefine these old growth forests.

Honey in the Appalachian Mountains of Eastern Kentucky

Compared to the Himalayas, which are still rising, the Appalachian Mountains are older and eroded. They formed when North America collided with Europe and Africa approximately 450 million years ago in three distinct stages. Its mixed mesophytic forests reflect the many changes as the region reacted to ice ages. Some pockets of the Appalachians became refuges for species that could not survive the ice. Just as the Himalayan mountains have major river systems, the Appalachians too have three major watersheds: the Big Sandy, the Kentucky River, and the Cumberland River. The result is a unique blend of temperate, quasitropical vegetation that is unlike any other place in the world.

Honeybees

Unlike India, which has a plethora of honeybee species, the Appalachian region has one predominant strain of European bees: *Apis mellifera mellifera* (European), especially a popular subspecies known as *Apis mellifera ligustica* (Italian). Native pollinators exist in the Appalachian region, but a honeybee species that was native to North America went extinct in the Miocene Epoch (Engel 2009). European honeybees *Apis mellifera mellifera* were introduced to North America in the seventeenth century. When European immigrants poured into the Appalachian Mountains and the Cumberland Plateau, they brought honeybees into the region, and these bees also advanced ahead of settlers because of their own swarming tendencies (Horn 2005).

Given the extensive Appalachian forests, many of the European forest-based beekeeping techniques transferred well, such as log gums for hives and pipes as makeshift smokers. The cultural traditions such as "telling the bees" and "tanging a swarm" were also popular. The bee charmer was and is a much-beloved

Fig. 22.2 A "bee gum" in Appalachia. Photo credit: Tammy Horn Potter

archetype of Appalachian literature, a holdover to a time when Appalachian people were reliant on the forests. The Appalachian tree and floral diversity provided very good habitat. Species such as redbud, red maples, tulip poplar, and black locust are prolific nectar-producing and pollen-producing trees. According to David Hughes of Rockbridge Trees, "One tree may equal 1-acre of ground forage. An acre of black locust can produce 1,000 pounds of honey. Two American Linden (Basswood) trees will equal an acre of sweet clover. The bloom withstands rainfall and an acre will produce 1,500 lbs. of honey!" (Hughes 2017).

As the rest of the United States developed an energy grid dependent on coal during the twentieth century, the Appalachian economy changed so that there were fewer agrarian landowners, and more livelihoods became dependent upon coal. In Harlan County, the first coal train was loaded and headed to the East Coast in 1911. Since then, the region has had a 100-year history with extractive technology impacting the forests by which people and honeybees live.

Deforestation is the most visible external challenge to bees in eastern Kentucky. According to one estimate by Steven Bullard of UK Forestry, Kentucky loses 134 acres of trees every day for a variety of reasons (Dott 2013). In 2008, Coal Country Beeworks started working with coal companies to provide more bee habitat in the Appalachian region by planting trees and wildflowers.

This multistakeholder effort began because pollinators in North America have been in precipitous decline since 2006. Pesticides, declining numbers of beekeepers, pathogens, the lack of queen bee diversity, and other factors make beekeeping very difficult. Conversely, many businesses have become more dependent on pollinator-dependent products. Agriculture is a $297 billion industry in the United States, and honeybees contribute at least $15.2 billion toward that number (Calderone 2012). The United States is the world's largest producer of almonds, a crop completely dependent on honeybees. Strawberries, cherries, apples, oranges, pumpkins, cucumbers, mustard, and tomatoes also benefit from pollinators, but many of these products also use agricultural chemicals. Kentucky has escaped some of the massive declines related to chemicals simply because it is so far removed from pesticide-dependent crops.

Compounding the problems of agricultural chemicals is the arrival of the varroa mite, an Asian parasite. Although the varroa mite species arrived in Kentucky in the late 1980s, honeybee colonies have not been able to develop resistance to it. Varroa mites weaken colonies because the mites reproduce in the brood chambers, underneath the wax cappings. Chemicals are not able to penetrate the wax cappings, and beekeepers are reluctant to alter the developing stages of bee brood in ways that are not organic. The varroa mites also vector viruses that impact the bees at all stages of development. Honeybees are developing minor levels of tolerance after thirty years, but much remains to be done. As the state continues to transition from tobacco to other forms of agriculture, such as soybeans, beekeepers can be poised to take advantage of this agricultural gap. While Coal Country Beeworks (employing Tammy Horn Potter) was operating apiaries on mine sites (2008–2014), coal companies were willing to incorporate native wildflowers and understory into the reclamation plan, in addition to high-value hardwoods as advised under the Appalachian Regional Reforestation Initiative. Since 2014, when the apiaries were closed as Tammy Horn Potter was named the state apiarist, the framework for Coal Country Beeworks has been successfully adopted in West Virginia for a military veteran–retraining program and, most recently, adopted by Appalachian Headwaters, a nonprofit that has decided to start a beekeeping collective in West Virginia.

Currently, beekeepers in the United States (including Kentucky) lose one in every three hives, according to the Bee Informed Partnership data (https://bip2 .beeinformed.org/geo/). Compared to visible threats to the hive (a pesticide kill, a bear, a spore), viruses that are vectored by varroa mites pose more complicated threats to the hive. Since 2015, Kentucky has participated in the US Department of Agriculture's Honeybee Health Survey. The reports from the first year of this grant indicate that all apiaries had varroa mites (no surprise), and approximately 50 percent of the apiaries had losses well above the threshold of what is considered manageable. In the USDA Honeybee Health Survey, 24 samples of honeybees are taken and analyzed. The samples taken from eastern Kentucky were not exceptionally high in mites and spores, but between the varroa mites and viruses present (all samples had at least one virus), eastern Kentucky beekeepers will have to remain diligent to keep mite populations low.

Fortunately, forest-based beekeeping is not complicated, nor is it a new economic plan. The Russians claimed that their "forests are the mantle of the poor" because they provided fruit and nuts, wood for shelter, and fuel for citizens and livestock (Williams 2002, 416). Ukraine especially has had an extensive forest-based beekeeping economy since AD 400. Where there have been forests, there have been beekeepers, so what has been unique about Coal Country Beeworks is its collaboration with UK Cooperative Extension in eastern Kentucky counties, coal companies, universities, and state and federal offices.

In working with the Office of Surface Mining and its annual Arbor Day celebrations, Coal Country Beeworks, which is now under the Green Forests Work, a nonprofit, that provides pollinator lessons at public schools in Knott, Letcher, Pike, and Perry Counties. Its current employee, Mary Sheldon, works with all groups, emphasizing not just one component of beekeeping, but a holistic process of planting trees and flowers and using honey in diets and beeswax for home goods.

Since 2008, the coal companies have planted at least 5,000 acres of trees and wildflowers. Green Forests Works planted its "2 millionth" seedling in April 2017. Grants have provided much of the funding to explore these efforts to transition away from surface mining to reforestation and apiculture. From 2011 to 2012, for instance, the Kentucky Governor's Office of Agricultural Policy sponsored a grant to collect royal jelly, the primary nutrition produced by the honeybees, on two surface mine sites. A Kentucky company named Alltech, Inc. produced a pollen supplement to use on an active surface mine site. A coal company, TECO, planted the other control site with wildflowers and undercanopy a year prior to the start of the grant.

Royal jelly was collected from queen cells in the fall of 2011 and then again from March to May 2012. Hives on surface mine sites had similar levels of protein, nitrogen, and carbon compared to hives in the Bluegrass (a central, pastoral region in Kentucky). From a preliminary standpoint, these results are a good indication that the honeybees have access to nutrients that they need. It suggests that habitat on surface mine sites can provide nutrition for bees, thereby supporting the larger goals of a bee industry. Coal Country Beeworks also provided queen production workshops that were well attended throughout the year.

Another grant focused on Appalachian native bees, such as squash bees, bumblebees, blue mason bees, and alkali bees. Native bees provide much of the pollination for native American fruits and vegetables, not only beans and squash but also alfalfa, pumpkins, and blueberries. Worried about the impact of bringing honeybee hives on to surface mine sites, Stephanie Bonner, a student at Oberlin College, received a grant to trap native pollinators from June to July 2011. In three weeks on four different mine sites, Bonner collected 599 individual bees representing five different families. Bonner had trapped native bees in Oregon in 2010, and brought with her not only experience, but a new type of trap to use on the surface mine sites, the blue vane trap. To her knowledge, the 2011 trapping was the first time that the blue vane trap had been used east of the Mississippi River.

This grant did not afford a comprehensive study of the native bees, and there were problems with timing. June is late in the year to begin trapping since many native bees appear in early and late spring. Also, the distance between the four trap sites made picking up the traps at a consistent time of day problematic. However, the variety of bee families represented suggested two conclusions: (1) the wildflower seed and undercanopy tree lists that the Kentucky Department of Fish and Wildlife was suggesting that coal companies plant may be attracting diverse bee communities, and (2) there seemed to be enough floral resources for native bees in addition to honeybees. Furthering such efforts nationally, the Office of Surface Mining has now published a reference article for all states to use as a guide to better reclamation practices that are inclusive of pollinator habitat (Horn, et al. 2017).

Coal

Both India and the United States have yet to define a responsible code of reclamation that includes the diverse ecological environments under which or on top of which vast coal reserves are located. In perhaps the best written document on the topic, American Electric Power (AEP 2010) commissioned a study of its coal suppliers in an effort to participate in the Global Reporting Initiative (GRI) framework. Of the 31 coal suppliers for which AEP has contracts, 14 suppliers responded, providing data for 52 mines and 10 facilities. These mines represented five of the six major coal production regions in the United States.

The report highlights the difficulty of defining sustainable practices. "There is more difficulty establishing trends, comparing performance, establishing statistics or identifying best practices with environmental performance because unlike MSHA, a national database of environmental performance data is not maintained at the federal level. The Office of Surface Mining Reclamation and Enforcement, the enforcement agency under the SMCRA of 1977 within the Interior Dept. does not maintain a historical record of noncompliance" (AEP 2010, 14).

The Office of Surface Mining provides oversight to the various primacy state programs, but the programs are individually managed by the states, have widely varying nomenclature, and are difficult to compare. The statistics that are maintained only include the outstanding or unabated violations, making comparisons on a nationwide basis nearly impossible.

Awards seem like the only formal way to acknowledge environmental plans. According to David Ledford (2013) of Appalachian Wildlife Foundation, "We don't have a culture of going above and beyond." The baseline often falls to the federal government to define: "The Surface Mining Control and Reclamation Act requires a final reclamation plan for all mines, and very few mines have a plan other than the required reclamation plan" (AEP 2010, 15).

The AEP survey also cautions readers to take its findings at face value. "The surveyed mines represent one-third of the coal being mined within the United States and demonstrate the broad reach of this Survey nationally to include a large portion of the mining community. . . . It should be noted that, although a portion of the results are available through public sources, much of the information is not available except through voluntary participation. Furthermore, the public data, other than the safety and health data available from MSHA, is only available through records within nine different states' regulatory agencies" (AEP 2010, 19).

It is certain that whereas India's conflicts with the coal industry could just be beginning, the eastern Kentucky region may be witnessing the denouement of a vitriolic and difficult 100-year industrial demise. Reporters for the *Lexington Herald-Leader* Bill Estep and John Cheves documented how quickly 10 eastern Kentucky coal counties are addressing declining taxes based on coal. "In the 10 Eastern Kentucky counties that produced the most coal in 2011," they wrote on January 27, 2013, "production in 2012 was down a total of 28.9 percent, according to information provided by the state Department for Energy Development and Independence, using federal production data."

Furthermore, Estep and Cheves continued, "Steep declines are expected to continue in the coming years. In a report released last June, the US Energy Information Administration projected that annual coal production in the region that includes eastern Kentucky would drop from the 2010 level of 186 million short tons to 132 tons in 2015 and to 92 million tons in 2018—a decline of more than half in less than a decade."

In view of this economic void, eastern Kentucky apiculture may be an economic sleeping giant. The United States currently imports beeswax from Africa (our domestic beeswax is inundated with pesticides), honey from Asia and South America, and queen bees from Hawaii. The Appalachian region will need to devote considerable funding for education to discuss the serious challenges to beekeeping, but it is possible to hope that this transition can be a beneficial one for pollinators and people.

Conclusion

The world's mountains are the heartbeat of floral and entomological wonders. Reclaimed-mine forests with pollinator-friendly plant species offer not just a return to ecologically diverse forests, but also opportunities for satisfying and sustainable livelihoods. India has the fifth-largest coal reserves in the world, and Kentucky accounts for one-tenth of all US coal production, so these two places will continue to be at the center of major extraction initiatives. But the reclamation patterns need not be reinvented. The Appalachian Regional Reforestation Initiative has provided good templates for communities transitioning to apiculture. As coal companies are transitioning into reclamation specialists, beekeepers and honey hunters' knowledge and experience can provide a crucial link between environmentalists and those working in extractive industries.

TAMMY HORN POTTER is state apiarist of Kentucky. Earlier, she founded and directed Coal Country Beeworks, facilitating the establishment of pollinator habitat as part of surface mine reclamation projects. She continues to work with others on reforestation with pollen-producing trees, surveying honeybee health, and the production of queen bees. Her books include *Bees in America: How the Honeybee Shaped a Nation* and *Beeconomy: What Women and Bees Teach Us about Local Trade and Global Markets.*

KUNAL SHARMA has worked on ecotourism for the Government of Karnataka, and on the honey trails in the Nilgiri Biosphere Reserve in India. His work is at the intersection of forestry, ecotourism, and community development at a grassroots level in mountain ecosystems. His long-term work involves understanding the complex issues surrounding forest livelihoods, conservation, and natural resources in the global ecological hotspot of the Western Ghats.

References

AEP (American Electric Power). 2010. *Sustainability Survey of AEP Coal Suppliers.* Columbus, Ohio: AEP.

Bradbear, Nicola, and Helen Jackson. 2002. *Strengthening Livelihoods: Exploring the Role of Beekeeping Development.* Cardiff: Beekeeping for Development Press.

Bradbear, Nicola, and M.S. Reddy. 1998. "Sustainable Beekeeping Development in Karnataka." In *Asian Bees and Beekeeping: Progress of Research and Development*, edited by M. Matsuka, L.R. Verma, S. Wongsiri, K.K. Shrestha, and Uma Partap, 266–270. Enfield, New Hampshire: Science Publishers.

Brammer, Jack. 2012. "Indian Company Plans to Buy Coal." *Lexington Herald-Leader,* August 15. http://www.kentucky.com/2012/08/15/2300027/indian-company-plans -to-buy-7.html#storylink=misearch#storylink=cpy.

Calderone, N. W. 2012. "Insect Pollinator Crops, Insect Pollinators, and US Agriculture: Trend Analysis of Aggregate Data for the Period 1992–2009." *PLOS ONE 7* (5): e37235. doi:10.1371/journal.pone.0037235.

Crane, Eva. 1999. *The World History of Beekeeping and Honey Hunting.* New York: Routledge.

———. 2001. *The Rock Art of Honey Hunters.* Bristol, UK: International Bee Research Association.

Denyer, Simon. 2012. "India Confronts Mountain of Coal Problems." *Washington Post*, December 23.

Directorate of Industries and Commerce (DIC). 1996. *Beekeeping Activities in Karnataka*. Bangalore, India: Directorate of Industries and Commerce.

Dott, Don, Executive Director. 2013. *Kentucky State Nature Preserves Commission Biennial Report*. Available online:naturepreserves.ky.gov/pubs/publications/2013%20 Biennial_Report.pdf

Douglas, J. C. 1884. *A Handbook of Bee-Keeping for India*. Calcutta: Superintendent of Government Printing.

Engel, M.S., Ismael Hinojosa-Diaz, and Alexandr Rasnitsyn. "A Honeybee from the Miocene of Nevada and the Biogeography of Apis (Hymenoptera: Apidae: Apini). *Proceedings of the California Academy of Sciences, series 4* 60 (3): 23–38.

Estep, Bill, and John Cheves. 2013. "Slumping Coal Business May Bring Tax Hike," *Lexington Herald-Leader*, January 27, A1–A2.

Horn, Tammy. 2005. *Bees in America: How the Honeybee Shaped a Nation*. Lexington: University Press of Kentucky.

———. 2012. *Beeconomy: What Women and Bees Teach Us about Local Economy and Global Markets*. Lexington: University Press of Kentucky.

Horn, Tammy, Patrick Angel, Carl Zipper, Michael Lyshen, Michael French, Jim Burger, and Mary Beth Adams. 2017. "Re-establishing Pollinator Habitat on Mined Lands Using the Forestry Reclamation Approach." *Appalachian Regional Reforestation Initiative Forest Reclamation*, advisory no. 14, February.

Hughes, David. 2017. Presentation to Pennyrile Beekeepers Association, Hopkinsville, Kentucky, April 10.

Islam, M. Nurul. 1998. "Beekeeping in Bangladesh." In *Asian Bees and Beekeeping: Progress of Research and Development*, edited by M. Matsuka, L.R. Verma, S. Wongsiri, K.K. Shrestha, and Uma Partap, 271. Enfield, New Hampshire: Science Publishers.

Ledford, David. 2013. "Mine Lands Initiative." Kentucky Professional Engineers in Mining Seminar, Lexington, Kentucky, September 6.

Nath, Snehlata, and Kunal Sharma. 2007. *Honey Trails in the Blue Mountains: Ecology, People and Livelihood in the Nilgiri Biosphere Reserve India*. Kotagir, India: Keystone Foundation.

Somerville, D. C. 1998. "Eucalyptus in Asia: A Beekeeping Resource." In *Asian Bees and Beekeeping: Progress of Research and Development*, edited by M. Matsuka, L. R. Verma, S. Wongsiri, K. K. Shrestha, and Uma Partap. Enfield, NH: Science.

Tudge, Colin. 1996. *The Time Before History: Five Million Years of Human Impact*. New York: Scribners.

Williams, Michael. 2002. *Deforesting the Earth: From Prehistory to Global Crisis*. Chicago: University of Chicago Press.

The Gap ($8,825 an Hour)

Si Kahn

Here I am spending my life
Down among the kielbasa
Making your lunch meat
Hot spicy sausage and dogs
You can count what I make
That's the reason they call it production
So how come it's you
That's living so high on the hog

Sometimes I wonder
What CEOs do in an hour
When I see your picture
You're talking away on the phone
Shaking some hand
Or jetting away to a meeting
You're sure not down here
On the floor with the gristle and bone

You make eight thousand eight hundred
Twenty-five dollars an hour
Seventy thousand and six hundred dollars a day
That's more than ten million a year

I just can't see it from here
What lets you deserve to be
Making a killing this way

Sometimes I dream
I'm sitting up in your office
You're working here on the floor
For the rest of your life
It's real work down here
But I know in my heart you can do it
The way you cut jobs
You've got to be good with a knife

You cut 500 jobs
And you say that you're being a leader
Me and my friends on the floor
Think it's old-fashioned greed
We can do the right thing
And hire them all back tomorrow
If we get cut back on you
We'll have all the payroll we need

CHAPTER 23

Agricultural Sovereignty and Arabica Coffee Production in Ethiopia

Aklilu Reda

DURING MY FIRST overseas trip to Italy in December 2010, I visited one of the Starbucks coffee shops located in the streets of the historic city of Rome to sip a strong Arabica coffee before starting my morning routine. I bought a cup of dark roasted coffee and experienced what it means to drink coffee thousands of miles away from the birthplace of the world's highly favored Arabica coffee. It was not a welcome experience for me, as a person from Ethiopia whose everyday experience is intertwined with culturally embedded coffee rituals and who passionately craves the right smell, aromatic flavor, and taste in a traditional sense. The mild coffee served in the transnational coffee retailer market made me realize that all coffee circulating in the global commodity network was not Ethiopian and that coffee differed at least in the way it is prepared, the courtesy with which it is served, the beans used to brew it, and the material artifact used in the preparation process. I was seeking to discover a cultural meaning inside the cup of coffee, and every sip had a defining moment for me as I realized the cultural variations involved in coffee consumption.

Located between 3 and 14 degrees above the equator, Ethiopia is part of the geographic region known as the Horn of Africa, made up of four countries—Eritrea,

Ethiopia, Djibouti, and Somalia—that lie toward the eastern tip of Africa. Ethiopia shares geographic and cultural boundaries with Eritrea on the northern and northeastern border, Djibouti to the east, Somalia to the southeast, Kenya to the south, South Sudan to the southwest, and Sudan to the west. Dotted with complex structures and fertile highlands rising up to 4,000 meters above sea level, the East African nation is one of the ancient centers of civilization that prevailed in parallel to other great Middle Eastern civilizations that emerged along the confluence of Tigris and Euphrates Rivers and the lower delta of the Nile about 5,000 years ago. Historically, the ancient civilization of Ethiopia began to develop as long as 4,000 years ago and reached its apex between the first century BC and the seventh century AD, marked by the rise and fall of the Axumite Kingdom. By about the fourth century, the Axumite Empire was able to establish a formidable civilization in the Red Sea region, extending its rule as far as present-day Yemen on the other side of the Red Sea and Sudan in its current western national boundary. Thus, the Ethiopian highlands constituted a rich context for the emergence of cultural boundaries and ecological diversity.

In this chapter, I focus on the southwestern Ethiopian highlands to describe the impact of global consumer behaviors on coffee production and marketing in the Ethiopian highlands. These terrains are undergoing rapid changes due to the influence of the transnational coffee market. My interest in the southwestern Ethiopian highlands was initially inspired by my personal coffee drinking habit, which I developed as an undergraduate at Dilla University, in the Gedeo Zone of the Southern Nations, Nationalities and Peoples (SNNP) regional state of Ethiopia, between 1997 and 2001. During this time, I became accustomed to drinking a strong Arabica coffee every morning to boost my day; that is how I became a passionate fan of Arabica coffee. With such inspiration, I used to go hiking in the Afromontane natural forests where coffee grows as a wild shrub under the shade of big tree canopies. Traveling more than 1,000 kilometers southward from northern Ethiopia, the place I call home, I found myself caught with excitement about the ecological contrast between the humid coffee-growing regions and the dry land in the areas where I was brought up. It was indeed an epistemic journey to rearticulate my conceptions regarding the ecological and social value of the coffee production processes, and to think about Ethiopian cultural and agricultural sovereignty as it related to the global coffee market.

Observing coffee beans being collected from wild shrubs that have grown under the shade of the Afromontane rainforests, I developed a commitment to advocate not only for the best-tasting coffee prepared in a culturally appropriate way, but also an appreciation of the natural landscape that produces the specialty coffee on which the Ethiopian cultural tradition and social interaction are built. Through extensive reading on the global coffee economy and my own coffee drinking experiences during travels to different parts of the world, including Japan,

Europe, and the United States, I became convinced that the southwestern highlands are not merely a unique geographic location, they also constitute a particular space where local and global connections on the one hand and human and nonhuman relations on the other hand converge and interact in a distinctive way. Above all, these terrains provide the gene pool for the highly traded gourmet coffee (*Coffea arabica*), and the sustainability of all of the world's coffee varieties depends on their well-being. The southwestern highlands are the cradle of Arabica coffee, and provide the gene pool for the genetic diversity of all coffee varieties circulated in the global commodity network; their sustainability has also been intertwined with the cultural and economic practices of the people who live adjacent to these terrains, which have enabled their sustainable preservation.

Nevertheless, Ethiopian coffee producers often feel that their product is not competitive because they believe that countries like Brazil, Guatemala, and Indonesia already control the market owing to an elaborate connection to the global north and adoption of modern production mechanisms that ensure quality and traceability in accordance with the standards set by international organizations. Hence, disregarding the socioeconomic and cultural significance of coffee production from wild forests in the southwestern Ethiopian highlands, two solutions are always suggested for Ethiopian coffee to make its way to the global market. The first is to watch for conditions that might reduce the presence of Brazil and other major coffee exporting countries in the global market such as natural calamities and unpredicted failures in production. In this way, Ethiopian coffee producers would hope to fill the market deficiency. The second option, perhaps is the most important one, is to ensure competitiveness by shifting from traditional means of production to employing modern techniques in line with the standards set by certifying organizations. While the southwestern highlands still provide the natural ecology for the reproduction of coffee, for the obvious reason that the wild coffee species used to reproduce coffee are not found in any of the other coffee-producing countries, other coffee-growing landscapes could not offer the same possibility as Ethiopia to sustainably conserve coffee. Taking the production of forest coffee out of the natural landscapes could imply unwise measures against the sustainability of coffee.

Traditionally, the cultivation and production of Arabica coffee in the Ethiopian landscapes epitomizes multiple agroecological values transcending the obvious economic significance of appropriation and extraction. Local production practices emphasize coffee's diverse uses, connecting the economic, cultural, and ecological functions under the rubric of conservation to create a perfect, pure, and sustainable natural ecology. Underpinning these values is the enactment of a web of meanings and expression revealed in the local tradition by which the coffee forest ecosystem is seen as a delicate blueprint of nature requiring protection to ensure its sustainable use (Buechley et al. 2015; Hundera et al. 2013; Mittermeier et al. 2004; Tadesse et al. 2014).

Ethiopians relate to a quintessential value revealed in their everyday ceremonial rituals. The Ethiopian coffee ceremony is deeply rooted in the people's cultural tradition and provides a space for social gathering. It also serves as a venue through which people build solidarity and strengthen social relationships. Participation in a coffee ceremony ritual is most often done voluntarily and can mean inclusion in a group through which mutual interdependence is sustained. The Ethiopian coffee ceremony is carried out on an everyday basis drawing on participation by neighbors and relatives living in nearby locations. The process involves the use of several material artifacts, each carrying a specific function for roasting, grinding, brewing, and so on. Although the entire process of the coffee ceremony is handled by women, men also attend the processes, giving blessings at the beginning of the ritual and sharing the brewed coffee with women.

The cultural interplay enshrined in the everyday practice of the coffee ceremony links people with nature in ongoing dialectical relationships. Thus, Ethiopian cultural practices are focused on protecting nature, which gives them coffee and all the grains produced in the agricultural fields, and by sanctifying the landscapes where they grow. One of the reasons coffee has been predominantly grown as wild forests is due to the popular perception of the landscapes as the hosts of species that care for human beings and deserve the same care in return. Thus, coffee is regarded not as a mere economic commodity subject to human action but as constitutive of different roles and values sustaining human life. Following Anna Tsing's (2015) notion of "life in the ruins of capitalism," I argue that in the Ethiopian tradition, in which forms of life other than humanity interact and coexist in different degrees of engagement, nature is not simply viewed as a passive cosmology on which human action thrives.

By virtue of its status as the place of origin of coffee, the southwestern Ethiopian highlands are considered a pristine environment where different species interact in a mutually interdependent collaboration to make life possible through natural regeneration. The significance of coffee in the everyday practices of the people also creates a space for a lively interaction between nonhuman species and humanity, producing a unique collaboration in support of mutual existence, as Tsing (2015) has vividly indicated in her study about the *matsutake* mushroom. The continuous interaction between human beings and nature, as well as the social value of coffee in the people's everyday life, shows that the Ethiopian Arabica coffee constitutes a space for multidimensional human activity, and it is not reducible to mere economic status in whatever sense stipulated by the encroaching transnational market order. Rather, it provides a particular lifeworld constituted through the cooperation of nature and human beings mutually shaping each other in a sustainable way. Thus, prior to any sort of thinking about the future that leads to the modification of the natural mosaic of the coffee forests in the southwestern highlands of Ethiopia, looking for mutual coexistence in the existing setting is of paramount importance.

The residents of southwestern Ethiopia tend to be skillful conservationists, in that they demonstrate practical knowledge and techniques regarding the ecology and biodiversity of the natural environment. Their livelihood is strictly linked with the well-being of the natural environment that provides them with coffee, and multispecies products thrive in the shade of the Afromontane coffee forests. Local peasants make a living by collecting coffee beans from the forest tracts close to their neighborhoods, both for the purpose of domestic consumption and to supplement their income from the local market. They also collect other food plants and material products used for construction, animal fodder, and agricultural utensils. To ensure a sustainable supply of both the economic and noneconomic value of the coffee forests, the people grow additional seedlings and protect the entire forest system from the risk of depletion (Stellmacher 2007). Southwestern Ethiopian farmers cultivate coffee with other edible indigenous plants to nourish the soil and help the forest ecosystem thrive undisturbed. Hence, forest coffee systems of the southwestern Ethiopian highlands provide a living space for diverse species' entanglement and interaction. Several studies support the idea that wild forest coffee grown in southwestern Ethiopia constitutes a unique genetic composition that no other coffee species circulating in the transnational coffee chain could (Aerts et al. 2017; Tesfaye et al. 2014). This area hosts a wide variety of species and the highlands are acknowledged as the sites of the global "gene house" for coffee species diversity (Aerts et al. 2017).

Fair Trade Movements, the Commodification of Coffee, and the Sustainability of the Southwestern Ethiopian Highlands

Although, to the best of my knowledge, no comprehensive assessments have been undertaken to determine the status of the forest coffee following the implementation of the fair trade scheme, scattered evidence on the status of southwestern Ethiopian coffee reveals that the local people have increasingly become dissociated from their attachment with the forest, and massive conversion of forest coffee into plantation agriculture is underway. As plantation agriculture has increased in importance, species diversity and area coverage of forest coffee has decreased. The shift in the production pattern of coffee illustrates that formalized efforts to link the coffee economy in Ethiopia with the transnational economy is contributing in undesirable ways to changes in the people's interaction with their natural environment and compromising the security of their livelihood. Stellmacher (2007) argues that the current coffee certification process, which requires standardization and labeling in line with the standards set by the fair trade certification organization, is responsible for the accelerated loss of the coffee forests. Aerts et al. (2017) list a range of factors, for example seed transplantation, "biotic homogenization," and the use of "improved cultivars" that contribute to rapid loss of the forest coffee ecosystem. The application of massive improved coffee cultivars in an attempt to improve productivity and to produce disease-tolerant species is severely eroding the genetic diversity and composition of the forest coffee. In recent years, natural forest coffee is increasingly losing ground to plantation agriculture, a practice that severely compromises the genetic stability of the entire coffee species in the system.

On November 6, 2006, a writer for *The Economist* published that Oxfam had launched a battle against Starbucks, accusing the American coffee firm of depriving Ethiopian coffee producers "of $90 million a year by opposing the Ethiopian government's efforts to trademark three types of local coffee beans . . . despite selling plenty of Fairtrade-branded coffee, it also buys other beans without a stamp of approval from these arbiters of fairness, in part because it questions the standards they apply in different parts of the world."

Underlying this bone of contention is an explanation of how the fair trade movement has transformed the relations between nature and human beings by reembedding them in the contexts of the transnational commodity chain. While consumers' actions are considered rational and economically necessary, producers are described as objects through which consumer logic is reasoned out. The rise of the fair trade movement has inherently been linked with concerns of uneven economic possibilities for the poor coffee growers in developing countries. Acknowledging the historical failure of the coffee market to address the economic suitability of the market, the fair trade movement has tasked itself with fixing injustices by transforming the North-South relationship into mutually empowering trading partnerships. Yet that work is undertaken in compliance with the standards set by consumers in the Global North; in that way, inequity, or a difference in the weight of people's voices and concerns, is built into the process.

The Ethiopian government is taking every possible action to improve the quality of the Ethiopian Arabica coffee in line with fair trade labeling standards, fulfilling the moral and ethical values of northern consumers. With the intention of meeting the requirements and expectations of ethical consumers, several projects have been implemented to improve the quality and productivity of the yield per unit area and increase the revenue from the transaction in the global commodity chain. In 2008, the Ethiopian Commodity Exchange market (ECX) was established to oversee the production and marketing of coffee in the domestic commodity network and serve as an outlet to the global market. Aimed at modernizing the coffee commodity exchange, ECX is, among other things, opening up Ethiopian connections to the international market as well as matching offers. Side by side, farmers are organized in unions and cooperative associations to enable them to produce the best quality coffee based on knowledge of the transnational demand. Yet these actions are not grounded in the understanding of local contexts and societal values that have nurtured coffee for millennia, since it was first discovered, and they are not facilitating the sustainable use of this delicate resource. Instead, the new intervention approaches are not only causing depletion of the coffee forests but also dramatically altering the entire ecosystem.

Living conditions of the people in the southwestern highlands in recent years have become increasingly full of uncertainties. More than at any time in history, their region has suffered from a loss of productivity and declining vegetation cover, as well as incidences of drought and food shortages. The commodification of land and the inadequacies of the interventions of development regimes have benefited the fair trade–certified growers at the expense of the well-being of the people and the natural environment. Claims of land rights and benefit sharing have become widespread as the intervention projects often emphasize improving the future with little regard to the current problems, subsequently giving rise to much more complicated challenges that will require a lot more energy to address. With local knowledge and value steadily ceding the space to conceptions of the fair trade initiatives, the latter are responsible for the broad-ranging repercussions of the modifications involved in its ascent to control of the local economy.

The Fair Trade Commodity Chain and Its Critique

Fair trade is becoming an attractive labeling enterprise in the global commodity chain. It is presented as an alternative development initiative expressed in the form of a social movement aimed at transforming the lives of the small-scale producers in the Global South. Fair trade emphasizes the central role of the small-scale economy and aims to safeguard the well-being of smallholding farmers in the Global South by ending the injustices incurred by exploitative markets. Wrapped in the motto of "trade not aid" Lyon 2011), the fair trade movement seeks to end the injustices of current market relations, which are often considered unfriendly to the farmers who are poor and disempowered by the complexities and inconveniences of the competitive global exchange pattern. Entrenched in neoliberal free market principles necessitating competition and appropriation, conventional markets negatively affect the coffee growers' social relations and ecological systems. These characteristics determine how fair trade more easily thrives over the agrofood commodity network than any other commodity in the world. It is also said that the fair trade initiative is a movement for the demystification of the global trading relationship that solely depends on price and restricting the transnational companies' control of the coffee commodity chain (Raynolds 2006).

The fair trade movement articulates the concerns and disadvantages of coffee growers and stipulates the creation of a transnational market that equally benefits the poor household coffee producers, whose benefit is usurped by the injustices of the market structure, so that they can harness economic gain proportional to their labor and capital investment. Proponents of the fair trade movement argue that such partnerships are vital to coffee producers in the Global South by empowering them to bargain and add value on their products. This process also involves the idea of protecting producers from abuses in the market, which they neither control nor create through their own discourses. Underlying the idea of protecting the coffee-growing farmers is the fair trade movement's endeavor to correct the injustices of the neoliberal capitalist market, where giant corporate enterprises amass unprecedented wealth and the poor farmers in the remote farmlands receive insignificant benefit. Fair trade provides consumers with choices in return for their commitment to environmental and social stewardships. However, whether fair trade could guarantee economic and ecological sustainability to southern producers is highly debatable. Although the fair trade movement appeared as a development scheme for the smallholder coffee-growing households through the incorporation of consumer values in the commodity network, in effect it is yet challenged from the viewpoints both of social justice and its inherently foundational alignment with global exchange values (Luetchford 2008, Raynolds 2000, 2009).

One of the inconspicuous reactions to the economic and environmental benefits of fair trade markets is that it is neither an efficient way to challenge what Raynolds (2009: 1083) argues to be the unequal market relations between the Northern "progressive consumers" and the Southern "marginalized producers" nor guarantees environmental sustainability as promised in the statutes of the movement. Instead, it portrays the apparent power hierarchy in which the responsible buyers in the North crowd their fellow producers in the South around the notion of ethical standards set and regulated by the moral values of the consumer society in the developed world. In effect, the concept of ethical consumption labels coffee producers as people in need of improvement and subjects them to economic and development programs targeting the creation of a socioeconomic stability through improved earnings (Carrier 2010).

These presumptive moral values in the coffee commodity chain locate ethics in the context of multiple relationships and manifestations in the people's everyday practices, transcending various contingencies of nature and economic practices. According to James Carrier (2010, 686), the idea of conservation stewardship works by disregarding certain "contextual realities" and confining the object (nature) to the services of the consumer's "moral values." Li (2007) also argues that discourses of development in the capitalist sense, as well the narratives and practices engraved in its operatives, assert their success by producing tensions and dislocating people from their traditional landscapes. This process is what she calls "rendering technical," a mechanism that objectifies humans as passive actors with no agency. Such standards are often undertaken through various forms of certification of farm-based activities such as labor wages, access to education and medical services, and controls on and modifications of the natural environment, subjecting them to the valuation and standardizations defined and executed by professional experts of ethical coffee.

Li (2007) clearly states that the neoliberal enterprise claims to transform the natural environment by subsuming it into the ethical rhetoric of transnational developmental assumptions. The developmental pursuit entailed in the fair trade programs is spearheaded by corporate organizations and NGOs who advocate and promote the preeminence of efficient markets that are capable of operating outside of state control. Put in a different way, this leads toward the privatization and corporatization of the natural landscape and the social cosmology at large, an action leading to commodification of nature. As fair trade succeeded in recruiting different groups of adherents drawn from different parts of global societies, it has been transforming both the economic justification of production and the people's social relations with the natural environment, creating new conservation and sustainability knowledge and approaches. Li (2007) indicates that such processes are conceptualized through expert knowledge, which subsequently generates discourses abstracting the meanings of livelihood and resource utilization. In this way, the role of the local people has become restricted to receiving knowledge and aligning their actions with the wisdom received from the group of experts who present their logic in technical statements. This trend gives way to what Escobar (2001, 46) termed the "decentering of place and locality" due to the global flow of knowledge exchange through the commodities exchanged under the auspices of the fair trade movement. The transnational nature of fair trade commodity exchange contributes to the deterritorialization of cultural boundaries along the lines of the capitalist rhetoric of globalization, which ultimately makes entry into neoliberal political economic space a mandatory prerequisite to harnessing the benefits of the new system (Appadurai 1996).

A visible sign of this deterritorialization process is the notion of ethical consumption by way of which local production standards are set to be certified by globally accredited certification bodies located in Western nations. Certification of a product requires adherence to the fair trade standards, acting and checking one's behavior in reference to consumer expectations. According to Carrier (2010), consumers expect producers to include their moral values in the production process, and the appropriateness of the production of a commodity is determined by assessing the degree to which the stated moral standards are included in the commodity. This requirement correspondingly applies to the actions of consumers, who in turn require fulfilling producers' expectations, paying fair price for the commodity sold in the commodity chain. In this way, transnational fair trade coffee chains enjoin two different groups of social categories, constituting new relationships between those people whose primary goal is to harness moral values and others who are concerned with the pressing need of eradicating poverty.

The Commodification and Integration of the Ethiopian Arabica Coffee in the Transnational Commodity Chain

In September 2013, Starbucks added three Ethiopian Arabica coffee cultivars to its single origin selection as the highest quality specialty signature coffee.

The news on Starbucks' official website read as follows:

> Starbucks' first whole bean packaged coffee available globally since the introduction of Starbucks Blonde Roast two years ago, Ethiopia coffee celebrates

Ethiopia's rich coffee tradition and delivers a taste in the cup unlike any other coffee offered in Starbucks' 42-year history. . . . With its high elevation, rich volcanic soil, and more than 10,000 coffee varieties, Ethiopia produces some of the most extraordinary coffee in the world, . . . Coffee was discovered in Africa more than 1,200 years ago and is where the first arabica beans were grown. Today, coffee remains central to Ethiopian culture and heritage and is shared with family and friends through daily coffee ceremonies often occurring throughout the day lasting up to several hours. Multiple steps in the ceremony include pan-roasting green coffee, grinding the roasted beans using a mortar and pestle, and preparing the roasted and ground coffee in a spherical-shaped pot called a jebena. The coffee is then served in traditional tasting cups.[1]

The incorporation of Ethiopian Arabica coffee into the global market as the finest specialty coffee demonstrates the highest achievement in connecting the Ethiopian economy with the transnational system, often regarded as a sign of modernity and a road for improvement. The new designation brought with it the precondition of ensuring the commodity's traceability down to the farm level and the application of scientific knowledge in line with the neoliberal conceptions of green development. As indicated in the Starbucks news release, the introduction of Ethiopian Arabica coffee was the formalization of the move towards the commodification of the product, assigning values to every aspect of its nature that can render economic gain. Introducing the coffee in its Single Origin selection, Starbucks presumed that it is honoring "Ethiopia's rich tradition," encapsulating its "taste" in a cup carrying the logo of Starbucks and sold in the market. As Hanson (2007) argues, this process is an example of the neoliberal conception of development, which appropriates its desired interest by commodifying the exchange of natural resources as capital objects. Their values are defined in technical terms using the capitalist institutional setup and practices. However, the technical specifications and institutional support fair trade provides to the producers in the remote mountain places of Ethiopia are selective, and target certain parts of the production chain. Mostly, it requires transformation from the traditional means of production to the modern system involving market-conscious decisions and an understanding of the desires of the company's strict code of quality control. With the rise of new preconditions in the transnational coffee trade, farmers are required not only to ensure their compliance with the standards but also to change their production behavior to ensure their products are traceable and ethical. This frame of thinking introduces new conceptions of biodiversity conservation stewardship, giving rise to multiple interpretations and discourses of nature.

Conclusion

In this chapter, I have discussed how the fair trade initiative is structured within the global market and how that impacts the producer's way of life in the southwestern

Ethiopian highlands. For more than a decade, Ethiopia has been making its way into the transnational coffee commodity chain and has successfully earned its claim to brand its coffee varieties. Although the global commodity chain has provided a space for Ethiopian coffee to prevail in an unprecedented way, the selective involvement of the fair trade actors and the differential power relations observed between the producers and the consumers is not without consequences. One of the major consequences is revealed in converting the natural coffee production into a distinct commodity form, hence inviting more vigorous modification of both the landscape and the production processes. Rituals and local knowledge have become less important as the local producer's positionality to set standards and negotiate power has been increasingly usurped by the moral values of the consumer society in the North. As a result, the people have started to shape their production practices by locating their social and economic desires within the context of the ethical consumption rhetoric. Assigning different meanings to specific values in the coffee commodity chain, fair trade has provided definitions of social justice, environmental stewardship, and ethical consumer behavior within the Western rhetoric that emphasizes the primacy of the market and the individual as opposed to collective values of the developing world that pay attention to the cooperative interaction between human beings and nature.

As coffee has been commodified, human labor has also become a commodity. As a result, farmers are obliged to make choices on how and when to invest their labor in the production processes. By locating consumers and their practices in the social and economic contexts in which they exist and that their ethical consumption affects, this volume presents a compelling interrogation of the rhetoric and assumptions of ethical consumption. People have started to decide their labor allocation in terms of how much they might gain in economic terms instead of the traditional labor that is structured less by market rationales than by collective social benefit. Therefore, in recent years we have seen a reduction in the historical connections of humanity with nature and the collaborative interplay of life with nonhuman species. Viewed in the context of shifting social relations, the increased frequency of natural crises such as drought, declining productivity, and claims of fair resource sharing, I conclude that fair trade has a lot more to do to ensure the empowerment of the farmers in southwestern Ethiopia. I suggest that the fair trade certification movement has to further redefine its standards to fully grasp the development need of the poor farmers in the Southern hemisphere. One area of redefinition that needs to be considered is the concept of ethical consumption. My recommendation is that by reinventing the definition of morality and ethics and approaching this concept from the producers' angle, fair trade could make a meaningful transformation towards a sustainable social and economic future.

As an Ethiopian, my overall concern with the well-being of Ethiopians in mountain communities and elsewhere in the country is linked with agricultural sovereignty. Coffee producers in Ethiopia should have the right to design their coffee production and other agricultural practices in an ecologically and culturally appropriate way. My long-term research is on the production of teff, another Ethiopian crop of local origin with a growing global market. European Union–based companies have already patented the intellectual property and production process for the grain, which has rich cultural and economic significance within Ethiopia. This seems to continue the postcolonial trend of controlling from outside the country the conceptualization and practice of Ethiopians' own agricultural engagement with global markets. Until Ethiopia's agricultural sovereignty is recognized by the Global North, it will be difficult for the lessons Ethiopia's culturally and ecologically sophisticated agroecological production offers to the world to be heeded.

AKLILU REDA is a PhD candidate in anthropology at the University of Kentucky. He taught ecological anthropology in Mekelle University, where he created the Department of Anthropology in the Institute of Paleo-Environment and Heritage Conservation, which he also directed. His research focuses on agricultural commodity chains and circulation of an Ethiopian grain, teff, in the US commodity network.

Note

1. From the Starbucks website. Accessed May 16, 2017. https://news.starbucks.com/news /starbucks-honors-the-birthplace-of-coffee-with-ethiopia.

References

Aerts, R., L. Geeraert, B. Gezahegn, H. Kitessa, B. Muys, H. De Kort, and O. Honnay. 2017. "Conserving Wild Arabica Coffee: Emerging Threats and Opportunities." *Agriculture, Ecosystems and Environment*, no. 237, 75–79 Accessed March 16, 2017. https://doi.org/10.1016/j.agee.2016.12.023

Appadurai, A. 1996. "Disjuncture and Difference in the Global Cultural Economy." In *Modernity at Large: Cultural Dimensions of Globalization*, 27–47. Minneapolis: University of Minnesota Press.

Buechley, E. R., C. H. Sekercioglu, A. Atickem, G. Gebremichael, J. K. Ndungu, B. A. Mahamued, T. Beyene, T. Mekonnen, and L. Lens. 2015. "Importance of Ethiopian Shade Coffee Farms for Forest Bird Conservation." *Biological Conservation*, no. 188, 50–60. Accessed February 27, 2017. https://pubag.nal.usda.gov /catalog/5361126.

Carrier, James G. 2010. "Protecting the Environment, the Natural Way: Ethical Consumption and Commodity Fetishism." *Antipode* 42 (3): 672–689. Accessed February 22, 2017. http://dx.doi.org/10.1111/j.1467-8330.2010.00768.x.

Economist. 2006. "Oxfam versus Starbucks: And, This Time, Oxfam May Be in the Wrong." November 7. Accessed April 2, 2017. http://www.economist.com /node/8129387.

Escobar, A. 2001."Culture Sits in Places: Reflections on Globalism and Subaltern Strategies of Localization." *Political Geography,* no. 20, 139–174 Accessed March 13, 2017. http://www.sciencedirect.com/science/article/pii/S0962629800000640.

Hanson, P. W. 2007. "Governmentality, Language Ideology, and the Production of Needs in Malagasy Conservation and Development." *Cultural Anthropology* 22 (2): 244–284. Accessed April 3, 2017. http://onlinelibrary.wiley.com/doi/10.1525 /can.2007.22.2.244/.

Hundera, K., R. Aerts, A. Fontaine, M. Van Mechelen, P. Gijbels, O. Honnay, and B. Muys. 2013. "Effects of Coffee Management Intensity on Composition, Structure, and Regeneration Status of Ethiopian Moist Evergreen Afromontane Forests." *Environmental Management,* no. 51, 801–809. Accessed February 12, 2017. https:// link.springer.com/article/10.1007/s00267-012-9976-5.

Li, T. Murray. 2007. *The Will to Improve: Governmentality, Development, and the Practice of Politics.* London: Duke University Press.

Luetchford, P. 2008. *Fair Trade and a Global Commodity: Coffee in Costa Rica.* London: Pluto Press.

Lyon, S. 2011. *Coffee and Community: Maya Farmers and Fair Trade Markets.* Boulder, CO: University Press of Colorado.

Mittermeier, R. A., P. Robles-Gil, M. Hoffmann, J. D. Pilgrim, T. B. Brooks, C. G. Mittermeier, J. L. Lamoreux, and G. A. B. Fonseca. 2004. *Hotspots Revisited: Earth's Biologically Richest and Most Endangered Ecoregions.* Mexico City: CEMEX.

Raynolds, Laura T. 2000. "Re-Embedding Global Agriculture: The International Organic and Fair Trade Movements." *Journal of Agriculture and Human Values,* no. 17, 297–309. Accessed April 4, 2017. https://link.springer.com/article/10.102 3/A:1007608805843.

———. 2006. "Organic and Fair Trade Movements in Global Food Networks." In *Ethical Sourcing in the Global Food System,* edited by S. Barrientos and C. Dolan, 49–62. London: Earthscan.

———. 2009. "Mainstreaming Fair Trade Coffee: From Partnership to Traceability." *World Development* 37 (6): 1083–1093. Accessed April 4, 2017. https://doi. org/10.1016/j.worlddev.2008.10.001.

Starbucks. 2013. "Starbucks Honors the Birthplace of Coffee with Ethiopia, a New Coffee Seeped in History," news release. September 23. Accessed May 16, 2017. https://news.starbucks.com/news/starbucks -honors-the-birthplace-of-coffee-with-ethiopia.

Stellmacher, T. 2007. *Governing the Ethiopian Coffee Forests: A Local Level Institutional Analysis in Kaffa and Bale Mountains.* Aachen, Germany: Shaker.

Tadesse, G., E. Zavaleta, C. Shennan, and M. FitzSimmons. 2014. "Policy and Demographic Factors Shape Deforestation Patterns and Socio-Ecological Processes in Southwest Ethiopian Coffee Agroecosystems." *Applied Geography,* no. 54, 149–159. Accessed March 13, 2017. https://doi.org/10.1016/j.apgeog.2014.08.001.

Tsing A. 2015. *The Mushroom at the End of the World: On the Possibility of Life in Capitalist Ruins.* Princeton, NJ: Princeton University Press.

The Flume

Si Kahn

Momma remembered
When she was young
How her Daddy'd get up
'Fore the rising sun
Up in the wagon
Off he'd go
Chasing the sunrise
Down that water road

Lord, Lord, down the road
Lord, Lord, down the road
Lord, Lord, down the road
Lord, Lord, down the road

Up Reddies River
There's trees so tall
No company on earth
Could ever cut 'em all
Straight heart poplar
By the wagon load
To float down to town
On that water road

Long about midnight
The sun gone down
They'd load up the flume
For the run to town
Step on a board
Grab a steady hold
Riding on home
Down that water road

The sawmills, the axes
The oxen teams
Iron boilers building up
A head of steam
Wagons and drivers
Who'd have ever known
They would all wash away
Down that water road

Creating Sustainable Post-extraction Livelihoods in the Central Appalachian Coalfields

Nathan Hall

THE MOUNTAINS OF Appalachia range from Maine to Alabama, existing as rolling foothills on the periphery and reaching peaks of over 6,600 feet (2,000 meters) in the central heartland. While many subregions within this relatively rough terrain have experienced varying degrees of marginality due to their inaccessibility and infrastructural challenges, the coal-producing areas within the central Appalachian interior have historically been the most marginalized for a host of reasons. This status has changed relatively little in recent years, and the rapid decline of the regional coal industry has highlighted social, cultural, and economic problems that have been developing for decades. It is an opportune time to address these challenges head-on in order to build a more desirable future for the inhabitants and environment of Appalachia. The possibilities for the development of sustainable livelihoods discussed in this chapter may also be relevant to other remote, marginalized post-extraction regions.

As an eighth-generation resident of the coalfields of eastern Kentucky, I have both worked directly on sustainable agriculture, forestry, and small-scale hydroelectric energy options in Appalachia and traveled (with a Watson Fellowship) to mountain communities elsewhere in the world to learn and exchange strategies for supporting sustainable livelihoods. The suggestions made here are based on those experiences. In my current work reclaiming postmined lands, I see sustainable agroforestry's potential to contribute to economic as well as environmental recovery from resource extraction in Appalachia.

Background

European immigrants have had a significant presence in the steep, remote hills and mountains of eastern Kentucky, southern West Virginia, southwestern Virginia, northeast Tennessee, and northwestern North Carolina since the late eighteenth and early nineteenth centuries. The indigenous Americans of the Shawnee and Cherokee nations inhabited these lands for hundreds if not thousands of years prior to the expansion of the United States' western frontier. A few European groups initially settled these remote forested hollows and hillsides to set up mostly self-sustaining mountain farmsteads. Among other immigrants who made a new home in Appalachia were many Scotch-Irish, who came to the region due to the similarity of the terrain to their homeland and because of their relatively marginalized socioeconomic status. The rough, mountainous terrain was not suitable for plantation-style farming as practiced in flatter regions proximate to the coastal centers of power, and was therefore less desirable. Economically disadvantaged newcomers to America were willing to live on marginal land with uncertain land tenure because of their social marginality (as indentured servants or deportees, for example) in other contexts (Williams 2001).

The American Civil War of 1861–1865 was a major turning point for mountain communities. Central Appalachia was an intense battleground wherein allegiance to the Union or Confederacy was often divided on a county-by-county basis and families were split by prolonged guerilla warfare. Besides damaging the newly forming social fabric of the region, the war also introduced wealthy New England elites to the vast untapped reserves of coal, timber, and gas that could be used to fuel a rapidly expanding and industrializing nation. In the decades that followed, massive tracts of land were transferred for pittances, sometimes through deceptive tactics (e.g., exploiting someone's low literacy level) from the hands of mountain farmsteaders to large landholding companies. Railroad, coal, timber, and landholding companies were created and often cross-linked in the boardrooms of Boston, Philadelphia, and other northeast urban centers with the intention of extracting the resources as quickly, efficiently, and profitably as possible (Eller 1982).

By the early 1900s, hundreds of thousands of acres had been transferred to corporate ownership and railroads had been extended to most of the major extraction points. The decades leading up to World War II witnessed an intensively active and convulsive period in the region's relationship to its resources.

Thousands of people were recruited to work in the coal mines and timber camps of Central Appalachia, wherein the towns were usually built and controlled by the coal or timber company and the company-controlled railroad was the only means of ingress or egress. Workers came from diverse regions and backgrounds, from the postslavery sharecropping American South to the farthest reaches of Eastern Europe, and all were subjected to harsh working conditions for very little pay by today's standards. Cross-cultural bonds were formed to create strong labor unions that provided a model for workers in other rapidly forming industries, as well as highly distinctive music that spawned entire musical genres (Eller 1982). With the onset of World War II the region saw a major boom as its coal, timber, and natural gas were in high demand for the wartime effort.

The boom quickly turned to bust as major technological advances (largely a byproduct of wartime engineering) soon replaced thousands of physical laborers with high-powered machinery and explosives. Continuous mining machines, roof bolters, auger machines, and ammonium nitrate that could blow entire mountains apart soon caused the layoff of thousands of miners (the valuable old-growth timber had largely been cleared by this point as well), resulting in the first of many waves of outmigration. The people who remained in the mountains had to compete in an increasingly limited labor market and lacked the land resources that their ancestors may have given up or lost a generation or two earlier (Eller 2008).

Current Situation

The general trend that began in the years following World War II has continued, with fewer and fewer humans needed to remove Appalachia's resources at ever-greater rates. Mountaintop removal, longwall, and continuous mining have resulted in the extraction of billions of tons of Appalachian coal over the past several decades and the permanent alteration of more than 1.5 million acres of land.

Previously, the decline in Appalachian mining employment was primarily caused by increases in efficiency, with larger and more advanced machinery and earth-moving techniques requiring fewer humans per jobsite. The decade leading up to the present (the spring of 2017) has seen not only job losses in the region's coal industry but also decreased production vis-á-vis other regions in the United States. Improvements in power plants' sulphur-scrubbing technology have enabled coal from the Powder River Basin in Montana and Wyoming as well as the Illinois Basin in Illinois, Indiana, and western Kentucky to be much more market-competitive than the thinner, expensive-to-access, yet higher quality coal found in the mountains of Central Appalachia. Instead, the latter's low-impurity bituminous coal is being shipped abroad for steel production in India and China, though even these rapidly developing countries cannot keep a full-scale mining economy afloat in Appalachia. Most important of all, advances in natural gas recovery known as fracking (pumping of high pressure or explosive materials deep underground to fracture rock strata, thus releasing bound-up natural gas) have opened up vast new gas reserves, greatly lowering the market price of natural gas. As a result, dozens of utility companies across the country have largely switched their generation capacity from coal to natural gas (Hansen and McIlmoil 2010).

There are different explanations in circulation in Appalachia for the region's current economic challenges. Some attribute their woes to the federal government's strengthening and enforcement of environmental regulations under the Obama administration, known as the "war on coal," whereas others believe that the flood of cheap natural gas onto the market has been the primary cause of the industry's downturn. Counties that had up to 50 percent of their working population associated with coal mining only a few years ago now have only 100 to 200 persons actively employed in the industry, a drop of up to 49 percent. The result has been another wave of outmigration and high unemployment for those who remain. Unemployment is not accurately reflected in official statistics due to the huge number of people who have simply stopped looking for work and therefore are not registered by unemployment agencies. Central Appalachia's economy includes broad informal activities—illegal trade in highly addictive prescription painkillers and homemade methamphetamines, for example—and there are numerous discussions about a lack of hope and pride in the region and ways to address that. There are several organizations, for instance, of young people imagining sustainable futures in the region.

Solutions Moving Forward

Central Appalachia is in desperate need of a cultural and economic re-visioning that values and respects the region's coal mining past while implementing viable sustainable options for livelihoods that both recognize the region's physical realities and create a rewarding life for even the most economically marginalized. To promote this re-visioning in a way that can be broadly inclusive of the region's residents, a few key principles are necessary:

1. *Respect for the past.* Multitudes of Central Appalachians have given their time, sweat, blood, and lives to the coal industry, and this contribution to the development of the United States and other nations should be valued. Emphasis should be placed on employing former coal miners and related workers, using their current skills to the greatest extent possible.

2. *Collaboration beyond ideological differences.* Divisions, represented as being between pro-environment and pro-industry, have fractured communities and communications within the region, and new, progressive ideas are often resisted based on the assumption that they are somehow part of an anticoal and therefore anti-Appalachian agenda. A more neutral path is more likely to lead to implementation of meaningful, long-lasting projects that benefit a greater number of Appalachians in need of opportunities.

3. *Equitable enterprise development structures.* While extractive industry workers have become accustomed to top-down hierarchical structures, the future of business development in the region could take a very different form. An opportunity now exists to implement more equitable business structures, such as hybrid for-profit/non-profit organizations and employee-owned cooperatives where workers would have a stake in the survival and profitability of an enterprise and their morale would be heightened as a result of a feeling of direct ownership of their work.

4. *Place-based approach to sustainable resource utilization.* The steep forested hills, narrow streambed hollows, vast expanses of flattened mountaintops turned into exotic scrubland savannahs, and small riverbottom towns scattered throughout the region call for flexible and location-specific strategies to create sustainable livelihoods based on the naturally recurring assets within the region.

I have chosen to group these strategies into three broad categories that can be linked in a number of ways: (*a*) sustainable agriculture and forestry, (*b*) energy (renewables and efficiency), and (*c*) remediation of damaged ecosystems.

With this framework in mind, the remainder of this chapter discusses one potential approach to regional improvement that intends to incorporate all of these themes into a single replicable model that could remediate thousands of mining-impacted lands and employ hundreds of unemployed and underemployed Appalachians throughout the region: reuse and remediation of surface mined lands for multifaceted agroforestry.

Over 1 million acres of the central Appalachian Mountains have been affected in some way by surface mining (Geredien 2009). From the smaller scale bench and auger (contour) operations of the 1950s and 1960s to the massive scale mountaintop removal and area mining methods employed from the mid-1970s on, the basic process has remained the same: (1) remove the trees (often without harvesting for timber), (2) drill large holes deep into the rock strata that overlay the coal seam, (3) fill the holes with powerful explosives and detonate, (4) push the exploded bedrock, or overburden, out of the way, either into nearby hollows to create valley fills or into stockpiles, (5) harvest the coal, and (6) "reclaim" the land by redistributing the stockpiled overburden over the former coal seam, intentionally compacting it with huge earthmoving machinery and spraying a mix of chemical fertilizer and seed (usually nonnative) over the compacted overburden.

The result has been a massive shift in geology, topography, hydrology, ecology, and land-use patterns throughout the region. Where there had been mixed mesophytic hardwood forests, there are now extended mesas of exotic scrub, such as tall fescue (from Europea) and *Sericea lespedeza*, autumn olive, tree of heaven, and Chinese silvergrass (from East Asia). Some game animals such as dove, rabbit, and the newly introduced Rocky Mountain elk can thrive on such cover, but many other native species, such as the threatened golden-winged

Fig. 24.1 Reclaimed mine scrubland.
Photo credit: Nathan Hall

warbler, Indiana bat, and many ecosystem health indicator species (e.g., caddisflies, water striders, and salamanders) struggle. These lands exist in a state of arrested natural succession wherein the native species have difficulty competing with the introduced exotics, and downstream water quality has suffered due to increased rates of sedimentation and erosion from compacted deforested landscapes. While schools, hospitals, and strip malls have been developed on a small percentage of these lands, most is abandoned land where unauthorized all-terrain-vehicle riding and little to no active management have become the norm.

Therefore, a significant opportunity exists to repurpose and remediate these lands in a way that equitably employs significant numbers of local people. While many potential projects can be carried out on these lands, my primary interest lies in a holistic, multifaceted approach to agroforestry that produces food and value-added products while returning the lands to native species that provide a greater variety of ecosystem services than the status quo in reclamation. The following describes the key steps in implementing such a project.

Step 1: Removal of Exotics and Land Preparation

The intensive competition from nonnative scrub and the heavy compaction of the overburden are the primary factors limiting the growth of native plant and tree species. Nonnative vegetation can be destroyed by repeated application of commercial herbicide, but this is harmful to the health of the ecosystem and is undesirable due to the damage to other plants and animals caused by broadcast

Fig. 24.2 Bulldozer ripping land.
Photo credit: Nathan Hall

application and because herbicide use precludes the land from organic certification for at least three years after application. An organic approach to exotic removal is more desirable because it can produce income without causing ecosystem damage while being as effective as the chemical approach to removal.

Two principal methods for organic exotic removal can be employed: mechanical or biological. Repeated mowing or cutting and tillage (mechanical) has higher associated costs due to fuel, equipment repair (rockiness of sites greatly increases damage to harvesting machinery), and so on, but the aboveground biomass (e.g., lespedeza hay or autumn olive woodchips) can be harvested and used for either livestock feed or for energy generation before eradication. Intensive grazing requires more active management since a solar-powered electric fence must be moved at least once per week, and thorough knowledge of animal husbandry is necessary, but it could potentially provide higher returns from meat and dairy products. Since goats, sheep, hogs, and birds prefer a complementary type of forage, they could effectively root up and decimate the exotic species.

Land preparation techniques vary based on intended use. "Ripping" will be required for areas that will be planted in woody species such as canes, vines, shrubs, and trees. "With this technique a set of 2- to 3-foot-long steel ripper shanks is pulled through the ground behind a large tractor or bulldozer, effectively breaking up the intensive compaction and allowing seedling roots to develop. This practice also reduces long-term erosion and sedimentation since rainfall is able to soak more deeply into the ground before traveling downgrade (Angel et al. 2007). Areas that will be planted in native grasses or noncompetitive grasses and legumes should have large rocks removed from the surface to avoid damaging agricultural equipment used for planting and harvesting.

Step 2: Plant Profitable Native and Noncompetitive Species

While each site plan will vary due to local postmining conditions and topography, a combination of agriculture and forestry in close proximity (i.e., alternating strips of woody plants and grasses), known as agroforestry, can create more diverse economic outputs and ecosystem benefits. For ripped areas, woody species (trees and shrubs) should be hand-planted since the post-ripping landscape is too rough and rocky for equipment. Blocks of fruit and nut species such as hazelnut, elderberry, and pawpaw can be alternated with canes and vines such as blackberry, raspberry, and grapes. Alleys between orchard rows should be planted with a mix of perennial native, or at least noninvasive, grasses, legumes, and brassicas to create a forage mix for rotationally grazed livestock species and to generate organic matter and improve soil health. Big bluestem, Canada wildrye, partridge pea, and nitro radish can be carefully managed by moving the grazing animals often enough that they do not harm the plants' ability to persist. Some areas will not be conducive to orchard establishment due to excessively steep or uneven terrain; these can be used for larger blocks of silvopastoral rotational grazing, wherein the grass and legume mix is planted with fast-growing native trees such as black locust, tulip poplar, and sycamore interspersed to regenerate soil carbon and promote ecosystem health. Certain high-value herbs such as lavender and echinacea actually prefer rocky, nutrient-poor soils, and could be integrated into the agroforestry system either in independent blocks or between the rows of woody orchard plants.

Step 3: Harvest and Utilize Outputs

Food and herbal outputs can be harvested and sold fresh in local and regional markets, or they can be processed into value-added products that will store and ship more easily. Examples include essential oils, wines, jams, pork, mutton, and sheep and goat milk products such as cheese, yogurt, soaps, and lotions. Honey bees can be intensively cultivated on these lands as well since they will collect pollen from most of the plant species mentioned. It should be noted that surface mined lands rarely have toxic contaminants present in the surface material in quantities that could affect human consumption, but any potential production site should be thoroughly tested for heavy metals before planting occurs.

An intensively managed agroforestry site will need a facility on the surface mine site for packaging, cold storage, and value-added processing. Many of these sites are at least a mile away from existing electrical infrastructure and may require an independent power source to operate. A renewable energy microgrid may be a viable option, wherein a battery backup array (such as the Tesla Powerpack) is charged by some combination of solar photovoltaic panels and biomass gasification, the latter of which involves using dry matter such as wood chips and grass pellets from invasive species as feedstocks for an electricity-producing engine system that creates carbon-sequestering biochar as its byproduct.

Step 4: Promulgate Model and Transition to Native Forest Cover

Ideally the above-mentioned processes will create a synergistic method that can be replicated throughout the surface-mined lands of central Appalachia. After establishment of a successful pilot project, intensive scaling up should occur to remediate and develop as many acres as possible and generate employment in the areas directly adjacent to project sites. The systems could be managed indefinitely since their resource utilization (soil health, productivity, etc.) is by nature and design sustainable, though the profitability of the output-based enterprises are somewhat tied to market conditions. The agroforestry approach will render the land in a much more suitable condition for native forest regeneration if active management ever ceases; the land preparation activities alone will constitute a significant remediation of these largely abandoned reclaimed lands.

Multifaceted Approach to Regional Improvement

There is no single remedy for the economic, cultural, and social challenges facing the Central Appalachian coalfields. The reuse and remediation of surface mined lands as discussed in this chapter is but one of many possible approaches to local development projects that can revitalize and rejuvenate not only the economy but also the soul and cultural identity of one of America's most misunderstood regions. Other possibilities include the development of small-scale sustainable agriculture on streambeds and river bottoms coupled with nontimber forest products from forested hillsides, the production of utility-scale solar power on surface-mined lands, and improvement of broadband internet access to facilitate new livelihoods in the technology sector in combination with, for example, agroforestry.

NATHAN HALL is an eighth-generation Appalachian from eastern Kentucky. He worked as an underground coal miner, studied at Berea College, then traveled through India, Europe, and Thailand as a Watson Fellow learning about sustainable development before becoming the reforestation coordinator for Green Forests Work. Following graduate work at Yale University in environmental management, he continues his work on sustainable economic development as the president of Reclaim Appalachia.

References

Angel, P., C. Barton, J. A. Burger, D. Graves, R. Sweigard, J. Skousen, and C. E. Zipper. 2007. *Loosening Compacted Soils on Mined Sites*. ARRI Forestry Reclamation, advisory no. 4. Pittsburgh: Appalachian Regional Reforestation Initiative.

Eller, R. 1982. *Miners, Millhands, and Mountaineers: Industrialization of the Appalachian South, 1880–1930*. Knoxville: University of Tennessee Press.

———. 2008. *Uneven Ground: Appalachia since 1945*. Lexington: University Press of Kentucky.

Geredien, R. 2009. *Assessing the Extent of Mountaintop Removal in Appalachia: An Analysis Using Vector Data*. Boone, NC: GIS Consultants.

Hansen, E., and R. McIlmoil. 2010. *The Decline of Central Appalachian Coal and the Need for Economic Diversification*. Morgantown, WV: Downstream Strategies.

Williams, J. A. 2001. *Appalachia: A History*. Chapel Hill: University of North Carolina Press.

Gone, Gonna Rise Again

Si Kahn

I remember the year that my granddaddy died
Gone, gonna rise again
They dug his grave on the mountainside
Gone, gonna rise again
I was too young to understand
The way he felt about the land
But I could read his history in his hands
Gone, gonna rise again

It's corn in the crib and apples in the bin
Gone, gonna rise again
Ham in the smokehouse and cotton in the gin
Gone, gonna rise again
Cows in the barn and hogs in the lot
You know, he never had a lot
But he worked like a devil for the little he got
Gone, gonna rise again

These apple trees on the mountainside
Gone, gonna rise again
He planted the seeds just before he died

Gone, gonna rise again
I guess he knew that he'd never see
The red fruit hanging on the tree
But he planted the seeds for his children and me
Gone, gonna rise again

High on the ridge above the farm
Gone, gonna rise again
I think of my people that have gone on
Gone, gonna rise again
Like a tree that grows in the mountain ground
The storms of life have cut them down
But the new wood springs from the roots underground
Gone, gonna rise again

CHAPTER 25

Reforestation Can Contribute to a Regenerative Economy in Global Mining Regions

Christopher D. Barton, Kenton Sena, and Patrick N. Angel

THE FORESTS OF the Appalachian region are some of the most biodiverse and valuable temperate forests of the world, but they are also some of the most threatened. Appalachian forests face challenges from invasive pests and pathogens (Ford et al. 2012; Flower et al. 2013; Anagnostakis 2001), large-scale land-use change driven by surface mining and urbanization (Wickham et al. 2013), and long-term stresses associated with climate change (Butler et al. 2015). Appalachian forests provide incredibly valuable ecosystem services and economically valuable products, including maintenance of high-quality water resources (Neary, Ice, and Jackson, 2009), flood attenuation (Negley and Eshleman 2006), carbon storage (Amichev et al., 2008; Littlefield, Arthur, and Coyne 2013), maintenance of soil health, wildlife habitat (Wickham et al. 2013), aesthetic value, ecotourism opportunity, and marketable timber and nontimber forest products (Zipper et al. 2011b). Degradation of these forests through deforestation and stresses contributing to declining forest health have been extensive; an estimated 600,000 hectares of previously forested land in Appalachia have been surface mined for coal and reclaimed to nonforest postmining land uses (Skousen and Zipper 2014; Zipper et al. 2011b; Zipper et al. 2011a). This wide-scale and long-term deforestation decreases the value of the ecosystem services and products provided, and high-quality forest restoration is necessary (Burger 2011).

Appalachian streams are also some of the most valuable in the world, home to biodiversity hotspots for crayfish, freshwater fish, salamanders, and mussels. Unfortunately, Appalachian streams are under significant stress from a legacy of surface mining, urbanization, and poor land-use management. Surface mining is the major driver of land-use change in Appalachia, contributing to wide-scale deforestation, burying hundreds of miles of streams (Bernhardt et al. 2012) and leading to long-term legacy impairments to stream water quality (Hopkins et al. 2013; Pond et al. 2014) and aquatic communities (Muncy et al. 2014; Pond et al. 2014; Smucker and Vis 2011). A study in southern West Virginia found that 6 percent of streams in the study area were buried by valley fills and 22 percent of stream miles drained watersheds heavily impacted by surface mining (Bernhardt et al. 2012). Degradation of Appalachian headwater streams has a cumulative impact on higher order streams downstream, with long-term impacts to human and nonhuman communities utilizing those water resources (Lindberg et al. 2011). Without intentional mitigation of these impacts, streams may remain heavily impaired for decades, perpetuating resource degradation into the future. While stream restoration is critical for maintenance of these and other crucial ecosystem services, stream restoration practitioners are not necessarily well acquainted with up-to-date stream restoration theory, and restored streams thus frequently fail to meet desired restoration goals (Bernhardt et al. 2005; Bernhardt and Palmer 2011; Palmer, Hondula, and Koch 2014; Palmer, Filoso, and Finelli 2014).

In addition to the environmental impacts of widespread ecological degradation, impaired ecosystems are economically devalued. Healthy ecosystems provide valuable ecosystem services, including carbon sequestration, wildlife habitat, water purification, aesthetic value, and recreational value (Benayas et al. 2009; Bullock et al. 2011). Projected total value (by 2050) of products and services provided by North American forests is estimated at $3.6–$4.1 trillion (Chiabai et al. 2011). When these valuable ecosystems are impacted, the value of the services they provide declines, posing significant economic cost on local communities inequitably burdened with this ecological impairment. In addition, the cost of drastically reduced land productivity accumulates over time, representing unrealized goods and services that could have been provided had the land been in good condition. For example, the cost of environmental damage caused by invasive species in the United States alone is estimated at $120 billion annually, including costs incurred by invasive plant, animal, and microbial species (Pimentel, Zuniga, and Morrison 2005).

Vast tracts of land in the Appalachian region and globally have been ecologically degraded, and represent both an economic burden to the affected area and an opportunity for economic diversification. While the Appalachian economy has traditionally been based in the coal industry, this industry has declined severely over recent decades, making a strong case for regional economic diversification (McIlmoil and Hansen 2010). Degraded ecosystems represent an opportunity for a "restoration economy," providing both jobs in the restoration industry via restoration work and monitoring (Holl and Howarth 2000) and improving long-term ecosystem productivity and associated goods and services (Thoemke 2016; Doyle et al. 2008; Yang et al. 2010; Tallis et al. 2008). The restoration industry is already burgeoning in the United States: stream restoration contributes over a $1 billion annually (Bernhardt et al. 2005). Forest management fuel reduction projects on national forests in the Southwest provided $40 million and 500 jobs in 2005 (Hjerpe and Kim 2008). Costs for similar fuel reduction treatments in the Southwest have been estimated at $35 to over $1,000 per acre (Rummer et al. 2003), and costs for reforesting mined land in Appalachia can be even higher ($1,000 to $2,300 per acre), with associated economic impacts and jobs to the nursery, tree planting, and geotechnical industries (Sullivan and Amacher 2013; Sullivan, Amacher, and Burger 2005). With an estimated 1.5 million acres of Appalachian surface-mined land available for reforestation, potential for economic investment in site preparation and tree planting alone (>$1,000 per acre) approaches $2 billion, not to mention associated impacts to related industries. Investment in ecological restoration breaks even or is economically profitable in most ecosystem types, with temperate forests, woodlands, and grasslands demonstrating the highest benefit–cost ratios (De Groot et al. 2013). Over time, as investment in ecosystem restoration continues to increase, this industry will continue to expand and diversify, offering jobs and extensive economic impacts to tangential industries (Aronson and Alexander 2013).

A Regional Restoration Initiative

Appalachia has experienced many hardships related to environmental degradation. At one time, virtually all of the land that has been mined in Appalachia was forested. Where once were forests, we now have abandoned grasslands that will take Mother Nature centuries to restore. Research has demonstrated that forested vegetation can be established on surface coal mines, and that it can be both productive and diverse. When properly prepared for forest vegetation, mine soils can provide a deep rooting medium and be rich in geologically derived nutrients that are capable of producing forests with growth characteristics similar to those of pre-mined native forest (Zipper, et al. 2013). Several studies (Torbert, Burger, and Daniels 1990; Angel et al. 2008; Emerson, Skousen, and Ziemkiewicz 2009; Wilson-Kokes et al. 2013; Zipper, et al.. 2013; Sena et al. 2014) have outlined best practices for planting trees on mine-impacted landscapes and the forestry reclamation approach (FRA) (see Burger et al. 2005; Burger et al. 2013) has become the accepted method for restoring forests in Appalachia.

The Appalachian Regional Reforestation Initiative, or ARRI, was created to promote the use of the FRA on active mine lands. Since the program started in 2004 over 100 million trees have been planted. In 2008, ARRI pledged the planting of 38 million trees on degraded mine land towards the United Nation's Plant for the Planet: Billion Tree Campaign—the largest pledge made in North America. By 2011 the commitment was fulfilled and great strides have been made in reversing the effects of forest loss and fragmentation in the region. Still, there is much more work to be done. We estimate that 600,000 hectares of land previously reclaimed as grasslands are in need of reforestation in Appalachia. Inspired by 2004 Nobel Peace Prize Laureate Wángari Maathai, who believed that "When we plant trees, we plant the seeds of peace and seeds of hope," a new green jobs and green economy program for the people of Appalachia called Green Forests Work (GFW) was established. As an economic development plan for Appalachia styled after the Civilian Conservation Corps of the 1930s, the GFW program will focus on restoring ecosystem services on mine-scarred lands and creating jobs in the process. Successful reestablishment of the hardwood forests that once dominated these lands will provide a renewable, sustainable multiuse resource that will create economic opportunities while enhancing the local and global environment. The jobs would include everything from nursery jobs, equipment operators, tree planters, forest managers, and wildlife biologists to managers of these sites for renewable energy and climate change mitigation.

Since the creation of GFW in 2009, many partnerships have been established with state and federal agencies, watershed groups, coal operators, conservation groups, environmental organizations, faith-based groups, and numerous universities, colleges, and K–12 schools, resulting in 273 tree planting projects and events throughout Appalachia. These events involved over 750 partner organizations and over 15,000 volunteers and participants. The result of these events and contractual for-hire services has been the planting of over 2 million trees on about 3,500 acres of previously reclaimed mine sites where reforestation was not attempted, or where the results were undesirable. These projects can empower local communities to participate in beautification and enhancement of land that is initially often abandoned. In addition, several million US dollars have been spent on these projects, which is an investment in a region of the United States that is economically distressed. The Appalachian Regional Commission has estimated that within 50 years nearly 17,000 jobs and billions of dollars in economic returns could be realized by this program.

Future Opportunities in a Global Context

Although the future of coal mining in the Appalachian region is a topic of great debate, there is no denying that coal mining production and jobs are at a 35-year low. Not only are the losses of these jobs of concern, but extraction of our region's abundant coal reserves has also negatively impacted the landscape, producing significant economic, environmental, and ecological challenges for future generations. Several recent initiatives by US state and federal governmental agencies have been implemented to facilitate the transition away from coal and provide "new" jobs in areas most affected by the downturn. What those jobs entail is a multibillion dollar question. Perhaps the forest, which largely defines coal-producing counties in Appalachia and is intertwined in the culture of the people who live there, will provide some answers. A recent analysis in the state of Kentucky revealed that the forestry industry provided nearly $13 billion to the Commonwealth's economy in 2015 and suggested that the forest industry could provide an additional $1.4 billion and over 7,000 new jobs to the region (Stringer, Ammerman, and Thomas 2015). These increases can be obtained through expanding current industries, improved use of degraded timber resources, which are abundant, as well as forest-based restoration activities on those lands affected by the mining. Restoring the forest for industrial use will certainly provide economic gain, but other societal values related to air quality, water quality, wildlife habitat, ecotourism, conservation, and hunting can also be achieved on these lands.

A reforestation program specific to the Appalachian region of the United States has been created and successfully implemented. Using basic principles of soil science, forestry, ecology, engineering, and agronomy, which are universal and applicable to multiple ecosystems, the global transferability of this program is being evaluated. Climate, geology, and soils will ultimately dictate which species are best suited for a particular ecoregion of the world, but the techniques described in the FRA as they pertain to determination of soil suitability, minimization of soil physical and chemical stressors, reduction of herbaceous competition, planting of early and late successional tree species, and use of good planting methods can be applied to surface-mined areas throughout the globe. Reforestation trials following the FRA are currently being evaluated in the Hunter Valley region of Australia (Christopher Barton, pers. comm.) and Patagonia, Chile (Eduardo Arelland, pers. comm.). As we learn from these global experiences, efforts will continue for developing a skilled green workforce to restore, protect, and manage the world's forests, which are vital to the current and future prosperity of mountainous mining regions. The inspiration provided by Wangari Maathai is encapsulated in her belief that "the act of planting a tree reconnects the human spirit to the beauty and importance of the natural world—the basis for all life on Earth." This belief is also at the heart of those who wish to return the forest to mine impacted landscapes across the globe.

CHRISTOPHER BARTON is director of the Appalachian Center and Professor in the Department of Forestry at the University of Kentucky. His research focuses on ecosystem restoration, reforestation and remediation, primarily in stream and wetland habitats and mined lands.

KENTON SENA is a PhD candidate in the Integrated Plant and Soil Sciences Program at the University of Kentucky. His research and professional experience has focused on ecological restoration, especially reforestation of mined lands. He received a National Science Foundation East Asia and the Pacific Summer Institutes fellowship.

PATRICK ANGEL, PhD, is employed since 1978 by the Office of Surface Mining Reclamation and Enforcement, US Department of the Interior, in London, Kentucky, now as senior forester and soil scientist. He promotes reforestation partnerships on active, abandoned, and legacy surface mines through the Appalachian Regional Reforestation Initiative and Green Forests Work.

References

Amichev, B. Y., J. A. Burger, and J. A. Rodrigue. 2008. "Carbon Sequestration by Forests and Soils on Mined Land in the Midwestern and Appalachian Coalfields of the U.S." *Forest Ecology and Management,* no. 256, 1949–1959.

Anagnostakis, S. 2001. "The Effect of Multiple Importations of Pests and Pathogens on a Native Tree." *Biological Invasions,* no. 3, 245–254.

Angel, P. N., C. D. Barton, R. Warner, C. Agouridis, T. Taylor, and S. Hall. 2008. "Forest Establishment and Water Quality Characteristics as Influenced by Soil Type on a Loose-Graded Surface Mine in Eastern Kentucky." In *25th National Meeting of the American Society of Mining and Reclamation,* 28–65. Lexington, KY: American Society of Mining and Reclamation.

Aronson, J., and S. Alexander. 2013. "Ecosystem Restoration Is Now a Global Priority: Time to Roll Up Our Sleeves." *Restoration Ecology,* no. 21, 293–296.

Benayas, J. M. R., A. C. Newton, A. Diaz, and J. M. Bullock. 2009. "Enhancement of Biodiversity and Ecosystem Services by Ecological Restoration: A Meta-Analysis." *Science,* no. 325, 1121–1124.

Bernhardt, E. S., B. D. Lutz, R. S. King et al. 2012. "How Many Mountains Can We Mine? Assessing the Regional Degradation of Central Appalachian Rivers by Surface Coal Mining." *Environmental Science & Technology,* no. 46, 8115–8122.

Bernhardt, E. S., and M. A. Palmer. 2011. "River Restoration: The Fuzzy Logic of Repairing Reaches to Reverse Catchment Scale Degradation." *Ecological Applications,* no. 21, 1926–1231.

Bernhardt, E. S., M. Palmer, J. Allan et al. 2005. "Synthesizing U.S. River Restoration Efforts." *Science,* no. 308, 636–637.

Bullock, J. M., J. Aronson, A. C. Newton, R. F. Pywell, and J. M. Rey-Benayas. 2011. "Restoration of Ecosystem Services and Biodiversity: Conflicts and Opportunities." *Trends in Ecology & Evolution,* no. 26, 541–549.

Burger, J. A. 2011. "Sustainable Mined Land Reclamation in the Eastern U. S. Coalfields: A Case for an Ecosystem Reclamation Approach." In *Reclamation: Sciences Leading to Success*, edited by R. I. Barnhisel, 113–141. Bismark, ND: ASMR.

Burger, J. A., D. Graves, P. N. Angel, V. M. Davis, and C. E. Zipper. 2005. *The Forestry Reclamation Approach*. Appalachian Regional Reforestation Initiative, US Office of Surface Mining. Forest Reclamation Advisory No. 2.

Burger, J. A., C. E. Zipper, P. N. Angel, N. Hall, J. G. Skousen, C. D. Barton, and S. Eggerud. 2013. "Establishing Native Trees on Legacy Surface Mines." US Office of Surface Mining. Forest Reclamation, advisory no. 11. http://arri.osmre.gov/fra.htm.

Butler, P. R., L. Iverson, F. R. Thompson et al. 2015. *Central Appalachians Forest Ecosystem Vulnerability Assessment and Synthesis: A Report from the Central Appalachians Climate Change Response Framework Project*. Gen. Tech. Rep. NRS-146. Newtown Square, Pennsylvania: U.S. Department of Agriculture, Forest Service, Northern Research Station.

Chiabai, A., C. M. Travisi, A. Markandya, H. Ding, and P. A. Nunes. 2011. "Economic Assessment of Forest Ecosystem Services Losses: Cost of Policy Inaction." *Environmental and Resource Economics,* no. 50, 405–445.

De Groot, R. S., J. Blignaut, S. Ploeg, J. Aronson, T. Elmqvist, and J. Farley. 2013. "Benefits of Investing in Ecosystem Restoration." *Conservation Biology,* no. 27, 1286–1293.

Doyle, M. W., E. H. Stanley, D. G. Havlick et al., 2008. "Aging Infrastructure and Ecosystem Restoration." *Science,* no. 319, 286–287.

Emerson, P., J. G. Skousen, and P. Ziemkiewicz. 2009. "Survival and Growth of Hardwoods in Brown versus Gray Sandstone on a Surface Mine in West Virginia." *Journal of Environmental Quality,* no. 38, 1821–1829.

Flower, C. E., K. S. Knight, J. Rebbeck, and M. A. Gonzalez-Meler. 2013. "The Relationship between the Emerald Ash Borer (Agrilus planipennis) and Ash (Fraxinus spp.) Tree Decline: Using Visual Canopy Condition Assessments and Leaf Isotope Measurements to Assess Pest Damage." *Forest Ecology and Management,* no. 303, 143–147.

Ford, C. R., K. J. Elliott, B. D. Clinton, B. D. Kloeppel, and J. M. Vose, 2012. "Forest Dynamics Following Eastern Hemlock Mortality in the Southern Appalachians." *Oikos,* no. 121 523–536.

Hjerpe, E. E., and Y-S. Kim. 2008. "Economic Impacts of Southwestern National Forest Fuels Reductions." *Journal of Forestry,* no. 106, 311–316.

Holl, K. D., and R. B. Howarth. 2000. "Paying for Restoration." *Restoration Ecology,* no. 8, 260–267.

Hopkins, R. L., B. M. Altier, D. Haselman, A. D. Merry, and J. J. White. 2013. "Exploring the Legacy Effects of Surface Coal Mining on Stream Chemistry." *Hydrobiologia,* no. 713, 87–95.

Lindberg, T. T., E. S. Bernhardt, R. Bier et al., 2011. "Cumulative Impacts of Mountaintop Mining on an Appalachian Watershed." *Proceedings of the National Academy of Sciences,* no. 108, 20929–20934.

Littlefield, T., C. Barton, M. Arthur, and M. Coyne. 2013. "Factors Controlling Carbon Distribution on Reforested Minelands and Regenerating Clearcuts in Appalachia." *Science of the Total Environment,* no. 465, 240–247.

McIlmoil, R., and E. Hansen E. 2010. *The Decline of Central Appalachian Coal and the Need for Economic Diversification.* Thinking Downstream, white paper no. 1. January 19. Morgantown, WV: Downstream Strategies.

Muncy, Breneé L., Steven J. Price, Simon J. Bonner, and Christopher D. Barton. 2014. "Mountaintop Removal Mining Reduces Stream Salamander Occupancy and Richness in Southeastern Kentucky (USA)." *Biological Conservation* 180: 115–121.

Neary, D. G., G. G. Ice, and C. R. Jackson. 2009. "Linkages Between Forest Soils and Water Quality and Quantity." *Forest Ecology and Management,* no. 258, 2269–2281.

Negley, T. L., and K. N. Eshleman. 2006. "Comparison of Stormflow Responses of Surface-Mined and Forested Watersheds in the Appalachian Mountains." *Hydrological Processes,* no. 20, 3467–3483.

Palmer, M.A., S. Filoso, and R. M. Fanelli. 2014. "From Ecosystems to Ecosystem Services: Stream Restoration as Ecological Engineering." *Ecological Engineering,* no. 65, 62–70.

Palmer, M. A., K. L. Hondula, and B. J. Koch. 2014. "Ecological Restoration of Streams and Rivers: Shifting Strategies and Shifting Goals." *Annual Review of Ecology, Evolution, and Systematics,* no. 45, 247–69.

Pimentel, D., R. Zuniga, and D. Morrison. 2005. "Update on the Environmental and Economic Costs Associated with Alien-Invasive Species in the United States." *Ecological Economics,* no. 52, 273–288.

Pond, G. J., M. E. Passmore, N. D. Pointon et al. 2014. "Long-Term Impacts on Macroinvertebrates Downstream of Reclaimed Mountaintop Mining Valley Fills In Central Appalachia." *Environmental Management,* no. 54, 919–933.

Rummer, B., J. Prestemon, D. May, et al., 2005. *A Strategic Assessment of Forest Biomass and Fuel Reduction Treatments in Western States.* Gen. Tech. Rep. RMRS-GTR-149. Fort Collins, Colorado: U.S. Department of Agriculture, Forest Service, Rocky Mountain Research Station.

Sena, K., C. Barton, P. Angel, C. Agouridis, and R. Warner. 2014. "Influence of Spoil Type on Chemistry and Hydrology of Interflow on a Surface Coal Mine in the Eastern U.S. Coalfield." *Water, Air, and Soil Pollution,* no. 225, 1–14.

Skousen, J., and C. E. Zipper. 2014. "Post-Mining Policies and Practices in the Eastern USA Coal Region." *International Journal of Coal Science & Technology,* no. 1, 135–151.

Smucker, N. J., and M. L. Vis. 2011. "Acid Mine Drainage Affects the Development and Function of Epilithic Biofilms In Streams." *Journal of the North American Benthological Society,* no. 30, 728–738.

Stringer, J., B. Ammerman, and B. Thomas. 2015. *SOAR—Analysis of the Forest Industry's Potential in Eastern Kentucky.* University of Kentucky Extension Report. https://forestry.ca.uky.edu/files/soar_forest_industry_analysis_2015.pdf

Sullivan, J., J. Aggett, G. Amacher, and J. Burger. 2005. "Financial Viability of Reforesting Reclaimed Surface Mined Lands, the Burden of Site Conversion Costs, and Carbon Payments as Reforestation Incentives." *Resources Policy,* no. 30, 247–258.

Sullivan, J., G. S. Amacher. 2013. "Optimal Hardwood Tree Planting And Forest Reclamation Policy On Reclaimed Surface Mine Lands In The Appalachian Coal Region." *Resources Policy* 38: 1–7.

Tallis, H., P. Kareiva, M. Marvier, and A. Chang. 2008. "An Ecosystem Services Framework to Support both Practical Conservation and Economic Development." *Proceedings of the National Academy of Sciences,* no. 105, 9457–9464.

Thoemke, K. W. 2016. "Career Development: Plenty of Opportunity, Plenty of Concern: The Short Term Future of the Environmental Job Market." *Environmental Practice,* no. 18, 75–77.

Torbert, J. L., J. A. Burger, and W. L. Daniels. 1990. "Pine Growth Variation Associated with Overburden Rock Type on a Reclaimed Surface Mine in Virginia." *Journal of Environmental Quality,* no. 19: 88–92.

Wickham, J., P. B. Wood, M. C. Nicholson et al., 2013. "The Overlooked Terrestrial Impacts of Mountaintop Mining." *BioScience,* no. 63, 335–348.

Wilson-Kokes, L., P. Emerson, C. DeLong, C. Thomas, and J. Skousen. 2013. "Hardwood Tree Growth after Eight Years on Brown and Gray Mine Soils in West Virginia." *Journal of Environmental Quality,* no. 42, 1353–1362.

Yang, W., B. A. Bryan, D. H. Macdonald et al., 2010. "A Conservation Industry for S ustaining Natural Capital and Ecosystem Services in Agricultural Landscapes." *Ecological Economics,* no. 69, 680–689.

Zipper, C. E., J. A. Burger, C. D. Barton, and J. G. Skousen. 2013. "Rebuilding Soils on Mined Land for Native Forests in Appalachia." *Soil Science Society of America Journal,* no. 77, 337–349.

Zipper, C. E., J. A. Burger, J. M. McGrath, J. A. Rodrigue, and G. I. Holtzman, 2011a. "Forest Restoration Potentials of Coal-Mined Lands in the Eastern United States." *Journal of Environmental Quality,* no. 40, 1567–1577.

Zipper, C. E., J. A. Burger, J. G. Skousen et al. 2011b. "Restoring Forests and Associated Ecosystem Services on Appalachian Coal Surface Mines." *Environmental Management,* no. 47, 751–765.

We're Still Here

Si Kahn

Evening hangs like smoke
On this mill town that I love
My thoughts they roll and tumble
Through the years
My heart drifts through the haze
Back to Youngstown's better days
The mills have gone away
But we're still here

We're still here
We're still here
The mills have gone away
But we're still here
With our neighbors and our kin
Right here where we've always been
The mills have gone away
But we're still here

Looking down the street
To the days when I was young
I can see my friends and neighbors
Strong and clear
People came from far away
Lives their lives from day to day

Through the good times and the hard times
We're still here

Dreaming down the days
'Til time circles home
When our children face
The future's hope and fear
Nothing went the way it should
But we did the best we could
When the whistle blows for courage
We're still here

CHAPTER 26

Palestinian Responsible Tourism for Cross-Cultural Understanding

Asma Jaber and Michel Awad

THOUGH IT HOSTS some of the world's most important religious, historical, and archaeological sites, Palestine rarely come to mind as a typical travel destination for tourists. Both comprehensive and ecofriendly, new experiential responsible tourism programs, such as hiking trails offered by the Siraj Center for Holy Land Studies in Palestine, enable deep cross-cultural exchanges while providing local residents sustainable livelihoods. The Siraj Center has driven the development of responsible tourism, while rebranding Palestine as a destination for experiential travel and human connection. Responsible tourism programs aim to engage tourists with the Palestinian people and land, while supporting local communities and going beyond the usual small number of iconic sites. Such cultural exchanges are at the center of community-based tourism in Palestine and provide unique value for excursionists and culture-seekers alike, as well as for those interested in witnessing Palestine's political situation on the ground. Still, due to travel warnings and commonly held misconceptions about Palestine, such tour programs routinely face challenges in reaching tourists.

Background

Palestine contains a high concentration of historical, religious and cultural heritage sites within a small geographic area. Approximately the size of the state of New Jersey, the country boasts an extraordinary range of ecosystems: from the fertile terraced hills of the north to the unique saline environment of the Dead Sea to the rocky Jerusalem Wilderness, Palestine has diverse offerings for cultural tourism.

Unfortunately, for the majority of visitors who travel through traditional tour operators to the Holy Land, their contact with local Palestinian communities is fleeting. While these tours stop in Bethlehem and Jericho, both of which are majority-Palestinian cities, their time there consists of quick, uninformative bus excursions. Little cultural exchange occurs, as tour operators fail to integrate the stories and livelihood of the indigenous Palestinian communities into the tourists' experience. Furthermore, the majority of the profits do not reach the community, and only a few private individuals benefit from the enterprise. Conventional tourism also ignores the contemporary culture and political realities of life in Palestine. Responsible programs, by contrast, invite visitors to deepen their understanding of the country's complex social and political landscape by meeting with and working alongside local people (PIRT n.d.). Responsible forms of tourism offer communities opportunities to share their cultures, tell their stories, request solidarity, and foster tolerance and greater understanding.

While tourists certainly discover the beauty, spirituality, and hospitality of the country, they also encounter some of the political, economic, and social realities that shape the daily lives of Palestinians. Such a genuine experiencing of both tourists and their Palestinian hosts serves to form a rich relationship between the two (PIRT n.d.). Responsible tourism programs aim to engage tourists with the Palestinian people and land to support local communities, while decreasing the exploitation of a small number of iconic sites. At the core of responsible tourism is respecting, protecting, and benefiting local communities, cultural heritage, and the environment. While tourists expect a life-changing experience when visiting the region's holy sites, the Siraj Center has learned that, through responsible experiential tourism in which cross-cultural exchanges are at the center, participation in Palestinian village life, family, food, and traditions becomes the life-changing experience. In light of the growing number of responsible community tourism operations, such as hiking and biking tour programs, Palestine's hidden gems are becoming increasingly accessible. More important, both local communities and the tourists are benefiting. Palestinian community members benefit economically by housing guests and participating in guiding expeditions and they benefit experientially by engaging in a unique opportunity to welcome visitors from across the world into their homes. By choosing socially responsible tour itineraries, visitors to Palestine have a hospitable, meaningful experience as they build connections with Palestinian people and gain knowledge about an otherwise unknown culture.

Hiking as Community-Based Tourism

The use of nonmotorized transport, such as hiking, virtually assures that tourism benefits will be decentralized and of broader benefit to tourists and local communities (Ibike Cultural Immersion, n.d.). Walking tours provide an enriching and well-rounded educational experience while bringing visitors deeper into the community and providing them the opportunity to support local businesses. With the barriers that accompany traveling via motor vehicles eliminated, walking and bicycling are ideal modes for learning, engaging with the community and environment, and supporting the hyperlocal economy. Walking and biking paths in Palestine often run through small peripheral villages and offer windows into local cultures and lifestyles that are unlike anything offered in regional urban centers. The primary reason for creating trails in Palestine is to enhance engagement between local communities and international visitors, which provides benefits for both sides.

The Siraj Center is one of three cofounders of Masar Ibrahim, a nonprofit with a mission to develop and promote community-based tourism in Palestine. The Siraj Center currently has three long-distance trails across Palestine, ranging up to 340 kilometers (Abraham's Path, the Samaritan Trail, and the Nativity Trail), and a network of shorter walks, from gentle afternoon strolls to challenging desert scrambles. Masar Ibrahim also works on development projects, such as enhancing the protection of local production processes and products, like embroidery. Together, Siraj Center and Masar Ibrahim provide programs centered on hiking and biking, as well as interfaith, cultural, educational, and political issues.

Cross-Cultural Understanding

Tourism is not merely an economic and commercial activity, it is also one of the world's principal instruments for human interaction (WTO 2011). Culture is an important dimension of tourism, both as an attraction for visitors and as a characteristic that influences visitor behavior and interaction with a destination's residents (Kang and Moscardo 2006). In the era of global tourism, greater cross-cultural awareness and understanding, which leads to acceptance of cultural differences, is very much needed. Triggering intercultural dialogue lies at the core of responsible tourism, as it leads to mutual understanding, helping tourists understand and appreciate other cultures and better understand their own.

Responsible tourism programs are designed such that they integrate visitors into the regular daily activities of the locals, who offer a wide window into the local culture. For example, as simple as it is, a tourist having a traditional meal with a Palestinian host is a great opportunity to experience the local cuisine while sharing personal and national histories and values. During hikes, which are led by local community guides, tourists have more opportunities to meet local Palestinians and encounter authentic Palestinian experiences than they would with a large commercial operator. The local guide's role is to accompany travelers along their journey, enriching their experience with information about the places they visit and the nature and landscape they encounter along the way. Since the hiking and biking trails of the Siraj Center are designed by local community members, the trails pass through local village stores, creating more opportunities for interactions between locals and visitors. Although not itself a cooperative, the Siraj Center works with several cooperatives, such as a women's center in Jericho, that regularly hosts visitors for meals and provides mud houses for visitors to stay overnight. In this case, income goes directly to the cooperative. Such programs, which create opportunities for meaningful communication and mutual understanding, can operate as a vehicle to appreciate foreign cultures. Furthermore, responsible tourism has the potential to bridge cultural and psychological distances that separate people of different races, religions, and socioeconomic classes (UNH n.d.).

Although responsible tourism plays a major role in bridging cultural boundaries through tourists-host interactions, it is also possible for cultural misunderstandings to emerge between hosts and guests caused by differences in behavior or perceptions. Although tourists may read various publications about Palestine beforehand, many Palestinian behaviors, norms, and frequently used expressions may still remain unknown to tourists. This could include attitudes and behaviors regarding religion and family, manners, facial expressions, and gestures.

Before visitors have contact with the host families, responsible tourism operators like the Siraj Center educate them that tourism activities should be conducted in harmony with traditions of the hosts and with respect for their practices, customs, and laws. At the same time, the host communities acquaint themselves with and show respect for the tourists who visit them and learn about their culture. The host families often undergo training during which various cultural behaviors and preferences of the potential visitors are presented and discussed in depth (Picard 2006). In this regard, local community guides play a crucial role, as they become the connection between the visitors and other members of their communities; they are often the key to visitors learning about local traditions and habits. For visitors who hold a negative view of Palestine and Palestinians prior to visiting, such interactions with hosts and local guides can change their perceptions completely. Most visitors realize the harsh reality of life under occupation, as they travel on the same trails and roads as Palestinians, encountering numerous checkpoints where Israeli forces can delay them for hours. The local community also feels empowered to realize its role in changing perceptions and educating international visitors about community traditions and the difficulty of life under military occupation.

Responsible Tourism Empowers Local Village Families

Responsible tourism is the vehicle for promoting lesser known destinations that complement visitors' experience in Palestine. The programs are designed to help explore Palestine's heritage in the company of experts and, of course, local people. The true strength of the programs are the local hosts and guides, who are an integral part of the tourism experience and are involved even in the early planning stages. For example, the Siraj Center and its partners did not rely on maps when initially planning the hiking trails. Instead, team members visited every nearby village council and sought advice about what path to take to a neighboring city or village. The Siraj Center and its partners did not work from "map to implementation"; rather, the work flowed from the local community to implementation on a map. Many of these local village families ended up becoming hosts or guides; thus, it was many of the host families themselves who decided the direction of the hiking trails. Accordingly, much of the success of the Siraj Center and its partners' hiking trails is a direct result of the host families establishing the paths of the trails through the areas they know best.

For these local communities, the hiking and biking trails brought tangible benefits to an area not traditionally involved with tourism due to their distance from traditional holy sites and related pilgrimage programs. Supporting responsible tourism initiatives has resulted in sustainable economic impact in marginalized regions of Palestine. Palestine's network of homestays is a vivid realization of community involvement in tourism development. The infrastructure required to accommodate visitors provides employment for large groups of community members. One of the local guides, Nidal, said, "Working with the Siraj Center allowed for my children to attend university in Palestine." Nidal is from a refugee camp near the West Bank city of Nablus and has six children. Prior to becoming a host and local guide, he worked with rehabilitation centers for people with disabilities, where he had a very limited income. Working as a guide enabled him to send three of his children to study at Birzeit University, the most prestigious four-year university in Palestine. One of his children recently graduated and is now working as a nurse. Nidal states emphatically that, "To have educated children is the most important goal for a Palestinian." He attributes his ability to achieve this goal to the responsible tourism industry. Furthermore, women are often the main hosts, as they cook meals for travelers and welcome visitors to stay the night in their family homes. This arrangement provides a unique opportunity for women to help support families in which the man may have been the sole provider of income.

Visitors can participate in local activities, such as learning how to bake bread over a fire or preparing a traditional dish. They may find themselves dancing at a traditional village wedding or partaking in a birthday celebration. These entry points into the daily life of community members humanize the region's people in a way that the media can never do. Also, responsible tourism packages often try to include rural and community-based festivals, which are platforms for cultural exchange and interaction between the visitors and the local community. Cultural heritage, agriculture, and harvest festivals in Palestine are more than an activity, they are innate representations of identity, traditions, and civilization, and serve as vehicles for the sustainability of cooperatives and artisans. These events also bring together some of the best Palestinian produce, artwork, textiles, glass, olive wood, and ceramics.

Challenges

Although there is no record of a tourist being harmed, there remains a strong false negative perception of Palestine as a destination for travel (Riyada Consulting 2016), a direct result of US and European media rarely showing Palestine in a positive manner (Rashid 2003). Unfortunately, the media's portrayal of places in the Middle East such as Palestine is usually accepted as "true" by viewers from the United States and Europe. Because the media functions as a main source of stereotypes and images associated with the Middle East, it can turn locations like Palestine into areas of concern among American and European tourists (Kaefer 2014). This makes quite difficult the work of recruiting tourists, especially school groups who must ensure the safety of students. The Siraj Center and its partners utilize international forums, church groups, tour operators, and school groups to advertise offerings to American and European travelers. To overcome the negative impact of travel warnings, organizations like the Siraj Center rely on spreading the word through previous visitors and testimonials from past trip participants to alleviate fear of danger.

The main challenge for responsible tourism in Palestine is Israel's military occupation, which impedes operations because Palestinians do not have access to borders and are under severe movement and building restrictions. For example, the Siraj Center and its partners were unable to develop trails in certain areas of the West Bank that are marked as restricted military areas. Such areas constitute 60 percent of the West Bank. Development in these areas would result in almost immediate demolition of any structures. Furthermore, nomadic Bedouin communities, although willing, are not allowed by the Israeli forces to develop and extend their tents to welcome visitors. Such movement and access restrictions impede development and expansion of tourism. Since little information about everyday life under Israeli occupation is portrayed in the US and European media, through offerings like those of the Siraj Center, Americans and Europeans can learn counternarratives.

Student-Led Responsible Justice Tourism

Responsible tourism, alternative tourism, and justice tourism are on the rise, especially among university students. These travelers seek an authentic experience to understand political and economic issues first hand and gain knowledge and further their future careers. Over the past five years, approximately 600 Harvard University graduate students traveled through the Siraj Center on Harvard student–led responsible tourism "treks" to Palestine. English-speaking tour guides from Harvard who had built relationships with hosts in Palestine beforehand were ambassadors to their fellow students. The ambassadors and the Palestinian hosts developed a justice-based curriculum together and implemented it within just 10 days. Students met with community leaders, human rights activists, businessmen and women, and politicians to learn what life is like for Palestinians under occupation. Often these trips consisted of home-stays, dining with local families, and traveling via roads and checkpoints on which ordinary Palestinians travel. Students return to the United States and share their findings with their peers back home.

There are other justice-minded trips similar to the Harvard Trek, such as the Boston College and Swarthmore College winter session (an undergraduate seminar led by a faculty member) and Go Palestine! (aimed at high school juniors and seniors of Palestinian descent who have never visited the region). These student-focused educational excursions have one common goal: to provide an authentic experience of what life is like for Palestinians.

Conclusion

The community and local guides are not simply an "offering"—they are at the core of responsible tourism. For those trying to organize similar tourism trails in other regions, community partnerships and authentic encounters with local people and cultures should remain at the center of the work. One should invest in these communities and genuinely enable them to become the core part of responsible tourism. When the local community trusts the organizers, tourists and the community arrive at the best experience.

MICHEL AWAD is an instructor at Bethlehem University and cofounder and executive director of Siraj Center for Holy Land Studies. He has represented Siraj Center as a member of the Steering Committee for the Palestinian Initiative for Responsible Tourism (PIRT) and the Network of Experiential Palestinian Tourism.

ASMA JABER is a student in the Harvard Law School, focusing on human rights advocacy. As a Palestinian-American entrepreneur inspired by Palestinian historic preservation efforts, she founded PIVOT, which allows users to see what a place looked like in the past using augmented and virtual reality. Earlier, she worked with the US Department of Justice Civil Rights Division and received her master's degree in public policy from Harvard's Kennedy School of Government.

References

Ibike Cultural Immersion. n.d. "Program Philosophy." Accessed May 15, 2017. http://www.ibike.org/ibike/philosophy.htm.

Kaefer, F. 2014. "Credibility at Stake? News Representations and Discursive Constructions of National Environmental Reputation and Place Brand Image: The Case of Clean, Green New Zealand." PhD diss., University of Waikato, New Zealand. http://researchcommons.waikato.ac.nz/handle/10289/8834.

Kang, Mihee, and Gianna Moscardo. 2006. "Exploring Cross-Cultural Differences in Attitudes towards Responsible Tourist Behaviour: A Comparison of Korean, British and Australian Tourists." *Asia Pacific Journal of Tourism Research* 11 (4): 303–320.

PIRT (Palestinian Initiative for Responsible Tourism). n.d. *The Context of Palestine.* Accessed May 15, 2017. http://www.pirt.ps/index.php?lang=en&page=123961689323.

Picard, David. 2006. *Tourism, Culture and Sustainable Development.* UNESCO. Accessed May 15, 2017. http://unesdoc.unesco.org/images/0014/001475/147578e .pdf,.

Rashid, S. 2003. *The Role of the International Media in the Palestinian-Israeli Conflict, Electronic Intifada.* Accessed June 26, 2016. https://electronicintifada.net/content /role-international-media-palestinian-israeli-conflict/4853.

Riyada Consulting. 2016. *Final Report 2016: Research Data Collection and Monitoring and Evaluation.* Abraham Path Initiative.

UNH (University of New Hampshire). n.d. Tourism and Global Understanding. Accessed May 12, 2017. http://courses.unh.edu/class/201650/51275.

WTO (World Tourism Organization). 2011. "Tourism—Linking Cultures." Accessed May 9, 2017. http://wtd.unwto.org/en/content/about-theme -tourism-linking-cultures.

A Time for Us All

Si Kahn

There's snow in the mountains
Winter's coming hard
But there's supper on the table
And dogs in the yard
The season is keeping
Its reason and rhyme
It's all in the timing
And all in the time

I am ready, I am ready
There's a time for us all
I am ready, I am ready
There's a time for us all

You can shout for justice
Stand all alone
But the power is greatest
When you stand with your own
For there's strength to sustain us
In all that we do
When we raise our expectations
To the power of two

You can work every issue
Take every stand
But morning is brighter
When you live hand in hand
You can make every meeting
Speak every part
But evening is sweeter
When you walk heart to heart

So read through the contract
Sign on the line
For this is the season
And now is the time
To join in this union
Though the numbers are small
When love's on the table
It's the finest of all

CHAPTER 27

Conclusion

CONVERSATIONS TOWARD THE
FUTURE IN GLOBAL MOUNTAIN REGIONS

Felix Bivens, Sasikumar Balasundaram, and Ann Kingsolver

WHETHER IN AFRICA, Asia, North America, or South America, mining and resource extraction appear as drivers of poverty, displacement, and violence rather than as forces of inclusive development. Marginalization of mountain regions is a form of structural violence that can be traced back to colonialism (*New Pittsburgh Courier* 2005). Many of the chapters in this volume exemplify these long roots of current challenges in mountain regions. While observing widespread reproduction of this global pattern, we also see the possibilities for resistance that grow from the alternative ways of knowing and building livelihoods that are evident in mountain communities across the world (Fisher 1993). The environmental justice movement documented in chapter 10, indigenous political actions leading to substantive political change documented in chapters 6 and 7, and communities exploring new livelihood possibilities described in chapters 19 through 26 provide examples of such possibilities. As activist scholars from marginalized regions, we see universities and other public institutions as having responsibilities to support mountain communities through research collaboration, exchanges, and community engagement globally and locally, joining dialogues already underway in those communities on current issues and future directions. Mountain communities, as this volume demonstrates, share not only many common histories and challenges—including the double burden of bearing the costs of the extractive practices that marginalized them in the first place—but also great potential for contributing to discussions of place-based postcapitalist livelihoods. Artists are important to envisioning futures in global mountain regions, as the poetry of Crystal Good and Jeremy Paden, the paintings of Pam Oldfield Meade, and the lyrics of Si Kahn threaded through this volume attest.

Land, Development, and State Violence

Since the beginning of the Industrial Revolution, mountain regions have been a primary target for the extraction of raw materials or cash crops. On the one hand, colonizers saw mountains as backward regions needing to be civilized; on the other hand, capitalists saw mountains as resource sites and assigned market value to them (Billings, Norman, and Ledford 1999). Both colonial and capitalist notions of understanding land have significantly influenced the way mountains are understood predominantly in state discourses today. Indigenous conceptualizations of human-environment relationships, featuring strongly throughout this volume, demonstrate that what many may call an alternative or new way of thinking is not new at all. If commons-based (cf. Reid and Taylor 2010) approaches had remained dominant, rather than being marginalized through capitalist logic and practice, there would be no need for Earth Day gatherings or protests in nations' capitals or at the United Nations to protect indigenous and mountain communities from expulsions (Sassen 2014) due to land grabbing and extractive industries. Oxfam International (2016), an advocacy NGO working on global poverty, has well documented the link between land grabs and poverty across several continents, yet long-term structural accountability does not generate the same news coverage as the drama of seemingly self-induced dispossession from "modernity."

This is not to say that there is a divide between mountain and indigenous communities and capitalism. As chapters in this book have demonstrated, there are complex strategies of capitalist engagement in all communities, and members of communities differ in political and economic views. What we are emphasizing in this global mountain region project—joining many other voices—is a conversation between those who valorize a social and environmental bottom line and the stewarding of resources for future generations rather than the dominant valorization in capitalist terms, emphasizing immediate profit margins for shareholders and financial bottom lines. There are many discussions of how these different bottom lines play out in relation to social movements and ways forward (cf. Rixecker and Tipene-Matua 2003; Isenhour, McDonogh, and Checker 2015; Kingsolver 2008; Shiva 2002; Johnston and Jorgensen 1994; Martinez-Alier 2003).

In recent decades, mountain regions have again become the new frontiers for corporate interests and battle zones for environmentalists. Corporations, governments, and environmentalists all are seeing the aesthetic and latent financial value in pristine mountain areas. Ecotourism, once a hopeful experiment of the Green movement, has moved from small-scale operations to large-scale corporate developments. In the early 2000s, Felix Bivens—who facilitated the plenary discussion of sustainable futures at the Global Mountain Regions Conference in 2012—did some community-based work on ecotourism in Monteverde, Costa Rica, and shares these observations. Monteverde is a strong example of how ecotourism could support local growth and prosperity. However, residents have been in a persistent struggle with the government and major developers who have wanted to scale up the tourism industry there and build massive resorts on the margins of the fragile cloud forest ecosystem. In the 1990s and early 2000s, community members staged mass demonstrations to stop government road crews from paving the single road up the mountain to the Monteverde community with the hope that as long as the road remained unpaved and challenging to navigate, larger scale development would remain too difficult and costly.

In another example, in 2012 the Indian government had to introduce a buffer zone in the Andaman Islands to protect the tribal members from being killed by tourists (Singh 2012). In 2014, Indian newspapers widely reported that ecotourists had sexually abused Jarawa tribal members in the Andaman Islands (Chamberlain 2014). Even though there is evidence that small-scale ecotourism helps local economy and communities, corporatization of ecotourism can endanger the identity and survival of indigenous people because of commodification and objectification of indigeneity.

Chapters in this volume have documented community-led experiences in economy development, but in many places corporate interests in ecotourism are getting much stronger and much more blatant. For example, in the Indian state of Odisha, the state government is in the process of trying to seize a 3,500-acre piece of property from a Dalit (oppressed) group that has lived in the area for generations. The business plan for the area includes a 27-hole golf resort that will sit on top of the mountain and occupy forest land that has until now provided livelihoods to residents threatened with expulsion. Meanwhile, as Annapurna Devi Pandey discusses in chapter 7, mining continues to be an issue in these same areas. Vedanta Limited has been fighting for the removal of Niyamgiri hilltops for 17 millions tons of bauxite. For centuries, the Kondhs revered the Niyamgiri Hills as their god who provides food and protection. The Kondhs fear what happened to the neighboring community in Lanjigarh, where Vedanta had established an aluminum refinery. Before the arrival of the factory, people of Lanjigarh had a subsistence lifestyle similar to the Kondhs', but now the vast majority of the people are living in impoverished villages and depend on aid. Kondh communities have refused to accept any false development initiative or any compensation. The conflict between a small group (just over 8,000) of indigenous people and one of the most powerful mining companies in the world, backed by the state, has become a symbol of resistance to neoliberal government policies and the unrestrained power and violence of corporations.

This wide-scale attention has sparked positive developments such as the emergence of Foil Vedanta (n.d.), a global network of activists from Delhi to London who are working through various legal channels to block Vedanta's development of new extraction sites. In a recent documentary, *Mine: Story of a Sacred Mountain* (n.d.), made by Survival International, an indigenous rights' advocacy organization, a young Kondh boy holding a traditional axe defends the fight against Vedanta saying "where will us children go? How will we survive? No. We won't give up our mountain." The small group has had surprising success against the powerful company, though on the ground in Odisha this has created a backlash, with the government ratcheting up violence against local groups and activists. Similar state violence in support of mining interests is common across mountain regions, as contributors to this volume have discussed.

Mountain Knowledge: An Epistemology of Place

While people in places like Niyamgiri are engaged in a forceful fight against the control of mountain land by the state and corporations, young people in other places like Appalachia are engaged in silent protests by creating alternative local economies and livelihoods. For example, some young people in Appalachian Kentucky are engaged in projects including reforestation, organic farming, media production, and the creation of mountain trails, museums, and art districts. Felix Bivens has worked with Marie Cirillo and the Clearfork Community Institute in Eagan, Tennessee, helping develop a program for community-led action research (CLAR), in which the research themes and projects are selected and carried out by young people in the community. Many of the projects have focused on ways to improve the local economy. Over time, young people in the group have come to question the dominant system of the cash economy and the devastating impact that coal mining has had on their community, families, and landscape. Concomitantly, they have recognized that being "cash poor" does not equate to poverty in all things, and that in many ways their valley and their community have resources, relationships, and traditions that have potential for sustainable livelihoods. Young people living in mountain regions, including Nathan Hall (author of chap. 24), have been arguing for an economy that goes beyond creating jobs to recognizing the "soul" and identity of the region itself. In other words, a noncapitalist economy that ensures the well-being of both people and the environment.

In Bivens' decade-long work on the Cumberland Plateau near Sewanee, Tennessee, he has frequently been struck by the lack of attention paid to rural areas, particularly if they are not an active part of the industrial agricultural economy, as is the case with many mountain communities. Stakeholders in the media, foundations, and universities all have a strongly urban bias in their interests. Moreover, policies created by the state and federal government to help mountain areas are often crafted with so little understanding of rural realities that the impacts of these policies are often a net negative rather than a net positive—the Clearfork Valley being a clear example, as this one unincorporated community is fractured across four counties, two states, and two development districts, the result being a lack of coherence in the policies that impact the area.

In recent participatory research, Bivens and others have focused on rural-urban knowledge divides and on how knowledge is created and valued as a critical part of the project of social justice. Through working in various mountain regions globally, he finds that these regions are the most marginalized in current political and economic systems. Likewise, he sees that the recognized, dominant engines of knowledge production are also often far from rural and mountain areas. Dipak Pant makes a similar argument in chapter 20, based on his research with people in marginalized regions. Knowledge economy hubs are in large cities. Think tanks and research universities, too, tend to be located in cities. As a result, the knowledge that is produced through these structures often has an urban bias and an ignorance of rural realities. Given the decline in government funding for universities and the increasing reliance on corporate support for research, even public university research is increasingly capitalistic in its function and serves the dominant economic paradigm.

Building on Stanley D. Brunn and Maria Paradiso's geographies of knowledge concept (chapter 14), Bivens also wonders if there might be a related concept of "epistemology of place knowledge and worldview" that is intimately shaped and reflected by a landscape and people's interactions with it. As with others included or mentioned in this volume, Bivens explores ways of thinking and knowing that can be broadly characterized as "mountain knowledge" and may be key to drawing connections between the many ways that different mountain communities function and how they organize themselves in response to the challenges that threaten their relationships with the land and, as a result, their traditions and livelihoods.

Looking toward the Future of Globalizing Mountain Studies

Interdisciplinary programs including area studies and international studies have waxed and waned in popularity within universities. As a result of austerity programs and neoliberal corporate restructuring of public universities in recent years they either have been cut because they are considered nonessential, or interdisciplinarity has been emphasized in response to administrative cost-cutting, leading to the combining of separate disciplinary departments into larger units. For those who are engaged in working in mountain regions, there is an opportunity—also by leveraging new media in the same way that social movements do—to globalize mountain studies and place marginalized voices at the center of interdisciplinary conversations. As climate change, environmental justice, organic food production and food justice, and sustainable livelihoods have become central themes in discussions about creating a better future for the next generation across many nations, mountain studies can play a crucial role—especially in bringing into the same frame social justice (like the Black Lives Matter and Native Lives Matter movements) and environmental justice concerns.

In a time when respectful conversations across opposing or differing viewpoints seem to be occurring less and less, rural and mountain communities have much to contribute to urban and university partners in showing them how to have these respectful discussions and move forward with conversations about the future. (Residents of rural communities are interconnected in many different ways and cannot simply "unfriend" one another and avoid conflict [Kingsolver 2011].) University–community partnerships can serve as meshworks (Harcourt 2003), that is, they do not always have to share an agenda completely but can serve as partners in projects with convergent goals and as allies in a much broader political sense, publicizing challenges faced in mountain regions and actively building the knowledge and capacity—moving equally in both directions—to resist the forces that are inflicting damage on a region and its people. There are a number of global mountain networks (including the one reflected in this volume) working to build a larger set of resources for those engaged in often-isolating struggles and to share the agentive solutions being implemented in so many mountain sites. Throughout the conference in 2012, particularly on the last day, we heard scholars and community members representing global mountain region communities calling unanimously for establishing global solidarity among mountain communities. Everyone agreed on the vital role young people are playing in the creation of alternative development planning processes and possibilities for mountain regions. Mobilizing young people from different communities to talk to one another through social media, a tool millennial youth widely use to organize, has since proven to be an effective platform for comparing notes on shared experiences of histories, traditions, marginalization, and the force of resistance and resilience. Cell phones, Twitter, Facebook, Skype, Instagram, and YouTube are being used to share stories and organize specific mobilizations globally and are crossing borders more effectively than was done in previous generations.

It is vital to use existing resources and networks to advance the concerns and strategies of mountain communities—rather than beginning a new website, we refer readers to many existing resources. The Mountain Partnership, for example, emerging from the 2002 International Year of Mountains, is a voluntary United Nations initiative that "addresses the challenges facing mountain regions by tapping the wealth and diversity of resources, knowledge, information, and experience, from and between its members, in order to stimulate concrete initiatives at all levels that will ensure improved quality of life and environments in the world's mountain regions."[1] Resources available through this initiative can be useful to mountain communities in communicating across global regions. Survival International (n.d.) is another useful platform for indigenous youth to advocate for their rights. There are many crises to be addressed collectively. Mountain regions are, for example, extremely vulnerable to the effects of global warming. Rural–urban and highland–lowland coalitions are vital in work to protect mountain ecosystems.

As Sasikumar Balasundaram learned as a young person in a financially resource-scarce mountain community, action for positive social change can be on any level and make a difference. Since most children could not do schoolwork because there was no electricity and candles were expensive, he organized a young persons' collective that made small cost-efficient free oil lamps that could be shared by households to make studying in the evening possible. A decade later, he is no longer the only student from his tea plantation to go to university. Now he is teaching university students and has these final observations about young people connecting across mountain regions to envision futures. Having worked with millennial youth so closely for the last several years, he sees them as an activist generation. Regardless of the rural-urban divide, or of gender and sexual identities, racial and ethnic backgrounds, nationalities, or political affiliations, many young people across borders are driven by creativity and commitment to social change, seeing the seemingly impossible as possible. Young people from mountain regions disproportionately serve in their nations' militaries, sometimes in conflicts that counter their own communities' interests, and have been hit hard by unemployment and a new heroin epidemic, for example; and still, many find positive ways to connect with each other across numerous divides. Short-term exchanges like the ones described in chapters 16, 17, 18, and 26 and longer term ones like those described in chapters 2, 11, 12, 14, 20, 21, and 22 can facilitate such connections, especially if they are made continually more inclusive.

The commitment of the Sinhalese and Tamil youth alliance in Sri Lanka to reconciliation after three decades of civil war, Hindu youths' fight for the rights of Muslims and Dalits in India, the undocumented youth who come out unafraid in the United States, the majority of white American youth who overwhelmingly elected the first black president of the United States, the Black Lives Matter movement, the Jewish and non-Jewish Youth Coalition for Justice for Palestine, the Austrian and German young people who wait day and night at railway stations to welcome refugees from Syria, the Native American youth who have fought against the Keystone Pipeline, the Dongriya Kondh children fighting against corporate invasion of their land, the Gujarat Dalit youth who refuse to do caste-based jobs, the Arab youth uprising for social and political change, US youth engagement in political revolutions for economic justice from Occupy Wall Street to "Feel the Bern" (support for Bernie Sanders in the 2016 election) movements, Rising Appalachia, and students working everywhere to address inequalities in their home areas—these are just a few examples of youth activism.

Many millennial youth reject the entrenched oppositions of dominant ideologies and are committed to working for an alternative agenda and finding some common ground. Of course, many of the problems discussed in this book are rooted in social and economic structural injustices and require structural solutions. Whether it was Rosa Parks' refusal to give up her seat, Indians' refusal to pay the salt tax during the British colonial era, undocumented youth refusing to be defined by fear of deportation (similar to the displaced described by Daniel Joseph in chapter 9), or workers and students protesting across the world in 1968—all have brought structural changes in big and small ways. The history of social movements shows us that everyday acts can initiate enduring structural changes.

Mountain communities should matter to everyone on the planet, not only because of climate change and watershed issues, but also because young people are creatively and persistently looking for ways forward, inspiring their elders. From the international, intergenerational, and interdisciplinary conversation we had in the Global Mountain Regions Conference—a conversation that has continued—it is evident that local mountain communities all across the world are challenging dominant structures in creative ways. Given that such gatherings are expensive and by their nature exclude many, in keeping with the challenge in this volume of the very capitalist models through which inequalities and marginalities have been sustained, it will be useful to continue to use platforms for cross-border conversations that minimize inequalities in access (including language). Using social media can be an alternative and affordable tool—which millennial youth already widely use—to organize a strong platform for the diverse voices of a global mountain community shaped by shared histories, traditions, experiences of marginalization, and the forces of resistance and resilience, recognizing the uneven access noted by Brunn and Paradiso in chapter 14. Everyday topics like food that put everyone on equal footing can be a way into challenging stereotypes and opening up conversation, even when people do not share a language, as we found in many situations during the Global Mountain Regions Conference.

As Sasikumar Balasundaram noticed on the streets of Mumbai at the 2004 World Social Forum—a consciously alternative and antihegemonic globalization movement advocating for a different world order—one thing that was very obvious was the diversity of its participants. Young and old, straight and gay, citizens and stateless, workers and managers, women and men, people who identify in many ways ethnically or racially, and people of all continents and languages gathered to voice that "another world is possible." The other world is possible not because of a single solution, but through millions of solutions that everyday people across the world have invented. Similarly, what young people are doing across mountain region communities is weaving a future—not a simplistically hopeful one, but one with generative possibilities. This is everyday work in global mountain regions. As Arundhati Roy (n.d.) said in her 2003 World Social Forum speech: "Another world is not only possible, she is on her way. On a quiet day, I can hear her breathing."

FELIX BIVENS is founder and director of Empyrean Research, a community-based research organization dedicated to enhancing the research and learning capacities of social change organizations and to working with higher education institutions to build better community–university partnerships.

SASIKUMAR BALASUNDARAM is Assistant Professor of Anthropology at Southern Illinois University, Edwardsville. His research interests include refugees, humanitarian aid, global health, engaged anthropology with children and youth, and contemporary issues of the Up-country Tamils of Sri Lanka.

ANN KINGSOLVER is Professor of Anthropology and past director of the Appalachian Center and Appalachian Studies Program at the University of Kentucky. Her research in the United States, Mexico, and Sri Lanka has focused on how people make sense of all that gets called "globalization" and act on those understandings. Her books include *NAFTA Stories: Fears and Hopes in Mexico and the United States*, *Tobacco Town Futures: Global Encounters in Rural Kentucky*, and several edited volumes.

Note

1. See the full text at http://www.mountainpartnership.org/about/en/, accessed May 15, 2017.

References

Billings, Dwight B., Gurney Norman, and Katherine Ledford. 1999. *Back Talk from Appalachia: Confronting Stereotypes*. Lexington: University Press of Kentucky.

Chamberlain, Gethin. 2014. "Jarawa Tribe Now Face Sexual Abuse by Outsiders on the Andaman Islands." *Guardian*. Accessed August 6, 2016. https://www.theguardian.com/world/2014/feb/01/andaman-islands-jarawa-sex-abuse-outsiders.

Fisher, Stephen. 1993. *Fighting Back in Appalachia: Traditions of Resistance and Change*. Philadelphia: Temple University Press.

Foil Vedanta. n.d. "Foil Vedanta." Accessed August 6, 2016. http://www.foilvedanta.org/.

Harcourt, Wendy. 2003. "The Impact of Transnational Discourses on Local Community Organizing." *Development: Journal of the Society for International Development* 46 (1): 74–79.

Isenhour, Cindy, Gary McDonogh, and Melissa Checker, eds. 2015. *Sustainability in the Global City: Myth and Practice*. Cambridge: Cambridge University Press.

Johnston, Barbara Rose, and Daniel Jorgensen. 1994. "Mineral Development, Environmental Degradation, and Human Rights: The Ok Tedi Mine, Papua New Guinea."

In *Who Pays the Price? The Sociocultural Context of Environmental Crisis*, edited by Barbara Rose Johnston, 86–98. Washington, DC: Island.

Kingsolver, Ann. 2008. "'As We Forgive Our Debtors': Mexico's *El Barzón* Movement, Bankruptcy Policy in the U.S., and Ethnography of Neoliberal Logic and Practice." *Rethinking Marxism* 20 (1): 13–27.

———. 2011. *Tobacco Town Futures: Global Encounters in Rural Kentucky*. Long Grove, IL: Waveland.

Martinez-Alier, Joan. 2003. "Mining Conflicts, Environmental Justice and Valuation." In *Just Sustainabilities: Development in an Unequal World*, edited by Julian Agyeman, Robert D. Bullard, and Bob Evans, 201–228. Cambridge, MA: MIT Press.

Mine: Story of a Sacred Mountain [film]. n.d. Survival International. Accessed August 6, 2016. http://www.survivalinternational.org/films/mine.

New Pittsburgh Courier. 2005. "Nigerian Women Win Out Against Oil Giant" In *Beyond Borders: Thinking Critically About Global Issues*, edited by Paula S. Rothenberg, 584–585. New York: Worth.

Oxfam, International Land Coalition, Rights and Resources Initiative. 2016. "Common Ground: Securing Land Rights and Safeguarding the Earth." Oxford: Oxfam.

Reid, Herbert, and Betsy Taylor. 2010. *Recovering the Commons: Democracy, Place, and Global Justice*. Urbana: University of Illinois Press.

Rixecker, Stefanie S., and Bevan Tipene-Matua. 2003. "Maori Kaupapa and the Inseparability of Social and Environmental Justice: An Analysis of Bioprospecting and a People's Resistance to (Bio)cultural Assimilation." In *Just Sustainabilities: Development in an Unequal World*, edited by Julian Agyeman, Robert D. Bullard, and Bob Evans, 252–268. Cambridge, MA: MIT Press.

Roy, Arundhati. n.d. "Arundhati Roy at the World Social Forum, Porto Alegre 2003."Accessed August 7, 2016. https://www.youtube.com/watch?v=uu3t8Z-kavA.

Sassen, Saskia. 2014. *Expulsions: Brutality and Complexity in the Global Economy*. Cambridge, MA: Harvard University Press.

Shiva, Vandana. 2002. *Water Wars: Privatization, Pollution, and Profit*. Cambridge, MA: South End.

Singh, Gyanant. 2012. "Supreme Court Ban on Intrusion into Jarawa Buffer Zone." *India Today*, July 4. Accessed August 7, 2016. http://indiatoday.intoday.in/story/ban-on-intrusion-into-jarawa-buffer-zone/1/203671.html.

Survival International .n.d. "The Movement for Tribal Peoples." Accessed August 6, 2016. http://www.survivalinternational.org/.

Index

www.ingramcontent.com/pod-product-compliance
Lightning Source LLC
Chambersburg PA
CBHW050625280326
41932CB00015B/2522